IMPOSSIBLE RETURNS

UNIVERSITY PRESS OF FLORIDA

Florida A&M University, Tallahassee
Florida Atlantic University, Boca Raton
Florida Gulf Coast University, Ft. Myers
Florida International University, Miami
Florida State University, Tallahassee
New College of Florida, Sarasota
University of Central Florida, Orlando
University of Florida, Gainesville
University of North Florida, Jacksonville
University of South Florida, Tampa
University of West Florida, Pensacola

# IMPOSSIBLE RETURNS
Narratives of the Cuban Diaspora

Iraida H. López

University Press of Florida
Gainesville · Tallahassee · Tampa · Boca Raton
Pensacola · Orlando · Miami · Jacksonville · Ft. Myers · Sarasota

Copyright 2015 by Iraida H. López
All rights reserved
Printed in the United States of America on acid-free paper

This book may be available in an electronic edition.

First cloth printing, 2015
First paperback printing, 2018

23 22 21 20 19 18   6 5 4 3 2 1

Library of Congress Cataloging-in-Publication Data
López, Iraida H., author.
Impossible returns : narratives of the Cuban diaspora / Iraida H. López.
pages cm
Includes bibliographical references and index.
Summary: This book examines the growing body of cultural works from Cuban exiles and Cuban Americans addressing the topic of return migration.
ISBN 978-0-8130-6103-0 (cloth)
ISBN 978-0-8130-6466-6 (pbk.)
1. Repatriation—Cuba. 2. United States—Emigration and immigration. 3. Cuba—History. 4. Cuba—Emigration and immigration. I. Title.
F1788.L577 2015
972.91—dc23
2015008378

The University Press of Florida is the scholarly publishing agency for the State University System of Florida, comprising Florida A&M University, Florida Atlantic University, Florida Gulf Coast University, Florida International University, Florida State University, New College of Florida, University of Central Florida, University of Florida, University of North Florida, University of South Florida, and University of West Florida.

University Press of Florida
15 Northwest 15th Street
Gainesville, FL 32611-2079
http://upress.ufl.edu

"Ithaka"

As you set out for Ithaka
hope the voyage is a long one,
full of adventure, full of discovery.
Laistrygonians and Cyclops,
angry Poseidon—don't be afraid of them:
you'll never find things like that on your way
as long as you keep your thoughts raised high,
as long as a rare excitement
stirs your spirit and your body.
Laistrygonians and Cyclops,
wild Poseidon—you won't encounter them
unless you bring them along inside your soul,
unless your soul sets them up in front of you.

Hope the voyage is a long one.
May there be many a summer morning when
with what pleasure, what joy,
you come into harbors seen for the first time;
may you stop at Phoenician trading stations
to buy fine things,
mother of pearl and coral, amber and ebony,
sensual perfume of every kind—
as many sensual perfumes as you can;
and may you visit many Egyptian cities
to gather stores of knowledge from their scholars.

Keep Ithaka always in your mind.
Arriving there is what you are destined for.
But do not hurry the journey at all.
Better if it lasts for years,
so you are old by the time you reach the island,
wealthy with all you have gained along the way,
not expecting Ithaka to make you rich.

Ithaka gave you the marvelous journey.
Without her you would not have set out.
She has nothing left to give you now.

And if you find her poor, Ithaka won't have fooled you.
Wise as you will have become, so full of experience,
you will have understood by then what these Ithakas mean.

—Constantine P. Cavafy, *Collected Poems*

Contents

List of Illustrations ix

Preface xi

Introduction: The Poetics of Return 1

1. An Uphill Battle: The Contentious Politics of Return 34
2. Daring to Go Back: In Search of Traces 61
3. Ana Mendieta: Chiseling (in) Cuba 90
4. Cuban Childhood Redux 121
5. Vicarious Returns and a Usable Past in *The Agüero Sisters*, *Days of Awe*, and *Loving Che* 159
6. Toward a Boomerang Aesthetic: The View from the Island 194

Epilogue 225

Notes 231

Works Cited 255

Index 279

Illustrations

2.1. Jaime Gans Grin, from Ruth Behar's *An Island Called Home* 72

2.2. *Cars in Havana*, from Tony Mendoza's *Cuba: Going Back* 86

2.3. *Boys in Old Havana*, from Tony Mendoza's *Cuba: Going Back* 87

3.1. Mendieta family in Cuba 94

3.2. "Mazapán de Matanzas" 99

3.3. Rubén Torres Llorca, *Nosotros, los de entonces, ya no somos los mismos* (1987) 105

3.4. *Maroya*, located at the same cave as *Bacayú*, as it appeared when the author and Cuarta Pragmática visited the site in 2011 106

3.5. Cuarta Pragmática students and the author at one of the caves in Jaruco 112

3.6. A local man helping to locate Mendieta's sculptures in Jaruco 114

3.7. Ana Mendieta performing *Death of a Chicken* (1972) 117

3.8. Tania Bruguera performing *El peso de la culpa* (1997–99) 117

4.1. Ernesto Pujol, *Los zapatos de Amparito* (1993) 126

4.2. Ernesto Pujol, *Tendedera* (1995) 129

4.3. María Brito, *El patio de mi casa* (1991) 133

4.4. María Brito, *Feed* (2001) 135

6.1. Abel Barroso, *Teoría de tránsito del arte cubano* (1995) 201

Preface

One afternoon, while my daughter and I were driving around the south side of Williamsburg, Brooklyn, we came to a street conspicuously called, in perfect Spanglish, El Regreso Way. As it turns out, it is a sandwiched street that, running between Bedford and Driggs Avenues along Third S. Street, stretches for just one block. Because it fleetingly evokes a homecoming without leading to any one route flowing into return, El Regreso Way fails to deliver drivers and pedestrians alike to any Promised Land. Appropriately enough, given widespread assumptions about the mythical nature of return, it remains within the realm of illusion.

For steering those captivated with the act of reminiscing fully into the sprawling field of returns, one need look no further than a number of narratives written from cities like New York, Michigan, Chicago, Miami, and London. These are narratives that have slowly but surely been placing not-so-subtle signposts pointing, perhaps unexpectedly due to the surge in the opposite direction, to Cuba as a destination. Such narratives are the cornerstones of my book. *Impossible Returns* attempts to recognize the robust quest for a home and homeland cultivated in one's imagination through stories of physical and metaphorical return. It represents an effort to understand Cuba's sway across borders, a sway made all the more startling given the personal circumstances of the writers and artists who penned the stories. Most left Cuba as children after the 1959 revolution, and some have since refrained from setting foot on the island. Through a critical reading of their work, this book highlights the affective ties as well as the tensions underlying the relationship between the authors and their native country decades after taking flight.

* * *

Though academic, the subject matter is personally close to me. I have dreamed about going back to Cuba. I have also traveled to Cuba more times than I can count since my parents, displeased with the turn of events on the socialist island, decided to flee more than four decades ago. A teenager at the time, I was devastated by their decision for purely personal and existential reasons. It would take me years to comprehend their well-founded apprehensions of a messianic undertaking whose shock waves are felt even today.

As soon as I could, but not earlier than eleven years after departure due to the travel prohibition, I went back to Cuba for the first time, and I have since returned under disparate guises: as an academic; as the head of a full-fledged City University of New York scholarly exchange program; as a member of organizations founded by progressive Cubans in the United States at a time when the desire to relate to one's homeland was dubbed a dishonorable act of betrayal; as an ordinary citizen to visit family; as a young feminist to attend regional meetings leading to the Third World Conference on Women; and as an affiliate in a delegation to donate medical supplies. And even at times when I was not physically present, Cuba prevailed in my life, as my academic research has paid particular attention to Cuba or, with more precision, Cuban America, *la América cubana*.

Yet in the literature on Cuban studies I found little that spoke to my experience and that of many others who underwent a similar process. To be sure, there is a hefty bibliography on post-1959 Cuba as well as Cuban migration. Less common, though, are critical works that bridge one and the other or view the diaspora as central to Cuba. To a degree, that silence led me to envision a study on the numerous narratives of return that have piled up through the years. In spite of my familiarity with the subject, I have made every effort to keep my distance and prevent my personal experience from clouding my judgment of other, different ideologies and economies of return. Being an insider is a double-edged sword that I have striven to use prudently.

All of the projects with which I have been involved sought to build bridges over what seemed at times like a colossal, intractable chasm between Cubans on the island and exiled Cubans. Given that background, I have friends and colleagues on both sides of the Florida Straits and beyond that answered my calls for support and feedback on the manuscript and whom I heartily thank. To begin, I am indebted to Jorge Duany and Andrea

O'Reilly Herrera for meticulously reading the entire manuscript for the University Press of Florida and offering expert advice. They urged me to finesse some of the arguments and tighten others with the help of additional sources. Moreover, Duany helped me navigate the dense universe of census and survey data. Thanks to him, I came out of this venture with renewed respect for social scientists.

Just as dependable as well as knowledgeable and admired colleagues agreed to read one or more of the book chapters. Rina Benmayor, Michael J. Bustamante, Karen S. Christian, Adriana López-Labourdette, Yolanda Prieto, Eliana Rivero, Raúl Rosales Herrera, and Miren Uriarte made insightful comments and proffered encouragement at different stages of the project. I am obliged also to Antonio Aja Díaz. My heartfelt gratitude goes to Monika Giacoppe, Paula Straile-Costa, and Lysandra Pérez-Strumolo, all three at my home institution, Ramapo College of New Jersey, who volunteered productive feedback on even rough drafts. Due to the generosity and intelligence of all of the above colleagues, the book is an enhanced version of the original manuscript. Additionally, I acknowledge the skilled help received from my gifted former students Francesca Baratta and Keysi Castillo.

Vitalina Alfonso knew which books, essays, and films on the Cuban side were critical for my research before I even imagined they had been published or released. She supported me throughout the past few years with exemplary dedication and friendship. Since details are crucial, I am indebted also to those friends and colleagues who lent a hand at some point or other in response to my smoke signals: Tony Mendieta, Rebeca Chávez, Senel Paz, José Hernández, Humberto Mayol, and Víctor Casaus, you can count on me, too.

My thanks go out to the following individuals on and off the island who agreed to be interviewed informally or who corresponded with me via e-mail: José Bedia, Joaquín Borges-Triana, María Brito, José Manuel Fors, Nereyda García Ferraz, Flavio Garciandía, Mariana Gastón, Rogelio López Marín, Raquelín and Tony Mendieta, Ernesto Pujol, René Francisco Rodríguez, Ricardo Rodríguez Brey, Leandro Soto, and José Veigas. Their knowledge and lived experience, shared freely, made a contribution to my study. The editors of the *South Atlantic Review* gave their permission to reprint "The Notion of *Volver* in Cuban-American Memoirs: Gustavo Pérez Firmat's *Next Year in Cuba* as a Case of Mistaken Coordinates," which appeared in issue 77.3–4 (2015). The essay is a slightly different version of the section devoted to this memoir in chapter 4. An earlier draft of chapter 3 appeared in the May/June 2012 issue of *La Gaceta de Cuba* under the title "Ana Mendieta, treinta años después: Al rescate de la memoria."

The Ramapo College Foundation extended several travel grants for on-site research. I am thankful to the Salameno School of Humanities and Global Studies for its ongoing encouragement and to the Provost Office at Ramapo College for supporting a sabbatical leave that allowed me to work full-time on the manuscript for a semester. During several fruitful months over the spring of 2012, I was a scholar-in-residence at New York University, made possible by the Faculty Resource Network (FRN), which sponsored another stint there in the summer of 2013. Deborah Szybinski and Anne Ward, of the FRN, went beyond the call of duty to give me unfettered access to the institution's plentiful resources.

A final, though no less expressive word goes to members of my family. Alejandra and Diego Íñiguez-López and Gabriela García joined me in the unforgettable pilgrimage to Jaruco and Varadero following Ana Mendieta's footprints and gracefully tolerated my long-term commitment to this absorbing project. Although second-generation Cuban Americans, the three have gone "back" to Cuba seduced by family stories. The late Yolanda Díaz, *mi querida tía,* and Jorge Urquiaga, *mi servicial hermanito,* were always ready to roll out the red carpet, unconditionally opening their home and hearts to me in Havana's Municipio Playa. The same applies to those located in my gateway to Havana, Miami: Iraida Rosa and María del Carmen López, and Amanda García, as well as Ofelia Costa and Ana Leyva. I extend my gratitude to all of the above. It takes a village to write a book.

I wish to dedicate *Impossible Returns* to all those intent on looking back without wallowing in nostalgia, in an "off-modern" mode nudging one to explore the meandering pathways of longing and memory. The off-modern mode dwells on "back alleys rather than the straight road of progress" (Boym xvi). Such a means of recasting nostalgia, devoid of sorrowfulness, blends in with the vision of a homecoming that is not quite out of reach if one believes in the power of narrative to make it happen. El Regreso Way may not take one far down the road, but good old return narratives, as old as storytelling itself, show an alternative way. This type of story originating in the Cuban diaspora measures up to other files in that rich, engrossing archive.

Introduction

The Poetics of Return

> es tarde para
> conocer ahora el nombre del árbol que
> siempre creció en el traspatio o el
> nombre musical de alguna fruta natural
> del país; yo les señalo el camino de
> los nombres
> [it is late
> for learning the name of the tree that
> always grew in the backyard or the
> musical name of some autochthonous fruit;
> I point to the way of
> the names]
>
> José Kozer, "Retrato sideral de mi casa"

Years after fleeing Cuba in the wake of the 1959 revolution, when many had lost hope they would ever set their eyes again on the beloved island, Cuban émigrés were finally allowed to reenter their homeland. Not every returnee has shared in writing his or her understanding of what must have been anything but a dull and uneventful sojourn. Were they able to rekindle personal relationships after such a long hiatus? How had the island fared all these years? How did the reencounter with their native city or hometown unfold? Were they successful in reconciling memories and reality? Did the trip bring about healing, disappointment, or both? And at a more abstract level, is return truly feasible? How is it represented? What is its lexicon and its syntax? Is there a typology of return?

These questions would remain virtually unanswered were it not for noteworthy accounts, written in particular by members of the "one-and-a-half generation" in exile, which indulge the age-old topic of return. The label applies to those who left Cuba as children or adolescents and reached adulthood in the United States. Since the first generation of exiles rarely tackled the representation of return trips for a confluence of reasons, the task has fallen upon the shoulders of the following cohort of Cuban Americans, especially, but also beyond, which have pursued the multifaceted notion of returning with increasing vehemence.

Notwithstanding the common ground shared by all return narratives, there are certain markers that distinguish the homecoming depicted by the one-and-a-half generation.[1] Many of the narratives include a family scene foregrounding the pronounced difference in attitudes toward going back across generations. In the typical scene, the older relatives are distraught at the behavior of their children whose desire to go back to the land of their ancestors is viewed as a betrayal. If the elders are not shocked by the intention, they are at least puzzled by it. After all—the script goes—if they sacrificed everything they had and ventured into the unknown in order to save their families from a life of repression and destitution under socialism, why would their offspring want to return to the cursed island, even to visit? What would they be looking for in that forsaken place? A tremendous amount of tension underlies such incidents, reflecting deep disagreements between the interlocutors. It is one thing to have personally made the decision to leave the country for political disaffection reasons and quite another to have been taken out of it.

Ingrained in the recurrent scene is an exile mind-set that erects insurmountable barriers for dialogue and interaction among those on opposite sides of the ideological divide, barriers that were raised in the aftermath of the Cuban revolution in 1959. Half a century later, that confrontational stance, though considerably softened, is still found among a segment of Cuban émigrés. The Cuban-American population has evolved over the years and now encompasses groups of migrants from various generations, social backgrounds, racial and gender composition, and dates of arrival. Yet, like in other exile communities, there are those who recoil at the mere thought of returning. Palestinian critic Edward Said claims to speak for all exiles when he states: "The pathos of exile is in the loss of contact with the solidity and the satisfaction of earth: homecoming is out of the question" (179). Said's statement has indeed been heeded by a sector of the Cuban-American community.

In her book *The Immigrant Divide: How Cuban Americans Changed the U.S. and Their Homeland* (2009), Susan E. Eckstein notes that exiles consider it unethical to step foot on the island, perpetually postponing their return to a Cuba without the Castros (141). Being faithful to their exile ethos, many of the early émigrés have remained adamant in their determination not to go back. On the opposite end, more recent arrivals lean toward maintaining their family ties and, by extension, support travel and the culture reinforcing it (142). Having fled in the recent past, many due to economic reasons or to a subtle combination of economic and political motives, they are reluctant to let go, persevering in their attempts to nurture, at all costs, a close relationship with relatives and friends left behind.

Eckstein singles out Cuban-American singer Willy Chirino's "Nuestro día (ya viene llegando)" as a song that captures the "new immigrant sentiment" about Cubans returning to their native land (142). Born in 1947, the singer came to the United States in 1960 through the Operation Pedro Pan. A teenager at the time of departure, Chirino is a member of the one-and-a-half generation. In the song, he feels nostalgic for the motherland and yearns to return to a new Cuba that would have at last rejoined the free world—in addition to Nicaragua, Hungary, and East Germany, all three countries once espousing a socialist political agenda. Yet Chirino's lyrics are not the best example of a post-exile sentiment given their underlying ambition to reenact the Cuba of yesteryear, overlooking the processes accountable for the current Cuba. Repeated references to competing worldviews underscore the political nature of the subtext.

By contrast, Raúl Paz's "En casa," a song from Paz's homonymous album released in 2006, conveys the singer's desire to return home to see his loved ones again, even if for a short while. Born in 1969, Paz represents a younger generation whose interests lie beyond exile politics. The singer left Cuba in the late 1990s, settling in Paris, and years later returned to resume his musical career on the island. In 2011, he joined forces with other well-liked returnee singers such as Descemer Bueno and Kelvis Ochoa to hold a momentous concert in Havana. One of Paz's most popular songs, "En casa," keeps at arm's length political quarrels, replacing them for the most part with intimate memories. Paz's lyrics are a better instance of the feelings shared by possibly a majority of post–Cold War Cuban émigrés. For them, matters of the heart (and opportunities) take precedence over ideological fault lines. While Chirino has spent a lifetime outside Cuba, Paz did not have to wait long before he, unencumbered by the stress of frayed memories, went back to his old haunts. Attuned to the rise of discourses less saliently nationalistic in the post-Soviet era, Paz is able to shift the center of attention toward other domains.

Setting aside the contrast between the two songs, Eckstein is correct in her assessment of a more permissive culture of return. Nowadays, in the 2010s, Cubans in Miami and elsewhere routinely exchange information in social media or through personal contact about the latest restrictions and requirements for travel, and many of the charter flights that make the trip back and forth are sold out. The eagerness to visit signals a promising future for travel to a controversial island only forty-five minutes away by airplane from Miami. If one considers that slightly over 50 percent of Cuban émigrés arrived in the United States after 1990, then surely there is a large sector of the Cuban-American population deeply invested in returning.[2] In spite of spirited talk about escaping from the island, there is a thriving culture of returning among Cuban émigrés. As Anders H. Stefansson writes, homecoming can be compelling for those in diaspora even if carried out under rather bleak, distressing conditions (2). Globalization and cosmopolitanism may have become major forces in the world, but home, homeland, and homecoming have not entirely surrendered their starring role.

Neither Hardliners nor Newcomers

While exiles and recent émigrés represent the two ends of the spectrum, there is a middle ground composed of the children of exiles that has received much less scrutiny in the secondary literature on migration and return. This diverse middle cohort, known by the moniker of the one-and-a-half generation, is this book's main though not exclusive subject. The term was concocted by sociologist Rubén G. Rumbaut and popularized by Gustavo Pérez Firmat, who put the group in the spotlight to offer his take on Cuban-American culture in his influential book, *Life on the Hyphen: The Cuban-American Way* (1994, 2012). Pérez Firmat's book grapples with the cultural hybridity of the generation with which the critic identifies through its manifestation in popular culture and literature, contrasting it with the cultural propensities of both the older and younger generations. A particular location straddling cultures provides the in-between generation with privileged insights into the nature of both Cuban and Anglo-Saxon traditions. It concurrently turns them into outsiders to each of the traditions.[3]

Yet what the members of the one-and-a-half generation have in common is not only their Janus-like duality, but also a certain sense of dislocation and dispossession that in the process of looking backward as part of examining several forms of homecoming comes fully into view. Mired in the passage between innocence and experience at the time of their departure from Cuba, many of its members' memories had not yet congealed. Unlike the older exiles' lives, theirs became truncated or bifurcated at an early age. Over fourteen thousand left their parents behind, following the U.S.-sponsored Operation Pedro Pan that brought them to unfamiliar places. Some in the one-and-a-half generation are still reeling from this unconscionable chapter in post-1959 Cuban history, an episode with the dubious merit of constituting the largest organized exodus of unaccompanied children in the Western Hemisphere.[4] Even when they left with their parents, their family support system and social networks came undone. Ejected from their homes, a majority in the one-and-a-half generation had to part with their most cherished treasures, such as the storybooks that fired their gullible imagination, and often even their family photo albums registering their first steps. They were all deuteragonists in the drama of exile:

> To the parent generation, as the protagonists (from the Greek *protos* and *agonists*, meaning "first actors") in the decision to leave, going into exile is a crucial act of self definition. . . . But to the generation of their children, deuteragonists (from *deuteros* and *agonists*, "second actors") in this drama, exile . . . represents a discontinuity with one's origins, less a personal commitment than an inherited circumstance. (Rumbaut and Rumbaut 340)

Holding onto what should have been second nature to them is a challenge for these deuteragonists. Mastery of the Cuban dialect was made all the more difficult in exile, and expert knowledge of their native city or hometown was suddenly forestalled. If they lived in the capital, locating in a city map streets of Old Havana with such incantatory names as Peña Pobre, Dragones, Lamparilla, and Compostela, not to mention Amargura, Aguacate, Amistad, Ánimas, and Alambique is nothing short of inconceivable now. As Lourdes Casal wrote in a poem about her recollections of Havana, what remains ten years after fleeing are "jirones," or shreds, of that urban landscape in one's memory (*Palabras juntan revolución* 50). Fast-forward to their return decades later and they surely will be carrying upside-down maps.

They grew up fearing, most probably in a different language, that they would never be able to go back and try to mend what had been broken by the farewell. A unique background, deeply informed by lack, absence, or trace, affects their approach to representing return. This scenario explains why, for some, the past becomes a mild liability rather than a foundation. It also explains why, in *Cuban Palimpsests*, José Quiroga turns to paradox and chiasmus to grasp the sense of being Cuban, indelibly seared "by interruption and traumatic absence," of the one-and-a-half generation (176). And why, in one of her essays on the subject Eliana Rivero resorts to a newly coined word, *Cubangst*, to capture the feeling of "deterritorialization, displacement, disenchantment, and dispossession" shared by Cubans of her generation ("Two or More [Dis]places" 198)—without the negativity that *angst* implies, I would append.

While one associates nostalgia as a sentimental, acute yearning for the past with classical exile, perhaps the Welsh word *hiraeth*, as untranslatable as the Portuguese *saudade* is said to be, best describes this subsequent generation's version of homesickness. Even more pointed than *saudade*, a craving for a missing someone or something that might not return, *hiraeth*, as defined by Pamela Petro, is an unachievable longing for a place, a "vague and constant desire for something that does not and probably cannot exist." It is a place attached to a "home-seeking imagination," to a homing desire borne by members of this cohort.[5] Like the Welsh who thus account for a homeland that was snatched away from them, if you will, by the British Empire, so too do these Cuban Americans pen stories about a native land that was off limits to them for what seems, from a young person's perspective, an exceedingly long time.

Features such as those mentioned above are shared in various degrees by all the members of the one-and-a-half generation even though the term applies to a wide range of individuals who arrived in the host society at different life stages: in early childhood, middle childhood, and adolescence (Rumbaut 1167).[6] When those who left Cuba as children or adolescents chose to return, breaking the rules of exile, the former homeland no longer felt quite like the home, providing a sense of belonging, nestled in their memory or imagination. Driven by an all-too-human homing desire nonetheless, their return narratives (both in textual and visual formulations) unveil elliptical forms that throw the fissures into sharp relief. This book is about the causes and consequences of those fissures and the largely unsuccessful attempts to close the attendant gaps. At the same time, the book is also about stubborn affection, a factor triggering the myriad forms in which Cuban-American writers and artists choose to go back. Among those considered are Ana Mendieta, Ruth Behar, María Brito, Cristina García, Carlos Eire, Achy Obejas, Ernesto Pujol, and Gustavo Pérez Firmat, all of them renowned artists, writers, and scholars.

Within the abovementioned cohort, some have defied their elders and gone back to the island multiple times. Others, however, have taken an uncompromising position and sworn not to return for political and emotional reasons or out of fear that Cuba will not live up to expectations hatched over decades.[7] All have made their positions clear in the memoirs that they have crafted. Those who dared to go back bore the brunt of the community's intransigence, sometimes translated into violent, even lethal actions, and thus laid the groundwork for later returns. They can be credited, indeed, with a pioneering role in the field of post-1959 returns, one that has not been sufficiently documented. Additional differences among worldviews just within the one-and-a-half generation will be taken up later in the book. Discerning between generations and waves of émigrés, as social scientists have been doing with regard to Cubans who settled in the United States, Puerto Rico, and Spain especially, yields critical information. Then again, acknowledging the intragenerational peculiarities of this and other cohorts makes the variegated character of a community that in the past has been portrayed as monolithic stand out. It is imperative not to lose sight of that diversity.

Many of the narratives included here are autobiographical in nature. Such type of subjective account constitutes a rich resource for the kind of inquiry I am proposing because, although fabricated like any other narrative, it draws from disparate personal and nontransferable *vivencias*—from very diverse experiences and political stances that, taken together, render a textured description. Tapping into a resource that has the *feel* of vérité, even if that vérité has been carefully airbrushed, as well as visual narratives and the fictionalized returns pictured in some novels, generates a number of possibilities about going back. In Spanish, these possibilities are subsumed in several terms derived from the verb *volver* rather than *regresar* or *retornar*.

Volver, Regresar, Retornar

All three words mean "to return" in Spanish, but the first, *volver*, besides being a synonym for *regresar* and *retornar*, "going back to the place one left," also implies "encircling or going around something," capturing key constitutive elements of the return imagination perused here. Some writers and artists portray "return" without setting foot on the island. This gesture of going back without literally returning is what social scientist Khachig Tölölyan partly alludes to in his essay "Rethinking Diaspora(s)." Tölölyan reminds us that "a repeated turning to the concept and/or the reality of the homeland and other diasporan kin through memory, written and visual texts, travel, gifts and assistance, et cetera" is a common trait among diasporic communities (14–15), Cubans included.

While Tölölyan mentions both abstract and concrete transnational practices that diasporic peoples conduct only to emphasize the latter as he gets deeper into his essay, my use of *volver* stresses the former, that is, the re-turn through memory and written and visual texts (Tölölyan, "The Contemporary Discourse of Diaspora Studies" 649). In *Life on the Hyphen*, Pérez Firmat claims that certain exiles "no tienen regreso" or will not partake of a return (19). And yet most exiles, including the often-quoted Cuban-American author himself, are willing to go back, in the sense of *volver*, to landmark events and recollections about their former lives in Cuba, or to discourses steeped in *lo cubano*. *Volver* gives free rein to the imagination, allowing writers to emotionally, spatially, and aesthetically shape Cuba to their advantage, according to present needs.

Moreover, *volver*, grammatically close to the reflexive verb *volverse*, "to become," evokes, however vaguely, the gradual and complex process by which one acquires subjectivities other than the one delimited by a single nationality overlapping with an erstwhile, bounded geography. Therefore, the verb *volver(se)* reverberates with the subjectivity typical of those for whom exile and migration involve changes in self-perception. Stretching its connotations even further, the lexeme *volver* is contained in *envolver*, 'to involve or influence someone,' as "Cuba" does with its long-lived aura of exceptionality. With the prefix *re*, it becomes *revolver*, whose actual meaning is "inquietar, enredar," that is, "to trouble, entangle."

These riffs on *volver* address even those unwilling to go back, yet seem equally haunted by Cuba, upholding the claim about the iteration of the homeland by both concrete and figurative means. Cuba becomes, for some, a meta-homeland or floating signifier distant from the actual island, a transformation that interrogates the fixity of a homeland or the superimposition of home and homeland. Indeed, some of the more accomplished narratives explicitly or implicitly question the modern convergence of identity and national territory. Finally, the word *revolución*, like *revolver*, comprises the verb *volver*. It comes from the Latin *revolvere*, "to turn, roll back," in the sense of an instance of abrupt change in public affairs. *Revolución* is, after all, the catalyst for fleeing and, therefore, everything else, including these remarks, flows from it.

On the other hand, missing from *retornar* and *regresar*—suitable to refer to actual returns, or to something that happens or is experienced again—is the connotation of "encircling or going around something" that *volver* optimally summons. *Regresar*, close to the English "regress," has the added meaning of reverting to an earlier, especially a less developed, condition or state such as childhood, which may be the intention of some return narratives, but surely not all. For semantic reasons, then, *volver* is a more apt term, one that encompasses the variety of returns available to the fractured one-and-a-half generation.

The manifold implications of revisiting the past without actually traveling to the island or engaging with it include making a clear distinction between diaspora and transnationalism, two terms that are often wedded, somewhat randomly, in the literature on diaspora. The resilient exile worldview still reigning in certain circles, though waning, impels this author to separate the two. Exiles, who join in some form of *volver* but not the actual *retornar*, can be accommodated within diaspora, perhaps not comfortably—a number of critics would argue—because the move obscures the political conspicuousness of exile. But they cannot be similarly located within transnationalism, as many refrain from engaging in practices across borders. The return motif shapes the labeling of writers of the one-and-a-half generation. Are they a part of the Cuban diaspora, a transnational community, or the Cuban exile or ethnic population?

A Diasporic Community or a Trans-Nation for All?

Broadly defined, *diaspora*, from the Greek *diasperien*, from *dia-* , "across," and *-sperien*, "to sow or scatter seeds," has historically referred to "displaced communities of people who have been dislocated from their native homeland through the movements of migration, immigration, or exile" and subsequently relocated in one or more nation-states, territories, or countries (Braziel and Mannur 1). Tölölyan points out that diasporas exhibit "a culture and a collective identity that preserves elements of the homeland's language, or religious, social, and cultural practice, either intact or, as time passes, in mixed, bicultural forms" ("The Contemporary Discourse of Diaspora Studies" 649). The term was originally applied to the Jews living in places other than Palestine, their homeland, and later to the descendants of African slaves who reached the Americas through the Middle Passage during a nearly four-hundred-year period since the beginning of the sixteenth century. For Dominique Schnapper, the term has, since the late sixties, designated "all forms of population dispersion, until then evoked by the terms *expelled, expatriate, exile, refugee, immigrant,* or *minority*" (225). Along with the critics cited above, Schnapper critiques the hazy application of the term for fear that it might render it meaningless. To avoid this pitfall, a brief detour to clarify the use of *diaspora* (and *transnationalism*) in the book is in order.

William Safran, whose early essay on diasporas is required reading in diaspora studies, counts the Cuban case alongside the Armenian, Turkish, Palestinian, and others, even though it does not fully conform to the Jewish diaspora model. Safran offers a general characterization of diaspora, indicating that for diasporic groups to coalesce they must share several elements, all of which revolve around the homeland, including an expectation of return.[8] With homeland as an axis around which everything else revolves, Safran's notion of diaspora corresponds to what Sudesh Mishra calls the "scene of dual territoriality" according to which the homeland state is "classically auto-centred, racially self-evident and ideologically homogenized" (16). By prioritizing the connection to the homeland as a territory unilaterally ensuring one's essential moorings, those thinking through diaspora in this fashion draw attention to the "roots" or "arborescent" side of the equation. Inversely, the "scene of situational laterality," in Mishra's nuanced, if dense, discussion about theories of diaspora, undermines the notion of bounded terrains inasmuch as national territories no longer furnish "privileged referents for identity constitution" (17). Rather, they are supplanted by the rise of lateral (not linear), shifting, and nonessentialist positionings one can correlate with "routes" or with a "rhizomatic" take on diasporic subjectivity.

Already in 1997, Robin Cohen critiqued Safran for placing the homeland at the center of his reflections. For Cohen, the collective identity of the diaspora musters its strength from the strongholds of place of origins *and* place of settlement, as well as from identifying with co-ethnic members in other countries where they have settled (23–26). In Cohen's critique, the source of diasporic identification has ceased to be exclusively the homeland. Thus framed, it appears that theories about diaspora are divided between the "roots" and "routes" distinction that Paul Gilroy identified in his well-known *Black Atlantic* (1993). Whereas the former refers to place attachment and the isomorphic link between identity and bounded territory, the latter denotes displacement, journeying, and evolving identities. In addition to Gilroy, other critics whose work, as per Mishra, is guided by the routes metaphor include James Clifford and Stuart Hall. However, it must be recognized that neither of these scholars cursorily dismisses the relevance accorded to roots; it is more a matter of emphasis.

Adding to the ambiguity of the signified is the connection some scholars now make between diaspora and transnationalism. As early as 1991, in the inaugural issue of the journal *Diaspora*, Khachig Tölölyan called diasporas the "exemplary communities of the transnational moment" ("The Nation-State and Its Others" 5), suggesting an intrinsic bond between the two terms. Aihwa Ong, another diaspora theorist, draws a distinction between "the classical 'ethno-diasporas'—Jews, Greeks, Parsis and Armenians—and large-scale dispersal of significant ethnic clusters witnessed in the time of advanced capital" (Mishra 19). It is the modern-day diasporas that Ong characterizes as transnational not only because they help spawn a new type of relationship between nation-states and capital but also because they bring in tow a "transactional," "translational," and "transgressive" behavior and imagination that go hand in hand with the new global economy (Mishra 4). Ong thus uses diaspora, transnationalism, and even globalization almost in one breath. Another scholar who draws parallels between the two is James Clifford: "Diasporic discourses reflect the sense of being part of an ongoing transnational network that includes the homeland not as something left behind but as a place of attachment in a contrapuntal modernity" (256). For

Clifford, discourses forged in diaspora envisage a transnational perspective. As the above examples demonstrate, there has been a tendency to conflate, or at least juxtapose, diaspora and transnationalism.

One must conclude that transnationalism, like diaspora, has become another slippery term applied, as it is, to a smorgasbord of realities. Some of these are as concrete and material as family visits and remittances while others are as elusive, intangible, and static as the absent but evoked homeland. While the former point to a reinvigorated engagement with the homeland and its peoples, the latter, being retrospective and introspective, are tagged onto exile.

This critic uses transnationalism not in the psychic, evocative sense but in the practical, prospective meaning. In order to be transnational, one must engage in a social network that spans two or more nations. The term specifically means "the process by which immigrants forge and sustain simultaneous multi-stranded social relations that link together their societies of origin and settlement" (Basch et al. 48). Sociologist Alejandro Portes adds that "transnationalism entails carrying out occupations and activities requiring regular and intense contact between two or more countries" (qtd. by Duany, "Networks, Remittances" 163). In addition to its human dimension, there is an economic implication, too, as the word also means "the construction of dense social fields through the circulation of people, ideas, practices, money, goods, and information across nations" with or without the intervention of the state (Duany, *Blurred Borders* 20–21). Further underlining the links, Juan Flores sustains that transnationalism dissolves the social distance between homeland and host country, merging the two poles "into a single arena of social action and determination" (22).

Moreover, transnational practices have implications for the meaning of homeland, as Purnima Mankekar notes. Since transnationalism speaks to the building of "alliances within the homeland *as well as* the diaspora," the center of attention is no longer circumscribed to a single territory. Implicitly, then, it brings about "a redefinition of *homeland* that challenges prevailing uses of the term either as a place of origin or authentic selfhood or, on the other hand, as a telos or point of return" (qtd. by Bettinger-López 160). A fluid back and forth movement characterizes transnational lives.

Spurring the movement across borders are the gamut of transnational activities that Cubans on both sides engage in, with telephone calls, mail, family visits, packages, and remittances being among the most common

(Duany, *Blurred Borders* 144–50). All of these activities offer opportunities for social and cultural remittances, that is, ideas and values that the displaced introduce in their former hometowns (Flores 4). Cultural remittances can be channeled in the opposite direction, too. Lisa Maya Knauer argues that the two-way flow breeds "a sense of belonging not coterminous with national boundaries" (160).

Furthermore, transnational interaction has an impact on affect since it feeds the emotional charge that flows between the island and mainland social spaces, as Elizabeth M. Aranda has written in relation with Puerto Ricans who straddle both societies (172). As Aranda convincingly argues, émigrés do not necessarily have to undertake frequent cross-border activities to be considered transnational actors. The emotional bridges that no doubt exist are strong vectors of transnational transactions (172). Despite the differences between Puerto Rican and Cuban migration patterns, an emotional rush colors the relationship between those who leave and those who stay behind. Indeed, in the Cuban case, it may carry even more weight given the numerous hurdles that have hindered reunification except for irregular periods of time. So far, Cuban Americans are allowed to return only for short visits, making postrevolutionary permanent migration largely a one-way flow from island to metropolis, unlike the Puerto Rican and Dominican migrations (Duany, *Blurred Borders* 139).[9] Most Cuban Americans have little choice but to opt for provisional or imagined rather than repatriated return in Oxfeld and Long's taxonomy (7–13). Cubans make fewer as well as shorter homeland trips than others in the region (Eckstein 149). With barriers to reunification still in place, there is a heightened sense of emotional tensions, and the returning, which in other cases may be physical, takes on other shapes and dimensions.

Given the breadth of views on the relationship with the nation within the Cuban-American community, the near equation of diaspora and transnationalism made by some critics is problematic for Cuban studies. Although the word *transnationalism* crops up in descriptions of the relationship between the Cuban community (purportedly including exiles) and their homeland, superimposing the two terms excludes a sector of the Cuban-American population from the diaspora designation that should encompass all Cubans, regardless of their ideology, date of arrival, or place of residence. Not all of them share or sanction the amalgam of practices typical of transnationalism—as evinced in a few of the narratives included here. Cuban-American writings suggest that a relationship with the home country has yet to develop for many, in which case there are no grounds for claiming a sweeping transnational relationship. Contrariwise, there is a growing number of Cuban Americans from different generations—especially among recent migrants—who automatically assert that relationship. The difference between the two sectors is substantiated by the dissimilar value they place on the issue of return, to which I turn momentarily. While keeping the label of diaspora for the heterogeneous Cuban community abroad, I choose to disentangle it from transnational practices unless called for, arguing that the idea of a trans-nation may be an assumption for many but not for all.[10]

Toward a Diaspora Rhetoric

Interventions by Cuban-American writers on the discussion about the use of labels illuminate the existing tensions. As politics tend to mediate every discussion in an exilic environment, and the Cuban case is anything but an exception, the term *diaspora* (and even the more impartial term *migration*, in some circles) is generally perceived as weakening or diluting the political edge of the word *exile* (O'Reilly Herrera, "The Politics of Mis-ReMembering" 181). Nevertheless, some show a preference for it. Not so, however, poet Lourdes Gil, who finds that the term accurately defines her experience, which she did not seek: "The concept of exile, from its Latin root 'exsul,' signifies its inherent condition: 'outside of.' The expatriate is, then, the perpetual outsider, the individual ousted from the community. I entered this exile space involuntarily (I was a child and others made the decision for me), yet the transition from the old to the new occurred in painful awareness" ("Against the Grain" 177). *Exul inmeritus* or an exiled individual undeserving of exile is how Pérez Firmat describes such a condition (*Cincuenta lecciones* 31). As for *diaspora*, the same writer retorts sharply: "Si me dicen diáspora, respondo: exilio" [If I hear *diaspora*, I respond: exile] (*Cincuenta lecciones* 108). Case closed.

Inversely, Ruth Behar began to use the word *diaspora* at the time she conceived her *Bridges* volume, published in 1995. She was drawn to it for its "undecidability, a refusal to submit to the tyranny of categories: Cubans outside Cuba are perhaps immigrants, perhaps exiles, perhaps both, perhaps neither," at the same time that it allows her to place the commotion caused by exile within a wider framework of streams of displaced migrants on the grounds of the loosening of borders ("Going to Cuba" 144–45). Likewise, Eliana Rivero privileges the elastic diaspora over exile. For Rivero, the prefix *ex* of *exilio* defines us by what has ceased to be or what is lacking; it essentially denotes an exclusion that she is willing to fight (*Discursos desde la diáspora* 17). As a longtime resident of the Southwest, where there is a strong Chicano or Mexican American presence, she dived into a generic Latinidad that was in the air, so to speak, but later embraced the term *diaspora*, which figures prominently in her volume of essays, *Discursos desde la diaspora* (2005).[11] Adding a twist to the debate, Adriana Méndez Rodenas accepts the idea of a diasporic consciousness among émigrés, but her recognition comes with a caveat. What sets the Cuban case apart, she argues, are the multiple hurdles for permanent return given the policies in place on the island since the early 1960s—as well as those owed to the U.S. embargo, one might add ("Identity and Diaspora" 147–48). The lingering political conflict is a stumbling block for alternative conceptualizations. And yet, although some still find it deficient for a number of reasons, the use of *diaspora* has spread among academics of Cuban origin.[12]

Cuban-American Provisions in the Roots/Routes Debate

More of a coming together is reflected among Cuban Americans around the roots versus routes debates sketched above. Quite a few reflections on the Cuban diaspora have paralleled in some ways the discussion around the need to broaden the national body, proof of the interest in keeping the nation and its diaspora linked. While roots continue to play a role in the discourse on identity, routes have been making inroads, providing at times the prime frame of reference. One need only contemplate the distance separating Behar's *Bridges to Cuba/Puentes a Cuba* (1995), stressing roots, with her coedited volume (with Lucía M. Suárez), *The Portable Island: Cubans at Home in the World* (2008), which foregrounds the routes by which one is Cuban in the world. The more recent volume, which includes contributions from Cubans around the globe, tacitly casts doubt on the reliance on roots in theories of *cubanidad* or *cubanía*. A growing diaspora hardly renouncing its ties to the island has questioned the usefulness of theories based on rooted, stationary subjectivities.

In his essay "Reconstructing Cubanness," Jorge Duany argues that discourses as varied as those of Fernando Ortiz and Manuel Moreno Fraginals, to mention only two of the intellectuals who have attempted to define "the" Cuban soul, emphasize the "rhetoric of roots" at the expense of "the dispersed landscapes of the Cuban nation beyond the island" (34–35). Instead of telluric images, Duany asserts, aerial or aquatic metaphors would be a better fit for a nation that has witnessed so much displacement throughout its history. Along with Pérez Firmat (*Life on the Hyphen* 15), Duany critiques the attempt to demarcate a national essence or core values. Pérez Firmat writes instead about the translational capabilities of the culture, about its ability to evolve and adapt. Perhaps less stationary, more mobile imagery would compensate for the shortcomings of current discourses that disregard the increasingly indeterminate boundaries of Cuban culture, their reflections suggest. If one narrates the nation, as Homi Bhabha and other cultural theorists maintain, the Cuba narration is due for an overhaul.

Another critic who strikes a similar note in her critique of a confining nationalism and an intersecting demand for the recognition of diaspora is Eliana Rivero. Rivero envisions a *Cuba (tras)pasada* or transnation summoning the active input of Cubans on the island and abroad on reconceptualizing the nation. As her choice of words indicates, the diaspora would have to be factored somehow into the revised concept ["Cuba (tras)pasada" 33]. Additional appeals include those of Rafael Rojas, who in his work has dwelled on the dispersals in both *exilio* and *insilio* forms that have characterized Cuban history, and Andrea O'Reilly Herrera, who has documented the ties that bind among Cuban artists and writers of the diaspora.[13]

On the same subject, it is interesting to note Ambrosio Fornet's concrete call for redrawing the boundaries of the Cuban literary canon. One of a few critics who have labored to keep track of Cuban-American literature from his residence in Havana, Fornet writes about the challenges posed by not only the new themes and discursive strategies turning up in the literature of younger generations of Cuba-based writers, but especially the literature of the diaspora.[14] The difficult access to a sprawling (and sometimes ideologically inflected) literary corpus, the partial knowledge of the context in which this body of work arises, and the need for translation in some cases are all obstacles that a renovated approach to the Cuban canon and national identity need to overcome. This is no small order. But as Fornet spells out, "¿Puede la identidad seguir definiéndose en función de territorios y de lenguas?" [Can identity still be defined in terms of territories and languages?]

("La crítica bicéfala" 25). Recent reflections emerging from both shores converge on this point, acknowledging both the audacity and complexity of the inquiry.

Additional critiques supplement the demands above. In their edited volume *Cuba: The Elusive Nation* (2000), Damián J. Fernández and Madeline Cámara make a point of using the neutral *lo cubano* instead of the feminine *cubanidad* or *cubanía* so as to demarcate a more spacious terrain for things Cuban. The term would presumably encompass the tension as well as the diversity that characterize Cuban civil society and which, as stated by the critics, have been sidestepped in discourses on Cuban nationality in favor of harmony and unity. Many of the narratives explored in this book echo the above critiques and question, tacitly or explicitly, a grounded cultural identity. Amid ever-expanding processes of migration, being Cuban can ultimately evolve into a performative endeavor. Yet the idea prevails of a durable, though less rooted, association with the native or ancestral homeland.

An Array of Returns

A befuddling experience, the return to the homeland does all but fulfill every promising expectation. Theorists of exile and diaspora have long argued that return is little more than a persistent myth or an exercise in futility. Safran, for instance, speaks of a permanent return forever hoped for but endlessly postponed by the diasporic subjects' own choice. Iain Chambers envisions the impossibility of a homecoming as the outcome of the blurring of borders amid processes of continuing global mobility. With borders collapsing, there are no clear points of departure or arrival in today's world. Chambers argues that it is not discrete travel but the forces of nomadism and migrancy currently at work that should garner our attention (5). Still other critics have called for a reassessment of homecomings on the basis of the obvious give-and-take inherent to transnationalism, arguing that not only do displaced peoples reincorporate themselves into their native societies but they can also upset the power relations that triggered migration to begin with. They bring the cultural capital earned abroad to bear on their revitalized relationships with fellow citizens (Flores 35–46).

Neither strictly exiles nor all-inclusive transnational subjects, the writers of the one-and-a-half generation entertained in this study hold mixed viewpoints about the feasibility of return. Their interstitial position precludes the possibility of identifying a uniform approach to the subject, with their narratives disclosing an assortment of conceivable returns. The scope becomes wider if we take into account other cohorts. Irrespective of their generation, however, some still operate within the framework of the myth of return, as the partial resistance to going back or becoming actually involved with insular Cuba strongly indicates.

This prevents me from consistently addressing the undeniable impact that returning émigrés as a critical mass have on their homeland, an influence that becomes increasingly blatant as one moves closer to the harsh realities of the post-Soviet era and, with it, a more comparable experience with regard to the rest of the Caribbean. What *Impossible Returns* does throughout is to evaluate the kind of return experience, physical or otherwise, written into the narratives, which demonstrate that there is ample room for acknowledging an ambivalent, ambiguous, and even impossible return. As Stefansson wisely remarks in his discussion of the unsettling consequences of homecoming, "there is no singular process of return" (4).

For the first post-1959 migration wave, returning was a matter of utmost concern. In accordance with the rationale of early émigrés, Cubans, unlike immigrants, were in the United States on a short-term basis, only until the socialist regime was overthrown. No sooner had the Castro regime been brought to its knees than they would resume their lives in Cuba. The exiles' expectation, naturally, did not come to fruition, so Cubans continued to be an indefinitely exiled people in the United States, harboring the illusion of return to a Cuba without Fidel Castro. Not until the 1970s did Cubans begin to perceive themselves as permanent residents (María C. García, "The Cuban Population of the United States" 85). Pérez Firmat's *Next Year in Cuba: A Cubano's Coming of Age in America* (1995), poignantly relates how the narrator's parents, after settling in Miami, lived with a pernicious excess of memory. They clung to an intact vision of Cuba that interfered with the adaptation process in the host society. The family's wait-and-see attitude in a Miami that felt like a halfway house in the end thwarted their cohesiveness as a unit, for each member of the family had to find his or her way out of the cultivated memory trap. Over time, the fantasy of return relished by the first waves of exiles would give way to the actual return of many, though ironically not of those identified more closely with an exile ideology.

As *Next Year in Cuba* suggests, some Cubans retain an exile identity for life—an idea encapsulated in Isabel Álvarez Borland's definition of the literary production of Cubans in the United States as "Cuban-American literature of exile," a definition that carves a plausible niche for Cuban-American literature under an inclusive U.S. ethnic literature while signaling the perpetuation of exile features.[15] The exile sentiment was so robust that it was often bequeathed to subsequent generations, along with a reluctance to visit the island. For those who still honor the set limits, Cuban-American subjectivity dovetails with an exile ethos—that is, for the purposes of this introduction, an exile identity embedded in oppositional politics as well as an aversion to returning. Uva de Aragón observed, in an article published in 2009, that exile "más que un status migratorio, o un lugar de residencia, se ha convertido en una posición de resistencia política [que] requiere de sus integrantes una condición incuestionable: no regresar a Cuba bajo el actual régimen" [more than a migratory status or a place of residence, has become a space of political resistance that requires of its members an unquestionable condition: to stay away from Cuba under the present regime] ("Distancia no quiere decir olvido" 206). If return is indeed antithetical to exile, as de Aragón argues, then it conflicts with a transnational imaginary—another reason to unlatch that imaginary from the one shaping a diasporic community that would include all émigrés.

Autobiographical narratives by Cuban and Cuban-American writers that appeared in the late 1980s and early 1990s, such as Heberto Padilla's *La mala memoria* (1989), Reinaldo Arenas's *Antes que anochezca* (1992), and Gustavo Pérez Firmat's *Next Year in Cuba* (1995), as well as more recent works like Carlos Eire's *Waiting for Snow in Havana* (2003) and Húber Matos's *Cómo llegó la noche* (2004) assert an exile identity. In the majority of these works, keeping the distance from Cuba is a moral obligation fulfilling the exile's mantra of not going back as long as the conditions that precipitated exile remain in place. Although increasingly rare, narratives infused with an exile spirit have continued to appear.

However, while many still adhere to exile, others move away from it in their writings. Ruth Behar's *An Island Called Home: Returning to Jewish Cuba* (2007), Tony Mendoza's *Cuba: Going Back* (1997), Román de la Campa's *Cuba on My Mind: Journeys to a Severed Nation* (2000), and Emilio Bejel's *The Write Way Home: A Cuban-American Story* (2003) are narratives exuding a diasporic and transnational imaginary that features a concrete homecoming. In all four cases, the past is literally a foreign country, a place to which the writers return out of curiosity about a land partly their own or to seek solace from the rupture and fragmentation brought about by displacement. Through their narratives, they reach that place, seeking to heal. Their return may also be future-oriented. The returnees may reclaim a presence in their natal homeland and make it part of their lives. Many narratives of the one-and-a-half generation align with a diasporic/transnational sensibility that consents to the idea of return even if the ideal conditions for it have yet to be met.

The claim applies to the various subgroups within the one-and-a-half cohort. Behar fled with her family as a small child, while de la Campa was in middle childhood. Being eighteen at the time, Bejel was at the threshold of adulthood, but he shares commonalities with the other writers. Mendoza is a borderline case. Born into a wealthy family, he attended a boarding school and college in the United States and was thus accustomed to traveling back and forth between island and mainland before the coming-to-power of the revolution. Like Bejel, he was poised to become an adult at the time he left Cuba permanently. Given his lived experience, he seems the farthest removed from Cuba while at the same time alleging an enduring relationship with it.

Prompted by their segmented views, the abovementioned Cuban-American authors fashion diverse new homes and homelands out of Cuba. These stretch from a rediscovered Cuban-Jewish community, itself the outcome of diaspora (Behar); a home built under the aegis of an unexpectedly lengthened exile (Pérez Firmat), and another that requires reinvention and a fresh start (Eire); images in the form of photographs that supply evidence of a lost but nonetheless conjured homeland (Mendoza); a hovering, overarching homeland that is no longer contained within geographical boundaries but spills over the borders of the island, shortening the distance between the island and the mainland (de la Campa); to the realization that home and homeland are continually being re-created through language, in narrative form (Bejel). A common thread to all is an underlying desire for home, as tenacious as it is elusive.

It is well to remember that narratives of return also worthy of note preceded the above examples. Early essays include those authored by individuals such as Lourdes Casal (1938–81), among the first to write about homecoming from the United States. A poet, writer, scholar, and public intellectual, Casal backed several projects that encouraged reconciliation between Cubans on both sides of the ideological divide, and she pursued this goal wholeheartedly at a time of fervid opposition to rapprochement. A charismatic mixed-race woman, Casal was a cofounder of *Areíto* magazine (1974–84), supported the launching of the Antonio Maceo Brigade (whose first visit to the island took place in 1977, establishing an important beachhead), played a major role in the Instituto de Estudios Cubanos, headed by María Cristina Herrera, and was a coeditor of *Contra viento y marea* (1978), a book of testimonials by young Cubans about their lives in the United States and their determination to restore their ties to Cuba. She inspired many who followed in her footsteps.

All Cuban Americans mentioned above bear witness to their trips in the autobiographical and testimonial genres, but the allure of *volver* pervades fiction as well. Fiction writers Cristina García, Achy Obejas, and Ana Menéndez dare to return not only physically as individuals but vicariously, too, through characters in their novels. Having left Cuba as small children, García and Obejas are among the younger members of the one-and-a-half generation. Menéndez, born in Los Angeles of Cuban parents, is technically of the second generation. Yet, as I argue in chapter 5, she partakes of some of the concerns regarding Cuba that suffuse the novels of García and Obejas, demonstrating the hold of a "post-memory," as Hirsch and Spitzer dub the memory shared by the descendants of Holocaust survivors. Menéndez, too, can be regarded as a deuteragonist.

Cuban-American visual artists have also been going back. In the 1980s Ana Mendieta exhibited her work in Havana and left behind samples of her ephemeral art. Inspired by *taíno* mythology, she left a testimony of her homecoming in the form of sculptures displaying the contour of indigenous goddesses carved in limestone caves on the island. More than a decade later, another visual and performance artist, Ernesto Pujol, returned to mount an exhibition titled *Los hijos de Pedro Pan* at a gallery in Havana.

This expansive second set of works by Cuban-American writers and artists is more reflective of a diasporic/transnational subjectivity or consciousness. The narratives may well reaffirm the lack of sympathy for the revolution one finds in the literature of exile. Indeed, some betray a highly critical stance, and most show a patent disenchantment over time. However, dissent does not rule out an intricate coming to grips with Cuba and the transnational character of migration today. In some cases, political differences are not regarded as roadblocks to an active engagement with insular Cuban culture and with the Cubans who stayed behind, although in other cases they do stand in the way of a fruitful dialogue, especially when Cubans closely identified with the Castro regime are involved (M. A. Torres, "Beyond the Rupture," "The Convergence of Time"). When a dialogue between the two parties takes place, differences of opinion may surface (M. A. Torres, "*Encuentros y encontronazos*").

Dystopian Returns

While there is no doubt a spectrum of return narratives, including some with a gratifying ending, texts that convey a feeling of estrangement are not all that uncommon in the Cuban and Hispanic traditions. In her essay on the literature of return, Adriana López Labourdette highlights works by José Donoso, Cristina Peri Rossi, and Alicia Kozameh where dislocation and disjunction constitute a literary staple. At the risk of being reductive, as the critic cautions, one can draw from the contrast between utopia and dystopia to depict what takes place in some of the texts written from a political or ontological exile perspective. Exiles typically hold two disparate visions, one utopian, revolving around their desired location (the homeland), and another dystopian to refer to their actual location, which they no doubt reject as a true home. But the return achieved in return narratives conjoin two opposing spaces at once: a utopian space, grounded in the place one travels to and wishes to recover, and another dystopian, that is, the place one has actually reached (33).

An example of the last type, where utopia and dystopia coexist in a geographic location, is Calvert Casey's short story "El regreso" (1962), a classic tale of return in Cuban canonical literature. The story exemplifies the doomed attempt of a socially isolated character to blend in a Cuba convulsed by prerevolutionary political strife. The character reaches the island seeking to escape the alienation that has haunted him on account of his "difference" (homosexuality). He deceives himself into thinking that Cuba, where the second half of the story is set, remains the place where he can lead an authentic life, free of prejudice. In the end, however, the illusion costs him his life. After falling into the hands of henchmen hunting for rebels, he is brutally tortured and left to die on the beach. The protagonist's utopian fantasies, then, are cut short almost as soon as he begins to anticipate the joy of a new life brimming with promise.

There are, of course, deviations to the described model where the coordinates of utopia do not collide but conflate with those of dystopia, as in the case of Casey. Another classic tale of return in insular literature is Reinaldo Arenas's novella "Viaje a La Habana" (1995), a title that recalls the memoirs of María de las Mercedes Beltrán Santa Cruz y Cárdenas Montalvo y O'Farrill (Havana 1789–Paris 1852), the Condesa de Merlín, about her own return to Cuba more than a century earlier. But in contrast with the Condesa de Merlín's constructive recollections in *Viaje a La Habana*, Arenas's homonym story offers a grim view of both departure and return, as if the two were indistinguishable. The story's protagonist, Ismael, a name that resonates with yet another classic of Cuban letters, José Martí's *Ismaelillo*, is driven out of Cuba after finally acting upon his long-repressed same-sex desire. Being true to himself after keeping up with appearances for so long, Ismael is willing to face the consequences of his actions. Many years later, upon his return, he makes the acquaintance of a young man whose eagerness to flee calls to mind Ismael's own. After spending the night with the young man, the protagonist discovers that he has had intercourse with his son, Ismaelito, whom he had not seen since he was a child.

Even though the narrator describes the discovery matter-of-factly, the incestuous conduct, developing as it does on the island, takes us deeper into a split and fragmented universe where *ser* and *estar* diverge, pointing to different geographic locations. As Antonio Prieto Taboada writes, playing with the double meaning of "to be" in Spanish (172), in "Viaje a La Habana" the homeland is defined as the only place where one can be (*ser*), a place where, simultaneously, one cannot be (*estar*). On the island, Ismael is always an abject figure. In Yolanda Martínez San Miguel's words, homoeroticism is presented as a limit that wounds the protagonist every time he finds himself within the nation's boundaries (364).

The dystopian view inscribed at first glance in Arenas's incest story gives way, though, to what Prieto Taboada persuasively calls a figurative representation of exile. Arenas goes beyond the political to bring into play an existential exilic condition, which he tries to overcome in the story with a metaphoric abolition of time and the fusion of bodies (178–79). However, despite the diffusion of limits that the critic pinpoints in his reading of the story, the transgression, subjugation, and deprivation that cut across the story remain with the reader, uncovering the island as the opposite of an ideally perfect place.

Scenes from other texts by Arenas reinforce that view. At the end of his autobiography, *Antes que anochezca* (1992), Arenas describes several dreams, or rather nightmares, entailing a return to Cuba. One of the nightmares ends with Arenas trapped in the room he has occupied upon returning, aware that the police will show up any minute. Anguished, he tries to break free, but all of his efforts are to no avail. Finally, he wakes up and, upon seeing the derelict walls of his room in New York, he feels nonetheless relieved (336). Nowhere are the feelings of confinement as vivid as on the island, unadulterated dystopia, where the author suffocates.[16]

More recently, Antonio José Ponte has put a post-Soviet spin to the theme of return in "Viniendo," a short story included in the compilation *Un arte de hacer ruinas y otros cuentos* (2005). Ponte's story invites the reader to reconsider the utopia/dystopia binary in light of post-1990s developments. As the title suggests, the main character in the story is neither leaving nor returning; he is merely "coming" from Russia, where he was on a student scholarship, one of the last Cubans to enjoy one, for the Soviet Union has ceased to exist. For those coming after him, the future is by all means precarious.

Although the character knows whence he is coming, he seems to lose his bearings as soon as he arrives in Havana. He is aware of the dissonance between who he was and who he is and between what was and what is, so he goes around searching, unsuccessfully, for a way to bridge the gap. At the end, it dawns on him that he has truly *returned*: "El tren suyo avisó que al fin saldrían de allí, y por primera vez, él estuvo seguro de haber vuelto" [His train announced that they would be leaving, and for the first time he was sure he had returned]. But it immediately strikes him that the discovery serves no purpose: "No sabía de dónde ni para qué. Perdió su tren y quedó solo en el campo" [He was unaware where he was coming from or for what purpose. He missed the train and was left in the countryside by himself] (124). He is utterly adrift.

An admixture of perplexity and anomie drives the Ponte story, where utopia and/or dystopia are no longer useful points of reference. Utopia, or the possibility of reaching perfection, has slipped out of reach, taking with it the opposite on which it, like a parasite, feeds. Free from any anchor, the story operates as a metaphor for that juncture in the island's history that transcends the binary to arrive at an unforeseen stalemate.[17]

Cuban-American authors who fled when they were still young after suffering repression write from a vantage point similar to the one adopted by Arenas. One such case is poet Magali Alabau, who left Cuba in 1966 when she was twenty-one years old after being expelled from the National Art School for her homosexual behavior. Having emigrated while transitioning into adulthood, Alabau is among the youngest of immigrants from the first generation. According to Rubén G. Rumbaut, those who were eighteen to twenty-four years old at the time they emigrated fall into this category (1166).

Upon her brief visit to Cuba in the early 1990s, Alabau is confronted with memories of that horrific experience, which she condenses in several stanzas of her book, *Hemos llegado a Ilión* (2013), a remarkable lengthy poem on the Cuban revolution seen from the other side of the mirror, in reverse (Rodríguez Gutiérrez 17). As she wanders through the city recalling familiar sites, paying visits to old friends, and delivering packages, all of these common tasks performed by a returnee, the persona in the poem focuses on what is missing from the urban landscape:

> La ciudad me recuerda los que faltan.
> Falta el conocimiento de los nuevos,
> el crecimiento de las contradicciones.
> Faltan más rostros, más risas al paisaje,
> falta algo que no sé descifrar, que no conozco.
> Falta la bulla, la esquina que se cruza,
> falta el círculo continuo,
> tropelaje del ruido de la risa,
> la música del claxon,
> el inquieto parpadear de la esperanza. (41–42)
> [The city reminds me of those who are missing.
> Knowledge about the new ones is missing,
> the growth of contradictions.
> More faces are missing, more laughs about the landscape,
> something that I do not know how to decipher, that I do not know is missing.
> The noise is missing, the corner that one crosses,
> the continuing circle is missing,

the snarl of the noise made by laughing,
the music of the claxon,
the restless blink of hope.]

So much is missing from the city that even that which is unknown is hyperbolically also gone. Hope, too, has withdrawn. What persists, however, are daunting feelings of enclosure that overshadow even the kindest of gestures, nipping in the bud every opportunity for redemption:

No es que no tenga miedo. En verdad, no estaba preparada
para el buen trato, para los buenos días de cada ascensor,
para el servicio portero de llaves repetidas.
Aún así, ¿por qué me siento como los prisioneros?
¿Por qué pregunto al techo si hay alguien deambulando en este sueño?
    Llego de madrugada.
Mal vestida ya estoy, un poco agria de tantas ocasiones.
Tiento a ver si soy la misma. Mi voz suena cambiada.
No llevo las acotaciones que creí aprendidas. (43)
[It is not that I'm not afraid. In truth, I was not prepared
for the good manners, for the good morning from each elevator,
for the doorman service of repeated keys.
Even then, why do I feel like prisoners do?
Why do I ask the ceiling if there is someone wandering in this dream? I
    arrive at dawn.
Badly dressed I am, a little bitter of so many occasions.
I feel to see if I am the same. My voice sounds different.
I do not carry the stage directions that I thought I had learned.]

In Alabau's universe, the present cannot be grasped outside of the framework provided by the past, which sets the terms of engagement. There are verses, like the ones cited above, that occasionally lapse into the light, but these are short-lived. Only at the end, as the visitor approaches her departure, does daybreak come through, and she is able to leave darkness behind.

Most of the narratives included in *Impossible Returns*, however, while equivocal about fitting in, are far from portraying dystopia on the island. The repeated returns evoked by the writers demonstrate that their trips are not deemed threatening. Nonetheless, the narratives confirm both the complexities of return and the desire to accomplish it. As López Labourdette argues in her essay, these texts create a narrative space that replaces the lost home/homeland: one is tempted to read the narratives not about identity but as identity personified; not as return narratives but as narratives that take the place of return (34). When Ruth Behar writes about saving Cuba for when she is not there, she proves the critic right: "I need to miss Cuba, conjure Cuba, struggle to remember Cuba in order to write. All my writing comes from not being there" (*Traveling Heavy* 224). For Behar, writing about return turns into her home away from home.

Return, the Stepchild of Migration Studies No Longer

Return migration has been called "the great unwritten chapter in the history of migration," as Stefansson, quoting Russell King, reminds the reader in his "Homecomings to the Future" (5), published in 2000. The overriding interest among academics lies in the processes of acculturation and assimilation in receiving countries, not on the opposite movement. Yet even before Russell King's essay was published, an increasing number of studies had addressed the topic of diasporic return, as Stefansson's bibliography makes clear. Most of the studies in the existing bibliography on homecoming, however, have been undertaken in the fields of anthropology and the social sciences, and for the most part have focused on lands other than the Hispanic Caribbean (Flores 37).

The new millennium has generated further research, occasionally addressing return migrants from Latin America and the Caribbean. Besides Elizabeth Aranda's and Juan Flores's books on Puerto Rico, there is a chapter by Gina M. Pérez on the role of gender in the dynamics of return migration to the island in *The Experience of Return Migration: Caribbean Perspectives* (2005), edited by Robert B. Poter et al. Takeyuki Tsuda's edited volume *Diasporic Homecomings: Ethnic Return Migration in Comparative Perspective* (2009) includes case studies on return migration from Peru and Brazil to Japan and from Argentina to Spain. Other titles are Mary Chamberlain's *Narratives of Exile and Return* (1997) about Barbadians leaving Great Britain; Solimar Otero's *Afro-Cuban Diasporas in the Atlantic World* (2010) about the return of Cubans to Lagos; and Belinda I. Reyes's *Dynamics of Immigration: Return Migration to Western Mexico* (1997). Silvio Torres Saillant's essay "El retorno de las yolas," included in his volume *El retorno de las yolas: ensayos sobre diáspora, democracia y dominicanidad* (1999), discusses the role of the Dominican diaspora in the country of origin, making a case for its modernizing and democratizing influence. Last but not least, Fran Markowitz and Anders H. Stefansson's edited volume *Homecomings: Unsettling Paths of Return* (2004) includes an essay by Ruth Behar on her return to Cuba and the making of her documentary *Adio Kerida* (reproduced in Ruggiero's *The Jewish Diaspora in Latin America and the Caribbean*). Behar delves into her trips to the island in the last chapter of her book *Traveling Heavy: A Memoir in between Journeys* (2013). This is far from an exhaustive review of the literature, which covers the return to ancestral lands and to a place where one once lived. It would appear that scholars are gradually paying heed to earlier calls for further research on homecomings.

A cursory review of the literature in other fields besides migration studies offers disappointing results. Of recent publication is Marianne Hirsch and Nancy K. Miller's edited volume, *Rites of Return: Diaspora Poetics and the Politics of Memory* (2011), a wide-ranging collection given the areas it covers, from digital technologies to memoir and photography to sites commemorating the past, such as museums and memorials. The focus here is on metaphorical return. Maria Antònia Oliver-Rotger's edited volume *Identity, Diaspora and Return in American Literature* (2015), addresses the work of writers of Vietnamese, Haitian, Mexican, Dominican, and Cuban descent, among others. Oliver-Rotger's book includes articles by Rocío G. Davis, Ada Ortuzar-Young, and Santiago Vaquera-Vázquez on Behar, Ana Menéndez, and Junot Díaz respectively, authors for whom narrating some sort of return is almost second nature. On the other hand, an essay by Marilén Loyola sees in the imaginary return of Severo Sarduy, Reinaldo Arenas, and Zoe Valdés such hopelessness and despair that it drives the main characters to a metaphorical death. There is no question these other returns are catastrophic.

Although focusing only partially on the topic, Yolanda Martínez San Miguel's *Caribe Two Ways: Cultura de la migración en el Caribe insular hispánico* (2003) treats the symbiotic nature of nation and migration in the cultural production of the Antilles, historically a crossroads in the Americas. Also worthy of note is Ana Serra's essay about writers in Spain, descendants of indianos (Spaniards who went to Cuba to try their hand starting in the seventeenth century), who describe follow-up trips to Cuba many years after their families went back to their native country. Finally, the equally perceptive essay by López Labourdette, cited above, applies suggestive theoretical considerations to the literature on return among mainly Southern Cone writers.

Returning as a line of inquiry has largely eluded Cuban studies. In "Distancia no quiere decir olvido: Viajes a la semilla," Uva de Aragón laments the fact that the return of many Cubans who were forced to leave their homeland over the last century-and-a-half has received neither the reflection it deserves nor the positive evaluation it warrants (204–5). Given its strategic position in the Caribbean and its history of colonialism, bouts of dictatorship, and foreign interventions, Cuba has withstood more than its share of one- and two-way journeys. In the 1800s, renowned intellectuals such as José Martí, Félix Varela, José María Heredia, José Antonio Saco, Gertrudis Gómez de Avellaneda, and the Condesa de Merlín left the island, some under trying circumstances, only to return, with exceptions, at a more propitious time.[18]

De Aragón asserts that even under the republic, fleeing Cuba became synonymous with treason, and so major writers such as Alejo Carpentier and Alfonso Hernández Catá, after living in France and Spain respectively for an extended period of time, were accused at first of having turned their backs on Cuba (205–6). As in the rest of Latin America, the political and social responsibility of the writer/intellectual rests (or used to rest in the past) on his or her place of residence and level of engagement with the native country (Zamora 11–12). Nevertheless, as de Aragón and other critics such as Rafael Rojas ("Diaspora and Memory") note, there is today a literature of reconciliation, or at least tolerance, that does not shy away from positing an eventual meeting of minds. As the equivalence between nation and bounded culture weakens due to myriad forces, one can only expect that changes in the understanding of fluid cultural identities will come to light.

The Many Facets of *Volver*

The chapters that follow take us on a journey through the land of return, with each of the six converging on a unique stopover. Chapter 1, "An Uphill Battle: The Contentious Politics of Return," provides the necessary historical background to migration and return. It offers a summary of postrevolutionary migration waves, succinct information on the Operation Pedro

Pan, the policies that have either eased or hindered travel both in Cuba and the United States, and the diverse attitudes toward return in the Cuban-American community. Additionally, it explores reports on the initial trips to Cuba undertaken by the Antonio Maceo Brigade and Grupo Areíto in the late 1970s, as well as others more individually focused that came after.

Chapter 2, "Daring to Go Back: In Search of Traces," looks at the ways in which the return trip is represented through autobiographical narratives such as the already cited memoirs by Behar, Mendoza, de la Campa, and Bejel. These narratives betray both a reclaiming of memory in spaces left behind and the slippery nature of that memory. Diverse in terms of content, voice, and style, they all reveal both the authors' keen interest in their "homeland" and the inevitable distance that has grown between their present selves and the land and culture from which they took flight. I rely on indexical markers and the post-indexical, an elliptical trope, to delineate the distance.

A number of Cuban Americans have trusted images rather than words to introduce the subject of return—to the island's syncretic cultures, to artifacts correlated with displacement such as boats and passports, to tropes and motifs that have come to stand for things Cuban such as tropical landscapes or colonial arches, and to objects that serve as a reminder of a childhood spent on the island. Chapter 3, "Chiseling (in) Cuba," examines the legacy of Ana Mendieta, the Cuban-American visual artist who became a feminist icon after her untimely death in 1985. Rather than addressing Mendieta's art proper, this chapter looks at the lasting impact of Mendieta's return to Cuba in the early 1980s, when she not only carved the so-called *Rupestrian Sculptures*, but also met with young Cuban artists whom she inspired. What are Mendieta's traces in Cuba more than twenty-five years after her death? Can one speak about her legacy on the island? Even though the focus here is on Mendieta, another émigré that fits the profile of the returnee visual artist is Ernesto Pujol. As his work in the 1990s revolved around childhood, it is included in the following chapter.

For some, the only possible return in order to recover a sense of *lo cubano* is through childhood memoirs. Chapter 4, "Cuban Childhood Redux," explores the work of Pujol and María Brito, who have treated the subject in their spellbinding artwork. It includes writers Carlos Eire and Gustavo Pérez Firmat, whose sense of rupture, loss, and discontinuity is exacerbated by the decision to stay away from the homeland. Their memoirs represent an effort to come to terms with a past that did all but prefigure the present of the narrative, set in the United States. Other memoirs enabling a return to a childhood spent in Cuba, such as *Exiled Memories: A Cuban Childhood* (1990) by Pablo Medina and *Spared Angola: Memories from a Cuban-American Childhood* (1997) by Virgil Suárez, would have provided rich primary material, but adding them to this chapter would have made it unwieldy. Faced with a choice, I selected those more clearly spanning Cuba and the diaspora.

Others choose to go back to Cuba on the shoulders of characters in their novels. Chapter 5, "Vicarious Returns and a Usable Past in *The Agüero Sisters, Days of Awe*, and *Loving Che*" surveys the fiction of Cristina García, Achy Obejas, and Ana Menéndez, the first two writers among the youngest members of the one-and-a-half generation, and the latter from the following generation. Despite their different generational location, most of the work penned by the three writers revolves around Cuba, demonstrating the island's continuing allure. The selected novels wrestle with somewhat overlooked aspects of Cuban culture such as *mestizaje*, marginalized religions, and the private lives of revolutionary icons, all from the vantage point of women characters. Donning metaphorical *guayaberas*, García, Obejas, and Menéndez draw from a "usable past" (Lois Parkinson Zamora) that infuses all three novels with *cubanidad*. Confronted with an assortment of novels built around a vicarious return, I chose these three in view of their similar narrative features and concerns.

Highlighting the representation of exiles and the one and-a-half generation as well as recent émigrés, chapter 6, "Toward a Boomerang Aesthetic: The View from the Island," explores the view from Cuba and the kind of reception those who decide to return can expect from the Cubans who stayed. For historical reasons, the understanding of exile and treason as synonymous terms embraced by the Cuban political leadership until the late 1970s has given way to a more open acceptance of emigration as well as returning. Unlike exiles, émigré artists and writers today are now able to engage in two-way travel with relative ease, making them receptive to a "boomerang aesthetic" that assimilates a variety of influences from around the world.

A final comment is warranted about the preponderance of memoirs in a study of return migration. As Álvarez Borland noted in 1994, autobiographical and semi-autobiographical genres have not only proliferated in the Cuban diaspora over the last two decades, they have prospered in the literature of the one-and-a-half generation ("Displacements and Autobiography" 59). Yet their critical reception has been lukewarm due perhaps to the marginal place reserved for such genres in Hispanic and even U.S. ethnic literary studies. Stephen J. Clark's *Autobiografía y revolución en Cuba* (1999) focuses on the memoirs of Padilla, Carlos Franqui, and other prominent expatriates, who write about a return of sorts to the early revolutionary period in order to settle old scores that point to an evasive universal truth. A chapter in Álvarez Borland's *Cuban-American Literature of Exile: From Person to Persona* (1998) and an article by the same critic are devoted to a handful of memoirs of the one-and-a-half generation. But there is no study of Cuban-American autobiography as a whole. Reflecting on the autobiographical genre would produce an enhanced appraisal of Cuban-American literature, with at least one memoir, Evelio Grillo's *Black Cuban, Black American: A Memoir* (2000), dealing overtly with a rarely addressed subject, racial relations. The omission prompts a scholar, Susan D. Greenbaum, to contend that black Cubans are still "the missing faces in the smiling portrait of Cuban ethnicity in the United States" (2).[19]

While this book does not aspire to remedy the lacunae, it will at least examine works with autobiographical or semi-autobiographical content across genres—literature, the visual arts, and film. My goal is to explore how return is "narrated" in each of these cases, without making distinctions among the various genres. I am far from arguing that memoirs and fiction are indistinguishable, if for nothing else than readers approach them with different expectations and assumptions. However, my aim here is to focus not on the differences between the genres, but on their common ground, that is, on their discursive representation of return.

Although a genuine effort has been made to identify primary sources on the subject of return in other countries where Cubans have settled, these are scarce thus far for reasons not exclusively stemming, I believe, from the smaller size of the émigré communities in those sites.[20] On the one hand, the publication of first-person narratives is not as common as in the United States, where the writing of autobiography has gone through a process of "democratization" (Fass), with ordinary but literate, educated citizens willing to disclose their private lives to the reading public. On the other hand, countries not as identified with immigration as the United States place limits on the kinds of mixed, hyphenated identities that foster reflections on biculturalism and the maintenance of ties to other homelands. Here, immigration is admittedly part and parcel of the U.S. experience. Émigrés in other countries may become more integrated into their new societies and therefore their identities may evolve in a completely different way. They may not recognize the existence of an ethnic literature that, by contrast, has been gaining ground steadily in the United States since the 1960s. Cuban Americans benefit from the growing acceptance of literature other than mainstream in publishing houses. But even with publishers devoted to Cuban studies, such as Verbum and, until recently, Colibrí, in Spain, there is no known bibliography on returning and little in the way of self-referential writings hailing from this Western European country. Interestingly, Enrique del Risco's memoir *Siempre nos quedará Madrid* (2012), although set in Spain and written in Spanish, was published in New York.

The emphasis, then, is on Cuban-American memoirs. I hope to show how one-and-a-halfers deploy an imaginary through which they lay claim to the homeland of their childhood and early adolescence without suppressing their ties to the receiving society. To that end, they either return to or evoke the lost homeland in their narratives. The authors embark on a journey of discovery, the type of voyage that has inspired human beings since time immemorial. As Cavafy's "Ithaka" insinuates, Cuba gave them the marvelous journey that they share with the reader through their writings. They may never truly reach the island of their dreams, one that is now sadly impoverished, but the unending search for home and homeland is, for the purposes of this book, what counts.

1

An Uphill Battle

The Contentious Politics of Return

> In the fifties, there was even a ferry that crossed regularly from the island to Key West; the *City of Havana*, they called it. But it stopped running in 1960, as hostility between the United States and Cuba began to flare. Thereafter, all movement between the two countries would become, in moral, psychological, and political terms, among the longest and costliest journeys in the world, no matter what it looked like on a map.
>
> David Rieff, *The Exile: Cuba in the Heart of Miami*

Florida senator Marco Rubio once cautioned that, as exiles, Cubans would do well not to travel to their former homeland lest they become regular migrants (Rieff, "Will Little Havana Go Blue?" 51). As Rubio's warning suggests, traveling to Cuba is ensnared in a web of significations that go well beyond family visits and tourism to include perils posed to the exile identity carved over half a century by Cuban émigrés in the United States. Since the exile identity masks other issues touching on class, race, and ideology, return trips to Cuba have ramifications unheard of in other contexts. Among exiles who, unlike immigrants, may enjoy certain privileges and have a measure of influence, the politics of return matter as much as the poetics of return, requiring special attention.

Yet, despite being a loaded issue in the community, return has been overlooked in most studies of the Cuban-American population. Because of the scarcity of studies shedding light on the topic, this chapter provides details about Cuba travel gleaned from a variety of sources that typically include only partial information. Even reliable statistics on returning exiles are hard to locate. My aim is to address historical grievances as well as policies both in the United States and Cuba informing the discourse on return in the

Cuban-American writings examined in the book and to do so as concisely as possible. The overall goal in the chapter is to frame the historical and political circumstances under which the flight, first, and later the return of the one-and-a-half generation took place. Also included is a review of collective returns that have materialized since the 1970s.

Flying the Unfriendly Skies, Braving the Choppy Seas

Either by air or by sea, more than a million Cubans have left the island since 1959.[1] The first wave occurred between 1959 and 1962, made up of the upper and middle classes who had the most to lose from the political and economic restructuring of society. Among them were Cubans with ties to the Batista regime escaping harassment, imprisonment, and summary executions.[2] During this period, over 248,000 Cubans fled. The increasing radicalization of the revolution, with policies ranging from the nationalization of Cuban-owned businesses to the closing of private schools, as well as the centralization of government and religious intolerance, antagonized many from the middle sectors of Cuban society who would have stayed had the revolution taken a different course. Censorship and shortages of basic foodstuffs began to have an impact as well. Since these were all earth-shaking events, Cubans continued to flee.

There was also an international dimension to Cuban affairs. The United States did not respond well to the threat represented by the revolution in power. Its long history of involvement in the region meant that there were vital economic interests to protect. By the 1950s U.S. companies controlled most Cuban mines and public utilities, in addition to a large percentage of the railways and sugar production (García Bedolla 48). After the revolution, relations between the two countries deteriorated rapidly, and Cuba confiscated U.S. businesses. It then drifted toward the Soviet Union. In addition to the already tense internal struggle among social classes and political factions, Cubans were inextricably caught up in the confrontation between the two Cold War superpowers. There was no easy way out.

No Cubans were untouched, including children. In 1960, rumors began to spread that the government would curb parental rights in order to facilitate the indoctrination of Cuban minors. Operation Pedro Pan, supported by the Archdiocese of Miami, the U.S. Department of State and, some argue, the Central Intelligence Agency (CIA), was introduced as a result with the ostensible purpose of saving as many children as possible from the clutches of communism. Conceived at first as a clandestine evacuation plan for the sons and daughters of Cuban fighters in the underground movement against the Castro regime, Operation Pedro Pan quickly became an all-inclusive program for the exodus of unaccompanied minors.

Between December 1960 and October 1962, 14,048 children and adolescents were extended visa waivers issued by the U.S. government that allowed them to enter the country. Those in charge of the program were expected to provide homes and scholarships. Family or acquaintances claimed about half of the refugee children while the rest were placed in temporary shelters (Conde 72). Children who were assigned to foster care outside of south Florida faced the most challenges, as the alien environment made it all the more difficult for them to adjust. The Pedro Pan program fell short of expectations in a good number of cases, with helpless minors suffering disastrous consequences, including emotional and sexual abuse. The lucky ones, however, thrived in their new milieu. Many parents were able to reunite with their children soon after they had left, but others were stranded when commercial flights to the United States were halted in the midst of the 1962 missile crisis. After the crisis, the United States maintained its economic embargo against the island, making travel all but impossible. Both Ana Mendieta and Carlos Eire were separated from their parents for what seemed too long due to the cutoff of ties. When they finally reunited, the damage to the family relationship was beyond repair. Parents who had initially feared losing control over their children had indeed lost control.

On 17 April 1961, shortly after Operation Pedro Pan was set in motion, the Bay of Pigs full-scale invasion of Cuba was launched from the United States. Seeking to overthrow the Castro government, it featured the return of over one thousand Cuban exiles trained and funded by the CIA-sponsored paramilitary organization Brigada 2506. The failed invasion brought about a hardening of positions on both sides. In the aftermath of the military intervention, the Cuban government proclaimed the socialist character of the revolution and its alignment with the Soviet bloc. By 1972, Cuba had joined the Council for Mutual Economic Assistance (COMECON), which enabled trade and integration among socialist member states.

The new developments, in turn, fueled the desire of middle-class Cubans to flee the island. Over 350,000 left either through the port of Camarioca and third countries in the period 1962–65 or through the Cuban refugee airlift (*puente aéreo*) initiated by President Lyndon B. Johnson in 1965. The airlift program ended in 1973. In the first exile wave of 1959–61, 31 percent of émigrés were professionals or managers. However, by 1970 the proportion had fallen to 12 percent for these two categories, and 57 percent were blue-collar, service, or agricultural workers (María C. García, *Havana USA* 35–44). Moreover, while the 1953 Cuba census revealed that blacks and mulattoes made up 27 percent of the island's population (44) the 1960 and 1970 "1 percent" U.S. surveys show that the black population amounted to 7.7 and 3.5 percent, respectively, of the Cuban community in the United States (Ruggles et al.).[3] The racial composition of Cuban society and the emerging Miami enclave further diverged during this period.[4] The children of exiles who became the one-and-a-half generation are the heirs of the racial, social, political, and educational profile of pre-1980 exile.

In 1980, thousands of Cubans occupied the grounds of the Peruvian embassy in Havana seeking political asylum. In response to the ensuing crisis, Cuban officials opened the port of Mariel to those who wanted to leave on boats arriving from South Florida. During the Mariel boatlift, over 125,000 Cubans reached U.S. shores. Even though there were common criminals who had been kicked out of prison in their midst, ordinary, hardworking Cubans made up the majority of the *marielitos*—along with writers and artists who had been marginalized due to their dissident politics or sexual orientation. Since many had grown up under the revolution, the *marielitos* were significantly different from the first two migration waves. They were also overwhelmingly from the working class (Pedraza, *Political Disaffection* 7–8). For these reasons, they were not fully accepted by the earlier émigrés, who felt that the latest arrivals had tarnished the image of model minority secured by the earlier cohorts in exile.

After a long interval, another mass exodus occurred in the summer of 1994. More than 34,000 *balseros* or rafters braved the shark-infested waters of the Straits and made it to the United States. Others were not so fortunate. Each of the four waves had a distinct social profile. Gradually, they evolved from upper and middle classes to working class, as well as from a disproportionate number of whites in the first wave to the gradually more mixed racial composition, more reflective of Cuban demographics, of subsequent ones (Pedraza, *Political Disaffection* 158).[5] In addition, thousands of Cubans have come into the United States as a result of migratory accords between the two countries.

Given this scenario of spurts migration, at least until the end of the twentieth century, Cuban migration was "more akin to the flow from a water faucet: abruptly turned off and on at the will of those in power in Havana and Washington in response to political considerations" (Grenier and Pérez 22). Opportunities to migrate became hostage to impromptu politics. Since mass migration in the wake of the revolution had a starting point and did not pan out on a continuous, rational basis, discriminating between attitudes toward acculturation and return among the various waves would seem to be somewhat easier than among other émigré communities. There is no discernible one-and-a-half generation in the Mexican American and Puerto Rican communities on the mainland. Also abetting the articulation of this generation's profile is the high level of education many of its members have attained. Given that background, they are in a position to formulate and disseminate the parameters within which such generational location ought to be understood. Their role in framing the boundaries of the discussion about their own cohort will become clear throughout the book.

Imbued as they are with symbolic value, labels remain important in the Cuban-American community. Especially over the first two decades following Castro's takeover, Cubans fleeing the island were branded as exiles, a label with profound political significance that brought them both advantages and disadvantages. Cubans could enter the United States as refugees and, once admitted, enjoyed terms of entry routinely denied to other immigrants at the height of the Cold War—and even today. The favorable treatment was due to geopolitical reasons: the Cuban exodus was tangible proof of the failure of the socialist revolution. The Cuban Adjustment Act of 1966, perhaps the most important privilege handed to the exiles, still in effect, postulates that any native or citizen of Cuba may be granted permanent resident status a year and a day following entry into the United States. Those who came before 1980 "benefited from some $957 million worth of official federal, state, and local level programs initiated to help their adaptation" (Eckstein and Barbería 804). The Cuban Refugee Program can only be qualified in superlative terms: it was "the largest, most expensive, and most ambitious program for handling refugees in U.S. history" (Y. Prieto, *The Cubans of New Jersey* 8). Exiles and their children benefited immensely from programs that have been out of reach to migrants from other countries.

Still, the federal support extended to Cuban émigrés does not diminish the hardships most have faced, as a host of Cuban-American memoirs more than sufficiently exemplify. Many émigrés had been persecuted in Cuba, and most had lost all of their possessions, arriving penniless in what was for them an unknown country whose language they did not speak. Additionally, because of their decision to leave or "abandon" the country, émigrés were banished from their native land. Having turned their backs for primarily political reasons, the first waves of exiles automatically became traitors to the motherland. Unlike other émigrés, Cubans were barred from going back even temporarily over the first two decades following Castro's takeover, a proscription that added to the anxiety of those who left. Banishment applied both to those who came to live within the boundaries of Cuba's archenemy, the United States, and to those who, joining the ranks of the diaspora, set their sights elsewhere.

Cuban Americans, a Distinctive Population within a Growing Diaspora

The one-and-a-half generation, whose adopted homeland is the United States, is only a fragment of an ever growing Cuban diaspora. Since 1959, hundreds of thousands of Cubans settled in Miami and other cities across the United States, making this community the third largest Hispanic population in the country after Mexicans and Puerto Ricans. According to the U.S. Census, the Cuban population grew from 1.2 million in 2000 to 1.8 million in 2010, comprising approximately 4 percent of the total Hispanic or Latino population in both 2000 and 2010. Thousands of other Cubans are dispersed throughout the world, part of a diaspora that has been the focus of several studies, such as José Cobas and Jorge Duany's *Cubans in Puerto Rico: Ethnic Economy and Cultural Identity* (1997), Andrea O'Reilly Herrera's *Cuba: The Idea of a Nation Displaced* (2007), Ruth Behar and Lucía M. Suárez's *The Portable Island: Cubans at Home in the World* (2008), Tanya N. Weimer's *La diáspora cubana en México* (2008), and Mette Louise Berg's *Diasporic Generations: Memory, Politics, and Nation among Cubans in Spain* (2011).[6]

In comparison with the United States, clusters of Cubans elsewhere seem small but not insignificant: there are roughly 90,000 in Spain, mostly in Madrid; 17,000 in Canada, especially in Toronto and Montreal; 9,000 in Germany, primarily in Berlin; 7,000 in France, above all in Paris; 3,000 in the United Kingdom, mainly in London; and about 20,000 in Venezuela.[7] The estimates are relatively consistent with those offered by Cuban researcher Antonio Aja Díaz, who found that 119,916 Cubans lived in Europe in 2007, while in South America the number was 84,715, and in Central America, 35,943 (Aja 203). Overall, more than 16 percent of the Cuban nation has relocated outside of Cuba since 1959. Although it is doubtful that Cuban émigrés shared all along a diaspora awareness given the infrastructure needed for such sustenance—media, festivities, and institutions stoking a certain identity—at the present time innovations in the field of virtual communications may well be enabling that awareness, alongside the above-mentioned volumes. *Diaspora* is likewise the term chosen in this book to name the scattering of Cubans throughout the world, even though most of the works analyzed here hail from the United States.

In the United States, the convergence of interests of the first wave of conservative, right-wing Cubans and the U.S. Cold War agenda gave rise to an alliance lasting several decades, one that has severely curbed the freedom to travel. According to Alejandro Portes and Alex Stepick, Cubans in South Florida closed ranks around the perceived threat of a communist conspiracy to take over the island, an idea propounded by conservative exiles (140–44). Related to the fear of a conspiracy, the theme of the betrayed revolution, foregrounded in the first historiography of exile, was also used to coalesce the anticommunist sentiment of the Cuban opposition, thus facilitating cooperation between the exiles and the U.S. government during the Cold War (Rojas, *Essays* 119–20). Comprised of a spectrum of political positions that included a right wing, moderates, and a left wing who espoused social changes short of socialism, the community was far from being homogeneous, yet came to be united in its opposition to Fidel Castro (García Bedolla 50). The coming together of interests between Cuban exile organizations and the U.S. government, which furthered access to the top echelons of government, distinguishes the United States from other nation-states where Cubans have settled. Here, travel and migratory issues have customarily been enmeshed with politics and ideology.

Other countries have followed a different approach. The relations of nation-states such as Mexico and Spain with Cuba have not always been friendly, yet Cuban émigrés there do not fall prey to dated politics of vindication. Émigrés in these other countries are unlikely to be confronted with threats to eliminate travel even though they may not speak with one voice about return trips. For instance, different views on the subject of homecoming are held among the members of the generation of the 1980s that chose to make Mexico their home and the émigrés who decide to return do so for various reasons (Rojas, "From Havana to Mexico City" 99). The United States, then, constitutes a special case that places heavy demands on the returnees.

Counterpoint between Politics and Returns: *Areíto* and the Antonio Maceo Brigade

The return narratives included in this study cover a broad historical period. As part of the Cuban-American community, their authors have been subjected to the ebb and flow that has characterized U.S. policy on travel to Cuba. The U.S. embargo against Cuba imposed in the early 1960s had a direct effect on travel. It placed restrictions on financial transactions related to travel to Cuba, effectively imposing a travel ban. From 1963 until 1977, the U.S. Treasury Department's Office of Foreign Assets Control (OFAC) prohibited travel as a means of enforcing the embargo.[8] However, defying the travel ban were individuals and groups that sympathized with Cuba, such as the Venceremos Brigade, a coalition of young Americans who proclaimed their solidarity with the revolution by traveling to Cuba through third countries and engaging in community service. Their first trip took place in 1969.

Likewise rebelling against the restrictions were young Cuban Americans who had fled of their own accord but had reconsidered their severance of ties with Cuba, as well as others who, as minors, had left involuntarily with their families or by themselves through Operation Pedro Pan. Like jetsam washed ashore after a shipwreck, they showed up unexpectedly beginning in the early 1970s, surprising many who believed that they were lost for the nation. Reports on the initial trips appeared in the pages of *Areíto*, a journal published by progressive Cuban Americans, most remarkably Lourdes Casal.[9] Although Casal was older than the one-and-a-halfers by a number of years and had personally made the decision to flee Cuba, as the activist and public intellectual that she eventually became she was instrumental in encouraging publications and organizations that sought to overcome the impasse in the relationship among Cubans.[10] One of the first to travel to Cuba (through Mexico) at the invitation of the Instituto Cubano de Amistad con los Pueblos (ICAP), Casal spent two weeks in Cuba in September 1973 and upon her return was interviewed by the editors of *Areíto*, who published the exchange in its 1974 inaugural issue. Given Casal's wide-ranging interests in the humanities and social sciences, the journey's main purpose was to critically assess major changes spearheaded by the revolution in the cultural, political, and economic spheres. The interview covers an eclectic and broad terrain.

Casal and others were inspired by the social achievements of the revolution, about which there was still a sense of excitement worldwide. The personal experiences that drove them to reevaluate its accomplishments and undergo "radicalization" are described in *Contra viento y marea* (1978), a book of testimonials based on some fifty responses to a survey conducted among young Cuban Americans who belonged to a handful of organizations, especially the Grupo Areíto gathered around the journal. Topics ranging from their "disenchantment" with the United States and specific instances of racism to their commitment to the Puerto Rican struggle for independence and their clashes with family members and the community due to their position are taken up in the book. Heavily edited, the testimonials themselves are incorporated anonymously into a single narrative, although most of the contributors' names are listed at the beginning. Among those who contributed to the volume were Lourdes Casal, Román de la Campa, Roberto González Echevarría, Adriana Méndez, Marifeli Pérez-Stable, and Miren Uriarte, who would go on to fill academic positions in reputable U.S. institutions of higher learning.

Many in this segment of the one-and-a-half generation were profoundly marked by the counterculture found on U.S. campuses, which gave rise to affiliations and networks that were anathema to Cuban ethnic, conservative enclaves. A period of confrontation with the paradoxes and incongruities of American society at home and abroad sharpened the conflict between parents and their offspring in Cuban-American households (Rumbaut and Rumbaut 341–42). The conflict derived partially from their clashing feelings on Cuba and the determination of these children of exile to embark on a passionate search for what they presumed to be legitimately theirs, a place in Cuban society. And this entailed engaging Cuba in a revolution. The revolution, moreover, was projected as an emancipatory program, a concept with which the youth especially, receptive to the demands of Afro-Americans and other minorities in their adopted homeland, could well identify.[11]

Additional narratives of return appeared, like Casal's, in *Areíto*, which provided a sense of collective identity needed to counteract the hostility these individuals encountered among older exiles. The journal helped build an imaginary homeland for what were then unorthodox views on Cuba in exile circles. Mariana Gastón and Regina Casal (no relation to Lourdes Casal), both of whom made a trip back in 1974, were also interviewed by the editors of *Areíto*. The interview covered an array of topics, from the articulation of academic programs and urgent social needs to changing family dynamics that threatened to undermine traditional gender roles.

The two women would go on to play a leadership role in the Antonio Maceo Brigade in the late 1970s and early 1980s, an organization made up of Cuban Americans in their twenties that appealed to many of their peers interested in experiencing Cuba firsthand. The Brigade represented about the only outlet for traveling to Cuba, thus attracting members who held diverse views about the revolution. While a majority saw the revolution through rose-tinted glasses, others were highly critical of it. All the organization required of them was to have taken a stand against the economic embargo as well as counterrevolutionary activities, and to support the reestablishment of diplomatic relations between the two countries. Another requirement was to have left Cuba by parental decision. For the most politically conscious among the youth, these trips imparted the credentials they sorely needed to assume their place as politically aware "Cubans" in the battle for the recognition of civil rights in the United States. Concern about the struggles in the host society drew them toward their native country, not away from it, as would have been anticipated (Torres, *In the Land of Mirrors* 91).

In December 1977 the Antonio Maceo Brigade, modeled after the Venceremos Brigade, made its first trip to Cuba. The impact of the trip cannot be understated, as Félix Masud-Piloto writes in *From Welcomed Exiles to Illegal Immigrants* (1995). Composed of fifty-five members, including some from well-to-do families who had left immediately following the coming-to-power of the revolution, it was the largest group of exiles to set foot on the island since the Bay of Pigs invasion, and it offered evidence that the Cuban community abroad was far from being monolithic. But the Miami exiles greeted with alarm the prospects of a dialogue with the Cuban government, accusing the Brigade members of selling out. They denounced the young Cubans as Castro agents (73–74).

The accusation did not deter the Brigade from organizing additional trips. Its members continued to recruit from among the children of exile in the United States and other countries for various contingents throughout the mid-1980s. There were 179 participants from the United States, Venezuela, Costa Rica, Mexico, and Spain during the summer of 1979. Some of their testimonials, focusing on family reunification, appeared in print in *Baraguá*, the official organ of the Brigade, as well as *Areíto*.[12] These two organizations advanced the process of return and reconciliation. As a critic notes, "Organizaciones como la Brigada Antonio Maceo hicieron evidente por primera vez la existencia de una ideología diaspórica que no se basara en el enfrentamiento al gobierno de Castro y la Revolución" [organizations such as the Antonio Maceo Brigade brought to the fore for the first time the existence of a diasporic ideology not based on confrontation with the Castro government or the revolution, Weimer 37]. Steering away from the aggressive politics of exile preempting any kind of discussion among the parties, the Brigade espoused dialogue as a tool for engagement, sometimes with positive results.[13]

A report on a community service project undertaken by the Brigade helps to illustrate the utopian proclivities of a sector of the returnees. On one occasion, the Brigade worked at a textile factory whose owners prior to the nationalization of businesses had been the parents of one of the *brigadistas*. This article, written by Maritza Giberga, marvels at the advances made by the regime in the pursuit of social equality. Underscoring the altruistic side of socialist policies, the author identifies with their egalitarian aims by working alongside the proletarians in whose name the takeover had been waged. Generally, what transpires in these narratives is the hope, curiosity, and admiration, in tandem with the trepidation at seeing social change in action, which the revolutionary process engendered among Cuban Americans who were bent on extolling the virtues of a Cuba in revolutionary struggle (while minimizing its flaws). For some, it was an effervescent time of utopian yearnings, turned sour upon the realization, years later, of the authoritarian tendencies of the regime, if not of the failure of socialism in meeting its own goals for the Cuban people.

But there was also a personal component to these pioneering trips undertaken against all odds. Although most of the reflections published at the time revolved around shifting societal values and mores, a handful of essays convey the emotional impact of coming into contact with past key people and places, such as relatives and the former home. "La casa vieja," an essay by Mariana Gastón, leads the reader into the family dwelling in Havana, a house designed by Gastón's father himself which, although abandoned nearly twenty years earlier, has the power to elicit a stream of memories, especially first memories. It was there, around the pool, that the narrator fell and broke her forehead, and it was there also when she learned about the particulars of human reproduction. Through a reconstructed walk around the house, those recollections come forth, confirming the paramount significance that a philosopher like Gaston Bachelard, in *The Poetics of Space* (1958), attributes to the house, particularly the house in which one was raised. All the other homes are only variations (15). If the house is "one of the greatest powers of integration for the thoughts, memories, and dreams of mankind" (6), the fact that it is one of the places prioritized in the itinerary of the returnee requires no further explanation. The house localizes and anchors memories; revisiting it is an integral part of the ritual of return. As it happens, visiting the lost home has provided the angle through which more than one return narrative has been structured.[14]

Needs both deeply emotional and intellectual were addressed by these trailblazing trips of the 1970s, which smoothed the way for others, more individually focused, that came later. José Quiroga writes about the tension between the personal and the political surely shaping these trips, with the returnees focused on their *petit histoire* and the revolution on its grand history (186). Reviewing the essays, testimonials, and films such as Jesús Díaz's *De la patria y el exilio* (1979) and *55 hermanos* (1978) on the return trips of the late 1970s and early 1980s, one senses that tension, while simultaneously coming across a genuine interest in and identification with the changes unraveled by the revolution in its initial stages. The returnees, many of whom felt they had been left out of an event of epic proportions and sought to rejoin it, were more than mere pawns in a political game.

The early trips helped set the tone for later reflections on biculturalism. In its editorials *Areíto* repeatedly claimed a Cuban identity, seeking to insert itself in the island's cultural history. However, some of these early narratives offer a clue about the incipient fluid identities of their authors. Yes, Cuban-American youth endeavored to reclaim their homeland, but they simultaneously—though obliquely—addressed their ambiguous cultural location. The ambiguity comes across vividly in the anecdotes collected in Jesús Díaz's book *De la patria y el exilio* (1979), which probes this very issue. Hints of the young Cubans' acquired identity pop up when least expected, such as the pronunciation of *son*, the Cuban quintessential musical genre, as *song* (146), as a brigadista remarks about another's accent; or linguistic borrowings like *friquiado*, from *freaking out* (180). Drawing from her own knowledge of the Puerto Rican community in New York, another one of their peers points out the difference: "Yo creo que sí que somos cubanos como los puertorriqueños que viven en Nueva York son puertorriqueños, pero no son como los puertorriqueños que viven en Puerto Rico" [I think that yes, we are Cubans the way the Puerto Ricans who live in New York are Puerto Rican, but they are not like the Puerto Ricans who live in Puerto Rico] (223). Though they considered themselves Cubans, many of them were aware of the difference between them and island-based Cubans.

One of the outcomes of the trip was that it allowed these children of exile to imagine that a Cuban subjectivity was not necessarily tethered to a geographic location. In their final communiqué of the first contingent, reproduced in *De la patria y el exilio*, the group identifies *cubanía* with the history of struggle for Cuban sovereignty running from the mid-nineteenth century to the revolution, a political fight they could conveniently carry on from afar:

> Hoy somos más cubanos que hace tres semanas, porque hemos visto de cerca cómo después de cien años de lucha el pueblo cubano ha rescatado su nacionalidad, su futuro, y ha tomado las riendas de su historia en sus manos. También nos sentimos más felices porque entendemos que la condición de cubanos no está atada a una definición geográfica sino a una tradición de lucha que comenzó Carlos Manuel de Céspedes, Antonio Maceo y José Martí, que continuó Julio Antonio Mella, Rubén Martínez Villena y Antonio Guiteras, y que llevó a su justa continuación histórica el compañero Comandante en Jefe Fidel Castro, el Movimiento 26 de Julio y las otras organizaciones revolucionarias.
>
> [Today we are more Cuban than three weeks ago because we have seen firsthand how the Cuban people have restored their nationality, their future, and taken command of its history after one hundred years of struggle. We are also more content because we understand that the Cuban condition is not tied to a geographic definition but to a tradition of struggle that began with Carlos Manuel de Céspedes, Antonio Maceo, and José Martí, then taken up by Julio Antonio Mella, Rubén Martínez Villena, and Antonio Guiteras, until it finally reached its honorable, historical climax with the compañero Comandante en

Jefe Fidel Castro, the Movimiento 26 de Julio, and the rest of the revolutionary organizations.] (243)

Their argument echoed the Cuban leadership's contention about one hundred years of struggle in the long road toward decolonization. But although phrased in political terms, the argument offered a way out of the identity quandary, an ideally suited resolution for all involved. These sons and daughters of Cuban exile could call themselves Cubans without necessarily having to return permanently to the island. With their steadfast commitment to the struggle, they could actually abide by the tenets of *cubanía* from elsewhere.

In the same vein, whereas in its first few years *Areíto* championed a Cuban identity superimposed to the island, over time it began to lean on a bicultural framework to express the symbolic location of its most faithful collaborators, themselves immersed in ethnic circles foreshadowing pan-Latinidad. At the beginning of the 1980s, joining the journal's editorial board were Puerto Rican and Chicano writers and academics who were also reflecting on their dealings with a multiethnic United States, not always to their satisfaction. Still, *Areíto* articulated its cultural hybridity in Spanish so as to emphasize the Cuban side of the cultural equation. Among Cuban Americans, it was Lourdes Casal who summed up the twin sense of identity and misidentity with respect to both her geographic and cultural referents in the last lines of her poem "Para Ana Veltfort,"[15] first published in *Areíto* in 1976 and later included in *Palabras juntan Revolución* (1981):

cargo esta marginalidad inmune a todos los retornos,
demasiado habanera para ser newyorkina,
demasiado newyorquina para ser
—aún volver a ser—
cualquier otra cosa.
[I carry this marginality inside me, immune to all returns
too much of an *habanera* to be a New Yorker
too much of a New Yorker to be
—or even go back to being—
anything else.] (61–62)

The poet immune to all returns was, ironically, one of the first to physically return. Casal's lines presaged the identity that later the moniker Cuban American would readily capture, one that was not an obstacle to myriad returns. Her insightful poem struck a cord and has been cited over and over since its publication.

Broadening Returns

Not until the late 1970s was travel for a wide sector of Cuban Americans possible. In 1977, the Carter administration softened the U.S. Cuba policy, lifting the travel ban and smoothing the way for the short-term trips that members of the Cuban-American community would take soon thereafter. Cuba and the United States agreed to open interests sections in Havana and Washington, D.C., for limited consular operations. In 1979, Cuban Americans were allowed into Cuba as a result of a dialogue between representatives of the Cuban-American community and the Cuban government. Held in November and December 1978 following an overture from Fidel Castro, who seemingly thought the time was ripe for such an encounter, the dialogue between the two parties aimed at reaching a few immediate goals. It served to negotiate not only the conditions for Cuban-American travel to the homeland but also the liberation of over three thousand political prisoners and far-reaching family reunification issues. While some weighed the invitation as a gesture worth considering, many denounced it as a ploy to divide the community abroad (María C. García, *Havana USA* 48).

Those who were part of the negotiations, which came to be known simply by the name of "el Diálogo," were ostracized from the community and became the victims of defamation campaigns. They were all accused of being *dialogueros*, a term of contempt for those wishing to engage in talks with the Cuban leadership. Prominent members of the *Diálogo*, such as Bernardo Benes, suffered the wrath of the opposition, as can be corroborated in the Benes Papers at the Cuban Heritage Collection of the University of Miami. Benes was vice chairman of the board of the Continental National Bank of Miami, said to be the first Cuban-American bank. In a letter dated 25 April 1979, addressed to Alberto H. Coya, Benes, who played a major role in the talks, complains about the "vociferantes del exilio" [strident members of exile] who tried to "aniquilar[lo] física y moralmente" [crush him physically and morally]. Benes and his wife received death threats and had to consent to police escort (Pedraza, *Political Disaffection* 146). They were but two of many who came under fire amid a surge in terrorist actions that swept through the Cuban communities in the United States.[16]

But their efforts paid off. In 1979 alone, over 100,000 nonresident Cuban nationals jumped at the opportunity to visit Cuba. Critics argue that the arrival of thousands of Cuban Americans carrying all kinds of presents for their relatives unleashed the ambition of many who then sought to leave Cuba by any means at their disposal, hence the Mariel exodus (Eckstein 23–24). At the same time, one cannot brush aside the discontent among the Cuban population that had been brewing for some time. There were legitimate political reasons for leaving as well.

Facilitating the trips were a handful of charter flight companies that set up shop for this purpose and that quickly became the objects of terrorist reprisal. In April 1979 Carlos Muñiz Varela, the head of Viajes Varadero, a travel agency in San Juan, Puerto Rico, was gunned down while driving a car. At twenty-six, married, and with a son, Muñiz Varela was a member of the Antonio Maceo Brigade and the Group of 75, entrusted with the task of overseeing the implementation of the *Diálogo* accords. Three and a half decades later, his murder, allegedly tied to his Cuba-travel activities, remains unsolved. It is no wonder that despite the high number of first-time returnees beginning in the late 1970s there were scant testimonials of return published at that moment of both opportunity and backlash. Travelers would have hardly put themselves at risk by publicly admitting their trips to Cuba.

Despite the tragic setbacks, travel to Cuba forged ahead, slowed down only by the unfavorable winds coming from the executive branch of government from time to time. After Carter, U.S. administrations either tightened the restrictions anew (the Reagan and Bush administrations) or relaxed them (the Clinton and, especially, the Obama administrations). Under Clinton, family visits were banned except for humanitarian reasons immediately following the *balsero* crisis of 1994. By 1998, however, President Clinton eased the restrictions to one trip per year and authorized direct charter flights to Cuba from U.S. cities other than Miami.

Regardless of their status as travelers, countless Cuban Americans of the one-and-a-half generation have followed the example set by their precursors and landed at some point or other on the island. In the 1990s a number of testimonials by Cubans who had made the trip appeared in *Bridges to Cuba/Puentes a Cuba* (1995), another landmark episode in the history of narratives of return. A collection of essays, photographs, poems, artwork, and interviews edited by the University of Michigan anthropologist Ruth Behar, *Bridges to Cuba* provided a space for bringing together Cubans from both shores. With a nod to Lourdes Casal and Grupo Areíto, the editor foregrounded the bridge as a space for the realization of such a project. For Behar, the generation of Cuban Americans, children of exile, who had answered her call for manuscripts, wanted to "go beyond the Castro fixation and create cultural and emotional ties among *all* Cuban people" (4). The fact that not only Cubans abroad but also island-based Cubans stepped forward and contributed to the project was seen as an optimistic sign, one that would pave the way for future collaborations.

A number of essays included in *Bridges* address a return to the island, displaying a gamut of reactions to a noteworthy event in the life of the authors. In "Beyond the Rupture," María de los Ángeles Torres writes about her multiple trips to Cuba (the first having taken place in 1978 after leaving in 1961 through Operation Pedro Pan), and her gradual disillusionment over the crude use of politics on both sides of the Cuban divide. Torres nevertheless insists on gestures of reconciliation with Cubans in civil society with whom she is able to connect. Flavio Risech shares his impressions through the prism of a gay, left-wing Cuban American walking the streets of Santiago de Cuba in the early 1980s in "Political and Cultural Cross-Dressing." He wears different "attires" as he moves from Boston to Miami and on to Cuba, each of these places vying for a piece of his identity. Risech and Torres both write with eloquence about the inextricably layered subjectivities that define them.

In "Finding What Had Been Lost in Plain View," Ester Rebeca Shapiro Rok reminisces about her first trip back to Cuba in 1990 after a twenty-nine-year absence, only to rediscover enduring bonds of kinship. Patricia Boero, the author of "Cubans Inside and Outside: Dialogue among the Deaf," offers a tale of hope followed by disappointment: she goes back to visit in 1981 after living in Sweden, Uruguay, and Australia, decides to move back to Cuba in 1985, and flees again in 1990 after losing faith in the Cuban regime. In "Queer Times in Cuba," Ruth Behar targets a series of visits in the mid-1990s aimed at deepening her social, cultural, professional, and political familiarization with her native land. Coco Fusco writes about navigating a fraught transnational art world in "El Diario de Miranda/Miranda's Diary," which provides snippets of impressions from several trying trips to Cuba. And Rosa Lowinger reflects on finding a comforting sense of place during her 1992 visit to Havana and Trinidad in "Repairing Things."

All of the voyagers feel entitled to travel back and forth as needed, in implicit recognition of their diasporic and transnational condition. All the while, some on the island contributed essays on the pain caused by the outbound migration of relatives and friends. They, too, were affected by loss and separation. Every one of the above essays appeared in *Bridges to Cuba*, published at a moment of flexibility toward Cuba travel. The circle of returnees was indeed broadening.[17]

However, after a brief opening under the Clinton administration, the pendulum swung back. During George W. Bush's second term, Cuban Americans were restricted to one trip every three years and money transfers were severely capped. The Cuban expansive notion of family was redefined by the new rules, as they were allowed to visit only immediate members of the family; aunts and uncles did not make the cut. During that period, many violated the law by flying through third countries such as Mexico and Canada.

As soon as Barack Obama assumed the presidency in 2009, the policy was eased once more. The U.S. Treasury Department began to allow Cubans to visit the island as often as they wished, lifted restrictions on the amount or frequency of remittances, and granted licenses for so-called people-to-people exchange trips generally catering to other than Cuban émigrés. It also added to the number of airports servicing charter flights to destinations inside Cuba. Despite the pressure of bipartisan lawmakers in Washington, including Cuban Americans, who have yet to let up in their efforts to obstruct travel, President Obama has been unwavering with regard to his Cuba policy. Although lifting the embargo requires House and Senate approval, in December 2014 Obama made use of his executive power to restore full diplomatic relations with Cuba and further ease travel, commerce, and banking restrictions. Seen as a turning point in the history of the two countries, the new measures include the expansion of travel under the general license.[18]

Shortly after Obama's 2009 inauguration, the first collective trip ever of Pedro Pans took place, adding to the trips made since the 1970s by Pedro Pans who either traveled individually or as part of other groups. Their testimonials of flight and return appeared in print in *Operación Peter Pan: cerrando el círculo en Cuba* (2013), a compilation of interviews made over the years by Cuba-based filmmaker Estela Bravo.[19] Edited by Olga Rosa Gómez Cortés, the book is based on Bravo's documentary with the same title, which focuses exclusively on the return of five individuals who were part of the program—Silvia Wilhelm, Flora González Mandri, Ed Cantel, Alex

López, and Dulce María "Candi" Sosa. The book, however, includes additional interviews conducted years earlier for another Bravo documentary, *Los que se fueron* (1980), which has a wider scope. Interviews with a number of individuals who participated directly or indirectly in the program, including parents and key players such as Monsignor Bryan O. Walsh (Miami director of the Catholic Welfare Service), James Baker (former director of the Ruston Academy in Havana), and "Polita" Grau Alsina (who was accused in Cuba of being an FBI agent and condemned to fourteen years behind bars), all three prominently implicated in the operation, are transcribed in the book.

About two-thirds of Bravo's documentary is devoted to the historical context that set the stage for Operation Pedro Pan through interviews and archival research. Well into the narrative, it follows five Pedro Pans as they land in Havana in a bid to seek closure. This is a diverse, if small lot of Pedro Pans, and what unites them is the emotional link to a life-altering event: the separation from their parents and departure from their homeland. Fleeing Cuba signaled the moment in which they ceased to be children, pressed by the responsibilities they would be obligated to take on in exile. Two of the returnees suffered at the hands of their caretakers in the United States, leaving permanent scars, and all of them decry the parental decision to send them away. They are still at a loss to explain it. Once in Cuba, the group engages in conversation among themselves and with others, still looking for answers.

Yet, despite its human dimension, the documentary succeeded in triggering a strong reaction (possibly heightened by the fact that the film originated in Cuba), from a group of Pedro Pans in California who saw it as a propaganda coup for the Cuban side. These are individuals who are most indebted to their parents for having sent them out, and they have refrained from going back. In a video that serves as a response to the documentary, they blame the Castro government for the painful, though unapologetic, parental decision and sing the praises of U.S. democracy, cherishing the opportunities they have enjoyed in exile.[20]

Evidently, squabbles over the responsibility and primary purpose of Operation Pedro Pan are still raging. There is no doubt, however, that the program was embroiled in politics and that it continues to be a subject of dispute for sparring sides. Shedding the political mantle with which it emerged does not seem feasible even today. Underlining the less than benevolent nature of the program, María de los Ángeles Torres describes the exodus as "a contest of ideas over the future of nations battled over the control of children's minds" (*The Lost Apple* 251).[21] From this perspective, children were used as a platform for political gains.

While social scientists have stressed the political motivations, the literature that has emerged around the Pedro Pan Operation focuses on the human cost of the heartbreaking separation. Plays by Eduardo Machado and Pedro Monge Rafuls (both Pedro Pans) as well as Nilo Cruz and Melinda López get their inspiration from the collective memory of the Pedro Pan affair, demonstrating its hold over Cuban Americans of the one-and-a-half and younger generations.[22] The sad episode continues to generate soul-searching interrogations at the margins of politics.

Lingering Opposition to Travel

The most recent trips occurred during a period of liberalization of the Cuba policy as well as a changing climate. Support for Cuba travel has grown as much among the U.S. population at large as within the Cuban-American community in Miami-Dade County.[23] A comparison of the Florida International University's Cuban Research Institute polls of 2000 and 2010 shows an obvious growth in support for unrestricted travel to Cuba among Cuban Americans in South Florida, up to approximately 62 percent from 50.7 percent. It increased even further in 2014, with the survey for this year showing that 69 percent of all Cuban-American respondents back such travel. Furthermore, only 48 percent are in favor of maintaining the embargo (compared with 87 percent in 1991), and 71 percent support people-to-people trips to Cuba.[24]

Such changing attitudes make the opposition that Cuba travel still garners among leading members of the Cuban-American community all the more reprehensible to many. The following examples show the lengths to which lawmakers from within the community have gone to rein it in. David Rieff's *New York Times Magazine* essay "Will Little Havana Go Blue?" delves into one such case. The article explores the impact that the generational shifts in Cuban Miami would potentially have on the presidential election of 2008. Over the course of an interview with Marco Rubio, then Speaker of the Florida legislature and a Republican senator from Florida since 2011 (as well as a rising star in the Republican Party), Rieff raised the question of travel. Rubio maintained that travel to the island undermines the image of exceptionality cultivated by Cuban exiles: "What makes Cubans different from Haitians who come here or anyone else . . . if they go back and forth, that is to say, if they're not exiles at all?" (51). As Rieff remarks, what Rubio meant is that "neither Washington nor the Cuban-exile community could accept a historical-political exile morphing into a contemporary economic migration" (51). By comparing them to Haitians, not only do Cubans cease to be exiles if they go back and forth, but apparently they are also stripped of their seeming whiteness; like Haitians, they become merely migrants of color.

Returning, then, and the concomitant weakening of exile chip away at the perception that Cubans deserve special treatment. As María Cristina García acknowledges, "When the Cubans called themselves exiles, it was a powerful political statement, a symbol of defiance that at the same time distinguished and isolated their experience from that of other immigrants" (*Havana USA* 84). In order to preserve the exile status of the Cuban community, Rubio's advice is to bar unrestricted access to the island. By making it difficult to return a year after arriving in the United States, politicians such as Rubio hope to expediently hold on to the idea that Cuban migration continues to be politically motivated. Addressing the favorable treatment of Cubans through the Cuban Adjustment Act, a legacy of the Cold War, has not been part of the plan thus far.

Rubio is not the only Cuban-American official opposed to travel. On 11 June 2008, a report by Mary Ellen Klas on the *Miami Herald* described a proposed bill that would have imposed new regulations on companies that arrange travel to Cuba—an onerous bill that would have pushed some of these companies out of business. Many Cuban families protested the bill. When asked about his reasons for proposing the new legislation, which failed to pass, then Miami representative David Rivera explained that, as exiles, Cubans should refrain from returning: "If somebody has asked for political asylum in the United States, they have no business returning to the country which they were supposedly fleeing."

Four years later, Rivera pressed the issue using a different approach. On 31 May 2012, at a hearing to amend Public Law 89–732 before the House Judiciary Committee, Subcommittee on Immigration Policy and Enforcement, he proposed legislation that sought to bar recent immigrants from traveling to the island, alleging their abuse of the 1966 Cuban Adjustment Act. Rivera agreed with Rubio on this point. Rivera argued that the residency status of those Cubans who, under the act, are approved for permanent residency one year and one day following their arrival should be revoked if they cash in on their status for family reunification purposes.

Prior to this date, another U.S. representative of Cuban ancestry, Mario Diaz-Balart, found himself in a swirl of controversy when he proposed an amendment that would have rolled back the comparatively lax Cuba travel and remittance policy adopted by the Obama administration to the harsh sanctions implemented by George W. Bush. President Obama, who had threatened to veto the Florida representative's rider on a spending bill, abstained from intervening when in December 2011 congressional leaders reached a compromise that allowed them to drop both the measure to tighten the screws on travel and another that would have made it easier for Cuba to purchase U.S. goods (Tamayo). In the end, both measures were shelved.

It should be added that the three officials mentioned, though sharing an exile ideology and having tenuous links with the island (the three were born in the United States), represent different generations, yet come together around the travel ban. And officeholders are hardly alone in siding with the cause of exile by denouncing return trips. As late as February 2012, Jaime Suchlicki, Emilio Bacardí Moreau Professor of History and Director of the Institute for Cuban and Cuban-American Studies at the University of Miami, lamented the demand for travel in an essay published in *El Nuevo Herald*, wondering whether the Jews who managed to escape Nazi Germany or the Russians who fled Stalinist Russia ever entertained going back.

The above-mentioned politicians may well be the last bulwark in the exile community against the full resumption of travel given the shifting attitudes of both Cuban émigrés and some sectors of government. As stated above, the 2014 Florida International University's Cuba poll shows that 69 percent of Cuban Americans support not only the lifting of travel restrictions but also reestablishing diplomatic relations with Cuba. Cuban enclave politics have slowly but inexorably changed, with a large percentage of Cubans, who have traditionally voted Republican, now willing to support the reelection of a Democrat, Barack Obama, who has shepherded like no other the loosening of regulations for travel to the island.[25] Some of the writers of the one-and-a-half generation beat the more recent trends to an opening by advocating for return to their former homeland.

The Other Shore: Cuba Warms to the Returnees

On the Cuban side, travel has likewise been captive to the flux of politics, emulating in some ways the U.S. conundrum. Current policy allows for unlimited trips and baggage, but it did not always do so. In fact, during the first two decades after the revolution, there were hardly any return trips at all, not even for brief visits. Legislation adopted in 1961 (Ley 98) and reintroduced in 1976 (Ley 1312) established the no return policy, codifying the permanent banishment of Cubans if they did not go back within the time limit stipulated in their mandatory exit permits (Aja 129). The stringent law had rhetorical ramifications. Cubans choosing exile were chastised by the Cuban government, which showered them with pejorative labels, such as *gusanos* (worms), *vendepatrias* (sellouts), and *escoria* (scum). With émigrés thus stigmatized, the distance between Cubans on the island and abroad feels wider than among other diasporas, a distance that some in the one-and-a-half generation sought to shorten with their travel initiatives.

In May 1985, visits by Cuban Americans were briefly suspended by the Cuban government as a response to the initial broadcasts of anti-Castro Radio Martí under the Reagan administration, but they were quickly reinstated in 1986. At this time, Havana imposed a cap on visiting émigrés. However, with the onset of the "Special Period in Times of Crisis" (hereafter called Special Period) a few years later, the cap was lifted and attitudes toward émigrés became more pliant, with officials in Cuba transitioning to the neutral term "emigration" or "the Cuban community abroad" in lieu of "exiles." Occurring shortly after the cutoff of subsidies from the Soviet bloc, whatever material contributions émigrés can make have arguably been a factor in the more welcoming disposition toward the returnees. Remittances represent, as they do for other countries in the Caribbean and Latin America, an increasingly crucial source of hard currency. In Cuba, they account for the third largest source of hard currency after fees charged for professional services rendered abroad and the tourist industry (Duany, *Blurred Borders* 148).[26]

Despite the relaxation, making travel arrangements is still an aggravation, for émigrés need either a current Cuban passport (in addition to proof of residency or citizenship in the United States) or a visa to enter Cuba, both of which are expensive to obtain and slow to process. At times, the processing of travel documents has been temporarily interrupted due to the repercussions of the embargo. Ruth Behar aptly refers to the "Kafkaesque regulations and emotional burdens" connected to travel to Cuba (*The Portable Island* 6). Moreover, there is no guarantee that the required entry permit will be granted or that it will arrive on time. The prospects of a visa denial have sometimes been used as a deterrent to the public denunciation of the one-party system or some other issue sensitive to the Cuban political leadership. To this day, some individuals have been blocked from returning to their homeland after making statements deemed hostile to the regime, such as advocating for a multiparty system. With the line separating the nation and the state rather blurred, decisions affecting one or the other have been hard to differentiate. Adding to the burden is the pricey airfare between the United States and Cuba due to the U.S.-enforced embargo and travel ban. Some of these aggravations will probably be lessened with the reopening of ties starting in 2015.

Also affecting return trips are the circumstances surrounding the exit. After the revolution, the notion of definitive banishment added to the trauma of fleeing. From 1961 until 2013, a visa was required to leave the country (Aja 129). Migratory laws have been revisited from time to time as part of the process of *flexibilización* or adjustment of the Cuban migration policy, which has made it increasingly easier for Cuban émigrés to leave and reenter the country (Aja 127).

After much anticipation since 2011 when additional reforms were announced, new measures meant to relax the regulations came into effect in January 2013. The most significant is that the costly exit visa requirement was rescinded. Cubans citizens need only a valid passport and an entry visa issued by the destination country, if required.[27] The latest reforms, part of a reshuffling of Cuban society under Raúl Castro, are a welcoming step with the potential of ushering in a new era in sanctioned Cuban migration. They may well have an impact on the number of Cubans who opt for circular migration, lifting the stigma of fleeing. Others may choose to leave permanently, expanding the extent of the diaspora. Whatever they choose, their experience of return will be markedly different from the one depicted in the return narratives of the one-and-a-half generation.

A Growing Demand for Travel

Starting in the early 1990s, the number of return visits to Cuba rose significantly, reaching levels reminiscent of 1979 when travel to the island first opened up. They ratcheted even further in the 2010s. The growth stems from a renewed interest among Cuban émigrés in visiting relatives and friends left behind and seeing their homeland after years of separation. Also contributing to travel is the more open acceptance of the émigrés at all levels of society. The upsurge coincided with the forbidding economic crisis that unraveled in Cuba after the fall of the Berlin Wall in 1989 and the collapse of the Soviet bloc immediately afterwards. Far from abating, the motivation to maintain personal ties with Cuba has steadily gained strength among Cuban Americans.

In "Networks, Remittances, and Family Restaurants," Duany tallies revealing statistics on travel, indicating that by the beginning of the new millennium one out of ten Cuban Americans had made the trip back to the island at least once, while in South Florida the proportion was one out of three. Eckstein and Barbería cite the same estimate while offering further statistics. Over the course of the 1990s, travel soared from approximately 7,000 to over 140,000, with an estimated minimum of 100,000 individuals making annual visits between 1996 and 1999 (813). Though not specifying a time period, Pedraza claims a pace of around 100,000 a year (*Political Disaffection* 301). As expected, longtime émigrés were less likely to travel to Cuba than recent immigrants, although an increase was also experienced among the former in spite of the fact that many of them have no relatives left in Cuba. The percentage of migrants who came to the United States in the period 1959–64 and traveled to Cuba went up from 18 to 26 between 2000 and 2001, while the percentage of recent immigrants rose from 31 to 45 between 2000 and 2004 (Eckstein 140–42). By now, more than one in ten Cuban Americans has traveled to Cuba. Supplementing the movement across the Straits is the large number of Cubans who are invited to come over to the United States to spend time with their families.

Reports from various sources leave no doubt as to the healthy interest in travel to Cuba. Based on a study conducted between 17 June and 17 July 2013, the Havana Consulting Group reported that Miami had finally outpaced Toronto and Montreal in the number of Cuba-bound flights. During the thirty-day period, almost 330 flights flew out of Miami to destinations all over Cuba. With six airlines offering their services, the number of visitors in 2012 included an unprecedented 400,000 nonresident Cuban nationals, according to one report from the Havana Consulting Group (Morales, "Miami Leads in Sending Flights to Cuba").[28]

These figures could very well swell if not only a majority of Cuban Americans but also some members of Congress get their way, even if small steps are actually taken. In April 2013, California representative Sam Farr sent a letter to Barack Obama, signed by fifty-nine of his colleagues, asking the administration to expand its Cuba travel policy. As reported by Dan Burns, the letter called upon the president to allow people-to-people travel and other forms of travel permitted by the law under a general license, thus encouraging a larger number of people to attempt the short trip. President Obama heeded precisely this kind of call when he proposed his latest liberalization of policies.

Meanwhile, the usual suspects are at work again. In July 2013 the House Appropriations Committee passed a financial services bill that included language proposed by Mario Díaz-Balart. The bill seeks to undercut the people-to-people licenses that allow all citizens to travel for educational purposes. It also requires OFAC to monitor and report details on Cuban-American travel and remittance flows to Cuba, whether by Cuban Americans or others. With the same diligence, Marco Rubio has vowed to derail Obama's current outreach to Cuba. These hardline tactics have been tried in the past with varied degrees of success. Even when lagging behind public opinion, Cuban-American as well as American officials who tout the advantages of curtailing travel are attempting to turn back the clock. It is doubtful, though, that efforts to keep a tight rein on the flow of visitors to Cuba will make much of a dent in the advances made toward the normalization of travel and those still to come with the restoration of relations. To be sure, much remains to be done by both sides to achieve full normalization, but the gates are wide open for change leading to it.

Conclusion

Addressing the political context of the return trips of the one-and-a-half generation, this chapter offers an overview of post-1959 migration and the causes that brought about the various exile waves as well as unprecedented programs such as Operation Pedro Pan. It also provides adequate details about the consequences of the political rift over the backing of policies hindering travel and regular contact both in Cuba and the United States.

Described in the chapter are various high points in the history of returns. Despite the tensions, a number of trips by young Cuban Americans broke new ground, confirming that the Cuban-American community was far from being one-dimensional. Grupo Areíto and the Antonio Maceo Brigade are credited for erecting the initial bridges for two-way exchanges, followed by others who, individually or collectively, also defied the travel ban. They all deviated from both written and unwritten rules that would have prevented them from reaching out to their former homeland. Some persisted in fostering dialogue in the face of opposition, and now a majority of Cuban Americans favor the same liberal policies for travel and engagement for which the forerunners fought, as surveys demonstrate.

Also introduced in the chapter are initial comments about the dual cultural subjectivity of the children of exile. While they aspired to reconnect with Cuba as Cuban subjects, hoping to smoothly recover their native land, they did so in ways that showed they were on the verge of becoming "Cuban-and-other" (Rivero, "Cuba [tras]pasada" 32). Heralding later calls for unspooling the intricate links between nation and identity, they arrived at the realization that they could be "Cubans" outside of Cuba. Although the realization was couched in political terms, it was nonetheless an original approach to a persistent dilemma.

Tenacious forces against dialogue have been at work to this day. I reviewed several of the attempts undertaken by different administrations and elected officials to turn back the clock on Cuba travel after the thaw in tensions between the two governments in the late 1970s. Since then, only the Clinton and Obama administrations relaxed the travel regulations, ensuring limited travel. Cuban Americans of the one-and-a-half generation and beyond continue to take advantage of the existing opportunities to reach an island that no matter the political tensions they perceive as partly theirs.

2

Daring to Go Back

In Search of Traces

> Odysseus thinks his landing at Ithaca is the commencement of a new adventure—as indeed it will prove to be. Half a lifetime's odyssey has been required for Odysseus to discover that life's signal adventure is the discovery of home.
>
> Jeffrey M. Perl, *The Tradition of Return*

> [I]t may often be easier to live in exile with a fantasy of paradise than to suffer the inevitable ambiguities and compromises of cultivating actual, earthly places.
>
> Eva Hoffman, "The New Nomads"

Like Odysseus upon his return to Ithaca, Cuban returnees must face the challenge of having to reacquaint themselves with the homeland after a long sojourn away from it. Before jumping right in, they must sift through memories, reactivate their relationship to people and places, make connections between the past and the present, figure out the role they might play in a new context, and see where—or whether—they fit in. This chapter delves into narratives that explore the physical return of four writers of the one-and-a-half generation, a return that makes multiple demands on the returnee. Because there are just as many different narratives, these texts depict diverse Cubas as homeland. They are vastly different from one another, yet related by the same search for connection to a long lost past. The yearning to reconnect meaningfully with the past urges the writers to identify people, sites, and objects capable of evoking even frayed memories and to single out equivalent narratives and discourses that resonate with their own.

Given that the interlude between fleeing and returning has stretched, sometimes over decades, the return is marked by the ambiguities and compromises that both Jeffrey M. Perl and Eva Hoffman point to in this chapter's epigraphs. It can indeed be a humbling experience to come across actual places that have little resemblance to those of one's most cherished dreams and memories. Because of their generational location within Cuban exile, this experience is most likely to take place among returnees of the one-and-a-half generation. All cohorts confront the challenges of return, but there are differences between the one-and-a-half generation and the ones that preceded and followed it.

As mentioned in the introduction, dates of arrival in the United States influence (along with age, education, race, occupation, and other categories) Cuban migrants' views of return trips and transnational ties. Exiles who left shortly after 1959 do not commonly support transnational practices. Many have no relatives left in Cuba and therefore do not feel obliged to visit, or they refrain from doing so due to their political allegiances. On the other hand, more recent arrivals embrace transnationalism in the form of regular communication, remittances, and visits to family and friends who stayed behind. They lived through the best and worst years of the revolution and are thus capable of empathizing with compatriots still on the island. When they visit, they do not have to familiarize themselves anew with their surroundings but rather resume their former lives on a temporary basis.

Written by members of an in-between generation, the memoirs of Ruth Behar, Román de la Campa, Emilio Bejel, and Tony Mendoza add complexity to the above distinction by highlighting the shifts that have been taking place over the last several decades. These narratives did not come out of a vacuum. Rather, they are the outcome of a process that took off when exiled Cubans first reached out to Cubans on the island in the 1970s. De la Campa's first trip to Cuba took place in 1977 as part of the Antonio Maceo Brigade, while Bejel joined the editorial board of *Areíto* early on, which offered opportunities for going back. Behar, de la Campa, and Bejel had been back to Cuba on numerous occasions by the time they wrote the autobiographical narratives contemplated here, while Mendoza reports on his first trip ever after almost four decades. The first three have conducted extensive research in Cuba for scholarly purposes and have presented their work there or published in island-based journals. They are clearly not unfamiliar figures in the intellectual arena in Cuba or abroad. On the whole, their reflections account for approximately twenty years of return trips, from the late 1970s to the late 1990s.

The four occupy different slots within the one-and-a-half generation. Since Behar was taken out of Cuba at age four, she is among the youngest members of this cohort. De la Campa, who left Cuba in 1960 when he was thirteen, follows Behar. Bejel had just turned eighteen when he came to the United States and is thus a borderline case between the first and the one-and-a-half generation, in accordance with Rumbaut's classification. In a similar fashion, Mendoza left Cuba permanently in 1960 at the age of nineteen. However, he had come to the United States to attend boarding school several years earlier, returning to his family in Cuba during the summer breaks. But despite the age differentials at the time of arrival, their narratives of return share a common ground conditioned by what I call post-indexical ties to the island.

Post-Indexical Ties

Unlike the one-and-a-half narratives espousing exile, these other memoirs illustrate the nurturing of a transnational relationship in particular ways and certainly not along the lines of the psychic, retrospective "transnationalism" that I argue in the introduction characterizes exiles, nor for the same reasons or in the same pragmatic fashion adopted by newcomers. The sections devoted to each of the narratives will elaborate on the characteristics of the transnational relationship, driven by back and forth trips.

Through these narratives of return, I seek to highlight the authors' implicit dis-identification with an exile culture attributed primarily to the first exile generation and, on the other hand, how distant they also are from accomplishing a smooth return to the homeland. Time has taken its toll, and the texts construct, with differing emphases, an imagined Cuba through diasporic and deterritorialized lenses. They speak of the unmet nationalist promise of a home wedded to a homeland. The memoirs authored by these Cuban Americans featuring an actual return show the fissures that have widened for political as well as personal reasons: cracks in the system brought to light by the Mariel exodus and the *balsero* crisis, if not before, and the change in the cultural makeup—the hyphenated identities—of the individual authors themselves.

Their return to the homeland is marked by a deep ambivalence whose final outcome is, paradoxically, a reaffirmation of bonds with the native land. Rooted in "shared longing without belonging," these narratives are close to what Svetlana Boym calls a "diasporic intimacy." An exiled Russian, Boym claims that diasporic intimacy "is haunted by the images of home and homeland, yet it also discloses some of the furtive pleasures of exile" (252–53). Theirs is a bifocal orientation or straddling position.

Given their interstitial location, the authors may share with Oliva Espín, a psychologist of their generation, a sense of deracination. After twenty-three years in exile, Espín arrived at a realization:

> It takes an experience like my going back to Cuba to realize that what you have mistaken for comfort does not compare with what the feeling of belonging really means.... [W]hat I learned once again is that who I am is inextricably intertwined with the experience of uprootedness. And what this uprootedness entails ... is an awareness that there is another place where I feel at home in profound ways that I did not even know or remember. That place, however, is not fully home anymore. (Qtd. by Rivero, *Discursos desde la diaspora* 86)

Because the homeland is not entirely home anymore, returning does not culminate in a simple reincorporation. Over the course of looking for a figure of speech or some such means of expression that would help to shed light on the ambivalence and even *extrañamiento* (estrangement) one finds in these narratives, I came across the notion of the post-indexical, whose natural home has been the visual arts. The post-indexical, as much as the indexical from which the term derives, can be applied also to the texts included in the chapter to mark their longer or shorter distance from the object or referent to which the two (the indexical and the post-indexical) are attached. It is in a continuum between the two that these memoirs oscillate, with the return trips providing the vehicle, at times, to keep the post-indexical at bay.

In *Making Memory Matter: Strategies of Remembrance in Contemporary Art* (2006), art historian Lisa Saltzman posits the intriguing idea that modern art of commemoration can be thought of as post-indexical. The term is drawn from the linguistic theory of American philosopher Charles Sanders Peirce. A pioneer in the field of semiotics in the second half of the nineteenth century, Peirce elaborated a triadic model of the sign as an alternative to the widely invoked dual structure of signifier and signified proposed by the French linguist Ferdinand de Saussure at about the same time. Peirce's lesser-known taxonomy of the sign contains three elements: icon, symbol, and index. For the purpose of my analysis, it is the latter that is of foremost importance. In Peirce's words, the index "furnish[es] positive assurance of the reality and the nearness" of its object or referent (251). Unlike the arbitrariness presumed between Saussure's concepts of signifier and signified, an index represents an object by being actually related with it. For Peirce, the footprint that Robinson Crusoe found on the sand was an index that stood for the presence of a creature (252), as a rap on a door is indicative of a visitor, or smoke of a fire. As in these examples, an indexical sign requires contiguity.

On the other hand, the post-indexical obviates that contiguity. The artists that Saltzman writes about are said to question the "indexical capacity" of the image through the foregrounding of form and structure, not physical relation or even resemblance. For Saltzman, the work of artists as diverse as Cuban émigré María Elena González, Kara Walker, Maya Lin, Rachel Whiteread, and William Kentridge are post-indexical, for "what we see ... in this art of the present is ... the index as a vestige rather than a viable means of representation" (13). One of González's recent installations, reproducing the floor plan of her childhood home from memory, relates to its subject not physically or geometrically (through the conventions of architectural design) but psychically, through memory (94). A separation occurs between the index and its object, with the index no longer providing a direct link to the once thought-to-be-adjacent object.[1]

One can make a fitting connection, as Saltzman does to an extent, between the notion of the post-indexical and the work of diasporic artists and writers who employ the power of narrative to come to terms with a host of issues stemming from a lost homeland. Do these artists have a choice if their work revolves around the self and part of their lives took place in locations some have rarely revisited? How do they remember without physical evidence and only through the memory of their ancestors in quite a few instances? Some of the narratives included in this study suggest that one of the prime purposes for returning is precisely to embark on a quest for sites enlivened with indexical quality. Places, people, and objects spark memories long forgotten that help reconnect with the past.

Cubans of the one-and-a-half generation also partake of the memories of exile. It is these memories that summon them back to the island, to family albums, to traditions. While trying to restore a link to the past, they have done so in ways that expose the loss as well as the gap that exists for them not only from that past but also from present-day Cuba. Some succeed in holding onto or re-creating some sort of indexical relation, while others lean toward the post-indexical. In the latter case, representation is problematical because it is vestigial and its ties to personal referents appear debilitated or severed.

All of these self-referential narratives were written in English, except Bejel's, which is available in the Spanish original and in the English and Portuguese translations. Critics have argued that, generally, first-generation Cuban immigrants write their works in Spanish, disclosing an affiliation to the Cuban literary canon while subsequent generations typically produce their body of works in their adopted country's dominant language. The latter group employs English as a means of "translating" or "explaining" their native and heritage cultures to the wider English-speaking public (Álvarez Borland, *Cuban-American Literature of Exile* 149–56).

However, while there may be a gradual movement toward English, Cuban-American writers of the one-and-a-half generation have not abandoned Spanish altogether. Bejel writes in Spanish, as does de la Campa. Even the younger Behar has published poetry in her native language. And they are far from being an exception. In an essay on such writers of this cohort as Pérez Firmat, Roberto G. Fernández, and Elías Miguel Muñoz, critic Karen S. Christian notes that all three have switched to Spanish even after publishing a number of well-received works in English. Their books *Cincuenta lecciones de exilio y desexilio* (2000), *En la ocho y la doce* (2001), *El príncipe y la bella cubana* (2014), and *Vida mía* (2006) were all published in the new millennium. Christian ponders about the inferences of the shift, arguing that language choice should not automatically determine the place of a writer in a single literary tradition, be it the Cuban or U.S. canon ("La lengua que se repite" 22). That would be an essentialist, binary move betraying, in a sense, what these writers stand for. Moving back and forth between languages is indicative, in her opinion, of the porousness of borders and the nonlinear, hybrid ways in which identities are assumed and expressed through language (Christian, "La lengua que se repite" 34–35). The process that the above-mentioned writers launch into should not be construed as straightforward, but informed by a diasporic, sometimes transnational perspective. These writers are ambidextrous in cultural and linguistic respects.

Also indicative, in my view, of a betwixt and between position is the intertextual nature of the narratives. A host of other accounts infuses the narratives, revealing how the native identities of the authors rub elbows with others. The result is a spectrum that brings diversity to bear: Behar draws from stories of the Jewish diaspora, de la Campa from Caribbean visions around two-way travel and transnationalism, Bejel from coming-out narratives, and Mendoza from contemporary photographic images of a Cuba in ruins. All of these writers' narratives have as much to do with Cuba as with diasporic vantage points.

Diaspora Counterpoint: Longing for Memories in *An Island Called Home*

Bridges to Cuba, discussed in the previous chapter, would stand as a first stage in Behar's trajectory in her quest for cultural identity and engagement with Cuba. Behar was four at the time her parents fled Cuba in the early 1960s. She then visited Cuba as a graduate student in 1979 and followed up with a second trip in 1991. Even though her ethnic and religious identities had remained subtly understated, at some point she began to embrace them passionately. This awareness led her to defy that sector of the Cuban community that supports the travel ban, using anthropology as an excuse as well as a shield: "Nobody could criticize me [as an anthropologist] for breaking with the Cuban exile position which held that no Cuban should set foot on Cuba" (*An Island* 18). However, Behar's parents, Sephardic and Ashkenazic Jews, have never gone back. After 1991, she continued traveling to Cuba, and years later she would address the topic of her Jewish background in a book, *An Island Called Home: Returning to Jewish Cuba* (2007), as well as an earlier documentary, *Adio Kerida/Goodbye Dear Love: A Cuban Sephardic Journey* (2002). Both projects required multiple trips that allowed Behar to more than make up for the time she stayed away from her native land.

One of Behar's objectives in going to Cuba was to gather evidence of the once lively Jewish community from one end of the island to the other. As an anthropologist, she conscientiously went after her leads, bringing to the attention of her readers what remained of the community's existence. The number of Jews in Cuba decreased from more than 15,000 in 1959 to about 1,000 today, with most having left by 1965 (*An Island* 9–10, 26).[2] At first sight, *An Island Called Home* seems to be a record of that search throughout the island, which Behar successfully carries on to the end. She seems to leave no stone unturned. But as in all of Behar's work, the personal and the collective are closely intertwined, with the ethnography becoming an autobiography and vice versa. Behar is such an avid observer of both her surroundings and her own thought processes that her books are superb examples of what Rocío Davis calls a "double-voiced text" ("Vulnerable Observation" 266). The narrative of the Jews in Cuba parallels, in a way, Behar's own narrative, supplying a language and an ethos for the depiction of diaspora.

There is no doubt that the search has a personal dimension. Researching the history of Jewish Cuba allows Behar to imagine, for one thing, what her life as a Jew would have been like had her parents decided to stay in their birthplace. It is her research on the Jewish community that enables the index to Behar's past in Cuba; it furnishes a reference to a way of life lost to her and her family. Through the remaining Jews, she hopes, in part, to recover her home:

> I was running toward the home that I and my family and thousands of other Jews had left on the island. I wanted to reclaim that lost home—the home in Cuba I believed was my true home.... What began as a vague desire to find my lost home in Cuba gradually became a more concrete search for the Jews who make their homes in Cuba today. (*An Island* 3)

The pursuit of home brings Behar to the actual homes of the remaining Jews, and from there she spins into a reflection on diaspora, which traverses Behar's family saga. Without diaspora, her Cuban nationality has no possible explanation. Her homing desire is the key to establishing a counterpoint between the Cuban and Jewish diasporas, a connection that animates Behar's work as an anthropologist.

Behar traces her ancestors on the island back to the early twentieth century, when Cuba offered refuge from anti-Semitism to Jews from Poland, Russia, and Turkey. Despite the safe haven that Cuba provided, it was considered merely a stopover for the Jews' final destination, the United States. For this reason, many called it Hotel Cuba. Arriving penniless from their countries of birth, Behar's forebears worked as peddlers and slowly made their way up the social ladder with relative degrees of success. When the revolution began to seize private businesses and properties, many of the Jews left, settling in the United States. Decades later, some of those who left would actively promote visits to the island, where a revival of religious observance has been experienced since the 1990s, not only among Jews but also among Catholics and practitioners of Santería.

An Island Called Home follows the Jews remaining in Cuba across the island, rescuing their life stories in words and images—photographs, postcards, and other objects that offer indexical proof of a story until then submerged and on the verge of succumbing. Many of the Jews Behar meets are elderly, and others might still leave the island for the Promised Land, taking with them the memories engraved in their souls. But how does the history of these people without history interact with Behar's story as a diasporic Cuban? How relevant are the return trips for who she is today? The following comments will delve into the relationship between the two diasporas, for it bears on the notion of home that Behar ultimately puts forward in her narrative, a home shaped by dislocation as much as the imagination. In a nutshell, the Jewish diaspora narrative provides the foundation upon which to build Behar's own narrative of displacement and return.

Behar's work presents a layered and overlapping approach to diaspora. This is evident in *An Island Called Home* as much as, in an emblematic way, in her choice of title for her earlier documentary on Sephardic Jews. *Adio Kerida* is a love song that, as Behar explains, references "many layers of goodbyes," those of the Jews who were forced to leave Spain in 1492, the Jews who left Cuba in the wake of the revolutionary takeover, and the Jews who were planning on leaving for Israel in the 2000s ("While Waiting for the Ferry to Cuba" 132). Dispersal is at the heart of all of these events.

Dispersal notwithstanding, the Jews are masters at preserving cultural identity, and Behar's project both capitalizes on and benefits from their lessons. The book is about the "intrahistory" or "the relationship people had with the Jewish past and the fierce ways they were holding on to this past" (34). Since Behar is an "inauthentic Jubana" ("Juban" 166) who had no memories of Cuba and only passive knowledge of Judaism at the time she embarks on this project, she plays the dual role of researcher and apprentice as she doggedly pursues her investigation. The Jewish diaspora is capable of suggesting the parameters within which Behar can make sense of her diasporic condition, hence the personal nature of the search.

Behar's late arrival to her Jewish and Cuban roots makes the quest all the more powerful. She acknowledges that both identities had taken a backseat while she collected ethnographies in Spain and Mexico in the 1980s. After a period of hibernation, so to speak, the anthropologist decided it was time to reclaim her family's ancestry. Over time, she recovered an identity that she had lost. In the words of a reviewer: "Behar has spent her life considering herself an outsider. As an academic she has pursued that posture studying different cultures, hiding her Jewish identity, and wondering where she could take root. In this, her sixth book, Behar reveals the child whose roots are photographs in a suitcase. In Cuba she finds a home" (Barr 209). In Cuba, Behar finds Jews who, "like herself, are not always sure how to be Jews" (Barr 209).

The ambivalent position of those who are between cultures makes self-definition all the more difficult. In her essay "Juban América" (Juban, or Jewban, stands for Jewish Cuban), Behar uses an example to illustrate this point. She comments about her grandfather's idiosyncratic use of Spanish (for example, "yo nació") and her own use of the language: "*Después de todo*, Spanish was my grandfather's language, in much the same convoluted way that it is mine now" ("Juban" 154). The remark points to the liminal position that both the grandfather and she occupy because of their seemingly conflicting subjectivities:

> I need to interrupt this third-person historical interlude to speak, again, as *yo*, at least momentarily. Like my grandfather, I keep wanting to situate myself somewhere between the third-person plural and the first-person singular. Indeed, "yo nació" seems exactly right for getting at the peculiar confluence of identity that is implied in the idea of being Jewish-Cuban, or "Juban," as they say in Miami. (157)

Skillfully, a parallel is established between both experiences even though they can be traced to different generations and personal circumstances. And there are further parallels in store. The stories gathered in *An Island Called Home* are all tales of resilience and cultural survival in the face of incredible odds. They are also narratives of figurative return, a return of sorts to a religion that some in the preceding generation had put on hold either because adherents were reluctant to practice it openly in an officially atheist society or because they had made a commitment to the advancement of the revolution above all else. These had wavered, but others held on to their beliefs over the years, albeit underground. Far from offering a master narrative about the life of Jews in Cuba, Behar offers a string of voices, with each Cuban Jew embodying a different story and a different way of living out their identities as Jews. Some want to "return" to Israel—although they have never been there. Behar brings into the narrative those who might not be easily pinpointed as Jews, such as Cubans of mixed blood, yet they, too, aspire to reach the Promised Land. The Cuban Jewish diaspora holds lessons for recognizing diversity even within such a small community. Highlighting a kaleidoscope of voices within the community, the book achieves a dialogic or polyphonic quality typical of diasporic personal narratives, as critics have noted. Two of the distinguishing characteristics that Susanna Egan finds in diasporic autobiography, dialogism as well as "its creation of strategic spaces for a network of people rather than linear time or a singular story" (123–25), are evident in Behar's work. Weaving in and out of the stories, on the surface or as a subtext, is Behar as both researcher and apprentice.

Yet another comparison can be made between the two diasporas, this time about the disjuncture between identity and territory. The meaning of Jewishness has shifted among many Jews, "from one based on land to a claim on the culture and heritage" (*An Island* 25). According to Behar, the nationalistic claim to land among the Jews in the diaspora is no longer feasible and ought to be replaced with one based on shared culture, history, and heritage. In the same way, discourses around Cubanness need to be revisited. The diaspora emerging from Cuba's recent history calls for a redefinition of the ties that bind. What common ground is there that allows Cubans everywhere to claim those ties? Are feeble links to the heritage enough for a definition? Like the Jews, diasporic Cubans wrestle with this type of questions.

Countless photographs inserted in the narrative reinforce the sense of displacement and their usefulness for keeping the erosion of memory at bay. And holding on to memory to fill the gaps caused by displacement is important for both the Jewish community in Cuba and for Behar: "I knew that I returned to Cuba with a longing for memory and I worried about imposing that nostalgia on Jews in Cuba, until I discovered that they too longed for memory" (*An Island* 34). The book is profusely illustrated with black-and-white photographs taken by Humberto Mayol, an award-winning Cuban photographer, and they play a major role in conveying the story that Behar chooses to tell (only a handful of photographs hark from Behar's family album). Behar sees in this artistic medium the instrument for salvaging memory. The photographs taken by Mayol as they made their journey across the island have the capacity to elicit the memories that Behar now has of Cuba,

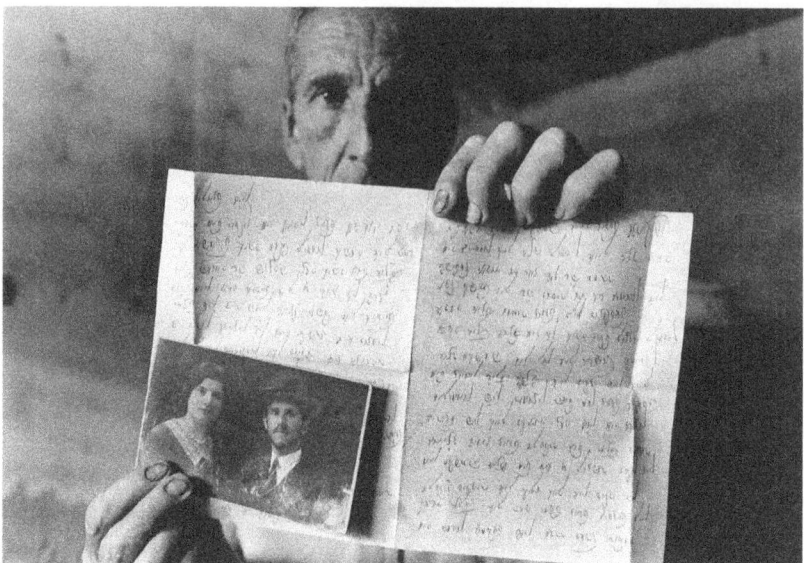

Figure 2.1. The son of Hungarian immigrants, Jaime Gans Grin is the only remaining Jew in Palma Soriano. The letter he is holding, written in Yiddish, is from relatives who were killed by the Nazis. Photograph by Humberto Mayol. Originally published in Ruth Behar's *An Island Called Home: Returning to Jewish Cuba.* Copyright © Ruth Behar; reprinted by permission of Rutgers University Press.

unlike those in her family album, which are only "surrogate memories of a Cuban-Jewish childhood" (Brink-Dahan 81). Those indexical photographs become, as photography does for Barthes, proof of the existence of the referent, evidence that keeps oblivion at arm's length: "because I was afraid of forgetting, I brought along a photographer on my journey—to make sure that the Cuba I was seeing would still be with me when I said goodbye again" (*An Island* 34). These photographs are producers of memory (Davis, "Vulnerable Observation" 281), Behar's "memoryscape" (*An Island* 261).

Many of the images replicate the layered approach to diaspora that distinguishes Behar's works dealing with the Jewish experience in Cuba and the interconnected Cuban and Juban experiences. The photographs capture not only the image of an individual but also indexical objects—another photograph, postcards, passports, letters, even a shirt worn by an inmate at a concentration camp—that the individual in question is usually holding in his or her hands, an object invested with great emotional value. The featured artifact invariably transports the viewer to another time and place, converting the evoked scene into a signpost for origins, a point of departure for a family chronicle that eventually dissolves into dislocation and diaspora. The author of *An Island Called Home* is twice removed from the "anachronistic" object contained in the photographs, yet is related to it by the nexus that Judaism provides. Likewise, she is connected to the subject in the photograph by virtue of nationality. There are bridges that span the various terrains.

Thanks to those bridges, Behar explores her own roots through her narrative of the Jewish community in Cuba. But paraphrasing Gilroy, it is not only about roots that Behar's work is about but also, and mainly, about paths and routes. Whereas the metaphor of the bridge was at the center of her first book on the island, *Bridges to Cuba/Puentes a Cuba*, with all signs in the U.S. portion pointing to Cuba as the final destination, in *An Island Called Home* that convergence is no longer a given. The emphasis here is not on straight lines, but on broken, meandering tracks covering a wide territory. Cubans of Behar's generation, like the Jews, are found across the globe. They may come and go while being spurred by a search for home that remains as such. In Behar's more recent book, *The Portable Island: Cubans at Home in the World* (2008), there are multiple bridges extending from Cuba to the rest of the world. The prominence of the Cuba-U.S. arch of the late twentieth century has given way, in the new millennium, to an awareness of a growing diaspora. And diaspora, as Ariana Hernández-Reguant writes in her review of *Adio Kerida*, problematizes the notion of home: "In this case, Cuba is not the place of origins, like one would find in similar ethnic narratives, nor the United States may be the final destination.... For Behar, migration—like exile for her parents—appears as a temporary element of Diaspora" (498). Ultimately, there is no single place one can call home.

In "Going to Cuba: Writing Ethnography of Diaspora, Return, and Despair" (1996), Behar had posed the question: "Return... to what? Or where? If there is no true place of origin, no native land, only diasporas layered on top of diasporas, what can return mean?" (*The Vulnerable Observer* 148). Now, more than a decade later, Behar concludes in *An Island Called Home* that the search, even if heartbreaking, never ends, because the search itself *is* home: "It's strange that there isn't a Kaddish [a Jewish prayer for the dead] a Jew can recite for a lost home. If there were, I'd utter that prayer. Without fear. Finally letting go in order to believe that the only true home is the one we have searched for inconsolably" (255). Behar seems to suggest that all that remains is to imagine a home built out of shards and transposed to the page, a Juba or home-like land where one can "create fictions, not actual cities or villages, but invisible ones" ("Juban América" 165). Behar's narratives render this imaginary homeland utterly intelligible by highlighting how the sense of home is under constant revision.

A Cuban Airbus by Way of a Latino Borderland

If Behar placed the emphasis on diaspora, in a similar vein it is spaces transcending nations and nationalities that the University of Pennsylvania cultural critic Román de la Campa underscores in *Cuba on My Mind: Journeys to a Severed Nation* (2000). This is a memoir that places the "greater" Cuba (the island and the exile community) in a hemispheric context while engaging the Cuba-Miami conundrum. The book is "an attempt to think through that period [1959–99] that is itself enveloped by questions not just on Cuba itself, but on the larger Cuban nation—the severed nation and its diaspora—and on the United States, where a considerable part of the Cuban nation now constructs its sense of Cubanness" (18). Thus the Latinos with whom Cubans interact in the United States will figure, too, in the equation. The book taps into a Latino imaginary that few writers with a Cuban background have acknowledged since they, too, along with other Hispanics, question the validity of the pan-ethnic label. Latino, though, is the moniker, a U.S. invention, that the narrator chooses to employ in order to place Cuban migration in a larger, hemispheric context.

De la Campa's hybrid memoir combines personal experiences with commentaries and reflections on scores of issues bearing on the reconfiguration of Cuban culture today. Here, as in Tony Mendoza's book, the balance is skewed on the side of the non-memoir; personal, intimate recollections are given the short end of the deal. What is different here is the link between the personal and the political. Lived experience, however succinctly, is used as a starting point to plunge into a public history of several decades—a strategy that helps to ascertain the writer's unmediated authority. By and large taking over the narrative, de la Campa's reflections about that history can be said to have a post-indexical effect accentuating the gap between places (especially sites imbued with a personal meaning) and their slippery traces in his memory, of which he nevertheless tries not to lose sight. Evidently, the academic musings close that gap, filling page after page of this hybrid memoir.

Unlike the memoirs of Carlos Eire, which focus on his Cuban childhood, or Behar's and Mendoza's, which deal with their recent experiences back in Cuba, de la Campa's book, the most political of the five, privileges the challenges he had to face in the United States. The children of a lawyer able to provide reasonably well for his family, de la Campa and his two older siblings were sent to boarding schools in the United States shortly after the arrival of the revolutionary forces in Havana. Once the family's resources were depleted, however, his parents arranged for Román to join the Peter Pan program in Miami in early 1961, and from there, the child was sent to a makeshift camp near Jacksonville. About a year later, he went back to Miami to reunite with his family, and then on to Pennsylvania and Iowa, where they settled. He eventually moved on to Minnesota to enroll in a postgraduate program.

After experiencing a radicalization process in the 1970s influenced by the war in Vietnam, the coup against Salvador Allende in Chile, and the civil rights movement in the United States, the narrator went back to Cuba with the first contingent of the Antonio Maceo Brigade in 1977, making him one of the 55 *hermanos* that Jesús Díaz featured in his 1978 film. The trip helped to upset the barriers to building a relationship between Cubans on both sides. At the same time, according to de la Campa, the trip served to ascertain, in hindsight, the existence of a growing number of Cubans whose identity does not overlap neatly with either the homeland or exile. Writing about *De la patria y el exilio* (1979), de la Campa concludes that "Díaz, along with other prominent figures in Cuba's cultural institutions, had trouble recognizing that between *patria* and *exilio*, one could find a Cuban diaspora that was neither one nor the other" (89). Diasporic Cubans occupy a third space, he claims, similar in characteristics to other Latino diasporas in the United States.

Implicated in this fluid third space is Cuban Miami as well. Cultivating a frozen image of Cuba, exiles in Miami fail to recognize diversity in their midst. They also tend to distort reality. The narrator critiques their denials about the profound social disparities rampant in pre-1959 Cuba, the intolerance toward internal dissent, and the assertion that it upholds the legitimate values of Cuban culture. However, de la Campa's assessment goes beyond the tension between Miami and Cuba to include broader parameters for debate on the Cuban nation, suggesting the rise of postnational imaginaries that coexist uneasily with the nationalist, official discourses still circulating on both sides of the Straits.

One of de la Campa's arguments is that the growing Latino presence in the United States complicates the landscape of diaspora, for it is not only the Cubans who claim an identity spanning two territories but also other Hispanics who, in a post melting-pot climate, similarly inhabit interstitial spaces between nations. All these pressures move the two hemispheres closer like never before. The resulting juncture, in turn, affects subjectivities developed on the mainland. In a context where Cubans come to interact with other Latinos and begin to question whether they, too, are perceived as people of color, de la Campa is hopeful that the well-defined exile identity may wither. The question may prompt a reflection on identity that rests just as much on other categories, not only political ideology. The author offers an example by way of his father, whose legal representation of Mexicans from the U.S. side of the border, in Iowa, had a tangential effect on his self-image and opened up channels of communication with his liberal son. For the critic, this mass of people becomes a "fluid diaspora of thirty-two million Latinos in the United States, a categorical ambivalence that often forgoes any attempt to distinguish between Latin Americans, American Latinos, exiles, immigrants, indigenous groups, rafters, refugees, and border peoples" (113). In such Latino borderlands,

> [e]ach Latino group may be unique, but all groups share a call for a different, if unstable, sense of ontological space—one characterized by a doubleness, one that is too American seriously to undertake a return to a real or mythical motherland, yet clings to that different cultural and linguistic heritage with which it maintains contact in multiple and contradictory ways. My own experience suggests that the distance between "Latinos" and immigrant groups of Latin America who see themselves strictly as exiles and foreign nationals will be reduced considerably with increased Latin American migration. (114)

It remains to be seen whether all these groups will eventually meld, as de la Campa predicted over a decade ago. What seems certain is that numerous Latinos span two or more geopolitical borders, as the extended bibliography on the subject demonstrates. For this reason, the critic argues, our hemisphere is being reconfigured to accommodate practices that can only be characterized as transnational.

De la Campa's personal relationship with Cuba constitutes an example of the shifting landscape he describes. Disillusioned with Cuban politics after the Mariel exodus, the critic stayed away from the island after 1982. However, in the summer of 1999 he makes another trip following an invitation to give a talk on the Latino diaspora in the United States. On this occasion, he devotes most of his trip to reminisce about his childhood. He spends endless hours strolling up and down the neighborhoods, schools, clubs, baseball fields, and churches that meant something to him as a child, going inside some personal landmarks that could help to rouse his memories. This is where *extrañamiento* kicks in, as he is not quite successful in his efforts. His old Marist Brothers School and his grandfather's former house are two of the places that resonate with childhood, but somehow the adult narrator cannot make them come alive, not even after stimulating his memories. On the contrary, he admits:

> The most striking aspect of these visits is that they never quite satisfy. I found myself walking by these places a number of times later on during my trip—not to go in again, but to look at them from different angles, as if to match the snapshots I was taking with the narratives in my memory bank. (158)

Challenging the narrator, the match between snapshots and recollections is never quite realized and the hollow space remaining between the two is filled with the post-indexical. Despite his willingness to close the gap, something went awry. Nonetheless, other experiences highlight the indexical quality of his search. In his ongoing quest for connection with the past, the narrator pays a visit to two black women who live in what used to be his aunt's house in El Vedado. Since one of the women lived there for many years looking after Aunt Mina, the narrator's only remaining close relative in Havana until she passed, the house is now hers, and she and her sister become his only remaining "kinship." Despite the obvious racial and class disparities, they serve as living indexes to a long lost world.[3]

Alongside the sites that used to spell home for him, de la Campa comes across *paladares, jineteras, boteros,* street hustlers, rappers, a dual currency economy, and buildings in ruins, all novel and distinct markers of a Special Period that contains the kernels of a post-Soviet return to a mixed economy.[4] De la Campa grapples with his feelings of bewilderment toward a transformed city and its disconcerting new denizens in a way that recalls an identically baffled Mendoza (see below). On his way back to Miami, as he goes over the experiences shared by his fellow travelers, de la Campa comes to the conclusion that the Cuban nation is at home in these very same travels and intersecting paths:

> [T]here is no real return or reunification left as far as Cubans are concerned, except in the dramatic embrace of these crisscrossing passages, travels, and flows that promise no clear direction, as well as the memories of separation they evoke. The plane ride back confirmed my suspicion that I was witnessing the Cuban nation at home, a state it can reach only in the act of traversing itself. (175)

The Cuban nation is at home in these very travels, a notion not at odds with the reality of transnationalism. Ironically, de la Campa's concluding comments echo the metaphor of the airbus proposed by well-known writer Luis Rafael Sánchez to evoke the constant back and forth movement of Puerto Ricans between the island and the mainland. For Sánchez, "la guagua aérea" becomes representational of the neocolonial status of Puerto Rico, whose population has halved due to migration to the United States. Endorsing the metaphor highlights not only de la Campa's debts to the Puerto Rican/Latino diaspora whose imagery he makes his own, corroborating his own analysis of a Latino imaginary, but also the absence of similar aerial metaphors in Cuban culture able to communicate the nature of the Cuban nation in the new millennium. It is, however, the kind of metaphor he longs for in order to get over the binary of exile or homeland and convey instead a transcending diasporic subjectivity: "[M]y life reads Cuban. Actually, it reads closer to what I call Cuban diaspora, a perspective that allows me to traverse the deep ideological divide between my two Cubas: homeland and exile" (4). De la Campa demands an in-between space that straddles homeland and exile, a space prefigured in other Latino narratives of ambiguous cultural belonging.

Home and Homeland: Making *Familia* in and from Diaspora

That the construction of a space in-between is in great part a "writerly" project is stressed in Emilio Bejel's *The Write Way Home: A Cuban-American*

Story (2003), first published in English and only later in the Spanish original under the title *El horizonte de mi piel* (2005). The front cover of the English edition shows a quill and an inkwell out of which the contours of the isle of Cuba emerge, its eastern tip comfortably resting on a chessboard—the drawing suggesting that it is through writing in addition to calculated, strategic moves that Cuba can best be imagined. Because of the liberties taken by the author, such as not revealing the true identity of some of the characters (*The Write Way Home* 237), Bejel's autobiographical account is designated as a *novela* in the Spanish edition even though the narrator/protagonist is still Emilio Bejel.

It is through verbal artifice that the narrator fathoms the possibility of re-creating home and homeland as well as shaping a persona whose notion of family is entangled with those of homosexuality and diaspora. Of the four self-referential narratives I have selected as examples of diasporic memoirs, *The Write Way Home* is the one most centered on the self and the body.[5] It is less nostalgic because it is also more forward driven and teleological in its search for a space of (sexual) liberation. In some ways, the story dovetails with the conventional coming-out narrative that follows the road toward a liberated gay subject, although one that is also from the Cuban diaspora, a twist that complicates the story.

Unlike most memoirists of the one-and-a-half generation, Bejel opted for exile of his own accord and left his family (his single mother, grandfather, and aunts) behind. Bejel was active in the Catholic Church as a teenager and fled Cuba in 1962 shortly after his eighteenth birthday when the relationship between the State and the Church took a turn for the worse.[6] Bejel's memoir offers details about his life in the United States, especially his graduate and postgraduate studies, both on scholarships. He also provides information about his teaching positions—particularly his struggle to secure tenure in the mid-1980s at the University of Florida in Gainesville, where he was unjustly accused of being a communist by a group of students. Details are also provided about a period of promiscuity following his coming out as gay. Bejel's central focus is the process that led to his coming to grips with his sexuality. Scenes taking place in Cuba are interspersed in the narrative; there is a to and fro movement between the two countries and between time periods.

Home and homeland are viewed as related though rarely compatible concepts. Exile or, rather, "sexile"—a neologism devised by Manolo Guzmán to account for those who leave their place of birth because of prejudice on the basis of their sexuality or gender (La Fountain-Stokes 296)—leads to a conflictive relationship between those two terms. Although Bejel's departure from Cuba was not the direct result of homophobia, he did have to repress his natural inclination to same-sex relationships. Perhaps a better phrase to describe the outcome is "lite sexile," used by Lawrence Fountain-Stokes in reference to his own exile from Puerto Rico (299). The phrase, an attempt to add nuance to the qualifier "sexile," implies a lack of persecution and even an unclear awareness of prejudice toward nonnormative sexuality that at the same time do not eradicate the feelings that something is amiss.

It was "lite sexile" that pushed Bejel to redefine the notions of home and family. This was quite a feat for an adult subject with no conjugal ties or progeny in the 1960s. He nonetheless committed himself to "making *familia* from scratch"—as the lesbian writer Cherrie Moraga adroitly puts it in one of her plays (35). However, his notion of family is determined by neither blood ties nor a union sanctioned by the law. Family is rather an aggregate of people who have come together by chance and who look after one another, a description Bejel himself offers in his book *Gay Cuban Nation* (48–49). Hence, free from various constraints, Bejel's families are always evolving as well as multiplying. For instance, his father, his only blood relative living in Havana, develops a close relationship with Bejel's Cuban partner, while Bejel's second gay lover's Cuban family in Tampa takes him in "like a son" (*The Write Way Home* 121). These are just two of the multiple, sometimes binational and biracial families that Bejel draws his strength from: there is another one in Manzanillo, Bejel's hometown, and two others in Colorado and Gainesville, thanks to his successive partners. As a gay person, as well as diasporic subject, Bejel sees the need to carry family on his back. Therefore, the post-indexical marker that in other cases surfaces around the coupling of place and family is downplayed in this narrative. See how fluid his understanding of family is and his ability to dodge any lack:

> In Cuba I would always hook up with Lázaro and would usually stay at my father's. He and his wife Iluminada became good friends with Lázaro, and I became very close to Lázaro's mother. It was a truly international family. One of the things I most appreciated about those acquired or recovered families was the very close friendship with my father and Iluminada. (*The Write Way Home* 219)

The right to enjoy a family, whether acquired or recovered, and home in the narrator's own terms is maintained throughout in ways that unlink the dyad of home and homeland. As a critic observes, "the concept of diaspora offers a critique of discourses of fixed origins while taking account of a homing desire, as distinct from a desire for 'homeland'" (Brah 16). The homing desire must take into account the narrator's body, its needs and desires, as if the homoerotic drive and the sublime welcoming of home finally came together, obliterating whatever feelings of past repression or heterosexual compulsion remained. What transpires from Bejel's narrative is an aspiration for a home that meets these requirements over the recuperation of a homeland with which he, nevertheless, stays connected—even if in ambivalent ways.

Bejel's sentiments toward the homeland remain equivocal for more than one reason. As queer, he is an abject figure in the national imaginary. His blood family was a source of inspiration and support while he was growing up in Manzanillo, but it also exerted control upon his behavior and gestures so as to stave off any hint of homosexuality in him. The rules were strictly enforced even though his family was far from being the conventional Cuban family. Headed by his mother, it was not patriarchal in the traditional sense, but it did foster heterosexual values. A loving family at any rate, it was bent on getting rid of young Bejel's deepest desires for "his own good," a misguided attempt proving that "'home' can be simultaneously a place of safety and of terror" (Brah 180).

Once in the United States, his sexuality fuels his bonding with an American society that in the 1970s experienced a transformation following the Stonewall uprisings in 1969. It is thus in Miami, after his first homosexual encounter, that Bejel's coming-out-of-the-closet is accomplished: "My life with Lauren at UM was the beginning of my true sexual coming-of-age, as well as the beginning of my most intensely accelerated Americanization" (*The Write Way Home* 110). Coincidentally, Bejel's acting upon his same-sex desire happens at a time when Cuba was clamping down on gays and throwing them in camps that sought to change their behavior. Diaspora is, in his case, in part the end result of a different type of exile—"lite sexile," to borrow La Fountain-Stokes's phrase again. But it is a sexile from which he returns to queer the homeland with his homosexual relationships and his hard-won, steadfast refusal to tolerate homophobic reactions, not to mention his scholarly contributions to the literature on gays in Cuba and Cuban literature. There are two unequivocal instances when the narrator confronts his relatives on the island after they make off-the-cuff remarks about gays. The indexical relationship between their hostile comments and the pervasive abjection of gays in Cuban society persists throughout the text, a situation that can only give rise to a discourse of anxious returns.

Similar to the experience of some of the writers above, Bejel's relationship with Cuba and with hardline Cuban exile is problematic. His involvement with the 1978 *Diálogo* and the journal *Areíto* came about as a result of his support for some of the progressive policies implemented in education and health care in Cuba after 1959. His upbringing made him appreciate the social change that was taking root on the island. At the same time, criticisms about the absence of personal freedom and vigilance made by other memoirists are voiced by Bejel, who also makes a severe judgment of the Mariel crisis in 1980, which brought about renewed homophobic reactions. His simultaneous critique of the intolerance of Cuban dogmatists in Florida recalls the tense relationship between exile and sexile that Reinaldo Arenas's *Antes que anochezca* (1992) makes all too clear.

Despite the critiques, though, defending the right to return to the island with relative ease is a primary issue in Bejel's memoirs, for he claims, in this poem and throughout his memoir, a transnational existence that redraws old maps:

> Then I said to myself: I have two countries
> and I told myself: nothing was actually drawn out
> with rulers and compasses. (*The Write Way Home* 181)

In lieu of coordinates, borders, and compulsory behavior, *The Write Way Home* deploys the limitless power of language to reimagine home and homeland from the diaspora. The reimagining of both requires, in Bejel, a concurrent critique of their limitations as they have been established until now.

Searching for Memories and Finding Post-Soviet Cuba

As Behar shows in her book, photography serves as a tool to jolt memory. Images in autobiographies of the Cuban diaspora are sometimes used as mere illustrations, while taking center stage at other times. This is the case in Tony Mendoza's *Cuba: Going Back* (1997), a photography book that reflects a similar lack of personal memories of Cuba. However, Mendoza, a professional photographer, fills that lack in a different manner. The notion of the post-indexical proves very useful in the specific context of this memoir, since there are few people and sites remaining on the island to which Mendoza can attach his remembrance of things past or his search for personal meaning. Indeed, instead of a memoirist, it is the chronicler of Cuba in the 1990s, under the Special Period, that ends up gaining the upper hand. As such, the book parallels other visual narratives on post-Soviet Cuba.

Combining over eighty black-and-white photographs and an essay, *Cuba: Going Back* records Mendoza's return trip to the island after thirty-seven years in exile. The trip takes place in 1996, coinciding with a "post-1995 image boom" of Havana brought about by the opening of the city to tourism and foreign investment (Dopico 452), a time when a particular version of Cuba became fashionable again. Mendoza spends twenty-one days in Cuba while shooting eighty rolls of film and recording a video. Mendoza, however, is no tourist, and he travels to the island in search of the "paradise" he left behind. In fact, one of the goals of the trip is to "confirm" his memory (*Cuba* 8), and this elusive goal is what makes the book an apparent return narrative to the abandoned homeland.

The accompanying essay includes background information about the author/photographer. Mendoza leaves Cuba permanently with his family in 1960 as part of the first wave of exiles. He had lived in the United States prior to that date as a boarding student at an elite New England preparatory school. Thus his last memories of the island were of vacations spent at the family summer residence in an affluent section of Varadero Beach where, in the 1950s, the spectacular houses of the well-to-do, with a splendid view of the ocean, graced the coastline. There, parents, relatives, and nannies presumably doted on a child who was largely absent from their day-to-day lives. Away from his family home and his homeland, Mendoza was pursuing a first-rate education on the mainland—as several generations in the family had done before him—one that eventually led him to Ivy League schools for degrees in engineering and architecture. He joins a commune in the 1960s and strays from his Cuban roots until he meets a Cuban woman whom he marries. He then goes through a period of "re-Cubanization."

Because of the lengthy separation from the island and the particularities of Mendoza's life in the United States, his return narrative differs from the "typical" homecoming described by social scientist Alfred Schutz: "The homecomer . . . expects to return to an environment of which he always had and—so he thinks—still has intimate knowledge and which he has just to take for granted in order to find his bearings within it. The approaching stranger has to anticipate in a more or less empty way what he will find; the homecomer has just to recur to the memories of his past" (qtd. in Stefansson 8). But Mendoza appears to have limited memories of Cuba, and the moments of remembrance tied to a personal history are few and far between.

Still, he honors the rituals of return. There is, of course, a *de rigueur* visit to the family mansion on the elegant Avenida de los Presidentes in Havana, which its former occupant finds well kept since it was converted into a government facility soon after the family flight. Significant changes have taken place, though, as if the index and object had come unglued. Mendoza's former room is now a kitchen, the furniture has been replaced, and, most important, the house's former dwellers have been silenced. Even though he is allowed to tour the mansion, little emotional reaction is recorded, and his brief comments, limited to a few paragraphs, soon move away from the personal domain (42–43). The other two scenes imbued with personal memories are also attached to houses—magnificent dwellings that used to be filled to the brim with relatives. As with the first, the family house of his ancestors at 31 Amargura Street in Old Havana, too, is now used for other functions (90). The only trace he finds of his family past is a brass plate that reads *Bufete Mendoza*, the law office of his great-great-grandfather, the first chief justice of the Cuban Supreme Court in 1902 and mayor of Havana before the turn of the century. Mendoza has trouble finding even the house, let alone the memories associated with it, because the numbers on the doorways have barely survived the ravages of time and the perverse effects of the latest economic crisis. The third and last house, in Varadero Beach, which Mendoza visits toward the end of his stay in Cuba, is the one that comes closest to triggering a common reaction among those undertaking a homecoming. Serving as a government guesthouse, it has been impeccably maintained. Memories rush through Mendoza's mind as he tours the house: "Every room brought forth memories, small incidents, family ghosts walking around, still laughing from a joke or their good fortune" (133). Just once do his memories spring to life.

Not only are there few vestiges or indexes left of the family history; the homeland itself, the nation as family, is hardly recognizable. Indeed, it sets in motion feelings of *extrañamiento*. Mendoza's ambiguous status is revealed in comments such as the following: "What impressed me the most was how clearly and eloquently Cubans speak. Every person I met had an amazing control of the language" (109). It is also revealed when Mendoza misses the point of a comment made in Cuban-style *choteo* in the middle of one of his casual conversations with people on the street. The self-deprecating humor goes over his head. Additionally, he has something to say about the changed racial makeup of the city, which, according to him, has injected black slang into the Cuban dialect, making it almost incomprehensible: "Cubans seem to speak faster now, and the intonation is different. Havana is now a predominantly Black city, so slang and idioms from Black culture predominate" (17). As if this were not enough, the video with the same title as the book shows scenes where ordinary Cubans identify him as anything (Spaniard, American) but a compatriot.[7]

If the essay does not amount to a full-blown, classic memoir, then what is it? A second goal of Mendoza's trip back is "to satisfy his curiosity about life in socialist Cuba" (*Cuba* 7), and it is this interest that takes over very quickly.[8] Mendoza goes around the city taking in the sights and he talks to over two hundred Cubans, inquiring about their lives during the Special Period. Since their reports fill page after page of the book, Mendoza comes across as a journalist going after that other story more than a memoirist retracing his steps. What ultimately takes over is a first-person travel account or travelogue of the Cuba, especially Havana, of the 1990s.

For the most part, the photographs back up this assertion. The photographic essay mirrors the narrative neatly enough, reinforcing the sense of the post-indexical. The one photograph that can be said to have personal connotation is the one of the porch overlooking the ocean in the Varadero summer retreat, which stirs the artist emotionally. But Mendoza's findings are for the most part far from any index, in Peirce's taxonomy, and fail to "confirm" his memory. He thus casts a wider net, replacing that erasure with scenes of the Special Period in Cuba—vignettes of a natural and built environment about to crumble, amid a national crisis of unprecedented dimensions that had to be *seen*, as Ana María Dopico notes:

> Havana has become synonymous with the photograph in the last seven years, and the journey there seems to demand a photographic eye, an instrumental lens, an archaeological instinct. The gaze of the lens in Havana has accompanied the eye of the market, reflecting the

fashionable status and historical exceptionalism of the city as living ruin, and the allure of a scarcity still set apart from the flawed and normative narratives of development, democratization, or global economic integration. (451)

Although surely with a style and technique all its own, many of Mendoza's photographs become an addendum to the visual archive that Dopico describes and, as such, bolsters the trope of the time warp commonly superimposed to the Cuba of the 1990s. As Damián J. Fernández remarks in his introduction to *Cuba Transnational* (2005): "One of the dominant images of Cuba, especially in the United States, is that of a geographically and politically isolated nation: an off-bounds place, caught in a retro time warp of the late 1950s and 1960s, quaint, romantic, shabby chic revolutionary, a sort of social Galapagos" (xiii). Except that the more somber aspects of that image prevail in Mendoza's photographs and essay. Images of the Chevys, Fords, Cadillacs, and Buicks from the 1950s abound, as well as those oozing with urban decay, "as if a new breed of concrete-eating vermin were loose in Havana" (Mendoza, *Cuba* 13). The photographs also show the by now predictable cracks in the Havana seawall, abandoned dogs, empty shelves, street markets, swaying palm trees set in the countryside, unkempt Cubans,

Figure 2.2. *Cars in Havana*, from Mendoza's *Cuba: Going Back*. Photograph by Tony Mendoza.

Figure 2.3. *Boys in Old Havana*, from Mendoza's *Cuba: Going Back*. Photograph by Tony Mendoza.

and makeshift boats. There are some exceptions, though, having to do with children in various settings, some of whom are cheerfully smiling, and of ordinary Cubans sitting in a park. These are the most appealing because they stand out amid the misery howled by the rest. Most, however, portray the shortages and coping mechanisms described at length in the narrative.

On the whole, the photographs present a slice of daily life in Cuba under the unforgiving crisis. Before his trip, Mendoza had been scrutinizing "pictures of Havana in photography books shot by European journalists" (*Cuba* 9), and it is as if the photographic essay in *Cuba: Going Back* had been mediated by a haunting grand narrative foregrounding ruins and bankruptcy. It is this subtext informed by an outside gaze that draws attention to the diasporic character of a book that originally sets out to "confirm" memories. The photographer/narrator stands at the intersection of the physical ruins of the city and the ruins of memory. And yet, despite waning memories, he hopes to make Cuba part of his life: "Someday Castro will die and socialism will wither away. I would guess that many exiled Cubans will return to Cuba, but many will stay in the United States. I would like to do both" (*Cuba* 153). His trip showed "how right the place feels" to him ("Going Back" 82).

The narrator has since returned, if not physically, at least figuratively. More than a decade after *Cuba: Going Back*, the author "returned" to Cuba through a coming-of-age novel set in Havana and Varadero. The novel, *A Cuban Summer* (2013), follows the well-to-do, charming protagonist as he deals with the onset of sexuality just before he is slated to leave for an exclusive boarding school in the United States. By taking himself back to Cuba to recount his alter ego's exploits, the author accomplishes the repeating "homecoming" that *Cuba: Going Back* hoped to enact at the end. Because it is accomplished in a work of fiction, the going back refrains from making any claims on reality and succeeds in offering myriad details about growing up in the Cuba of the 1950s. Unconstrained by limits of any kind, the novel achieves a smooth landing, reimagining at will what an advantaged Cuban childhood would have been like. The novel sidesteps the ambivalence and contradictions pervading memoirs written in the diaspora. As a qualifier, ambivalence is, as a critic states, a striking mark of diasporic memoirs, where parallel spaces are routinely carved (Egan 120–58).

Conclusion

The four narratives examined seek out indices to a Cuban past. Ruth Behar embarks on this quest through the remains of the Jewish community throughout the island, which provides a link to her Jewish childhood in Havana as well as to an enhanced understanding of dispersal and memory building among Cubans. Behar battles against the erosion of memory resulting from diaspora by locating or fashioning indexical markers, such as the photographs of her informants and the photographs taken by Mayol of Behar's own journey. While Behar seeks out those indices as if her life depended on them, Tony Mendoza takes us into a post-indexical narrative where things aren't what they seem. *Cuba: Going Back* is not exactly a memoir of a Cuban childhood; there is little left in Havana that Mendoza can lay his hands on to reconstruct his past. Instead, he sets his photographic gaze on the rundown city of the 1990s, a gaze that adds another layer of mediation to a distant past. Many of the images in the book echo those found in photography collections on a Cuba deep in crisis.

Similarly to Mendoza, de la Campa addresses both personal and nonpersonal concerns in his *Cuba on My Mind*, a book where Havana becomes a largely post-indexical city where places, people, and objects enabling a passage to the narrator's past are rarely found. There are, however, plenty of reflections about the role played by Cuban Americans, among other Latinos, in closing the distance between the United States and the Southern Hemisphere. The back and forth movement between Miami and Havana that de la Campa predicts will become commonplace in the future resonates with other paradigmatic Latino tales of two-way travel between island and mainland. Finally, Emilio Bejel draws from coming-out narratives to offer his memoirs of growing up in a homophobic society, recognizing and self-disclosing his sexual identity in exile, and going back and confronting multiple indexes to homophobia. Bejel's narrative is not just another coming-out story; it takes place at the intersection between homosexuality and diaspora.

These memoirs all converge in expressing a deep ambivalence about returning. If returning grants the returnees a measure of fulfillment, it also underscores the subjects' defamiliarization, in some cases, and distancing, in others, from a land and people they nonetheless approach as their own. The narrative paradigms from which they draw inspiration are largely unrelated to the island, yet they are cleverly and conveniently brought into the fold. It is often repeated that bicultural subjects are both outsiders and insiders with respect to the host culture, and the narratives showcased in this chapter illustrate that the reverse statement can also stand up to scrutiny: it can be extended to the way migrant subjects enter into a relationship with their birthplace as well. The outcome of multiple causes, this ambivalence stands as a hallmark of Cuban-American self-referential narratives of return.

Speaking about someone who, married to a Cuban woman now has strong, unmistakable bonds to the island, Ruth Behar wonders about the rationale for her identity claims:

> What can I say? Who now has a stronger claim to Cuba: I who left the island as a child and no longer have family in Cuba, or my friend, a Michigan native, still unable to speak Spanish, who now has family "down there"? If an identity, like a library book, has an expiration date, mine is surely past due, and the fine for clinging to it can only get heftier. (*Traveling Heavy* 195)

Despite the mounting ambivalence that permeates their pages, the return narratives included in this book demonstrate the willingness of their authors to let the fines accrue.

3

Ana Mendieta

Chiseling (in) Cuba

> Cuando está de veras viva, la memoria no contempla la historia, sino que invita a hacerla. Más que en los museos, donde la pobre se aburre, la memoria está en el aire que respiramos.... La memoria viva no nació para ancla. Tiene, más bien, vocación de catapulta.
>
> [When it is truly alive, memory does not contemplate history but extends an invitation to creating it. Rather than in museums, where the poor thing gets bored, memory is found in the air we breathe.... Living memory was not born to be an anchor. It has, rather, a catapult vocation.]
>
> Eduardo Galeano, "La memoria viva"

In one of the most moving scenes in Estela Bravo's documentary *Los que se fueron* (1980), Ana Mendieta reminisces about the day of her departure from Cuba on 11 September 1961 when she was close to thirteen years old. She remembers being confined to *la pecera*, the glass-enclosed space known as the "fishbowl" inside the airport, built to keep Cubans who were flying out of the country from mingling with those who remained. Once past the threshold of the fishbowl, passengers reached a point of no return. After going through the immigration authorities, they had turned into noncitizens, no longer regarded as part of the nation by virtue of their "abandoning" it. Mendieta's parents were on the other side of the fishbowl with their hands against the glass, in all likelihood agonizing over their decision to send their girls away, while Ana and her sister, Raquelín, tried unsuccessfully to make contact.

The two girls would arrive shortly in Miami and be placed in camps and foster homes in a string of cities in Iowa, far from the fledgling Cuban enclave in South Florida, which perhaps would have offered a more hospitable environment for Peter Pan children. They would not see their mother for five years. And it wasn't until nineteen years since that day at the airport that Mendieta would go back to Cuba and single-mindedly try to restore her bonds to kin and the nation with her work. She was finally breaking free from the glass enclosure, although later events would make it all too clear that some partitions had not budged. In the end, Mendieta's case agrees with the volatile character of return.

Between January 1980 and July 1983, visual and performance artist Ana Mendieta (1948–85) went back to Cuba seven times. The remarkable intensity with which she undertook the project of reconnecting with her former homeland naturally calls for special attention in a book about homecomings. This chapter treks into Mendieta's attempts to insert herself in the island's art milieu, pursuing opportunities to show her work, forging professional relationships, and crowning her labor with the *Esculturas rupestres* or *Rupestrian Sculptures* in the Jaruco limestone caves, a capstone achievement inspired by indigenous mythology. "Chiseling (in) Cuba" explores the reception and impact of Mendieta's work in Cuba in order to determine how successful she was over time, and it concludes with a mixed appraisal of the full balance of her struggle. The artist's aspiration to gain a rightful place in the nation's art no doubt came to fruition during the time of her visits, when she received the attention of the media, local artists, and the art establishment. However, Mendieta's traces today are to be found not in the art institutions whose relationship she cultivated but on the margins, in alternative spaces where her memory has been passed down, albeit rather unconventionally, through generations. Both Maurice Halbwachs's and Pierre Nora's conceptualizations of collective memory and sites of memory, respectively, will assist in appraising how those alternative spaces have been configured and what is their function.

Given the scope of Mendieta's artwork, it is not surprising that her work still casts a spell on new generations of artists in Cuba and beyond. Mendieta was part of a cohort of artists who experimented with performance, earth, and body art at a time when these innovative forms were still viewed as experimental. Prior to her trips to Cuba, she worked in Iowa and Mexico, drawing attention for a series of unusual performances, some of them riveting. Through her pieces and performances, she sought to make a statement about violence, power, and indifference in society. Her works in this area include self-portraits using blood as a medium; enacting a violent rape scene;

transforming herself into a sacrificial cock by covering herself with white feathers; standing naked while holding a dead, bloody rooster in her hands; making ritualistic tracks on a white wall with her hands and arms spilling blood; and having a steady stream of blood flow from underneath a door onto the street while monitoring the reactions of passersby.

She was interested in normativity and the socially constructed nature of gender as well. In two of her self-portraits, she pasted hair onto her face to simulate a beard and a moustache, and in another project she distorted her face against a glass surface. She also conveyed the vulnerability and ephemerality of human existence through the short-lived silhouettes that she made outdoors, availing herself of whatever nature bountifully supplied: sand, water, mud, tree branches, grass, dirt, and leaves, in addition to gunpowder. Animating Mendieta's life and work was the quest for change and transformation at various levels, in art as well as life. She knew firsthand how disruptive politics as usual could be on individuals and the family.

Backdrop to Mendieta's Return Story

Mendieta's return in 1980 was made possible by the Círculo de Cultura Cubana, created in 1979 by Cuban Americans who shared an interest in cultural exchanges between their native and adopted homelands as a means to bridge the divide. Ana Mendieta was a founding member of the Círculo de Cultura Cubana along with others who had also left Cuba as children, some, like her, through the Operation Pedro Pan.

From a cultural point of view, these were auspicious times for exchanges as Cuban cultural production was just recovering from the slumber of the 1970s. At the beginning of that decade, state cultural institutions promoted socialist realist aesthetics in support of the large-scale revolutionary project, thus making the cultural sphere subservient to politics. Alas, rather than fostering social transformation, the policy produced a stifling environment that hindered the development of works (both in the visual arts and literature) whose outlook overstepped the boundaries of orthodox criteria. The period, which stretched beyond 1975, received the moniker of *quinquenio gris*, a term intended to showcase the dullness of works produced under its banner.[1]

By the early 1980s a breath of fresh air was sweeping across the Cuban cultural landscape. Cutting-edge, experimental works of art began to come out of workshops, galleries, and art studios on the island. According to Luis Camnitzer, those accountable for the shift in direction were a new generation of visual artists who would make an outstanding contribution to the image of Cuban art worldwide. The eleven artists—José Bedia, Flavio Garciandía, Tomás Sánchez, Leandro Soto, Rubén Torres Llorca, Ricardo Rodríguez Brey, Juan Francisco Elso Padilla, José Manuel Fors, Gustavo Pérez Monzón, Israel León, and Rogelio López Marín ("Gory")—behind the renewal came to be known as Volumen I, the title of a group exhibition of their work launched in Havana in January 1981.

Mendieta's second trip to Cuba crystallized at the time of the Volumen I exhibition in the framework of a specialized exchange of U.S. artists and critics organized by the Círculo de Cultura Cubana. Mendieta, who led the exchange, met the young Cuban artists, who were her junior by just a few years, befriending some of them. There is a photograph of Mendieta surrounded by several of the artists—Bedia and Garciandía, among others, along with American art critic Lucy Lippard—taken at the time by López Marín. Like a happy family picture, the photograph conveys warmth, affinity, and bonding. Showing them huddled in a tight group, the photograph transmits the idea that the artist had naturally assumed her place among peers. To be sure, both Camnitzer and Olga Viso comment on the strong ties that developed between Mendieta and this group of artists. One of them, in fact, led her to Jaruco, where she would later carve her *Rupestrian Sculptures*.

Return, Personally Speaking

For Ana Mendieta, Cuba contained the key to understanding her peculiar, traumatic experience of exile and parental desertion. Based on careful research, Viso asserts that Mendieta began to ruminate about her return to Cuba at the time of her reunion with her father, a former political prisoner, in April 1979 after eighteen years of separation (*Ana Mendieta* 78). Perhaps her reencounter with the homeland would yield more consolation than the reencounter with her father, which neither healed the pain nor bridged the emotional distance caused by the lengthy separation they had experienced. Mendieta herself disclosed the rift in an interview with Cuban journalist Roger Ricardo Luis published in *Granma* during one of her visits.

At about the time of the father's arrival, Mendieta met other Cubans her age who, as college students, had become involved in campus protests

Figure 3.1. With members of the family during one of Mendieta's trips to Cuba. *Left to right*: María Victoria Cambó (cousin), Kaky Mendieta (cousin, deceased), Elvira Cambó (cousin), Paulette Oti (aunt, deceased), Ana Mendieta, and Raquel Costa (aunt, deceased). Courtesy of Tony Mendieta.

against the Vietnam War and in the national struggle for civil rights. The political and social unrest in the United States during this period called into question many assumptions, likely contributing to Mendieta's later determination to return to Cuba with her peers in order to see with her own eyes the accomplishments of the revolution. Mendieta's first trip in January 1980 took her not only to Havana but also to Trinidad, Cienfuegos, Bahía de Cochinos, Camagüey, and Santiago de Cuba, in addition to Cárdenas and Varadero, where her ancestral roots are located. In Havana, she honored one of the rituals of return: she passed by her family's former home, asked to be let in, and sat in her old bedroom. Overcome with emotion, she broke down in tears.[2] Even if for the returnee children of exile "home" was, as José Quiroga writes, a "constructed fiction, an imaginary landscape" (186), the truth is that emotionally, upon arrival, it seemed all too real. Only later would the occasion present itself to determine whether first impressions would stick.

After an interlude of nearly twenty years, Mendieta reunited with her grandparents, aunts, uncles, and cousins with whom she had had a nurturing relationship as a child. Hers was a large, extended family with artistic inclinations. Both her maternal grandmother and her mother studied art and practiced it for a while, while a paternal uncle kept an art studio. But their lives also revolved around politics. Their paternal grandfather, Pablo Mendieta, was a colonel in the Liberating Army during Cuba's last war for independence. After the war, he was appointed Mayor General of the Army and later Chief of the National Police. His brother, Carlos Mendieta, was president of Cuba in 1934 after the fall of Gerardo Machado. Mendieta's childhood memories are linked to their maternal grandparents' large house in Varadero, where the family would gather from time to time, as Raquel Mendieta, her sister, recounts. It was there, at the beach, where Ana began to make silhouettes, arms and legs extended, in the wet sand (Raquel Mendieta Costa 73).

The initial trip was intensely stirring. When Mendieta came back to the United States, she felt she had regained Cuba, only to lose it again. Her visit made her relive the initial moment of departure, and subsequent trips afforded the repossession of memories and relationships. Ana's cousin, "Kaki" Mendieta Costa, fills in details of Ana's trips in a touching essay included in *Bridges to Cuba*:

> Those were nights of painful conversations, nostalgic memories, anecdotes forgotten and reconstructed. Nights of non-stop partying, especially for you and me. We roamed the streets of the city, the Apostolado School, the old house in El Vedado. Then Cárdenas, grandparents, our roots and history, the *mambí* great-grandfather. You searched for the old museum, but it wasn't there anymore; it had changed but you could recognize yourself in the new one, too. In the sand on Varadero beach you recovered the detailed profiles of your silhouette, and you left your definitive outline in the small caves of the southern coast. (75)

In accordance with her cousin's recollections, Mendieta laid a claim to both the past, through her memories, and the future, on the basis of her artwork. Not only did she reaffirm memories and recover her old turf. She would also leave her imprint in previously uncharted spaces such as the Jaruco caves. Becoming part of the Cuban art scene, which she sought actively at a moment when brokering a close relationship was viewed with suspicion both inside and outside the island, was a major item in her agenda. Her nearly absolute effacement from institutional spaces in Cuba today is all the more glaring because of it.

Staking a Claim to a Place in Cuban Art

Mendieta's interpersonal connections with Cubans on the island went beyond her family. As stated, during her second trip she met the Volumen I artists and key players in the art world who may have had a part in helping her obtain invitations to exhibit her work on the island, even though those invitations were rarely extended to Cubans from the diaspora. She received not only invitations but permits to work there as well. Personal notes from Mendieta to José Veigas Zamora, a researcher who worked in the International Relations section of the Ministry of Culture's Visual Arts and Design department in the early 1980s, attest to Mendieta's intense interest in showing her art on the island. In her personal correspondence with Veigas, she mentions time and again that she is awaiting word about exhibitions that she expected to be mounted in Havana, going into details about curatorial arrangements.[3]

The obstinacy and perseverance with which she followed up on whatever opportunities arose bore fruit. Her successes included an invitation to participate in the Small Format Salon at the Habana Libre Hotel in September 1981, at which time she presented a work made in Cuba consisting of five heart-shaped figures made out of roots from areca palm trees grounded in 25 square centimeters of the red soil found in Cuba (Mosquera, "Esculturas rupestres" 56). There was also an exhibition of four photographs documenting her *Silueta* series in the *Premio de Fotografía Cubana* sponsored by Casa de las Américas in mid-1982; a solo exhibition of her work, *Geo-Imago*, in the Salón de Trabajadores of the Museo Nacional de Bellas Artes in April 1983; and her participation in the show *Artistas Latinoamericanos en Nueva York*, also at Bellas Artes, as part of the I Havana Biennial held from 22 May to 9 June 1984.

Taking place over a short period of time, these exhibits, in addition to the many sculptures she made outdoors during her visits to Varadero, Guanabo, and other sites, were meant to gain a foothold in the Cuban art world parallel to the one Mendieta already enjoyed outside of Cuba. She had studied and worked with prominent artists such as Hans Breder in Iowa; had won recognition for her performance, earth art, and body art; and had been admitted to the exclusive A.I.R. (Artists in Residence) Collective in 1978. Founded in 1972, A.I.R. was the first women's collective gallery in SoHo, and many renowned visual artists, such as Nancy Spero, who became Mendieta's friend, were affiliated with it. It was there that Mendieta later presented solo exhibitions, including one devoted to the *Rupestrian Sculptures*. Notwithstanding the inroads she had already made in the art world, being acknowledged as an artist in Cuba seems to have been of paramount importance to Mendieta, although not only for professional reasons. According to Viso, the invitation to participate in the "Premio de Fotografía Cubana" alongside local artists was a significant achievement, highly symbolic for that side of Mendieta's self-fashioning that factored in exile. In fact, Mendieta was the first Cuban exile on which such a privilege was bestowed (*Ana Mendieta* 95), even though she was the daughter of a former political prisoner. Her family background raised questions in some circles.

Mendieta's left-wing ideology probably helped to speed up her reincorporation in Cuba. Her thoughts on the intersection between art and politics, which have been preserved in writing, offer a window into her political views. In her essays "Art and Politics" and "The Struggle for Culture Today Is the Struggle for Life," she contrasts the spiritual role that, in her view, should be the driving force behind art, to the commodification of art made by the "ruling class" in western civilization. Mendieta's candid views about the interplay of politics and the arts nevertheless possibly gave a de facto license to Cuban media to interpret her artistic innovations as a critique of a hostile and oppressive environment toward human beings presumably prevalent in the United States.[4] The profound antagonism between Cuba and the United States fed this kind of facile, reductive assumption.

Regardless of the political context in which her visit was framed, Mendieta felt she had been warmly received. According to her cousin Tony Mendieta, a sculptor who lives in Varadero, Ana declared in one of her first trips that she would have felt totally at ease had she brought the slides of her work with her. Such a guileless comment bares both her feelings of identification with her surroundings at that particular time and the weight she attached to faithfully documenting her actions.[5]

Glitches to a Soft Landing

Mendieta was one among many who returned with a mixed cultural history—a history that occasionally elicited a measure of ambivalence and even distrust on the island. This tension would eventually get in the way of an uneventful, sustainable integration. Due to the nearly twenty years that she had spent in the United States, Mendieta's inventive art tended to trespass any set border (Viso, *Ana Mendieta* 21–32). As Jane Blocker has demonstrated, engaging Mendieta's multifaceted work within the parameters of any one category of analysis lessens its overall expressive richness. Mendieta's explorations unraveled out of the multiplicity of subjectivities that made up her self, and the result was simply more than the sum of its parts. Her aesthetics were of a hybrid nature (Camnitzer 91), as was her identity. Mendieta's work spans cultures and shores, impugning a strictly nationalist approach.

Pages of Mendieta's sketchbook from 1976 to 1978, many of which Viso reproduces in *Unseen Mendieta*, contain multiple clues about her double consciousness. In it, she jotted down ideas for further development. Her entries reveal the contamination and mutual interference of the Spanish and English languages at multiple levels: morphological, syntactic, orthographic, and semantic. This was happening at a time when others, such as the writers identified with the Nuyorican movement, were experimenting with linguistic borrowing and code switching as a means to convey their bicultural allegiance. Within this circle, Spanglish was an enabling language, an inevitable creole, the product of a contact zone. In Mendieta's notes both languages appear side by side in a veritable display of Spanglish: "Tambien la misma idea, hacer la figura de metal pero como si fuera un *icon* parado y *weld* en las manos un lugar para poner velas (*containers*)" (Viso, *Ana Mendieta* 183). [A variation of the same idea—make the figure of metal but as if it were an icon standing and weld in the hands a place to fit the candles—containers.] (The words in English inserted in the Spanish notation, which is devoid of diacritical marks, are highlighted).

In one striking example she even goes so far as musing about re-creating out of mud the "Mazapán de Matanzas" (Marzipan of Matanzas), apparently referring to an easily recognizable hill in Matanzas, the province east of Havana, her ancestral home. Oddly enough, the topographical accident is known as "Pan de Matanzas" (Bread of Matanzas), presumably because of its elongated, puffed shape, not *Mazapán* as Mendieta wrote, giving a hint about her frayed memories or the way her memory encoded the name when she was a child. She intended to place the malleable mud on a tree trunk in Old Man's Creek in Iowa, thus merging two of the topographies that resonated deeply with her. This particular entry reads, in part, with all accent marks omitted: "En el rio O. M. Creek—con barro hecha el Mazapan de

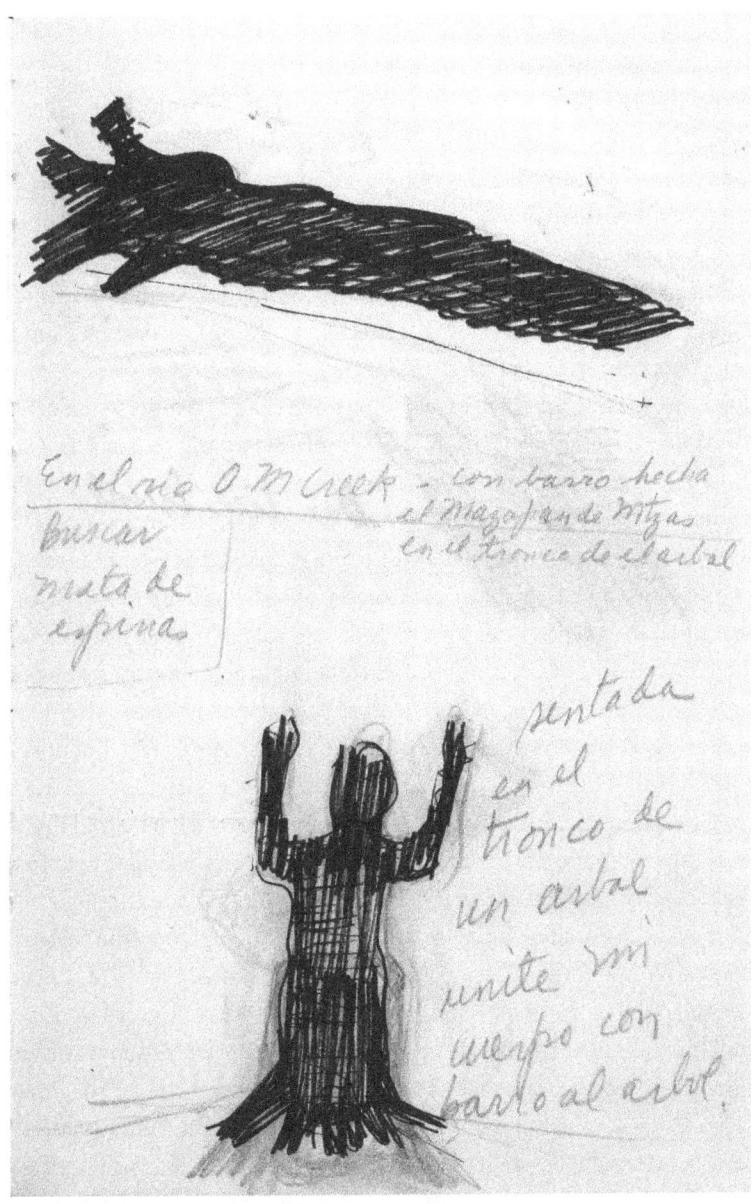

Figure 3.2. "Mazapán de Matanzas." "On the river of Old Man's Creek—the Mazapan [sic] de Matanzas made out of clay on a tree trunk. Look for a tree with thorns. Sitting on a tree trunk merge my body with the base of the tree." Page from artist's sketchbook *Ideas para siluetas*, 1976–78. Ink and pencil on paper. Hardcover black leather-bound sketchbook © The Estate of Ana Mendieta Collection. Courtesy of Galerie Lelong, New York.

Mtzas en el tronco de el arbol" [On the river of O. M. Creek—the Mazapan de Matanzas made out of clay on a tree trunk.]

Even though Mendieta's written Spanish was far from being flawless (having interrupted her formal education in the language at age eleven), she clung to it, a clue to her desire to hold on to a crucial marker of cultural and national identity. This, in spite of the fact that by the time she wrote the entries she had spent more years abroad than in the land of her forebears. Not surprisingly, Camnitzer characterizes Mendieta's work as "Spanglish art" (91), and she herself acknowledged her cultural hybridity: "I am between two cultures, you know?" (Brett 181).

Due to such hybridity there was a part of her and of others similarly bicultural that raised questions on the island. During my research in Cuba, I came across an article on *Areíto* published in 1984 in *La Nueva Gaceta*, the official journal of the Cuban Writers and Artists National Union (UNEAC), which lays bare the uncertain feelings that many island-based Cubans harbored toward the return of exiled Cubans. It did not help that, prior to that time, all exiles had been publicly denounced as traitors. Although the author commends "el cariz progresista de la publicación" or the progressive slant of the journal *Areíto*, he adds: "Entre nosotros, cubanos castristas furibundos, la revista nos resultó sospechosa. Alguna vez pensé: 'bueno, para qué se fueron'" (Moya 22). [Amongst us, fervent supporters of Castro, the journal raised suspicions. At one point I thought: after all, who told them to leave?] Several members of the *Areíto* editorial board belonged also to the Círculo de Cultura Cubana to which Mendieta was affiliated.

Of course, suspicions likewise arose on the other side of the Straits. In a letter published in *El Miami Herald* in the early 1980s, Carlos M. Luis critiques the publication of an article written by journalist Lourdes Meluzá on Mendieta's exhibit at the University of Miami's Lowe Art Museum and wonders how to reconcile the revolutionary art of Mendieta with "su simpatía retrógrada hacia el sistema imperante en Cuba" [her retrograde sympathy toward the prevailing system in Cuba]. There were challenges on both sides for people who, like Mendieta, attempted to circumnavigate the divide.

Even though the artist was able to exhibit her work individually in *Geo-Imago*, the show was barely promoted and poorly attended, having been set up in a secluded back room, not easily reached, at the Museo Nacional de Bellas Artes.[6] As a Cuban American, she had to apply for an entry visa to her native country every time she wished to travel there, and in March 1983 she did not receive a visa on time to pay her last respects to her beloved grandparents, who passed within days of each other. However, a month later she was granted an entry permit to inaugurate her solo show. On her way out of Cuba in July 1983, Mendieta's luggage was searched and pieces of china from her grandmother's estate were seized by Customs (Viso, *Ana Mendieta* 99), in addition to artwork by Flavio Garciandía that he had given to her as a present.[7] Even though Nancy Morejón, in her emotive poem dedicated to the artist, offers her the motherland "as never before" (117), Mendieta was standing on rather shifting ground. Addressing some of the work made by Mendieta in Cuba, Martínez San Miguel maintains that Mendieta's initiatives are embedded in the dialectic of return. Her art stands as both a testimony of her efforts at reinsertion and a trace of an anomalous presence in the Cuban cultural imaginary (229).

Some opine that Mendieta evolved in her views about the Cuban revolution and became frustrated by the obstacles she encountered along the way. Disillusioned after that last unpleasant experience, she vowed never to return, a statement not at odds with her impetuous, passionate, and occasionally hot-tempered (as some of those who knew her well claim) character. Although her work was shown at the 1984 Biennial, two other projects were left pending.[8] Sometime after this last trip to Cuba, Mendieta left for Rome on a scholarship, and on 8 September 1985 fell to her death from the thirty-fourth floor of a skyscraper located in the West Village in New York City. Thanks to the foothold she had established, Mendieta was still a force to be reckoned with in Havana.

Stoking Memory: Volumen I Recollections of Mendieta

In the summer of 2010, I took off for Cuba to retrace some of Mendieta's steps and conduct research on her legacy on the island. I intended to begin at the source and interview the Volumen I artists about their recollections. What I was unaware of at the time was that out of the eleven artists in the group, only José Manuel Fors remained on the island. Juan Francisco Elso passed away prematurely years ago, and the rest were dispersed throughout the world. At that moment Rodríguez Brey was in Belgium, Bedia and Torres Llorca were in the United States, Garciandía and Pérez Monzón were in Mexico, Sánchez was in Costa Rica, and Soto was in the West Indies. Ironically, tracking Mendieta's footsteps in Cuba led me, in an unexpected boomerang effect, not only to locations distant from the island but also far from one another.

José Bedia, whom I interviewed in Miami, touched upon the reasons for the dispersal, explaining that the departure of the Volumen I artists from the end of the 1980s onward was motivated by cultural policy changes that brought about even the marginalization of bureaucrats in favor of artistic innovation.[9] Art exhibitions that dared to violate certain boundaries would be forced to close down just days after opening. Toward the end of the 1980s, official tolerance toward artistic experimentation was once more wearing thin, and the Volumen I artists eventually left Cuba—as did Consuelo Castañeda, Arturo Cuenca, and others—packing into their suitcases their memories of Ana Mendieta.

Nevertheless, the artists I was able to interview share a collective memory about Mendieta and her times. Useful to describe such a relationship, the notion of collective memory, elaborated by sociologist Maurice Halbwachs, has contributed to an understanding of shared memory by foregrounding the relevance of groups in keeping alive the past—a past always liable to revisions. It is in society that individuals normally acquire their memories, and it is in concert (and in tension) with others that they recall, recognize, reaffirm, and/or revise those memories. It is through groups and social networks drawing from an archive of common memories that individuals are capable of the "act of remembrance" (38). While the task of constructing shared memory has fallen under the purview of nation-states in modern times, Anne Whitehead points out that it is incumbent upon small communities rather than individuals or the nation to define what should go into the making of collective memory and memorialization (137).

Furthermore, for Svetlana Boym there are telling differences between national and collective memory. National memory provides "a coherent and inspiring tale of recovered identity" that tends to leave out the gaps and discontinuities typical of recollections. Conversely, collective memory offers "mere signposts for individual reminiscences that could suggest multiple narratives. These narratives have a certain syntax (as well as a common intonation), but no single plot" (53). While these narratives contributing to the archive of collective memory share a core, they also give rise to multiple storylines. When it comes to Mendieta, those multiple storylines underscore her bridging or mediating function as well as her diasporic condition, her exemplary commitment to art, and her feminist affects.

Among the groups and individuals that have ensured Mendieta's survival in the Cuban cultural imagination are the Volumen I artists she met and Cuban artist Tania Bruguera as well as the students associated with the "Pragmáticas" of René Francisco Rodríguez. All of the actions they have collectively launched around Mendieta are located for the most part at the fringes of national memory, that is, far from the spaces aligned with official, institutional promotion.

It was the Volumen I artists who knew Mendieta personally and benefited, as she did, from the relationship who collaborate in guarding those memories. Mendieta aimed to connect with her Cuban peers in fruitful ways, engaging wholeheartedly. The artists with whom I communicated in person or via electronic mail underscored Mendieta's strong opinions about art, which she shared freely. Bedia indicated that her views helped him and others to develop or hone their ideas. Garciandía mentioned how Mendieta gave herself wholly to art, as if it were some sort of "priesthood" and how her deep commitment was as much a source of inspiration as a challenge for other young artists. He also commented on the high standards and rigor with which she approached her profession.

Common interests in certain subjects also came up over the course of our exchanges. Bedia and Rodríguez Brey, in addition to the late Elso Padilla, shared her passion for Afro-Cuban and indigenous cultures while Pérez Monzón learned from Mendieta's reliance on natural elements and later, as a teacher, turned nature into a boundless classroom. Others referred to Mendieta's political "naiveté," expressing their dismay at what they thought was the artist's readiness to play into the hands of the Cuban bureaucracy, which allegedly used her return for political purposes—to proclaim the sympathy of even Cuban exiles toward the revolution. However, Rodríguez Brey provided a glowing portrait of the artist in an electronic message:

> Primero Ana para mí era mi amiga, una gran amiga, de la cual tuve el privilegio de ser confidente y que fuera la primera voz con autoridad ante mis ojos que valorara lo que estaba haciendo en esos momentos yo con mi arte. Gracias a su intervención fue posible mi viaje en el '85 a los EU, ella fue el puente ideal entre la inquietud de los artistas plásticos cubanos de los 80 (Volumen I) y el mundo exterior, la vanguardia que en ese momento se definía en NY. Fue un intercambio en los dos sentidos fructíferos; Ana empezó a tener una real vinculación afectiva

y artística con su país y para algunos de nosotros su relación agudizó y "limpió" los instrumentos con los cuales estábamos haciendo el arte dentro de Cuba.

[First of all, Ana was a friend, a great friend, and I had the privilege of being her confidant. She was the first authority figure who valued what I was doing with my art at that moment. Thanks to her efforts I was able to travel to the United States in 1985. She was the ideal bridge between the restless Volumen I Cuban visual artists of the 1980s and the world, specifically with the avant-garde that was then being defined in New York. It was a productive exchange for both: Ana began to have both an affective and an artistic link with her native country, and we sharpened and "cleaned" the instruments with which we were making art inside Cuba.][10]

Through this and other relationships, Mendieta opened up space for herself in Cuba. She also drew from her blossoming knowledge of the art world abroad to clear the ground for many. More than exerting a formal artistic influence, she played the role of ambassador and brought to Cuba influential artists and critics from the United States, including Carl Andre, who became her husband, Lucy Lippard, Ruby Rich, and Rudolf Baranik, thus helping advance the interests of the young Cuban artists. Some would receive invitations to come to the United States as a result.

Although scattered in an ever-growing diaspora, the Volumen I collective memory has outlived the brevity of their encounter. In 1987, Torres Llorca recycled the 1981 photograph of Mendieta flanked by some of their peers taken outside of the Volumen I exhibition in a collage titled "Nosotros, los de entonces, ya no somos los mismos" (What We Were Then, We Are No Longer), equally recycling Neruda's oft-quoted line from "Poema 20." All around the original photograph is what appears to be faded wallpaper in gold tones, with an electric outlet on the left. Although there is a wire plugged into it and attached to the right side of the wallpaper, it is not connected to any source of energy on that opposite side, displaying a broken circuit. The mixed-media piece is a commentary on the effects of time, natural evolution, and the forces at work that dissolve relationships given the upheavals experienced by the group between the years inscribed underneath the electrical devices, 1981 and 1987, on each side. However, despite the patina-like atmosphere that encircles the artwork, Torres Llorca

Figure 3.3. Rubén Torres Llorca, *Nosotros, los de entonces, ya no somos los mismos* (1987). Mixed media on cardboard with electric outlets and wires. Permission courtesy of the artist. Photograph: The Farber Collection.

succeeds in commemorating and holding on to the memory of a key, collective moment filled with courage, confidence, and coalescence.

The *Rupestrian Sculptures*, a Return to *la tierra* and *su tierra*

If Mendieta's role vis-à-vis the Volumen I artists was deemed rather circumstantial, her intervention in Jaruco was meant to leave an exile's signature in a place charged with historical meaning, skillfully adding a diasporic component to its history. Rodríguez Brey fortuitously introduced Ana to Escaleras de Jaruco, a national park about thirty kilometers east of Havana that the Cuban-American artist found optimal for a series of earth sculptures. Probably between July and September 1981, Mendieta worked on the

Figure 3.4. *Maroya* as it appeared when the author and Cuarta Pragmática visited the site in May 2011. Photograph by Iraida H. López.

Rupestrian Sculptures, no doubt her boldest and most elaborate accomplishment on Cuban soil. No less important in the context of her whole oeuvre, the series is composed of ten sculptures whose poetic names hearken from the indigenous *taíno* mythology: Maroya (Moon), Bacayú (Daylight), Guabancex (Goddess of the Wind), Iyare (Mother), Guanaroca (First Woman), Guacar (Our Menstruation), Atabey (Mother of the Waters), and Itiba Cahubaba (Blood of the Old Mother), among others (Clearwater 13). Mendieta drew the deities from José Juan Arrom's *Mitología y artes prehispánicas de las Antillas* (1975) and Salvador Bueno's *Leyendas cubanas* (1978). Some of Mendieta's previous works had been named after feminine icons from the Yoruba pantheon, a religion that she also found stimulating due to its intimate connection with Afro-Cuban culture. In naming the *Rupestrian Sculptures* after indigenous goddesses, the artist was reasserting her links to ancestral Cuban traditions.

The work, supported by a Guggenheim Foundation fellowship and authorized by the Cuban Ministry of Culture, was, in the words of Shifra M. Goldman, "reminiscent of ancient Caribbean petroglyphs" (238). Mendieta sculpted and painted the contours of the goddesses in the limestone caves of Jaruco, in a steep zone inhabited centuries before by indigenous peoples and which later offered refuge to runaway slaves and the brave *mambises* who fought for Cuban independence. Renowned art critic Gerardo Mosquera points out that the *Rupestrian Sculptures* represent the fantasy of Mendieta's return to her origins:

> Las obras que aquí pueden verse representan una desenajenación; con ellas culmina—del único modo posible—todo un proceso interior. . . . Lo que allí hizo no representaba ya una vuelta a la tierra. Era algo más: una vuelta a *su* tierra. Las cuevas de Jaruco recibían a un nuevo rebelde, eran el lugar apropiado para un inusitado rito de comunión y autorreconocimiento, para la integración de un artista—y un ser humano—en el *humus* de sus orígenes. ("Resucitando a Ana Mendieta" 55)
>
> [The works that can be seen here represent a des-alienation; they crown, in the only way possible, a whole interior process. . . . What she made no longer represented a return to the soil (*la tierra*). It was something more: a return to her homeland (*su tierra*). The Jaruco caves would welcome a new rebel; they were the appropriate site for

an unusual rite of communion and self-knowledge and for the integration of an artist—a human being—into the hummus of her origins.]

By the same token, art critic and artist Luis Camnitzer, who knew Mendieta personally, posits that the sculptures represent the consummation of a process that, although initially subjected to wounds and extermination, ultimately led to healing, integration, and reincarnation. He sees in them "fertility goddesses" that replace the "sterile, maimed, and emptied" (98) silhouettes made before Jaruco. Goldman concurs with Camnitzer when she states that this project helped Mendieta achieve "a reintegration of her divided self, a sense of fulfillment and positive growth [that] began with her first return to Cuba in 1980" (238). All three critics (Mosquera, Camnitzer, and Goldman) evaluate Mendieta's homecoming as a return to her origins that allowed the artist to make peace with her past and move forward, even if her work was always about more than Cuba. Restating its ultimate outcome a bit differently, I would conjecture that, first and foremost, the work Mendieta completed in Cuba allowed her to inscribe herself in the Cuban landscape with the intention of bringing Cuba into her present, a present filled with silhouettes she had been making elsewhere. It was Mendieta's present that shaped or reshaped her Cuban past.

The wish to affirm her subjectivity as a woman, as Cuban, and as artist seems to have pushed Mendieta to go down the path of rescuing the original cultures with which the caves are associated. As she wrote in the brochure for her exhibition *Geo-Imago* (1983) at the Museo Nacional de Bellas Artes: "Estos actos obsesivos de reanudar mis vínculos ancestrales son realmente una manifestación de mi necesidad de ser." [These obsessive acts to renew my ancestral ties are really a manifestation of my need to be.] An admirer of primitive art and cultures, she wanted to connect with the *taínos* in a special way. Unquestionably, the Jaruco project was unique for Mendieta, for she wanted to follow it up with a book that regrettably did not come about (Clearwater 39).

In essence, Mendieta was enacting an almost atavistic homing desire that urged her to revitalize her cultural identity across time—in terms not only of her personal trajectory but also of the distant collective past of the Cuban people. The memory work she engaged in is in line with the work of many others likewise inclined to recodify the past by making it meaningful to the present. But it was an ephemeral present. Sadly, a handful of these sculptures are about the only remnants of her art still existing in Cuba more than thirty years after her death.

The *Rupestrian Sculptures* as a *Lieu de Memoire*

Given the transient nature of most of Mendieta's art, it is unlikely that she would have wanted the cave sculptures to be preserved. The question is whether the site should have been marked in some way to call attention to its significance. Somewhat unrealistically, Gerardo Mosquera defends the idea that the *Rupestrian Sculptures* should have been declared a national monument because of their historic, artistic, and cultural implications. He deplores that

> a pesar de los ribetes místicos que ha adquirido su figura, en Cuba [Mendieta] no es bien conocida entre los más jóvenes. Esto se debe al silencio en que se le mantiene en los medios de comunicación y la cultura oficial, desinterés que ha llegado hasta a permitir la destrucción de una parte de sus *Esculturas rupestres* en las Escaleras de Jaruco, y el abandono de las restantes. Hoy hasta resulta difícil localizar el sitio. ("Resucitando a Ana Mendieta" 55)
>
> [despite the mystical aura that surrounds her, Mendieta is not well known among younger Cubans. This is due to the silence of the media and the official culture, a disinterest that has allowed the destruction of part of her *Rupestrian Sculptures* in Las Escaleras at Jaruco, and the abandonment of the rest of the works. Today even locating the site is difficult.]

Mosquera's suggestion to solemnize the site implicitly draws from Anne Whitehead's and Pierre Nora's observations about the preservation of memory through its association with sites enabling that memory, among other existing strategies to accomplish this lofty goal. Whitehead recognizes the strong power of cultural artifacts as well as institutional commemorations for ensuring remembrance. More important, Pierre Nora adds *lieux de mémoire* or sites of memory, that is, the designation of certain locations and tangible objects, to the list of contemporary practices aiding in securing the future of memory. It is no longer sufficient to experience memory internally or spontaneously, as Nora claims that premodern societies did. Therefore, the *lieux de mémoire*, all of which arise out of "a will to remember" (Nora 19), function as substitutes for an authentic and unmediated collective memory. Built into gestures and habits, vocations kept through generations, and immediate memories and reflexes, "true" memory has been replaced by another that is willful, individual, subjective, indirect, and representational (Nora 13).

Nora appears resigned to the existence of *lieux de mémoire* as a device to protect the latter memory, in no way more disposable because it is less "authentic." But when addressing the typology of topographical sites engendering memory (there are abstract and portable ones, too, such as anniversaries, lineage, or the Tablets of the Law), he makes an important distinction, for my purposes, between the "dominant" and "dominated" loci honoring such memory. The former—imposing, spectacular, and triumphant—are officially designated and serve to celebrate with gravitas ceremonies imbued with power. They are also prone to idealizations (Boym 17). On the other hand, the dominated are "places of refuge, sanctuaries of spontaneous devotion and silent pilgrimage, where one finds the living heart of memory" (Nora 23). The dominated are sites that can rarely be relocated because their worth is embedded in them.

Going back to Ana Mendieta, it is understandable why Mosquera would want to make a *lieu de mémoire* out of the Escaleras de Jaruco or even out of the similarly abandoned large rock in the Varadero highway, in the vicinity of the legendary Hotel Internacional. On this other site, the artist etched and painted three silhouettes whose remains can still be made out, especially one in the shape of a woman in a relaxed position painted in black. That *lieu de mémoire* located in Jaruco would have to be understood as of the second type described by Nora, and in fact, it has operated as such. It has become a destination for spontaneous peregrinations, where Mendieta's presence has taken root despite the absence of monuments or plaques to her memory. There is no marker to designate its relevance and no sign to reveal its transcendence on account of either official negligence or indifference. Ironically, the very lack of gimmicks has done nothing but spur the desire to remember and honor. There are no written signs there that sanction a terse mode of remembering that tends to leave out the gray, problematic zones, or gloss over them. Rather than being induced to take in the experience in a preordained way, one is free to conceive one's own narrative, contrived only by collective memory which provides, paraphrasing Halbwachs, a "checks and balances" function to the memory of individuals (183).

The negligence or indifference with which these sites have been treated is illustrative of the fate to which Mendieta's work in general on the island has been subjected. The only piece by Mendieta found in a public space, the drawing of a silhouette in a *copey* (*Clusia major* or *rosea*) leaf that she contributed to the I Havana Biennial en 1984 and later donated, hangs from a wall in the office of the director of the Wifredo Lam Center in Old Havana. It is, therefore, off limits to the general public. There is no doubt that most of Mendieta's art, made outdoors in nature, using the elements it inexhaustibly supplies, was tied to a specific time and place. It was meant to be transient. Nonetheless, the artist documented her site-specific art zealously and consistently through the use of still and video cameras, which furnish the imperishable image. The action is left behind, in the past, but the technology conserves it for the future, thus safeguarding the survival of memory as well as the ad libitum reproduction of the image. Those images that document the original action are missing from Cuban galleries and museums. On the other hand, Mendieta's works have been preserved through these means in other art venues worldwide, including the collections of Rosa de la Cruz in Miami and the Guggenheim as well as others in New York.

It is possible that this method of conserving art, still unconventional in the 1980s, was not taken seriously by Cuban art institutions at the time. But later there was nothing that would have prevented curators and other professionals from going out to the sites where Mendieta left her silhouettes and using photographs as substitutes for her own documentation. There was no attempt made to preserve her work through mechanical methods or in its original locations. Art books, usually expensive, that could also help to affirm Mendieta's presence in Cuban art history are scarce, while they are readily available outside of Cuba.[11] These lacunae impinge on memory, interfering with the potential influence of her innovative art. But if in the more sanctioned realms Mendieta's presence has been almost erased, there are other symbolic spaces, such as in collective memory, where her figure still has the power to inspire.

Beyond Return: Mendieta's Standing at the Turn of the Century

In May 2011, I made arrangements to visit the Escaleras de Jaruco with a group of students of René Francisco Rodríguez's "Cuarta Pragmática," from the Higher Institute of Art (ISA) in Havana.[12] The trip represented, from beginning to end, a remarkable homage to Ana Mendieta. On the bus to Jaruco, one of the students, Yamisleisy "Yami" García Socarrás, described an excursion to the caves that she had made in October 2010 with the goal of retracing Ana's footsteps until reaching the *Rupestrian Sculptures*. Traveling alone, she had trouble identifying the isolated site, but after a few false starts she finally stumbled upon a stone sculpture that Mendieta named *Bacayú*, depicting, like the one in Varadero, the outline of a reclining woman. Mendieta had accentuated some features to connote femininity, using a chisel as well as black paint. Yami's intention was to honor Mendieta in that "dominated" *lieu de mémoire*. Her plans included getting undressed and, nude, lying on top of this sculpture with the intention of creating "a relationship between woman and woman." Emphasizing forms used by Mendieta, such as body art, another one of her actions was to lie on the ground with her body completely covered with mud, as if she, too, intended to submerge

Figure 3.5. Cuarta Pragmática students and the author at one of the caves in Jaruco. At the center, *Bacayú* as it appeared in May 2011. Photograph by Suri Vázquez Ruiz.

herself in nature. Also like her predecessor, Yami documented her action in video. In one of its segments, another one of Mendieta's sculptures, the rounded *Maroya*, appears in the background, carved on the wall of the same limestone cave.[13]

Once we arrived in Jaruco, Yami led the group to that faraway and rustic site. The two sculptures found in that cave, *Bacayú* and *Maroya*, have evidently suffered the adverse effects of time and exposure. The former, a freestanding sculpture, is easily recognized, but one can overlook the latter, carved in the cave wall. While the rock, up front, that became *Bacayú*, is an accident of nature that Mendieta used to her advantage, the sensual *Maroya* with prominent genitals is the sole product of Mendieta's imagination and skills as a sculptor. The black paint used to emphasize the contours of both sculptures has faded, and the chiseled lines themselves have been softened, but the hollow tracks made by the hand of the artist are still visible.

Thus, in the midst of the rough landscape of Jaruco, there are still vestiges of an art that agrees with the nature that surrounds it, as if art were susceptible to evolving parallel with the environment, far from the spaces consecrated by human beings to contain it. The resulting harmony with the cosmos that transpires in many of Mendieta's works was not fortuitous but part of a holistic view of nature. This is what the artist wrote in the introduction to her proposal for a project on G and Farallones del Castillo del Príncipe that did not come to fruition:

> For over ten years my art consists of a dialogue between nature and me, using the feminine figure to explore the relation between the artist, the work of art, and its environment. I generally work by myself, utilizing in the creation of the works the very same suggestions that natural forms provoke in me. Working with the context of a mental landscape, I identify with nature, accepting its values and limitations and working harmoniously with them.

Mendieta abided as much as possible by what nature had to offer, altering it as little as possible. This is a technique that the *taínos* also used, according to Viso (*Ana Mendieta* 89). And like nature, their artwork was bound to evolve.

Just as unconventional as the concept of art held by Mendieta was the experience that the students from the Higher Institute of Art had the day of the trip. The dearth of signage, and even of cleared roads, made the search

Figure 3.6. A local man helping the group locate additional rupestrian sculptures in Jaruco. Photograph by Suri Vázquez Ruiz.

invigorating. A local peasant tried to help us find other caves with the help of the vivid photographic spreads included in Viso's *Ana Mendieta*, which we brought as a precautionary measure. However, we found no other traces. Some affirm that part of Mendieta's work was destroyed when a highway was built through the woods, but the young artists from the Institute promised to return to carry on the search. One of them was motivated to draw a silhouette on a *copey* leaf, similar to the one made by Mendieta for the 1984 Biennial, and he gave it to me as a present for having shared with him and his peers my memories of Ana and of the time that witnessed other returns. The site is intrinsically transformative: none of the actions undertaken by the students would have occurred in places dedicated to the exhibition of art.

Even though my initial exploration in galleries and museums had made me fear that very little of the artist remained in Cuba, after this field trip I came to the realization that her memory has survived, and even thrived, in spaces and groups located at the periphery of art centers and that it continues to circulate through semi-subterranean corridors. Moreover, the students' interest helps to correct the discontinuities produced by the flight of memories and official indifference.

More than a decade earlier, in December 1997, in an excursion led by René Francisco Rodríguez, Gerardo Mosquera, and Lupe Álvarez, students from the "Tercera Pragmática" class arrived at the Jaruco caves where they found, according to Rodríguez, vestiges of several of the *Rupestrian Sculptures*.[14] René Francisco, who has been behind initiatives meant to introduce the younger generations to Mendieta's work, was still a student when he visited Mendieta's "Geo-Imago" exhibition in 1983, which he found compelling. Among his former instructors at the Higher Institute of Art were members of Volumen I, such as Garciandía, Bedia, and Torres Llorca (Fernández, "René Francisco" 18). Later, a Mendieta retrospective at the Kunsthalle Düsseldorf Museum in Germany in 1996, as well as a performance by Tania Bruguera based on the artist, strengthened his interest. In the 1990s, already as an instructor at the Institute, he developed a pedagogy that, taking into account the sociohistoric context of art, contemplates the integration of art into daily life. Such pedagogical strategy received the name of "Desde una pragmática pedagógica" or DUPP.

The projects undertaken by the Tercera Pragmática class were dedicated to Mendieta, in homage to a Cuban artist "from outside." Rodríguez was hoping to motivate his students into thinking about the relationship between the market economy and art during the 1990s, when that relationship had surged to the forefront. As Anne Raine indicates, art made out of dirt, in nature, represents an inherent challenge to the mechanisms for the commercialization of the artistic product (232). For this reason, it lends itself to a questioning of the primary raison d'être of the art object and the distortion that it has suffered in consumer society even though, ironically and paradoxically, it reverts through reproductions to the venues it was attempting to avoid in the first place. Additionally, with the example provided by Mendieta's return to her homeland, René Francisco set out to question the seduction for fleeing in search of other horizons at a time when fleeing was treated as definitive. Through Mendieta, the art instructor believed that a number of concerns pivotal to that moment in time could adequately be addressed.

Another artist who set out to confront the challenges of the late twentieth century through art, specifically through Mendieta, is Tania Bruguera. Born in 1968, twenty years after Mendieta, Bruguera took on the responsibility of rescuing the Cuban-American artist in order to bring her back to the island and to reimagine her art for other generations, thus keeping her in "the collective imagination" (Mosquera, "Resucitando a Ana Mendieta" 55). In the mid-1980s, Bruguera organized several exhibitions and performances under the title *Homenaje a Ana Mendieta* with the explicit intention of bringing about her vicarious return. Most of all, she wanted to conjure up the tragic disappearance of the artist and to recuperate her figure for the history of Cuban art inside the island (Bruguera 171).

Bruguera drew from the life and work of Mendieta to reflect on loss and displacement, which were then vital topics among Cubans. Ana's exile became the metaphor for the predicament that Bruguera's generation was experiencing: "Can you belong without being there?" (170). Bruguera writes that the flight of so many artists at the end of the 1980s and the beginning of the 1990s, which prefigured her own in 1998, affected her profoundly.[15] The loss led her to believe that subsequent generations had an obligation to keep afloat the memories of the displaced. Because there were few tangible signs of their accomplishments, Bruguera reaches the conclusion that "the legacy of the artists who had left belonged almost exclusively to the realm of memory and oral history" (171). Her words suggest that many other erasures happened as well, creating a loss for the island. Hence the homecomings of Mendieta and others acquire added value, for they serve to stimulate memory in both directions. In a sense, Mendieta and Bruguera engaged in a dialectical back and forth movement, as Bruguera suggests: "Ana was interested in rescuing the idea of Cuba from the outside [while] I was interested in rescuing the idea of the Cuba that was abroad" (Zaya 254). Their efforts were mutually supportive.

Given the erasure of Mendieta and others precipitated by exile, Bruguera's work, in addition to addressing the feminist concerns for which she is known, has played with the block of wax that constitutes memory, as Plato dubbed it. She has peppered her installations with old letters, discarded clothes, flags, maps, and flimsy boats. She has even invited a group of Cuban Americans to participate in one of her performances by pushing around carton boxes representing parts of a house in constant movement to signify migration, displacement, and deracination. Between 1985 and 1996, Bruguera reenacted some of Mendieta's works, serving as a "medium," as critic Fadraga Tudela describes it, in explicit recognition of Mendieta. According to another critic, Eugenio Valdés Figueroa, Bruguera's art owes much to Mendieta's, being as it is at the intersection of personal memory and the allegorical reproduction of social, political, and cultural situations

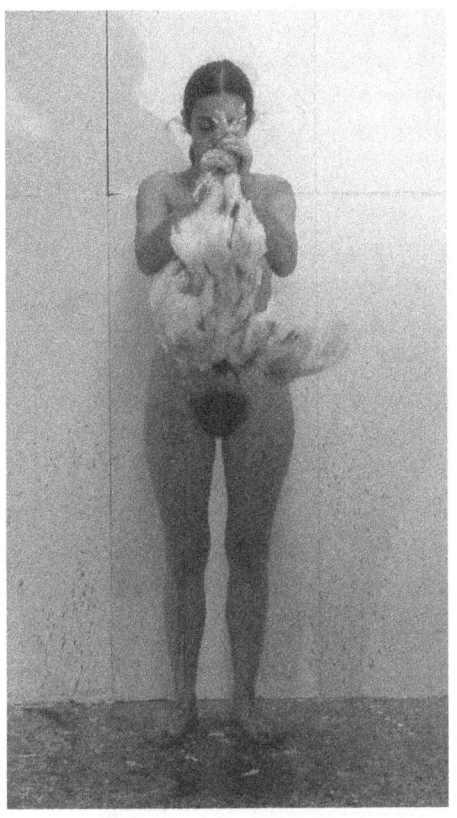 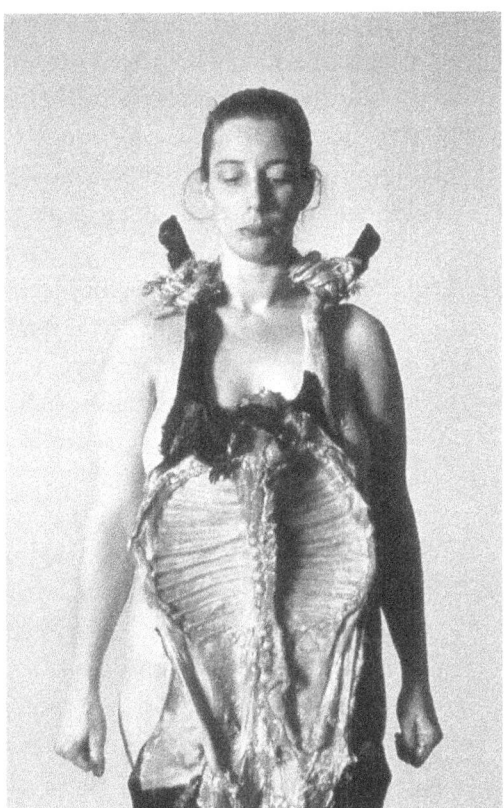

Left: Figure 3.7. Ana Mendieta performing *Death of a Chicken* (1972) at the Intermedia Studio, University of Iowa. Copyright © The Estate of Ana Mendieta Collection. Courtesy of Galerie Lelong, New York.

Right: Figure 3.8. Tania Bruguera performing *El peso de la culpa* (1997–99). Reenactment of a historic event. Decapitated lamb, rope, water, salt, Cuban soil. Courtesy of Studio Bruguera. Photograph: Museo de Bellas Artes, Caracas.

(156). She drew inspiration from an aesthetics based on the body that Ana had assimilated and put into practice, questioning the deceiving dividing line between the public and the private, and in so doing acknowledging the importance of the naked body for feminist art, as Yolanda Wood asserts.

Bruguera utilized her own body like Mendieta, occasionally bringing the abject into relief.[16] Far from culminating in an art capable of pulling viewers away from their immediate reality, some of Bruguera's performances, like those of her predecessor, attempt to emphasize the "crude" and "perturbing" power of an art that pays attention to an often pathetic or piercing reality (Jay 64). In one such performance, *El peso de la culpa* (1997), the carcass of a headless lamb hangs from Bruguera's neck while the artist, completely naked, swallows balls of dirt covered with saltwater, a gesture that evokes indigenous resistance against abuse and slavery by means of collective suicide. The only escape for the indigenous population was to eat dirt until they died, weighing death as an escape (Zaya 245). Just like the Mendieta who, also naked, holds in her hands the bloody rooster following primitive religious practices, Bruguera brings into relief what is rejected or expelled for not submitting to the symbolic Law of the Father. Paraphrasing Julia Kristeva, this is the terrain of the maternal pre-symbolic, in which subjectivity can be reconfigured. As such, it is of interest to feminist criticism.

Besides Tania Bruguera, some of the critics and artists I interviewed mentioned Consuelo Castañeda and Marta María Pérez as artists over whom Mendieta could have had an influence. José Bedia pointed to Adela González, an aspiring Cuban-American artist whose first solo exhibition, *Así de natural*, took place in July 2010 at Nkisi Project in Miami. Olga Viso also lists María Magdalena Campos-Pons and Coco Fusco, besides other artists from various nationalities (*Ana Mendieta*, 126–34).

For all of these reasons, and despite her misleading invisibility, Mendieta's legacy in Cuba has endured. But her presence is not to be found where one would expect it, in museums, galleries, or beautifully illustrated art books. In part, it inhabits the myths inspired by the artist, as an informal comment made by a resident of Jaruco suggests, "A young woman used to pass by here carrying a large hammer" to make "handicrafts" (Fernández, "René Francisco" 22), or the passing remark that Yami García Socarrás heard about the young woman "who made her art and died."

Mendieta is also present in her absence, as Quiroga suggests after describing his efforts to reach the caves: "And even though the pieces were not there, I knew that . . . she was everywhere, having gained the privilege of ubiquity that is the privilege of all those who register their disappearance and allow us to learn what it means" (195). She is conspicuously present in some remaining locations where she worked, becoming a magnet for admirers of her work. These sites of memory are difficult to locate and can be reached with the help of those who in turn were led by others who knew Mendieta personally and knew how to find them, as in a chain reaction, in an off-modern, artisanal mode. It was Mosquera who led Rodríguez to the

Jaruco caves, Rodríguez who lured García Socarrás, and she who showed others, both Cuban residents and nonresidents of the island, the way to the sculptures. Mendieta's impact also penetrates the porous walls of art institutes and universities where, some assert, she is an essential part of the curriculum.

We are facing, then, a legacy built on oral tradition and collective memory, which obviates official inaction or the dominant *lieux de mémoire*, to use Nora's taxonomy. Evidently, this is one way of sustaining memory, even if in alternative spaces. Notwithstanding the existence of these other spaces for channeling memory, it would not be gratuitous to foment further knowledge about Mendieta on the island. Rather than erecting a monument, as Mosquera at one point urged, or a dominant *lieux de mémoire*, this could be accomplished through the preservation, or at least the public acknowledgment (if honoring the ephemerality of the art is deemed vital), on site of the remains of the *Rupestrian Sculptures*. This would count as a contribution to Cuban national patrimony—even if from an artist of the diaspora. Not much more is needed, as the continuing impact of her work demonstrates even in the absence of official support and recognition.

There are, of course, more traditional channels to guarantee its survival, such as the splendid anthological collection of Rosa de la Cruz consisting of sculptures, drawings, photographs, and videos of Mendieta at the Contemporary Art Space in Miami, at quite a distance from Jaruco. This collection offers an overview covering the 1970s (there are photographs of silhouettes made in Mexico and the *Body Tracks* series) up to the time of Mendieta's death in 1985, when Mendieta was experimenting with forms of durable art. It also includes several photographic blowups of the *Rupestrian Sculptures* hanging from immaculate white walls. Confined by multiple frames—those of the photographs, the walls, the museum itself—but also undisturbed by the more tranquil built environment on the opposite side of the Florida Straits, the *taíno* goddesses seem out of place, in a perplexing milieu. Yet the space devoted to these black-and-white images can be envisaged as a *lieu de mémoire* that the technologies of memory have engendered more than ninety miles away from the original. Moreover, it signals the victory of art over geopolitics, since this space devoted to art transcends the schism between the prevailing politics in the community (of Cuban Miami, frequently intolerant) and dissidence (Mendieta's progressive ideas).

Conclusion

Retracing Mendieta's steps since her years in Iowa yields the picture of a Pedro Pan artist intent on preserving certain markers associated with a Cuban identity. In spite of great obstacles, she maintained her native language, actively using it for personal as well as professional purposes; sought out the company of other Cubans of the diaspora; was inspired by Afro-Cuban and *taíno* mythologies, thus bringing the island's cultural patrimony into the fold; went back to Cuba as soon as there was an opening, showing her work and making it there, too; and opened doors for her Cuban peers in her adopted country. However Mendieta's actions were eventually disregarded in official circles, they have not been obliterated. Time has taken its toll on the remaining Jaruco sculptures, but their contours have not disappeared, the signature of a Cuban artist from the diaspora whose homing desire pushed her to go back to Cuba following an all-too-elusive goal.

The framework this chapter uses to engage with Mendieta's work points to the imperative of approaching the artist, and Cuban culture generally, from a transnational and diasporic perspective. Given the mayhem that has characterized migration history on the island, the collective memory that provides an account of the relationship between Ana and Cuba is found where those who knew her or appreciate her work are located, on the island or abroad. Being far and wide apart, they exhibit what André Aciman calls "a diaspora of memory" that "no longer has a single anchor in the native city but unfolds through superimposition of native and foreign lands" (qtd. in Boym 258). Cuban art has been overflowing the contours of the island for decades. This is what a Cuban artist like Antonio Eligio Fernández, known as Tonel, suggests when in his essay "La isla, el mapa, los viajeros" he distinguishes between the "minor map" and the "major map" of Cuban art. The new cartography spills over the minor map of the island, with the major map containing other territories where Cuban art is produced, exhibited, and remembered. Both maps are integral to an understanding of Mendieta's contribution to the arts and to her involvement in intersecting localities in a revealing chapter of Cuban history.[17]

Cuban Childhood Redux

Perhaps the chief risk of privileging the exilic narrative is a psychic split—living in a story in which one's past becomes radically different from the present and in which the lost homeland becomes sequestered in the imagination as a mythic, static realm.

Eva Hoffman, "The New Nomads"

The truism that one can never go home again becomes a special predicament for the young exile: my childhood lies inside the bowl of distance and politics, unapproachable and thus disconnected from my adulthood. The two revolve around each other like twin stars, pulling and tugging, without hope of reconciliation.

Pablo Medina, Exiled Memories: A Cuban Childhood

The self-evident truth to which Eva Hoffman and Pablo Medina point becomes particularly wrenching for those Cuban-American writers who make the decision not to go back to their birthplace, even to visit: childhood becomes, indeed, disconnected from adulthood, as if the two pulled in different directions. This is, at least, what some Cuban-American narratives on *souvenirs d'enfance* by the one-and-a-half generation establish. Chapter 4 delves into three such narratives by Carlos Eire and Gustavo Pérez Firmat in order to highlight rupture and continuity factors in the exile experience. This is preceded by comments on the visual art of Ernesto Pujol and María Brito, who graphically exemplify the heartrending consequences of permanent displacement.

Staying away and returning give rise to different dynamics. Returning enables some of the displaced to confirm the elusiveness of home in concrete ways. Given the passage of time between departure and return for the one-and-a-half generation, spanning between one and four decades, there are few physical vestiges left that one can attach to that past, a lost world. Still, there are some advantages that can be drawn from the search for home. For instance, Gabriela Ibieta, a Cuban American of the one-and-a-half generation, writes about the self-awareness she gained from her trip to Cuba:

> For almost thirty years I had felt that my life had been split in two when I left Cuba; once I became conscious of this doubleness, what pained me the most was the fact that I couldn't connect the two parts, that what I left behind in Havana was completely separate from my life in the U.S., and that I might never be able to integrate the pieces or to write about my experiences. My journey to Cuba bridged the gap between these two separate spheres of my life; it was as healing as it was painful.... The exile's return does not bring closure to the conflict of identity, but it does heal the pain of fragmentation. (76)

The journey, then, can give rise to narratives seeking to bridge the gap between the past and the present, between memory and reality. The mere account of attempting to reconcile recollections to reality seems a remedy, even if what it confirms in the end is the waning of indexical relationship between memory and location (see chapter 2). Examining the loose ends of memory without succeeding in reconstructing the whole fabric resonates with the Cavafy poem used as an epigraph to *Impossible Returns*, for what matters in "Ithaka" is the entelechy of return in the Aristotelian sense. In the poem, the reward resides in the search, always enriching, in which we embark upon leaving home, rather than in the return, whose actuality can be disappointing, even irrelevant. This search, the substance of the narrative, is or ought to be rewarding in and of itself. Closer to home, one is also reminded of O'Reilly Herrera's comment on the effect that the journey *is* home, that what matters is the process, not the always unfulfilled sense of completeness and contentment one associates with one's dwelling, with being at home ("The Politics of Mis-Remembering" 179). Taking on the journey allows many memoirists to put the past to rest, so to speak, move on, and even catch up with time. As Flora González Mandri has noted with regard to her trips to Cuba: "Each time I return I get to live a little more in the present and less in the past" (77). I suspect that many other Cuban-American frequent travelers to the island would endorse González Mandri's statement.[1]

In the absence of return, émigrés may be hounded by nostalgia or, better still, *añoranza*, the term Milan Kundera insightfully associates, in his novel *Ignorance* (2000), with those who have long been away from their birthplace. The noun comes from *añorar*, which derives from the Catalan *enyorar* and originally from the Latin *ignorare*. As the root implies, émigrés afflicted with the sentiment tend to miss or be unaware of what is happening there (Kundera 6), as if they were cut off from the present. They miss the place, but by staying away they are also "ignorant" about it, without the knowledge that firsthand *vivencias* impart. And because of their reticence toward return, they can be consumed by "the demons of nostalgia," as Eliana Rivero writes, utilizing the word in its modern sense of wistful yearning for the past. The best cure for those demons, according to Rivero, is more than one return trip (*Discursos desde la diáspora* 81). Yet abstaining from returning does not stop these émigrés from imagining a home.

The visual and textual narratives on childhood analyzed in the current chapter do not represent an actual return to the island (except for Pujol's) and therefore leave unresolved some of the tensions that a trip to Cuba foregrounds. But they do go back to a different time and place through a return to childhood, which also yields some comfort. A whole subspecies of autobiography has been built around childhood memories. Revisiting childhood in a story can afford the advantage of suturing a splintered history, as Ruth Behar suggests: "Inevitably, living a childhood and writing about it as an adult are fundamentally different experiences, but the value of autobiography is that it creates forms of embodied knowledge in which the (adult) self and the (childhood) other can rediscover and reaffirm their connectedness" ("The Girl in the Cast" 237). And even when that connection is not fully realized, the narratives serve to palliate the rupture and separation. Since memoirs create a neat, elegant plot out of shards of memories, they generally supply coherence and a prolepsis of the present.

That cohesion is more difficult to accomplish when childhood occurred elsewhere. The three written narratives selected for this chapter feature a U-turn to childhood from the vantage point of adulthood as a means to recuperate—or lay to rest—not just one's childhood but also a *Cuban* (or *Cuban-American*) past. Revisiting that period of their lives grants some authors the license to revisit Cuba (and/or Cuban Miami, in one case) metaphorically. While Eire rewinds until reaching his affluent childhood in Havana, Pérez Firmat sets his sights on an older childhood in Little Havana, a detour that nevertheless allows him to reach "Cuba" as well given the saturation of the enclave with things Cuban. On account of their particular circumstances, both autobiographies deviate from some of the standard features of memoirs on childhood (Coe, *When the Grass Was Taller*). In particular, they highlight the salient discontinuities, as well as the politics, that permeate the narratives. They seem to fall into a category all their own, here identified as the "Exile's Childhood."

Conjuring Images of a Cuban Childhood

Matters of continuity and rupture that mark reflections on a childhood lived elsewhere come to the fore in the works of visual artists Ernesto Pujol and María Brito. Their artwork substantiates, in a concentrated fashion, some of the struggles that writers Eire and Pérez Firmat wage in the more expansive form of a full-fledged narrative. Both artists have drawn from childhood memories to make some of their most poignant art, and those memories bring into relief issues of sexuality, gender, class, and race in vivid ways. These issues, in turn, remit the viewer to a past that is retrievable only, in the case of Brito, through an exploration of memory, given her long absence from Cuba. Pujol, on the other hand, has been able to lure residents of the island into helping him to re-create at least the physical ambiance of his childhood in installations he has made in art venues in Havana.

Ernesto Félix de la Vega Pujol is a Cuban-American performer and artist who left Cuba as a four-year-old in 1961 and has made Brooklyn his home for some time. He has a long list of exhibitions and performances to his credit starting in the 1990s. He shares with María Brito, Carlos Eire, and Gustavo Pérez Firmat an interest in childhood reminiscences, while his return to Cuba in the 1990s separates him from the three. With an intensity that rivals Ana Mendieta's, Pujol visited Cuba five times between 1995 and 1997. His work, influenced by feminist theory, has run the gamut from the paintings and installations that characterize his early interventions to site-specific performance art and "social choreography" more recently. The elegiac, albeit spirited, tone of his earlier works, all steeped in personal and collective deprivation and displacement, has given way to a more assertive and socially engaged art that brings to light such issues as war and mourning, the precariousness of urban space, and the sustainability of the environment. David J. Getsy, a well-regarded professor at the Art Institute of Chicago, finds that a queer sensibility seeking to bring the private into public view informs Pujol's performances and projects. His earlier work, however, revolves primarily around memory.

Pujol's first trips to Cuba were meant to "demystify his memories." Having grown up surrounded by his grandmothers as well as four aunts, who looked after the young Ernesto and his brother while his parents were at work, he absorbed endless stories about a family past rooted in the Cuban countryside where his ancestors served as administrators of sugar plantations. The six women, "memory machines," were able to nourish his imagination with countless "illustrated memories" in the form of photographs.[2] Cuba thus acquired mythic proportions, taking on the aura of an Atlantis, a kingdom lost in the middle of the ocean.

Growing up in Puerto Rico, he had supported its independence and was estranged from the Cuban community on the island.[3] Pujol was in his late thirties when he made his first trip to Cuba in 1995, and while he sought to come to terms with that past, he was also curious about Cuban politics and culture as well as the fate of gay writers. Preoccupied with the idea of not fitting in, Pujol sought to "reclaim the right to a voice within the cultural life of Havana, as the son of Cuban exiles," as he expressed in a published interview (Watson 261).

Prior to his first arrival in Cuba in 1995, Pujol completed *Taxonomías/Taxonomies* (1995), a collection of paintings and installations in which he began to explore what Gerardo Mosquera dubs a "mnemonic construction of identity" ("Mi tierra/My Homeland"). By this he means that Pujol turns to artifacts and characters bearing on his white, bourgeois background and, multiplying them on the canvas, ventures to reenact a period of his life that stirred him profoundly. Since he has lost that world, an "intellectual restoration of memory" takes place. All of the paintings in the collection stress repetition, as if depicting multiple objects of identical shape and size on each canvas afforded some kind of solace or compensation. The strategy suggests a ritual meant to preclude disappearance and forgetfulness. In other words, abundance is brandished as a weapon against erasure. Alternatively, the repetition of identical items side by side could indicate how widespread in Cuban culture is the image or practice depicted on the canvas.

The works validate both interpretations. In one painting, the viewer is confronted with eight rows, each of the same five shoes, which harken back to his beloved grandmother, Amparo, presumably in order to recuperate her evocative gait. Other paintings aim to recover the colored subaltern

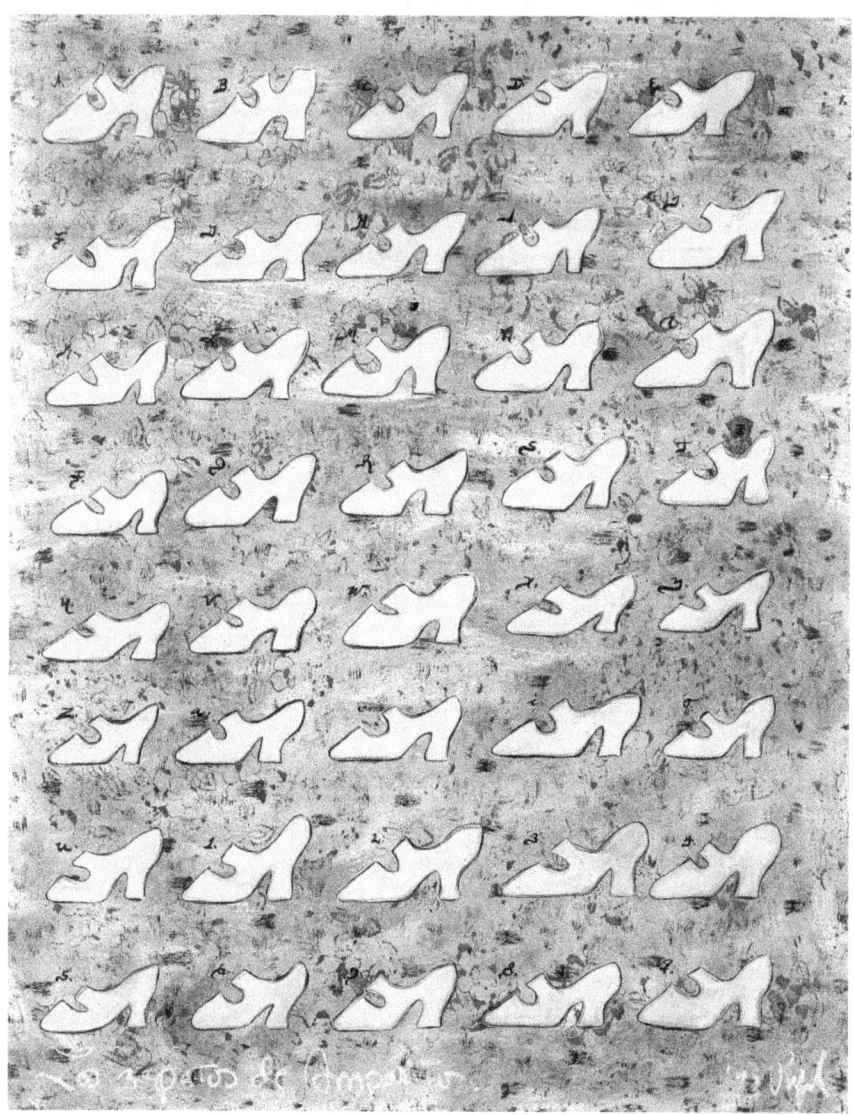

Figure 4.1. Ernesto Pujol, *Los zapatos de Amparito* (1993), from the *Taxonomías/Taxonomies* solo show at the Galería Ramis Barquet, in Monterrey, México, in 1995. Photo courtesy of the artist.

buttressing the privileged white environment. In *Nanas y cunas*, Pujol assembles multiple profiles of cribs and black nannies, while in *Cocineras mulatas*, twelve black women face the viewer, all with their heads covered with handkerchiefs. The indispensable contribution of Afro-Cubans to the maintenance and, even more, the nurturance of a white, middle-class Cuban way of life is one of the themes addressed in Pujol's paintings, where childhood occupies a prominent space. Also of note is the partial view of subjects in the paintings where the human figure is evoked, as well as their nonpersonalized identity, as if a fragmented memory were incapable of capturing the entire picture.

Other paintings in the same collection ring with an abrupt disruption. As a prelude to his delving into the trauma experienced by the children who were sent unaccompanied to the United States through Operation Pedro Pan, these other paintings, such as the blood-spattered *Nacimientos* and *Cunas y Tijeras*, are informed by violence. They visually outline the bloodiness of birth as much as the wounds resulting from violent expulsion, an ejection possibly alluding to both birthing and birthplace. Pictorially, the sentiment the paintings exude is akin to the split subjectivity conveyed by way of text in Eire's and Pérez Firmat's memoirs.

In April 1995, Pujol presented a solo show entitled *Los hijos de Pedro Pan* at the Galería Latinoamericana, Casa de las Américas, in Havana. He was the second Cuban-American visual artist, after Mendieta, to have received an invitation to mount such an exhibit. As the brochure prepared for the five room-size installations reads, the exhibition was dedicated to Mendieta for, in Pujol's words, "daring to search for a space within the history of contemporary Cuban art," as well as to Cuban women around the world who have managed to hand down their cultural legacy despite the odds, a reference to his own female relatives.

During my interview with the artist, Pujol remarked that he would have been a Pedro Pan, along with Mendieta, Carlos Eire, María Brito, and Román de la Campa, had parental plans for his departure come through, but the flight on which he and his brother were scheduled to leave for Miami was unexpectedly cancelled when it was about to take off. However, along with other exiled children, Pujol was not spared the pain of loss and deprivation. Published comments about *Los hijos de Pedro Pan* converge in pointing out that for its creator the installations stand as "a signifier of childhood memory" (Bleys 211) coinciding with the loss of Cuba. Writing in 1995, Gerardo Mosquera asserts that Pujol's work "is characterized by an obsession with childhood memory which in turn is an obsession with Cuba as his lost foundational myth" ("Ernesto Pujol"). Some components of the installations that were part of the exhibition evoke a distinct, unequivocal fracture; critics see in them an act of psychological and physical castration. A good example is *Peter Pan's Table* which shows rows of detached male genitalia made out of clay. As Edward J. Sullivan has written, Pujol is "intrigued by memory's dark side" (123). Another installation, *Varones*, made up of an arrangement of twelve heavy old wooden chairs, the kind found in many Cuban homes, each with a male sex organ on top of the wicker seat, also represents castration. A third installation, *Armarios*, consists of several large antique wardrobes that showcase childhood objects from a foregone era such as a baseball bat and glove, pairs of children's shoes, a doll house, and a christening gown.

As powerful as these installations are, however, they fall short of transparently conveying the link between childhood and nation that critics have highlighted in Pujol's work. For that, I turn to another one of his installations, *Tendedera*, which so strikingly portrays the link. Pujol's "clothesline" shows more than a dozen children's well-worn school shirts suspended from the ceiling, hovering over the outline of the island drawn with tempera on the ground. The shirts, all white, look like disembodied objects that, despite their benign character, cast a persistent shadow over national territory. These are garments no one will care to pick up. The human figure is nowhere to be found, yet overwhelmingly present in its absence. Only the objects remain, as traces. One cannot help but wonder if these traces will ever disappear as they live on among those who were affected. Many of Pujol's installations and paintings represent the vacuum left by the flight, making sure the emptiness does not vanish altogether, but is made to reverberate in one way or another. Given its breadth, the exhibition had such a powerful effect on the public that it was extended to four months from one that had been planned originally.

Some of the other shows that Pujol was able to organize in Havana overlap with the above themes. *Trofeos de la guerra fría* showed his installations alongside the artwork of island-based artist Manuel Alcaide. The exhibit was held in 1995 at Espacio Aglutinador, a venue that boasts of being "the oldest ongoing independent art space in Cuba."[4] A third, *La mesa de Saturno*, sponsored by the Ludwig Foundation, was mounted in 1996 at the

Figure 4.2. Ernesto Pujol, *Tendedera*, an installation from *Los hijos de Pedro Pan*, a solo show at Casa de las Américas in Havana in 1995. Photograph courtesy of the artist.

Centro de Desarrollo de las Artes Visuales (Center for the Development of the Visual Arts), also located in the capital, while another, *El vacío*, was part of the sixth Havana Biennial in 1997. In Pujol's "emptiness," the walls and unoccupied rooms of a typical middle-class Cuban house stand on soil gathered by the artist while on the island.

Although successful from a professional and personal point of view, Pujol's trips brought him face to face with the challenging, and at times disconcerting, politics of return. In Miami the Cuban-American art community ostracized him, and the Fredric Snitzer Gallery, which represented the artist, dropped him from its roster.[5] On the island, he was expected not to engage in "improper conduct," staying within the boundaries set by his official hosts.[6] After his joint exhibition with Alcaide in Espacio Aglutinador, a venue that cultural authorities viewed with suspicion at the time, Pujol began to receive the cold shoulder. Juggling these competing demands was onerous, as they conflicted with what he calls "critical neutrality" (Watson 261), a position that necessitates using his leverage as an artist to critique aspects of the system. In Cuba, the critique involved conjuring away obliteration by summoning what was of upmost concern to him as a person and artist: exile and diaspora.[7]

Pujol's intention was to drive home the compelling topic of fleeing by stressing how mutually implicated the exiles' friends, relatives, and lovers left behind really were. The flip side of the Cuban migration story had also been understated from the outset, as if only the ones who left suffered the bitter repercussions of fleeing. What the artist intended was to create a narrative that made everyone partake of the malady of separation, thereby collapsing the distance between the two opposing shores. The artist borrowed pieces of clothing and furniture from local residents in order to elucidate the themes of loss, dislocation, and return. For the Peter Pan exhibition he borrowed the children's shirts used in *Tendedera*, whereas for the *El vacío* installation he furnished the home with pieces borrowed from local residents, inviting them to visit the site with the purpose of eliciting empathy for the absent dwellers. A trope for exile, *El vacío* resembles a home that has been suddenly abandoned (Sullivan 125). Pujol also intended to open up space for diasporic Cubans because "if a so-called foreigner like me, a son of Cuban exiles, a Cuban American, a North American of Cuban descent can conceptually re-create a Cuban domestic environment that people there can identify with, then maybe I am not so foreign to them; maybe I am not such a foreigner after all" (Watson 263). He was seeking recognition of his Cubanness.

The overarching themes Pujol chose for his work were rather novel at the time, since travel and deracination as motifs in the fine arts, film, and literature on the island were only then beginning to emerge. They would erupt with full force shortly thereafter in the work of such artists as Kcho and Sandra Ramos, both contemporaneous with Pujol, who began to fill their artwork with boats, oars, suitcases, rafts, fish tanks, and glass bottles. Because of Pujol's itinerant life—having lived in various countries throughout the years—these are migration-related objects and imagery with which the artist could identify. In fact, it would appear that little more than artifacts remain of Pujol's life as a child on the island. Throughout the years, he has kept a handful of objects that he was able to take out of Cuba, including his passport, an old Cuban flag, and the name tag from his grandmother's suitcase (Aparicio 152). Appropriately, these point to national symbols as much as travel, a combination that suggests a portable national identity. Pujol no longer travels to Cuba (his last trip was in 1997), but the trips he made allowed him to come to grips with his family past and personal memories, which had acquired a ghostly presence, signaling a stage in his personal life and career. The Cuban-American artist has since moved on to other life projects.

Inextricable Links Between the Present and the Past

Objects play a major role, too, in the arresting work of María Brito, another Cuban-American artist who has addressed childhood memories in her art. A Peter Pan child who left Cuba as a thirteen-year-old with her younger brother in 1961, Brito is identified closely with the generation of Cuban artists who emerged in Miami in the late 1970s. She has won prestigious awards and grants over the course of her career, and her paintings, sculptures, installations, and assemblages have been acquired by major U.S. art museums and collections. While she has held numerous solo shows since 1980, Brito's feminist concerns, although downplayed in interviews she has given, justified her inclusion in two exhibitions that also featured the work of Ana Mendieta and other female artists.[8] O'Reilly Herrera asserts that Brito's work "inadvertently lends itself to a critique of the oppressive social roles imposed on women" (*Cuban Artists Across the Diaspora* 154). Far from pretending to shed new light on Brito's expansive oeuvre, amply scrutinized by art critics, I shall comment briefly on a few pieces associated with this chapter's subject, drawing in part from Juan A. Martínez's enlightening study of her art.

Even more than the early Pujol, Brito shows a fondness for houses, interiors, and the domestic environment. In an interview with Martínez, she explains that, following Jungian psychology, the house serves as a metaphor for individuals seeking some sort of transcendence (26). That may be the case, although the argument may not be all too apparent to the lay viewer. What is evident is that Brito uses images, such as the crib motif, and household objects found inside a house to reflect on fragmentation, transformation, and identity as they bear on the present. She relies on a layered approach that does not discard the past but entwines it to the present, both in terms of content and form. For instance, in *Party at Goya's/First Arrivals* (2006), a sculpture inspired by Goya's *Caprichos*, a figure representing the artist appears next to another character portraying Goya, the two having a lively conversation conveyed through their body language. Part of Brito's work provides a commentary on contemporary issues through the utilization of models supplied by the Spaniard as well as other European painters from the Renaissance and Baroque periods. The original drawing or painting, whose trace does not disappear altogether but resonates in the new context in one way or another because of its reminiscent power, seeps into Brito's freshly minted characters, setting, or structure. The concurring strategy aptly connects the past and the present.

Likewise, in *Self-Portrait in Grey and White* (1982), Brito juxtaposes two generations in a mixed media, three-dimensional piece enclosed in a wooden box with a hinged door. The work represents the artist's different facets in a concentrated fashion. Once the door is opened, the viewer sees various compartments, arranged horizontally. Cutout figures of her two sons and her former husband's two boys appear at the bottom, with only one of them showing facial features; the artist and her spouse are situated in the middle, on both sides of a smaller box containing a red heart; and they reappear, though as shadows, in the top compartment. Brito argues that the interior signals her identities as mother, wife, and artist, with the top section, which includes a ladder, representing the ethereal place in which she dwells during the creative process (Martínez 29). In a rather small space (24½ × 14½ × 6½ in.), Brito manages to squeeze in the various facets of her identity, achieving a measure of condensation. In both *Self-Portrait* and *Party at Goya's*, Brito contracts time and space in what could be interpreted as a struggle against rupture, dispersion, and fragmentation. Whereas Pujol sought to replicate an object evocative of a time period ad infinitum, Brito aims for condensation or compression. The box itself of *Self-Portrait*, as well as many others used in her collages, filled with compartments, lends containment.

Fragmentation is, in fact, the subject matter of *The Room Upstairs: Self-Portrait with Two Friends* (1985), which is built in another box, this time divided into two compartments. The larger compartment at the bottom includes a wall and a white door with no knob, and the smaller one on top contains three black-and-white images of young girls, the one at the center split in two. According to Martínez, the piece reflects the themes of domestic interiors, childhood memories, and divided self and duality characteristic of the work made by Brito in the 1980s, a period in which the deep influence of "the abrupt separation from parents and homeland, the

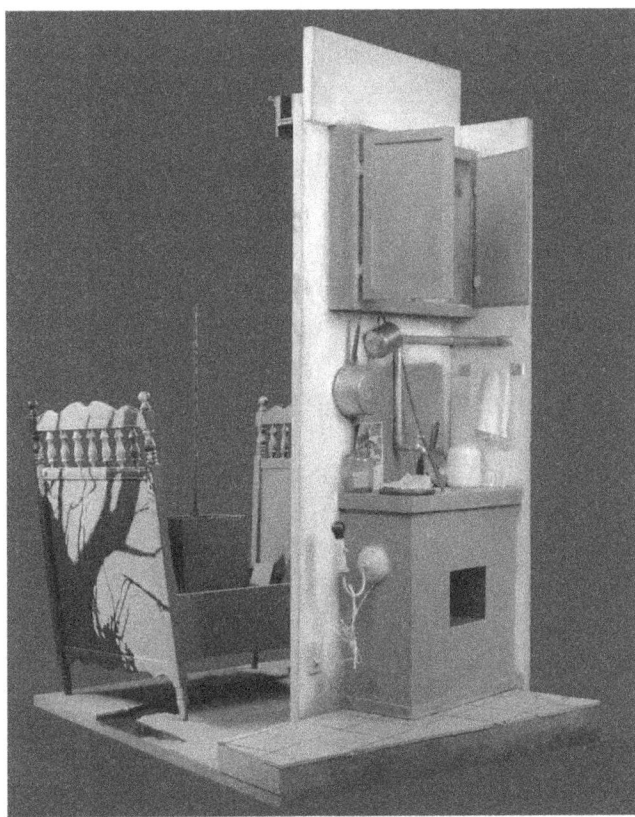

Figure 4.3. María Brito, *El Patio de mi Casa* (1991). Permission courtesy of the artist. Photograph: Smithsonian American Art Museum.

entrapment in a children's camp, and the unfriendly surroundings of her new life in South Florida" (8) left an indelible mark. The artist's interaction with her children brought back memories of her own childhood (Martínez 30), giving rise to another piece, *Come Play with Me*, utilizing the crib motif. In her interviews with the art critic, Brito, who has chosen not to return to Cuba, confessed how painful it was to open the vault of repressed memories from her Peter Pan childhood: "I now realize that a lot of my memories from that time, as important as they are to my life, have blurred. I have gaps in my memory, so it must have been quite painful. Today, I can only look back and see the pain in a very objective way" (7). It took time to deal with the agony of a particular kind of rupture.

That agony may be why gloominess envelops the past in one of her better-known pieces, *El patio de mi casa* (1991), inspired by a popular nursery rhyme in Spanish. The installation represents an attempt, according to the artist, to break away from that past or from childhood (Martínez 40). It is composed of a bright kitchen filled with utensils such as pots, a cutting board, and a jar, and a bedroom/backyard with a dark bed or crib resting over a cracked floor. These two areas are separated by a wall. The artist's own assessment indicates that the bedroom constructed outdoors represents the past while the kitchen, where change occurs, stands for the present (Brito, "The Juggler" 45). In it, layers of skin have been peeled off of a plaster cast of the artist's head with a knife. There are elements that link both sides of the installation, providing a semblance of connection between past and present or between exposed and sheltered spaces.

Brito cautions against readily injecting Cuba into interpretations of her work, claiming that she leaves her Cuban identity at the door of her studio.[9] But the temptation to bring her personal history into play given the presence of the self in her work is hard to resist, and art critics have succumbed to it. For Lynette Bosch, the "theme of *El patio de mi casa* can be summed up as Cuba/Miami" (106), with Cuba, if that is the case, presented in an unfavorable light. Juan Martínez goes beyond the strictly personal interpretation of *El patio de mi casa* to tie it to concerns of immigration and biculturalism, especially in regard to continuity and disruption:

> To every exile or immigrant, a significant part of the past is the moment of rupture, producing a sense of "before and after"; this is suggested in *El patio* by the cracked floor and dividing wall. An important part of the migration experience is also the sense of continuity between past and present, here suggested by the connection between the two María Britos in the photo and the mask, between the rain and faucet water, and between the Cuban bedroom/backyard and the Cuban-American kitchen. *El patio* effectively expresses these views and feelings about the past, continuity, and identity as they regard the experience of exiles and immigrants from Cuba and other countries. (41)

It may well be that Brito chooses to underline continuity in this installation inspired by childhood memories, but the darkness in which she bathes her past as a child and a young woman would indicate that it is a period of her life best left behind, perhaps because of the painful memories to which Brito alluded before. Unscrambling the two sections of the installation is quite a challenge, of course, here boosted by the full-blown, sturdy

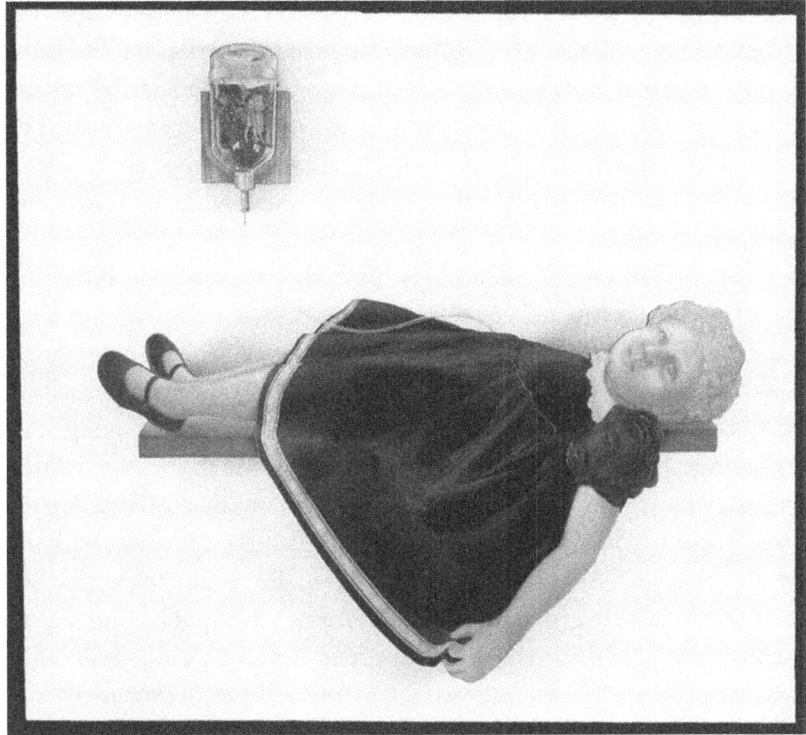

Figure 4.4. María Brito, *Feed* (2001). Photograph by Teresa Diehl.

tree painted in a dark color on one side of the bed or crib, and the small twig carried over to the kitchen sink (not easily discernible in figure 4.4). If nothing else, the lone twig suggests a lopsided, if inextricable, relationship between past and present and the impossibility of completely eliding or burying memory.

Also reflecting the links, for better or for worse, between past and present is a piece with the suggestive title of *Feed* (2001), combining painting and sculpture. In *Feed* the figure of a girl lying on a wooden shelf is attached through a plastic tube to an intravenous bottle that feeds her. Inside the bottle, there is a scene inspired in a section of the Renaissance painting *The Annunciation*, by Fra Angelico, depicting Adam and Eve at the moment of being expelled from the Garden of Eden. With its biblical reference, *Feed* is an explicit critique of a Catholic upbringing haunted by the primal experience of the Fall. Brito wanted to comment on "the tainting of children's innocence when the idea of sin is introduced in early life" (O'Reilly Herrera,

Cuban Artists Across the Diaspora 156).[10] The piece, therefore, highlights the vulnerability of children who are "fed" these visions. It refers, by extension, to any power that seeks to enforce control by wielding dogmas. No sooner does a breach occur than serious consequences are felt, here signaled by the loss of paradise. As in *El patio de mi casa*, an interpretation that contemplates exile as a concept informing, however tenuously, Brito's installation is difficult to resist.

If the past and tradition are conceived as somehow menacing and a break with them is what the above pieces are about, Brito has something in common with the Cuban-American memoirs that follow, where a rift prevails. Brito's dark imaginings have more in common with Eire's when it comes to childhood, but there's rupture in Pérez Firmat as well. This is a split that although deeply personal and subjective is embedded in the political matrix, which comes to the fore in written narratives in a way that the visual artists do not openly communicate despite the fact that they, too, flirt with the political domain.[11] As in good poetry, politics in the visual arts are generally more connotative than denotative. The far from oblique politics impregnating the literary autobiographies warrant characterizing them as exilic writings, setting them apart from those analyzed in chapter 2, even though all of the authors are from the same generation. While these two writers are entitled to blame exile for bringing about the breakup or distention of their families, that impact does not explain their choice of an exile ethos. Ana Mendieta's family was subjected to extreme pains, yet she chose to engage Cuba. Rather than identifying politics as a scapegoat, I prefer to see the two writers' oppositional stance both as proof that their cohort is as diverse, politically and otherwise, as any other and the impracticality of denying continuing exile subjectivities in sectors of the one-and-a-half generation and beyond.

The "Exile's Childhood" as a Sub-Sub-Genre

Although at no point reneging on their Cuban identity, both Carlos M. N. Eire and Gustavo Pérez Firmat succeed in detaching childhood from adolescence in their memoirs, with their formative years lived on the island and the rest in the United States. Time, geography, and language conspire to widen the gap between the two. Childhood took place many years ago in a seemingly faraway Spanish-speaking land to which these authors have not and in all likelihood will not return. Álvarez Borland correctly asserts that in their autobiographical writings Cuban-American authors attempt to reconcile "past experiences in their country of birth with present circumstances in their adopted country" (*Cuban-American Literature of Exile* 62), quite a feat for those who choose to stay away from their birthplace. The transition from one to another time period, or one country to another, in some of these texts belies James Olney's assertion that "autobiographers see in their childhood the outline and the embryonic promise of all that follows in terms of life and career"(42). In other words, in the typical narrative the child fathers the adult. But here, the authors' circumstances as Cuban exiles defy all expectations.

Leaving Cuba as an outcome of the revolutionary takeover constitutes a parting of the ways, with everything else either leading to or resulting from it. The rupture recalls the split between bedroom and kitchen, or Cuba and the United States, in María Brito's *El patio de mi casa*. In this regard, these childhood memoirs are clearly different from the usual *souvenirs d'enfance* in that their structure does not reflect the precise development of the writer's self, which begins often—to paraphrase Richard N. Coe—with the first inkling of consciousness and concludes with the attainment of maturity (*When the Grass Was Taller* 8–9). According to Coe, who has written a monograph on the subject focusing on works by Nabokov, Naipaul, Ionesco, and Leiris, autobiographies on the experience of childhood are expected to show such evolution.

Rather than the attainment of maturity, Cuban-American narratives on childhood reflect especially on how distant or close their protagonists are said to be to their native culture in order to express particular subjectivities. Coe called childhood memoirs simply "the Childhood," claiming that it forms a sub-genre of autobiography, and James Olney contends that within "the Childhood" there is a "sub-sub-genre" of works that merits being called "the Writer's Childhood" (*When the Grass Was Taller* 41). Similarly, one could argue that the autobiographies focusing on childhood written by political exiles constitute a second sub-sub-genre. This specific category would be called "the Exile's Childhood," one under which both Eire's and Pérez Firmat's memoirs would be listed. In "the Writer's Childhood," according to Olney, writers return to their childhoods to see how they became the writers they are (42), but in "the Exile's Childhood" it is rarely the case that the past prefigures the present. There is little or nothing in these "Childhoods" that foreshadow later developments.

Moreover, if conventionally in the Childhood the loss of innocence comes with the arrival of adolescence (Silos Ribas 170), in the following Cuban-American memoirs the critical turn will be determined by one significant event: departure from the island. Even in childhood memoirs such as Pablo Medina's *Exiled Memories: A Cuban Childhood* (1990), where the personal realm is not as juxtaposed, at least overtly, to politics, or Mirta Ojito's *Finding Mañana*, where the individual takes a backseat to the journalistic chronicle of the Mariel exodus, departing Cuba (and arriving in New York, in Medina's case) becomes at once the towering and triggering moment. It functions as a kind of freeze-frame after which the former self is pivoted away. The framework certainly resonates in Virgil Suárez's *Spared Angola: Memories from a Cuban-American Childhood* (1997), a hard-hitting "Exile's Childhood" that does not gloss over the dark side of childhood. Its title refers to the Angolan Civil War (1975–2002) in which thousands of Cuban soldiers fought and died before Cuba ended its military engagement in 1991.[12] In the book, the protagonist's parents take him out of Cuba a few years before the onset of the war, saving him well ahead of time from being conscripted (Suárez was born in 1962). Fleeing, then, represents a potential life-saving strategy, one to which the protagonist retrospectively owes his adulthood. These writers, then, depict a return to that decidedly crucial moment in their lives.

Inevitably, all of these authors are concerned with symbolic rather than literal truth given the events they evoke, built around the child-self, a distinction that applies to all narratives of childhood (Coe, *When the Grass Was Taller* 80). These authors thus draw from private, subjective, and largely unrecoverable experience to enact a useful and usable public identity. Finally, they share with some Jewish and Irish writers a concern with the political realm. According to Coe, unless political situations "actually cause a rift within its own family, the child, comfortable in the heart of its 'small world,' is to all intents and purposes immune from political debate. . . . But the exception to this is to be found when the political history of a country or of a culture is so consistently tragic that it penetrates, as it were, into the communal subconscious—in which case, once again, it acquires the status of 'Myth'" ("Childhood in the Shadows" 7–8). This is no doubt the case with the narratives that follow.

Textual Representation of an Interrupted Childhood

The centrality of departure in these texts can be verified in Eire's accounts of childhood, the first of which covers just enough ground before the grand event—departing—occurs. There are perhaps no autobiographical accounts in the Cuban-American canon as imaginative and vivid as *Waiting for Snow in Havana: Confessions of a Cuban Boy* (2003) and *Learning to Die in Miami: Confessions of a Refugee Boy* (2010), by Carlos M. N. Eire, T. Lawrason Riggs Professor of History and Religion at Yale University. The former, winner of the 2003 National Book Award for nonfiction, is set in Havana, involving the first eleven years in the life of the author. The latter takes place mostly in Miami, but also in Indiana and Chicago, where Eire lived as a child and young adult. About to turn fifty at the beginning of the millennium, Eire wrote his first book of memoirs in a mere four months, and seven years later he followed up with a second installment. Both narratives are set against the backdrop of radical change, which imposes a break with the past.

As expected, radical change is brought about by the revolutionary initiatives adopted early on. *Waiting for Snow in Havana* describes like few other autobiographical accounts the cost of revolution for an upper-middle-class family. The book's focus is concisely stated by the author in an interview with Susana Paternostro: "What I wanted to do in the book was show how a political system can try to crush an individual soul and also how it can crush and demolish families and the price one has to pay for an ideology." Downfall and revolution are thus inseparable in Eire's account. The day of the triumphant arrival of the revolutionary forces in Havana is, for the narrator, the instant his immediate world begins to crumble. As Paternostro points out, there are "rabid, unapologetic anti-Castro rants in Eire's book. 'Fidel's Cuba is the deepest circle of hell,' he writes." In some ways, Eire's is a Fidel-centric book in which the Comandante becomes the main source of evil.[13]

In April 1962, Eire and his older brother fled Cuba under the auspices of Operation Pedro Pan. Eire's mother would arrive in the United States in 1965, after a three-year separation. His father, a judge, remained in Cuba looking after his prized art and fine porcelain collection. He passed away in 1976 without ever having seen his family again. Although the narrator's family carried within itself the seed of destruction, the blame for the family turmoil rests squarely on the revolution. It was the revolution that callously unleashed disruption and chaos: "God-damned place where I was born, that God-damned place where everything I knew was destroyed. Wrecked in the name of fairness. In the name of progress. In the name of the oppressed, and of love for the gods of Marx and Lenin" (*Waiting for Snow* 51). However, the narrator's well-being hangs in the balance with or without the revolution, given his particulars: his adopted brother, whom the judge picks up from the streets, is a sly and contemptible young man who makes sexual advances to his helpless younger brother.[14] Even worse given their blood ties, his father's love of material possessions sadly takes precedence over his loyalty to his family. He stays behind to guard them, waiting in vain for his sons to return.

The story is made all the more poignant given the child's point of view, one belonging to an eight-year-old at the time of the coming-to-power of the revolution. The boy's fear of change and disruption colors the entire narrative, influencing the narrator's choice of symbols and metaphors. The highly impressionable character has an irrational apprehension of lizards, the ubiquitous reptiles in the Caribbean with the ability to camouflage. The shape of the lizard also resembles the elongated contours of the island of Cuba because of its similarity to an alligator, thus making it an appropriate symbol. It is, however, the capacity for concealment that makes the lizard especially nimble to anticipate the changes that the child will be going through as his world shatters around him: "I'm turning into a chameleon, or into one of Addison's brown iguanas. I'm camouflaged. I blend in so well as a respectable Cuban boy from a good family, but underneath I am a rebel, a worm, and a refugee in the making" (*Waiting for Snow* 308). Given the appalling prospects of turning into someone else, the child holds on steadfastly to the illusion of permanence:

> I'm still the same though my friends have all vanished.
> I'm still the same though my favorite school will never exist again.
> I'm still the same even though my first childish love vanished overnight.

I'm still the same even though I have no comic books, ice cream, baseball cards, Coca-Cola, chewing gum, toys, good movies, or decent shoes.
I'm still the same even though I don't have the right to say what's on my mind inside my own house, let alone in public.
(*Waiting for Snow* 342)

And the litany goes on in an attempt to cling to the self-deception that he has changed not one iota despite the turmoil. But, of course, the commotion does take its toll, a fact that becomes more threatening once he arrives with his brother in the United States, where his musings about "rich boys who become poor orphans" (56) are no longer an abstraction. Such quotation on the loss of social status is not gratuitous; it captures one of the protagonist's main concerns. Once in his adopted homeland, the narrator's idyllic yet vulnerable childhood is all but forgotten, and he soon gets more than what he bargained for, such as juggling study and menial work, both full time; being labeled a spic; lacking health insurance and medical assistance when needed; being turned down for welfare benefits; and seeing his brother lose touch with reality. All of these daunting challenges stress the dissonance between childhood and adolescence, making Paula S. Fass's comment about disconnected time frames nothing but compelling: "Eire presents a Cuban child separated from his future, a child left behind in another world" (113). Through his autobiography, he demands his boyhood back.

An interesting feature of Eire's *Waiting for Snow in Havana* is the emphasis on the loss of social standing over cultural differences. While the first will serve to highlight the changes our protagonist must confront, culture will in effect smooth over the transition because instead of actual cultural differences, it is the familiarity with U.S. culture that is reiterated throughout the book. His familiarity is understandable given that Eire's insulated world danced to a tune that, by virtue of Cuban neocolonial standards, had little to do with vernacular culture. "We had no movies about our own history" (72), he acknowledges at one point. The older generation seemed to be partial to what the Old World had to offer—fine porcelain and classical music. The narrator's parents went by the names of Louis XVI and Marie Antoinette and, as such, were conversant about the mayhem of revolution. It is no wonder that in such a colonial mind-set, Cubans were "being cheated out of snow" (188). Simultaneously, American popular culture—Hollywood movies and their stars, comic books, Disney characters, Christmas trees—gained ground steadily among the younger crowd. To be up-to-date meant to be "as American as possible" (86), perhaps because "everything was perfect in the U.S." (210).

The environment described in the book is not all that rare given the awareness of Cubans in general, and the urban middle and upper classes in particular, of the United States, whose reach was so deep that "becoming Cuban" was predicated on a systematic awareness of it, as historian Louis A. Pérez has elaborated in his book by that title. But while U.S. culture was ubiquitous, what passes for authentic Cuban culture since at least the second half of the twentieth century, especially its Afro-Cuban components, was found only on the outer reaches of Eire's world. We learn early on that Cuban popular music was restricted to the kitchen and another room not directly connected to the main house where a black maid, sexualized in the description, kept her quarters (*Waiting for Snow* 3–4).[15]

Surely such a colonial mind-set—whether one chooses Spain or the United States as the colonial power is not all that relevant—must have an impact on the split and continuity factors underscored in this chapter, as the identification with that other culture becomes an asset easing the transition. The narrator's cognizance of mainstream culture is likely to cushion, however slightly, the rupture caused by all of the other factors. When Eire was asked recently in an interview with Isabel Álvarez Borland about authors who might have had an influence on his writing, he acknowledged his unfamiliarity with Latin American and Cuban luminaries such as García Márquez and Cabrera Infante, listing instead Verne, Stevenson, Twain, Dickens, Shakespeare, Hemingway, Conrad, the Brönte sisters, Dashiell Hammett, and Raymond Chandler as those writers he has admired and tried to emulate (127).

Because of his upbringing, Eire feels "as Cuban as an eleven-year-old Cuban boy who has lived the rest of his life apart from other Cubans and in very limited contact with Cuban culture" ("Thinking in Images" 127). Yet he claims a Cuban identity: "I yam what I yam. *Soy Cubano. Cubanus sum*" (*Waiting for Snow* 223). Due to the intimacy with U.S. culture that comes across in the narrative, there is a gulf between Eire's memoirs and many others written by autobiographers of Hispanic background. A particular strand of Latino memoirs (Norma Cantú's *Canícula* and Ernesto Galarza's *Barrio Boy*, both authored by Chicanos, come to mind) takes the form of a disguised ethnography in the first person; like all ethnographies, it dwells on cultural capital in order to render difference all the more palpable. This type of memoir is redolent of unique values and traditions, food, and family celebrations as a way of bringing difference to the fore, at the same time that it claims a right to retain a culture distinguishable from the mainstream. It affirms an entitlement to cultural citizenship not necessarily paired to the legal, functional citizenship usually enjoyed by the authors.[16]

Eire accomplishes a different goal. As Paternostro points out, he succeeds in getting across "to non-Cubans that Cuba is a place they could recognize, that what happens in this book didn't happen in some far-off place that's very different." His narrative supports the idea that Cuban culture is "appositional," amenable to merging or coexisting with North American culture (Pérez Firmat, *Life on the Hyphen* 6). It is not "oppositional," like perhaps other less pliant and more restive Latino cultures. Rather than underscoring cultural uniqueness, Vitalina Alfonso affirms that in Eire's memoir there is a prevalence of the vital day-to-day that communicates the mental and even physical devastation let loose upon the children ripped away from their families and sent to the United States through Operation Pedro Pan ("Redescubrimiento de la infancia" 44). If culturally Eire happened to have arrived at a place not entirely new to him in light of his education, in all other respects exile dealt him a heavy blow.

Learning to Die in Miami: "What English word do you use when you kill yourself and become a new *you*?"

Even though the narrative goes back and forth between Cuba and the United States, *Waiting for Snow in Havana* focuses mostly on a Cuban childhood. Because of Eire's sparse reflections on his life in the United States, Silvio Torres Saillant's comments about Pablo Medina's autobiography would apply here as well: "What we do not get is any inkling of the life the author has lived between the loss of his world of childhood and his subsequent coming to terms with the loss. Interestingly, the omitted portion of the life is precisely the one that would yield material for ethnic autobiography" ("The Latino Autobiography" 71). Focusing on the *before* of migration, Torres Saillant seems to imply, is what distinguishes exile from ethnic memoirs, and the emphasis on times passed in Eire's memoir seems to confirm the critic's insight. However, there is at least one exception to the norm: Eire's second autobiographical volume, *Learning to Die in Miami: Confessions of a Refugee Boy*, although wholly set in the United States, is also distinctly shaped by a sense of exile.

Whereas in *Waiting for Snow in Havana* it was the chameleonic lizard that signaled the metamorphosis of the child, in *Learning to Die in Miami* the transformations are brought about by successive metaphorical deaths experienced by the narrator in his new homeland—"necessary" deaths that help him to gradually cast off his recollections of a lost paradise. In his review of Eire's book, Bernardo Aparicio García points out that "the central paradox in the book is how true life cannot be reached without death, the same apparent contradiction that lies at the heart of the Christian view of reality—in a word, Resurrection" (64). The notion of resurrection, as well as other religious beliefs and philosophical reflections, informs the book, a fact that the Spanish translation of the title reflects more accurately, *Miami y mis mil muertes: Confesiones de un cubanito desterrado* [Miami and my thousand deaths: Confessions of a Cuban refugee boy]. Indeed, the narrator "dies" repeatedly over the course of the narrative, which takes place for the most part in the Cuban enclave of South Florida over three years in the early 1960s.

Eire is not new to death, having researched the topic as part of his scholarly endeavors; among his publications is a book about the art of dying in sixteenth-century Spain and another about the history of eternity. But Eire succeeds in blending his interest in dying from a Christian point of view, in the sense that Aparicio García notes, with the figurative dying that any new immigrant ought to endure upon giving up his former life, language, and customs and being reborn, if you will. In Eire's case, such a jolting experience is heightened by the separation from his parents.

However, Eire is surely not just any immigrant. He is an exile, a fact that will not slip his mind. As in *Waiting for Snow in Havana*, the narrator will dot the narrative with anti-Castro caustic denunciations, and his admiration for the American way of life comes across even more robustly than in the previous volume: "All of my life I'd longed to be *here* in the United States of America because the place had thrust itself upon me through movies, television shows, comic books, and a thousand and one products, from baseball cards to model trains and soft drinks. I'd been seeing images of this place, playing with its toys, and consuming its goods and entertainment since the day I was born" (*Learning to Die* 8). As a child, he becomes enamored of objects that are new to him or that he had forgotten, such as colorful soda cans, cereal boxes, sprinklers, and more. (Eire the author has a flair for constructing a child's point of view as well as for dialogues with children as interlocutors, a novelistic feature of his memoirs.) But despite the distractions, Carlos, the child narrator, cannot shake off his loneliness and sense of abandonment, which over time lead him to an almost pathological feeling of helplessness.

Meanwhile, death and dying lurk over the narrator from the minute he steps on the U.S. side of the Straits. The first death strikes on page 1: "Having just died, I shouldn't be starting my afterlife with a chicken sandwich, no matter what, especially one served by nuns." Carlos has just arrived at a camp for Cuban children in South Miami where he is offered the one nourishment he viscerally rejects. However, it is during his stay with a Jewish family that takes him in for several months that he starts on the road to becoming someone else. No longer fearful of change, as in *Waiting for Snow in Havana*, he begins to call himself Charles while making an extraordinary effort to master the English language so that he can assimilate as quickly as possible: "I've become an expert at separating my present life from my previous one. Charles has vanished Carlos to the grave in which he belongs" (65). But Carlos does not fade away, at least not yet.

Eire's second death actually arrives when Carlos must leave his foster family's home and he and his brother move on to their third residence, a cockroach-infested home where orphans, among them several delinquents, struggle to survive. The narrator delivers a stirring account of the humiliations suffered at the hands of the abusive Cuban couple that oversees the home, all the more painful for the abyss between his past and present dwellings. One of his most vehement wishes is to eliminate Carlos once and for all:

Living in the *Palacio de las Cucarachas*, surrounded by Cubans at home, and being called Carlos at school only makes me wish more fervently for a total immolation of my former self. If I were able to strangle Carlos in his sleep, I'd do it. What a thrill that would be.

> Forget about strangling Lucy and Ricky Ricardo [the hosts' nicknames] or the Three Thugs. The one death I hanker for most intensely is my own. (*Learning to Die* 159)

Mastering the English language and getting rid of his accent would make the death of Carlos that much easier; it would make "such an enjoyable death. Or should I call it murder? Or is it all right to call it both a death and a murder? What English word do you use when you kill yourself and become a new *you*? *Selficide*?" (*Learning to Die* 163). He craves to crush his former self. When the protagonist and his brother move on once again, this time to join their uncle and his family in Bloomington, Indiana, Carlos takes on the name of Chuck Nieto. Years later he will assume the name of Carlos M. N. Eire or simply Carlos Eire, as if he has come to terms, partially, with his past (he drops the paternal surname). But the conflicting identities will haunt him through the end of the narrative. Even though Eire, unlike other memoirists that purport to speak for a community, speaks only for himself, his split self recalls a "we": "If all we are is memory, and memory contains one death after another, rebirth upon rebirth, how can we ever hope to speak of 'I,' 'me,' or 'myself'? Shouldn't we speak of 'we,' 'us,' or 'ourselves'?" (302). But the "we" that the speaker invokes is in truth a bundle of refracted Carloses adept at recombining and conjuring someone else from the ashes within himself. The Cuban-American self that Eire takes to inhabiting is indeed densely populated.

Such an arduous tale of conflicting identities brings about a similar tension between past and future. The narrator's fervent desire to speed up assimilation in order to annihilate the boy who he was—as a defense mechanism against his feelings of despair—mediates between events and recollections, giving rise to competing interpretations. In a revealing scene, while visiting many years later the Jewish family that took him in, he reminisces and expresses his gratitude to them for assigning him responsibilities around the house, instilling in him an American work ethic, and making him feel like a true American child. But they contradict him and assure him that he had disliked having responsibilities and protested about them, arguing that he was above the task; in his home, it was the servants who were in charge of domestic chores. The disagreement per se is not the issue, with incompatible versions of the same incident naturally arising in many a memoir. What is striking in this case is the gist of the narrator's interpretation, which rests on his urgency to carve a new, all-American identity for himself. In another chapter that touches on the manipulation of memory, Eire decides to delete from a home video a scene in which his two children, having become ill, vomit over their Christmas presents. What moves him to do so is his wish to discard any evidence of unhappiness, even at the risk of distorting or editing reality. Past events need to conform to his idea of which memories ought to be kept for future reference.

Lorena Silos Ribas, who has researched similar accounts marked by trauma in a different context, has observed that the narrative discourse in such texts reflects

> la lucha por enfrentarse a estos recuerdos dolorosos para intentar comprenderlos y, en última instancia, superarlos. Los relatos de infancia adquieren en estas ocasiones una calidad terapéutica, pues el recuento de acontecimientos traumáticos permite exorcizar los demonios del pasado y construir una subjetividad íntegra, liberada del dolor y del miedo. En estos textos, resulta evidente que la infancia ha dejado de ser la grata patria espiritual que la persona mantiene como refugio en su recuerdo, no constituye ya la *Heimat* que la lengua alemana asocia a una noción muy precisa de 'hogar,' sino que se ha convertido en un infierno, al que no es posible regresar. (10–11)
>
> [the battle in confronting painful memories to strive to understand them and ultimately to overcome them. In these instances, childhood memoirs take on a therapeutic quality, since recounting traumatic experiences helps to exorcize the demons of the past and build an integral subjectivity, free from pain and fear. In these texts, it is evident that childhood has ceased to be a pleasant spiritual homeland that the individual maintains as a refuge in his recollections, no longer providing the *Heimat* that the German language associates to a precise notion of home, but has turned into hell, and therefore returning is not possible.]

Like others in the present chapter, Eire has lost the homeland in both metaphorical and literal senses. The dual losses compound the challenge. The fact that he wrote his first volume of memoirs in a matter of months after four decades in exile underlines Silos Ribas's contention about their cathartic value, allowing the writer to put the past behind him. Contributing to the trauma he must overcome are the elements in the book that convey rupture and transformation, such as a radical shift in social status, a different language, and the metamorphosis and camouflage capabilities of the narrator, mirroring those of the lizard. Some evoke the death and resurrection imagery that are at the core of Christian experience, accentuating the distance between child and adult. On the other hand, ensuring a comforting continuity is a Cuban culture steeped in U.S. popular culture, at least for the social class the writer occupies. The familiarity with the American culture and way of life surely helps to soften the impact of the transition.

Disappearing Acts: A Childhood in Havana

The autobiographical narrative *Next Year in Cuba: A Cubano's Coming-of-Age in America* (1995) allows Cuban-American Gustavo Pérez Firmat to revisit his childhood and adolescence from afar. It affords him the opportunity to reconsider places that reverberate with intimate memories, namely, Miami and Cuba. But while Miami, where he came of age, is a location that Pérez Firmat visited frequently after he moved away from the city, Cuba, or more properly Havana, stands as an exclusively figurative return. The author has not visited Cuba since his family fled in 1960, less than two years after the coming to power of the socialist revolution. Even though Cuba remains as a key subject in his work, he has refrained from joining scores of Cuban Americans who have made the trip back across the Florida Straits.

Next Year in Cuba offers the vehicle to ponder not only the rupture and continuity issues running through the chapter but also how Cuban exiles go back to Cuba metaphorically through their enclave in the adopted homeland. By identifying with Havana through Little Havana, they manage to uncouple the modern dyad of national identity and physical territory that still drives nationalist discourses, positing instead a rather mobile subjectivity.[17] They may keep their identity as political exiles, but as Pérez Firmat's memoir implies, they also partake of a diasporic subjectivity that revolves around the island from a distance.

If in Eire's case it was estrangement from his absent parents that forced him to seek a way out and secure a clean break from the past, in Pérez Firmat's example it is his parents' refusal to procure such a distancing that made it problematic for him and his siblings to meaningfully engage their new surroundings in Miami. The owners of a food wholesaling business or *almacén* in Havana that provided the extended family with a privileged lifestyle in the upscale Reparto Kohly in Havana, Pérez Firmat's parents, who fled Cuba with their four children in 1960 after the confiscation of large Cuban-owned businesses, held back from engaging in the host society, awaiting an imminent return to Cuba after the overthrow of the Castro regime. The parents relied on short-term planning and improvisation to lead their lives as exiles, not realizing the need for a road map to functional acculturation that the young members of the family sorely craved. The need becomes imperative for someone like Pérez Firmat who feels that often "there is no going back to the country or the culture of one's origin" and, furthermore, that for most immigrants and exiles, there "comes a moment when we must begin to define ourselves not by our place of birth, but by our destination" (9). Thus the narrative the author constructs has as its centerpiece the tug-of-war between two visions, one that looks backward, the other forward; one toward Havana, the other toward Little Havana. In fact, the underlying conflict has to do with time as well as place.

In his memoir, Pérez Firmat goes back to childhood like many other Cuban-American and Latino writers, but his narrative is set apart from the rest by the fact that the first eleven years of his life, spent in Havana, get amazingly short shrift. They occupy just a handful of his close to three hundred pages of narrative. Only a tiny part of the book is devoted to the writer's Cuban childhood, an intriguing tactic for someone whose public identity is so obviously marked by a concern with Cuba and whose scholarly output, moreover, revolves around Cuban and Cuban-American topics. Given that the present life of autobiographical subjects dialectically shapes the past, as William Luis reminds us in his essay on *Next Year in Cuba*, why is this Cuban-American narrative paradoxically unhinged from a Cuban childhood? Why is Cuban childhood expunged for the most part from Pérez Firmat's book?[18]

The narrator explains in the book that he is unsure as to why Cuba does not figure in his memories, but offers several explanations: his "embargo" on Cuban memories (35) may be the result of the geographical discontinuity between the two locations, the different language in which he spent his early years, or his family's reluctance to let go of the fixation on their Cuban past. The narrator acknowledges his parents' obsession with their lost privileges and rebels against it, concluding: "Since Cuba wasn't where I was, I began to put it out of my mind. Cuba became someone else's memories. I sliced my life in halves and threw away the bitter half" (34).

Evading Cuba seems to represent, indeed, an attempt to undo his many years of vicarious immersion in a Cuban past and strike back at his parents for putting their lives on hold in the name of their native land. The parental gesture shapes some of Pérez Firmat's arguments in his *Life on the Hyphen: The Cuban-American Way*, a book in which the author celebrates the hyphen, arguing about its advantages. In an interview, Pérez Firmat states that *Next Year in Cuba* is, in fact, a spinoff of that book of essays, issued only a year before the publication of his memoir. He wrote the book in response to a request for another manuscript from his editor at Doubleday. Instead of mounting a new project, Pérez Firmat decided to write a more personal version of his previous book, drafting an autobiography in the shadow of his more theoretical *Life on the Hyphen* (Booher).

Thus, Pérez Firmat's autobiography is informed by his prior musings about cultural evolution and the festive character of biculturalism. Lingering over the period spent in Cuba would have brought *Next Year in Cuba* closer to an account that could have been written by Pérez Sr., who is incapable of fathoming a home away from his homeland. On the contrary, Pérez Jr.'s book should reflect, and in fact does reflect, the separation from Cuba that has occurred culturally and otherwise ensuing from the possibility of constructing a home abroad, while at the same time foregrounding a second-generation exile still shunning engagement with Cuba. Pérez Firmat feels strongly about wielding the word *exile* as opposed to *diaspora* to describe the Cuban experience (*Cincuenta lecciones* 108). In his *Cincuenta lecciones de exilio y desexilio* (2000), *desexilio* does not stand for "un-exile," or the unmaking of exile that a return to Cuba would represent, but for assimilation into American culture (Weimer 45).

In line with the disaffection vis-à-vis Cuba, the book's narrator keeps replaying in his mind the day of his departure from the island, when he and his family boarded the ferry that used to make the routine trip between Havana and Key West. He acknowledges that the family was hard hit by the sudden change. The split between the child who stayed behind and the one who fled is so stark that he imagines he is literally in two places at once, eloquently expressed in the following passage that captures like no other the spirit infusing all of the exiles' childhoods:

I realize that this boy on the dock is me. Somehow, in my dream, I'm in two places at once. I'm on the dock and I'm waving: I'm on the ferry and I'm waving. From the dock, I can see myself on the ferry, getting smaller and smaller, until what is left is no bigger than a swallow's flutter. The last image in my dream is of me on the ferry, with my hands gripping the deck railing and my head barely above it, looking toward the shore and seeing the Cuban boy I was, the Cuban boy I am no longer, fade to a point and then to nothing. Finally, the only kid is the one on the ferry, which has sailed out into the open sea. (*Next Year in Cuba* 21)

Still, the Cuban child, lost in mist, segues into the Cuban-American older boy and young adult. By an unusual sleight of hand, a Cuban-American coming-of-age story is somehow untethered to a Cuban childhood. While Carlos Eire belabors to re-create endless details of his life in the Cuban capital in *Waiting for Snow in Havana*, Pérez Firmat makes Little Havana, instead of Cuba, the object of not only his recollections but also his abiding affection. As the writer concedes in an interview with Álvarez Borland: "[W]hen I grow nostalgic, it's not for the Havana of my childhood but for the Miami of my adolescence. I have very fond memories of the early years in Miami, hard as they were" ("What Sounds Good" 140). It would not be until many years later that the critic would outgrow his nostalgia for Miami.

However, Cuba does not evaporate; on the contrary, Cuba looms large, casting its spell from beginning to end. Cuba is, in fact, the dazzling, sizzling absence at the heart of the narrative. *Envolver* (to involve or influence someone) is what an evanescent Cuba does to the narrator, keeping him on a short leash all along. It does not help that the family has settled in Miami, specifically in what would become Little Havana, where Cubans would concentrate and a version of the island unfurl.[19] A portion of the narrative takes on the hue of an ethnographic account of the emerging locale that consistently draws Pérez Firmat's attention, since this is where his sweet memories lie. In that fledging ethnic enclave, Cuba, or more properly its capital, Havana, was reinvented by the exiles, masters of substitution:

Exiles live by substitution. If you can't have it in Havana, make it in Miami. The Cuban-American poet Ricardo Pau-Llosa writes, "The exile knows his place, and that place is the imagination." Life in exile: memory enhanced by imagination. Like Don Quixote, every exile is an apostle of the imagination, someone who invents a world more amenable to his ambitions and dreams. It's no accident that for over twenty years the most popular eatery in Little Havana has been the Versailles restaurant, which is all cigar smoke and mirrors. Surrounded by reflections, the exile cannot always tell the genuine article from the hoax, the oasis from the mirage. Exile is a hall of mirrors, a house of spirits. (*Next Year in Cuba* 82)

The result was a feat of the imagination, the means to accomplishing a *volver*. Even if deluded by mirages, exiles were capable of ensuring the neighborhood's self-containment, independent of whatever lay beyond its borders. At times, the neighborhood feels more Cuban than the real Cuba. In one instance, an exhibition of photographs of Havana organized by a Miami museum stops at the year 1958, perhaps, as Pérez Firmat puts it, because the history of the city after that point was supposedly taking place in the very same neighborhood where the museum was located. In that case, to "continue the overview of the city, all one had to do was to step out on Calle Ocho. Little Havana U.S.A. was perhaps small in size, but it was large enough to contain some of what was best and most typical about Cuba. The diminished city, the truly little Havana, was the one that languished in the Caribbean" (87–88). As in *Next Year in Cuba*, today's Havana was kept out of the picture, and the idealized exhibition itself constituted an "imagined return," as opposed to a provisional, actual return—to borrow Oxfeld and Long's nomenclature on return (8).

The beloved South Florida neighborhood, regarded by critics as the "foremost example in the United States of a true ethnic enclave" (Lisandro Pérez 90), becomes a surrogate Cuba to which Pérez Firmat owes allegiance, returning to his stomping grounds time and time again, even after leaving for Michigan as a graduate student and for North Carolina to assume his first faculty appointment. His loyalty to the city explains why William Luis notes that the book could have been better entitled *Next Year in Miami* (95). What the protagonist tries to re-create in other states is an ambiance evocative of not La Habana but Little Havana, and the music he plays is not Los Van Van's or Silvio Rodríguez's but Willie Chirino's and Gloria Estefan's. The family returns to Miami several times a year in order to mitigate the pain of a second exile. What the protagonist finds in Miami, according to Luis, is "his and his father's recollections of a bygone era. They find comfort in the few signs that allow them to read and interpret the distant past. In either case, the physical past is inaccessible and lost forever" (106). Those recollections are very important, though, for they help to keep the emptiness and despair of a certain kind of nostalgia at bay. According to Milan Kundera, himself a displaced writer:

> [F]or memory to function well, it needs constant practice: if recollections are not invoked again and again, in conversations with friends, they go. Émigrés gathered together in compatriot colonies keep retelling to the point of nausea the same stories, which thereby become unforgettable. But people who do not spend time with their compatriots... are inevitably stricken with amnesia. The stronger their nostalgia, the emptier of recollections it becomes. (*Ignorance* 33)

Given its potential for offering a plethora of family and communal recollections, Miami fulfills the nourishing need identified by Kundera. At the same time, however, and because of its self-sufficiency, it can feel as an obstacle on the road toward outgrowing a Cuban identity. As Lisandro Pérez notes, the institutional completeness of the enclave had the effect of stymieing the process of acculturation (93), giving greater relevance to the resilience of a Cuban identity.

No matter how much our protagonist wishes to move away from the past, the identity he harbors within himself, linked to that past, weighs him down. Not surprisingly, Pérez Firmat's narrative centers on subjectivity in a parallel way to Eire's. However, instead of the battle of names and surnames waged in Eire's second memoir, various significant incidents in *Next Year in Cuba* will convey the author's anxiety toward an identity tying him to Cuba from which he wants to break free and his ardent desire to embrace another that entices him with its allure.

Aiding in this effort is the notion expounded by Pérez Firmat of discrete cultures along a continuum: Cuban, Cuban-American, and American, with subcultures in between (Cuban-bred Americans or CBA and American-born Cubans or ABC). Can the narrator-protagonist leave behind enough of his Cuban side to become Cuban American? Is the give-and-take a legitimate operation? The concern about a cultural compromise, connected to his search for home weaves together the three incidents bearing on the subject, involving an impostor brother, the theft of index cards at a university library, and the narrator's divorce from his Cuban wife and second marriage to an American. All three are embedded in the sense of ambiguity of his own self: the fact of being Cuban (without Cuba, mind you) in America and the questions the disconnect raises about authenticity and wholeness.

In the first incident, the narrator offers temporary shelter in North Carolina to his younger brother, who needs a place to stay. Time goes on, however, and his sibling is still around. After giving him an ultimatum, the brother finally leaves, but not without taking with him the narrator's credit card numbers, which he uses to make several purchases in his brother's name. The experience gives the narrator pause to ruminate about imposture and about the shifting ground on which he stands as someone who straddles two cultures. Is he not as much of an impostor as the brother who stole his identity, being that he is a professor, a profession he would not have dreamed of pursuing in Cuba, and a Carolina resident, no less?

The second bizarre incident takes place at the University of Michigan while the narrator is conducting research for his dissertation on Hispanic vanguard literatures. The index cards with his notes go missing from his carrel, after which he begins to receive puzzling written messages from an anonymous source who threatens to dispose of his cards if he does not fulfill certain demands. The incident makes him wonder about his choice of profession, a point of contention within himself and also with his father, who expected him to inherit his *almacén*. Is the narrator really who he says he is? Is the library incident not insinuating that the academy is not truly his place?

Finally, the third passage has to do with the narrator's divorce from his first wife, a *cubana* from Miami, and his extramarital affair and subsequent betrothal to a woman from New Jersey. The whole incident is couched in cultural terms as the need to move away from a Miami past that, although not strictly Cuban, feels as such, toward a less burdensome present and future grounded in the United States. In the cultural chart envisioned by the author, marrying an American woman meant accepting the inevitable: embracing the majority culture to which he and his progeny were destined with varying degrees of integration.

The three incidents show the weight of a Cuban past that is eloquently absent from the narrative, as is the Cuban present. If the exiles' attitude of being stuck in the past and waxing nostalgic for Little Havana is discomforting for Pérez Firmat, returning to the island of his birth is no less so. When he is alone with his father, one of the questions that Pérez Sr. asks repeatedly is whether he will return to Cuba. The answer to this question is found in his reaction to the short trips made by Pepe, his older brother, to the island. He becomes incensed by Pepe's praise for the changes that have taken place in Cuba as well as by his indifference to the fate of their former possessions in the capital. He also refuses to look at the photographs of the family's house and *almacén* that Pepe has brought for all to see. His excuse is that he wants to keep intact his memories of their home (173). These memories, however meager or faded, are evidently not for sharing with the public, perhaps as an attempt to circumvent his family's wallowing in nostalgia. He simply skirts the subject.

For personal as well as political reasons, then, the South Florida enclave where Pérez Firmat grew up indeed becomes the Cuba he knows best. His attachment to Miami is rather unique among Cuban-American memoirs. Most other narratives rely on Cuba for a sense of *cubanía*, but in *Next Year in Cuba*, it is Miami that plays that role, providing the means to preserve a Cuban self-identity. In the narrative, home trumps homeland, an uncoupling that rests on the author's fluid sense of place.[20]

Returning to Miami, then, is a way of going halfway back to the island, as it is for one of the informants in David Rieff's *The Exile: Cuba in the Heart of Miami* (1993): "For a guy to grow up in Cuba, and then live among sights and sounds that are totally foreign for years, and then return to a place where it's 'Varadero' this and 'La Habana' that and 'Pinar del Río' the other, is like going halfway back to Cuba" (136). This is a city that, as a simulacrum, is bonded to Cuba. The experience represents a return (in the sense of *volver*) to Cuba through Miami. In order to reach "Cuba," the exile who refuses to go back to the island must *retornar* to Miami so as to experience the idiosyncrasy, if you will.

It is in Miami, a kind of cultural mecca or epicenter of the Cuban population in the United States, where Pérez Firmat can indulge in the Cuban tastes, sounds, and accents that adorned his past, even as he recognizes that "[w]hat's 'little' about Havana is not only its size (Miami is actually the second most populous Cuban city), but its diminished status as a deficient or incomplete copy of the original" (*Life on the Hyphen* 7).[21] The displaced homeland is so intertwined with the island close by—Cuba is so much in "the heart of Miami" (Rieff, *The Exile*)—that it is difficult to extricate the two. This is due, perhaps, to the enclave's embodiment of Cuba, even if it is a Cuba frozen in time. As Rieff remarks, the paradox is that it is far easier "to get away from Cuba in Cuba itself than in Miami" (43). And so the details of the narrator's life on the island are kept out of sight, but Cuba and its avatars crisscross the narrative from beginning to end, demonstrating its sway.

Since *Next Year in Cuba* was published in 1995, Pérez Firmat has moved on and, after spending twenty years as faculty at Duke University in Durham, accepted another position at Columbia University. He now lives in New Jersey. When the writer feels nostalgic nowadays, he and his family return (in the sense of *retornar*) to North Carolina. As he expressed in his keynote address at the South Atlantic Modern Language Association 2012 congress in Durham, "When I became a part-time northerner, an unexpected thing happened. I became homesick for North Carolina, a place that I'd never considered home" ("A Cuban in Mayberry").[22]

The nostalgia he now feels for North Carolina drove him to watch episode after episode of *The Andy Griffith Show*, which is set in Mayberry, a fictional place two hours away from Durham. One of the things the author likes about Mayberry is how its residents share a sense of communion:

> Watching episodes of *TAGS*, I developed a sense of what it must feel like to enjoy such intimacy, to feel attached to the ground under your feet, and to know that the person you are talking to is similarly attached. Everyone was born someplace, but not everybody has a hometown, for the term designates an intensity of connection that not everyone enjoys." ("A Cuban in Mayberry")

The remark alludes to the affinity found among individuals who have a similar ethnic, social, and even racial background and therefore recognize a common set of references that makes communication and understanding an easy task. This familiarity or connection is lacking for the writer anywhere he goes. Since he fled his birthplace long ago and cultures are constantly evolving, it is doubtful that the author would attain that connection even in Havana, a city he left more than half a century ago.

Pérez Firmat's ongoing quest for a place that would recognize him as one of its own, a place he has yet to find, turns him into a "chronic exile" ("A Cuban in Mayberry"). As a Cuban American, he moves from one adopted, displaced home after another. Cuba, at least, was subsumed in Miami, but in North Carolina, this is no longer the case. Cuba is twice removed from the place he now considers home.

The new development, however, does not mean that Cuba has disappeared from Pérez Firmat's writings. After all, he is still a *Cuban* in Mayberry. Cuba stands as the distant homeland, where home is no longer found. Yet Cuba is a hovering idea, one to which the critic returns, or *vuelve*, time and again. Steering away from the original homeland, then, Pérez Firmat's reflections provide a preview of a brave new world in which the modern isomorphic relation between national identity and territory suffers a blow. The resulting dent allows a fluid sense of Cuban diasporic identity to shine through.

Conclusion

Even though Pujol, Brito, Eire, and Pérez Firmat are part of the growing Cuban diaspora, they refrain from engaging in transnational practices. Only one, Ernesto Pujol, returned to show his work in Havana and develop a professional relationship there, accomplishing what only a handful of Cuban artists of the diaspora have achieved. What these visual and textual narratives have in common are the depiction of a childhood left behind in another place, one to which most of their creators will not return for political reasons. Broadly speaking, politics underlies these narratives, giving rise, in the case of the autobiographies, to the sub-sub-genre of the "Exile's Childhood" that draws attention to multiple reasons for the figurative divide between childhood and adolescence.

Eire's and Pérez Firmat's narratives should be construed not as exceptional but in line with discourses espoused by many Cubans who claim an exile identity in the United States and other countries. In her interviews with Cuban informants who settled in Spain in the year following the revolutionary takeover, Mette L. Berg finds some of the characteristics that are also present in Eire's memoirs: a racialized narrative that privileges whiteness, filled with tropes of prerevolutionary affluence and modernity, turned upside down by the strongman (Castro) on whom everything hinges (74–75).

Comments made by Berg's interviewees and Pérez Firmat's memoir share some ground. Many exiles appreciate the food, the products, and the institutions that have been refashioned outside of Cuba to cater to the emotional needs of nostalgic émigrés. By contrast, the photographs that those who make the trip back bring with them to share show an unrecognizable, deprived, and ruinous Havana that has little resemblance to these migrants' memories. Berg points out that the Havana remembered by one of her informants "was clearly different from the one he saw in the photos, which he seemed to keep as proof of what he had lost, the decay and rubbish standing for the moral decay of revolutionary Cuba" (83). Their position upholds the argument that space is a physical category as much as a perceptive and cultural entity (García Calderón 27). Instead of placing themselves in the position of decrying the decrepitude of the existing Havana, some exiles simply refuse to look at photographs that visitors to the island bring back with them so that they can retain memories of their past. As Susan E. Eckstein puts it in reference to exiles in the United States, "Visuals of Cuba under Castro were too much for them, for fear that they might destroy the beloved Cuba of their imagination" (152). A parallel can be established between these exiled Cubans in the United States and Spain and Pérez Firmat, who also turns down the opportunity to see the photographs taken by his brother of the old *almacén*.

Eire and Pérez Firmat's autobiographies may well be representative of Cuban-American literature, but they are also cautionary tales about the dangers of generalization. Both show how a sense of Cuban Americanness and an exilic perspective are not mutually exclusive. These narratives are generated by writers of the one-and-a-half generation, but they still contain vestiges of an exile sensibility embroiled with overt politics. Exile, in these texts, becomes a mode of narrating that discursively exacts a chasm difficult to bridge, one that withholds reconciliation. Admitting that there is no single but multiple Cuban-American ways, as the personal narratives of the one-and-a-half generation insinuate, does justice to this body of work.

5

Vicarious Returns and a Usable Past in *The Agüero Sisters*, *Days of Awe*, and *Loving Che*

> The past is full of life, eager to irritate us, provoke and insult us, tempt us to destroy or repaint it.
> Milan Kundera, *The Book of Laughter and Forgetting*

> A contemporary Russian saying claims that the past has become much more unpredictable than the future.
> Svetlana Boym, *The Future of Nostalgia*

In all of the narratives on return analyzed thus far, author, narrator, and protagonist overlap, upholding the autobiographical pact (Lejeune). Although retouched and filtered through the lens of the present and the deployment of literary devices, the narratives set out to depict actual journeys to the island. These journeys serve as vehicles for an encounter with a past that is as full of life as it is unpredictable, as Kundera and Boym's epigraphs powerfully convey. The past does not store memory as much as it generates memory, thereby becoming a site for contention.

Chapter 5 targets a different kind of representation, one that relies on a fictionalized usable past. Its focus shifts from autobiographies to fiction in order to explore promising returns to Cuba in novels by Cristina García, Achy Obejas, and Ana Menéndez, the first two among the youngest members of the one-and-a-half generation, and the latter belonging to a subsequent generation. Born in 1958 and 1956, respectively, García and Obejas came to the United States as small children. Born in 1970 in the United States to Cuban parents, Menéndez is viewed as an American-Born Cuban or ABC, presumably a Cuban "in name only, in last name" (Pérez Firmat, *Life on the Hyphen* 5).

Although not strictly of the one-and-a-half generation, I include Menéndez in the chapter for two reasons. On the one hand, her novel shares with the other two similar narrative strategies in the pursuit of comparable goals, suggesting that there is some dovetailing among approaches to the literature inspired by Cuba across the younger generational cohorts. On the other hand, Menéndez illustrates the resilience of the idea of Cuba among a sector of young Cuban Americans with feeble actual links to the island. According to Eckstein and Barbería, even children who emigrated as infants talk about "going back" to visit relatives whom they have never met (816–17). Many of these children learn how to be "Cuban" by hearsay.

An example is Andrea O'Reilly Herrera, an ABC of mixed Cuban and Irish heritage who has described how her sense of *lo cubano* comes from listening to her relatives passionately talking about their way of life on the island at weekly family gatherings. Underscoring her hybridity, she argues that "Cub*ands*" like her are the recipients of a "second-hand exile condition" ("The Politics of Mis-ReMembering" 179). In her edited volume *ReMembering Cuba: Legacy of a Diaspora* (2001), there are several testimonials from other "Cub*ands*" who, having been born in exile, have no personal knowledge of Cuba yet have developed a Cuban diasporic consciousness. O'Reilly Herrera draws from theorists such as Antonio Benítez-Rojo and Nicolas Bourriaud to conceptualize the paradoxical claims to Cuban cultural traditions of these contributors to the volume. These claims conflict with the modern superimposition of cultural belonging to a discrete geography, a quarrel that prompts the critic to adopt the metaphor, in a later book on Cuban artists, of a movable or transportable tent representing the island and its culture. Cuba becomes a portable island. With this conceptualization, the critic adds to the growing list of demands for a more expansive sense of *lo cubano*.[1]

Regardless of their precise location among the exile waves, García, Obejas, and Menéndez are writers who by dint of their literary output have gained a rightful place in Cuban-American and Latino/a literature, at the same time that they have been applauded in Cuba, where the three have been interviewed and their work discussed in local journals. Island-based critics have also published essays about their fiction in volumes published overseas.[2] The three are among a handful of Cuban-American writers who have questioned the divide between Cubans on the island and abroad, and they have been to Cuba more than once.[3]

Through such novels as *The Agüero Sisters* (1997), *Days of Awe* (2001), and *Loving Che* (2003), García, Obejas, and Menéndez debunk dominant narratives circulating in Cuba and/or its diaspora by tapping into the ambiguous nature of reality and engaging in the type of rewriting of the past suggested by this chapter's epigraphs. The novels showcase a return to relatively overlooked aspects of the culture, such as *mestizaje*, marginal religions, and the private lives of revolutionary icons, respectively, from the vantage point of women characters in order to subvert the grand narrative of both Cuban and Cuban-American exile culture, with its emphasis on a homogeneous past. In addition to figurative returns, there are also literal *retornos* represented by the homecoming of the characters to the place where they were born. Though not quite the authors' alter egos, the characters share a family resemblance of sorts with their creators. Thus, these authors accomplish a vicarious return under a fake name.

The three authors are driven not by an ill-conceived notion of a naturalized homeland or essentialist identity but by a diasporic consciousness that all too often revamps official discourses.[4] As Cubans of the diaspora, they are obstinate in both drawing from and altering the reservoir of discourses built around the greater Cuba. A scholar of diaspora, Khachig Tölölyan, describes what happens when time has taken its toll and the people in the diaspora have to resort to a renewed sense of identification:

> [E]ither old national tropes are refurbished or new fictions of shared identity are invented. The community endures as a distinct diaspora, not because its members individually remember grandma or the village, but thanks to the collective work of memory and commemoration, the performance of difference, the cultivation of ideologies of identity, and the institutionalization of practices of connection to the homeland. ("The Contemporary Discourse of Diaspora Studies" 650)

This chapter touches on those changes, examining especially the performance of difference and the cultivation of ideologies of identity mentioned by Tölölyan. Although these are far from being the only fictional works addressing return, the three selected novels share additional elements, namely, a family secret, a preoccupation with the historical past, and women as active subjects.[5] These commonalities, which afford an overlapping critical reading, influenced my choice of works among the many that envisage a vicarious return.[6]

A Family Secret

Going back to Cuba leads these characters to uncover an elusive secret. In García's novel, the secret involves the death of the co-protagonists' mother. The Agüero sisters have grown up—and apart from each other—with a different as well as a deceitful account of that disappearance and the tragedy of their father's suicide two years later. In *Days of Awe*, by Obejas, the protagonist goes back to the island at first as an interpreter, becoming reacquainted with family friends who gradually reveal to her the rich Jewish background of her family—a faith proudly embraced by some of her ancestors, but not by others, including the main character's father, who has shrouded it in secrecy. In Ana Menendez's novel, *Loving Che*, the main character returns to Cuba after a frustrated search for her mother. She has received in Miami an enigmatic package containing a journal and photographs. These documents lead her to believe that she will find her mother, from whom she was separated when she was an infant, on the island. According to her mother's account, she is Che Guevara's daughter, conceived out of wedlock.

Deemed worthy of keeping under wraps, carefully protected from intrusive eyes and ears, the information withheld is prized, and in these three novels that knowledge relates to issues of identity: Is Ignacio Agüero only the respected, brilliant naturalist known the world over, or is he also an assassin accountable for the violent end of his own wife? Is Alejandra's father in *Days of Awe* a Cuban exile with faint links to the Jewish community, or is he just too terrified to fully assume and defend his vigorous faith? Is the narrator in *Loving Che* the illegitimate daughter of a revolutionary icon put on a pedestal on the island for daring to dream of a new man in a just new world, or is she the offspring of an executioner of foes, despised as such in Little Havana, USA? Perhaps more important for the three Cuban-American writers, what relevance do the secrets have for the hybrid, diasporic characters who cannot escape the ambiguities of truth and appearance?

Indeed, secrets point to valuable information, maybe as precious as one's self-definition. And just as significant as the substance of the secret is the line it draws between those in the know and those outside that privileged circle. The separation mirrors the one ensuing among Cubans in the aftermath of the 1959 revolutionary takeover. As Obejas notes in an interview, "I was born on an island that had a revolution which shook and inspired the world and split its own people in two: those in, those out" (Shapiro 20). The divide is embedded in the very etymology of the linguistic sign *secret,* for the Latin *secretum* derives from *secernere,* which originally meant to sift apart, to separate as with a sieve (Bok 6).

It follows that once the secret is revealed, the lines previously drawn dissolve and the separation dissipates. When this stage is reached, the characters are *in* as well as *on* the island, where the secret originates. However, they are in only up to a certain point: while the details of Blanca Agüero's last moments are revealed, the motives for the murder remain inconclusive for the Agüero sisters in García's novel, for they never learn explicitly what motivated Ignacio Agüero to pull the trigger. Like the reader, they have to cobble together an explanation out of subtle clues. And in Menéndez's novel, Che's relationship to the protagonist fails to be ascertained. Could this be read as a symbolic drawing of the boundaries for diasporic writers—with a foot inside but astride two traditions?

Obviously, a concern with concealment and verity is paramount in all of these works written from the diaspora. The narrators find the available accounts about the past untrustworthy and set out to take them apart.

A Preoccupation with the Past

In addition to wrestling with lingering mysteries bearing upon the nature of fact and subjectivity, these narratives grapple with a historical past associated with Cuba, the land of the protagonists' ancestors. Countless references to the island's history in the three novels prompt a reflection about the relevance and recasting of that past for contemporary Cuban-American writers. All three writers zero in on a family saga enmeshed in a history that has largely eluded them. As one of Ignacio Agüero's granddaughters wonders, "Why is it that everything interesting in my family happened long before I was born?" (García, *Agüero Sisters* 205). Because of the relative weight of that past in the stories, Lois Parkinson Zamora's reflections on the powerful notion of a usable (and useful) past shed light on the implications of claiming ownership of it.

Zamora's arguments arise from her critique of Harold Bloom's claim about an anxiety of influence afflicting writers in the western world, an anxiety that coaxes them to steer away from the past in their quest for innovation and, ultimately, progress. Zamora, on the other hand, argues that writers from the Americas can hardly disown their precursors. Even when these appear obscure, contradictory, or unsatisfying due to a history of colonization and miscegenation, American writers' anxiety about origins is anything but troubling, and the narrative strategies they use in order to account for multiple origins or "absent ones" due to colonial legacies are imaginative as well as forceful (8). "Origins," for Zamora, signify "acceptable sources of cultural authority, communal coherence, and individual agency," and "anxiety" denotes "the efforts of American writers to establish such sources by various strategies of research, restitution, revaluation, renovation, and resistance" (5–6). An anxiety about origins marks the authors examined here, who narrow the distance between the two hemispheres. Zamora finds that rather than discarding the past, that anxiety "impels American writers to search *for* precursors (in the name of community) rather than escape *from* them (in the name of individuation), and to connect *to* traditions and histories (in the name of a usable past) rather than dissociate *from* them (in the name of originality)" (5). The search for precursors, traditions, memory, and history buttresses their stories.

Situated in the Americas, the three Cuban-American writers seek to do the latter—connect to traditions and histories, in this case written in a different language. But they both reconstruct and re-create so as to address their current circumstances. As Cristina García openly acknowledges: "This story [*The Agüero Sisters*] gave me an opportunity to explore the extent to which the past continues to inhabit the present and how we transform the past to accommodate it with our current sense of self. How do we live with the past? How do we tailor it so we can go about living our daily lives?"[7] Past stories serve as a catalyst for gaining a better grasp of self. Although in fiction mode, these authors comb the past to fashion a cohesive narrative and add complexity to the stories they choose to tell.

It can thus be argued that Cuban-American narratives mirror the inclination to advance while simultaneously walking backward, a feature that Antonio Benítez-Rojo identifies in Caribbean literature. In a similar way to the anxiety of origins, walking backward, which resembles the locomotion of the crab, is a retrogressive move that does not let us off the hook. Rather than merely moving ahead unencumbered, there is always the past to contend with, one that is often embroiled with the African substratum of Caribbean cultures (*The Repeating Island* 221–25)—as *The Agüero Sisters* illustrates. Hence there is always a historicist as well as a constructivist bent to these authorial deeds.[8]

García, Obejas, and Menéndez draw inspiration from Cuban precursors, although they were naturally first exposed to Anglo writers from whom they learned their craft. Writing about *The Agüero Sisters*, Adriana Méndez Rodenas points out that the portrayal of the island as a naturalist's dream reenacts the long tradition of scientific writings sparked by the work of Cuban naturalists like Felipe Poey and continued in travel writing and modern scientists' accounts ("En búsqueda del paraíso perdido" 396). Achy Obejas nods to Reinaldo Arenas, José Lezama Lima, and Virgilio Piñera, among other Cuban writers, through ingenious literary allusions in *Days of Awe*. The idea, Obejas states in her interview with Ilan Stavans, was to pay tribute to those writers to whom she owes a debt. As for Ana Menéndez, Isabel Álvarez Borland claims that it was Guillermo Cabrera Infante's *Vista del amanecer en el trópico* that provided the scaffold for *Loving Che* ("Figures of Identity" 42). In this regard, the narratives align nicely with Zamora's and Benítez-Rojo's ruminations.

More often than not, these writers look south, toward the island, as a source of inspiration to explore the past. They do so for various reasons, in addition to those pointed out by Zamora. First, since they write from the diaspora, Cuba may hold the key to suturing a fragmented genealogy resulting from displacement and the breakup of the family. Second, due to the authors' cultural location, all things Cuban may acquire a prominence that island-based writers simply take for granted and therefore disregard. Because these novelists write from a distant position, they are sometimes direct in terms of their national/ethnic identity, however ambiguous and seemingly contradictory the statement may be. As Achy Obejas remarks: "I'm Cuban, Cuban American, Latina by virtue of being Cuban, a Cuban journalist, a Cuban writer, somebody's Cuban lover, a Cuban dyke, a Cuban girl on a bus, a Cuban exploring Sephardic roots, always and endlessly Cuban. I'm more Cuban here than I am in Cuba, by sheer contrast and repetition" (qtd. in Shapiro 20). At times, there is a measure of excess in statements about identity and the uses of Cuba, particularly if these are meant to "perform" difference (Christian, *Show and Tell* 18). Third, these authors profit from the possibilities afforded by a multicultural society whose public discourse values difference and multiple identities and therefore enables statements such as Obejas's to mark that difference. Finally, these writers take advantage of the fact that Cuba has become fashionable in the United States as one of the last bastions of socialism worldwide, making it conspicuous, contradictory, and controversial. In short, there are emotional, existential, and pragmatic reasons for bringing Cuba into the narratives.

At the same time, the authors capitalize on their family bonds to Cuba because these serve a purpose. The past is usable because it can be dialectically molded to fit present intentions, as García suggests above. And these writers can reshape the past with comparative ease on account of their being simultaneously unburdened by a direct involvement with it. These are memories that can be tinkered with, as Carmelita Tropicana, performance persona of Alina Troyano, notes in an interview:

> [W]hat you have is sort of like my parents' memory of this wonderful romantic Tropicana, of what Cuba was like in the fifties, which we all know wasn't so beautiful. And I can take it and don't have to be romantic with it because it was not my time. So I can take liberties with it and I can break it every which way. If you were living in the period you can be very romantic and very precious with that kind of material. But that's not what we do; we take it to town. That way we give it more of a clear vision perhaps, because we put the good and the bad taste in, and sometimes bad taste is actually good. (Qtd. in Dorson)

To an extent, García's blunt critique of Cuba's foremost writer and patriot, José Martí, ensues from a condition, which she shares with Tropicana, not of disengagement proper but of engagement from afar: "I've read a lot of his poetry and a little about his life and so on, but to be honest—and I think this will be sacrilegious—he is so overrated. In the Cuban context, everybody claims him for himself" (qtd. in Kevane and Heredia 74). Writers on the island would most likely think twice before making similarly irreverent statements given Martí's monumental stature in Cuban letters.[9]

García is nonetheless aware of the "sacrilegious" character of her judgment because her work is driven by a mediated history. As a daughter of exile, she treads into memories distant from her in time and place but near in terms of kinship. Her gesture brings to mind Marianne Hirsch and Leo Spitzer's notion of post-memory, which refers to the unspeakable legacy of the children of the Holocaust who struggle with their parents' memories. The term can be extended to the younger Cubans who partake of the memory of exile without, of course, the genocidal implications that the Holocaust connotes. Post-memory is described as "a secondary, belated memory mediated by stories, images and behaviours . . . which never added up to a complete picture or linear tale. Its power derives precisely from the layers—both positive and negative—that have been passed down . . . unintegrated, conflicting, fragmented, dispersed" (Hirsch and Spitzer 85). The lives, stories, and images of the ancestors, without, in this case, the burden of genocide, make up an archive that has been bequeathed in snippets and needs to be pieced together—as well as fiddled with.[10] Reflecting on the boundaries of individual and family memory in *Memory Mambo*, Obejas's protagonist is unsure where her family's memories end and hers begin: "I no longer know if I really lived through an experience or just heard about it so many times, or so convincingly, that I believed it for myself—became the lens through which it was captured, retold and shaped" (9). The communal memories that the writers recycle constitute a post-history, an archive that has been passed down away from the sites generative of those memories. Yet they do not take those memories at face value.

Key events of a historical nature are folded into all three narratives. *The Agüero Sisters* is framed in the wider context of both Cuban natural history, a saga characterized by survival as well as extinction, and a cultural history built simultaneously on inclusions and exclusions. The novel affords a rereading of the counterpoint between sugar and tobacco, the two most important crops in Cuba, which inspired Fernando Ortiz's reflections in *Contrapunteo cubano del tabaco y el azúcar*, originally published in 1940. The balance is here tipped toward sugar, what with its implications of *mestizaje* and syncretism. This claim will be further elaborated in the section devoted to the novel. Moreover, the mission of the protagonist of Obejas's *Days of Awe*, born on the island the very same day as Fidel Castro's triumphant march into Havana, will be a return to her homeland in order to unwittingly detect a history of abasement of Jews on the island. Finally, Menéndez's *Loving Che* centers on a passionate, but in all likelihood fictive, love affair between Che Guevara and a woman, the mother of the unnamed narrator, who records in her diary sporadic but notable events in Cuban history over a period of several decades.

García, Obejas, and Menéndez take advantage of the latitude inherent in the construction of historical and cultural narratives to tamper with them, making some of these usable for themselves. As Zamora argues:

Usable implies the active engagement of a user or users, through whose agency collective and personal histories are constituted. The term thus obviates the possibility of innocent history, but not the possibility of authentic history when it is actively imagined by its user(s). What is deemed usable is valuable; what is valuable is constituted according to specific cultural and personal needs and desires. (ix)

Uses of the past are far from being innocent and may clash, as this chapter's epigraphs by Kundera and Boym suggest. Documents, photographs, and diaries, while important as archival material, can and do give rise to competing interpretations—as the narrator of *Loving Che* learns in due time. All three writers come from an exile community that has made almost an art form out of constructing conflicting historical narratives out of the same fabric, along with contempt and disparagement toward counternarratives—a less than ennobling predisposition that sectors of the community have upheld time and again. Cristina García has denounced in interviews the intolerance of the Cuban exile population in the South Florida enclave. García's liberal views, travels to Cuba, and opposition to the U.S. embargo against the island cast her as an outsider when she moved to Miami to assume the position of *Time* bureau chief in 1987. Because of it, she became an "other Cuban": "As far as Cuban identity goes, there are three concentric circles—the Cubans, the Miami-Cubans, and the other Cubans. I'm in the third ring three times removed!" (qtd. in Kevane and Heredia 71). García notes, however, that the community has become more broadminded and diverse in recent times ("Con frecuencia se simplifica" 157).

The younger Ana Menéndez speaks about the paradisiacal Cuba of yesteryear that she grew up hearing about, a tall tale difficult to reconcile with credible, highly regarded historical accounts of underdeveloped, prerevolutionary Cuba. Doubting that story, "las verdades múltiples se convirtieron en las únicas verdades posibles" (Alfredo Prieto 39) [multiple truths became the only possible truths]. In some ways, the authors use the ambiguous nature of memory and reality to, subliminally or otherwise, demystify overriding narratives and offer counternarratives that challenge the essentialist tendencies at the core of any imagined community (Christian, *Show and Tell* 8–9).

Female Characters as Interpreters

In addition to a usable past and an equally usable secret, both of which pull the characters to the island, the three novels share an interest in strong female characters who challenge normative behavior, patriarchal precepts, and official histories. They make dogged efforts to dispel the unknown, going after an ever-evanescent truth in some cases, and they are resourceful in their use of the historical past to weave a cogent narrative for female diasporic subjects. As female writers, García, Obejas, and Menéndez offer a counterbalance to a long record of exclusion from interpretive frameworks. Commenting on feminist historian Gerda Lerner's thoughts on women and history, Zamora points out "the contradiction between women's centrality on creating culture and yet their marginality in the meaning-giving process of interpretation" (171). Both Lerner and Zamora conclude that the contribution of women to that development has been largely dismissed.

Along with writers such as Rosario Ferré, Sandra Cisneros, Maryse Condé, Isabel Allende, and Elena Garro, these Cuban-American novelists draw attention to that erasure. One of García's female characters grumbles about the historians' highly selective focus: "If it were up to me, I'd record other things. Like the time there was a hailstorm in the Congo and the women took it as a sign that they should rule. Or the life stories of prostitutes in Bombay. Why don't I know anything about them? Who chooses what we should know or what's important?" (*Dreaming in Cuban* 28). And García posits in an interview with Iraida H. López that "[t]raditional history, the way it has been written, interpreted, and recorded, obviates women and the evolution of home, family, and society, and basically becomes a recording of battles and wars and dubious accomplishments of men" ("And There Is Only My Imagination" 107). What if we thought anew and rearranged the order of things according to a different set of priorities?, García asks. Placing women in the spotlight, all three novels examine the impact of historical events and grand narratives on the lives of female characters.

The Continuing Centrality of Cuba

Drawing from a usable past, all three writers don figurative *guayaberas* through their fictional narratives of return. While inserting themselves in a U.S. ethnic literature market that feeds on multiculturalism and difference, they rely on a usable post-history to offer substitute readings of Cuban cultural and historical accounts.

Written in English, their narratives revolve around Cuba even though their personal memories are anchored in the United States. García was two years old when her family left Cuba, Obejas was six when her family fled Cuba on a boat, and Menéndez was born in the United States. The three grew up away from Miami: García in a non-Hispanic neighborhood in Brooklyn; Obejas in Michigan City, a coastal town in Indiana, and then Chicago when she was in her twenties; and Menéndez in Los Angeles and later Tampa, where she attended high school.

Most of the novels these authors have published focus on the island. García's first three novels, *Dreaming in Cuban* (1992), *The Agüero Sisters* (1997), and *Monkey Hunting* (2003), form a trilogy on Cuba. Although two of her novels published thereafter, *A Handbook to Luck* (2007) and *The Lady Matador's Hotel* (2010) only tangentially deal with Cuban characters, in 2013 she returns, with *King of Cuba*, to a prototypical Cuban subject. The novel's main characters are a hardheaded Fidel Castro still in charge and an octogenarian Miami exile determined to free Cuba of the Castro dictatorship.

Informed by a different aesthetic, Achy Obejas's fiction revolves around the lives of gay characters, most of which are Cuban American or Latino, who are part of a larger U.S. multicultural community. *We Came All the Way from Cuba So You Could Dress Like This?* (1994), Obejas's short story collection, includes a story about cultural conflict across generations, while her novel *Ruins* (2009) is set totally on the island. Her anthology of detective fiction, *Havana Noir* (2007), includes short stories by both island and diaspora writers. In her work, Obejas seems to move back and forth with ease between English and Spanish as well as across the Strait of Florida.

On the other hand, Menéndez, who was born in the United States, deals with the Cuban exile community in her first book, *In Cuba I Was a German Shepherd* (2001), as well as in *Loving Che*, which is partly set in Cuba. In *The Last War* (2009), she veers away from Cuba to address war conflict in Iraq, but returns to the island in *Adiós, Happy Homeland!* (2011), a book of intertextual vignettes that deal with translation and misinterpretation. Saturated with the mind-numbing "tema" (the theme, Cuba), given her immersion in things Cuban, Menéndez nevertheless concedes that she has been lured back to the same topic repeatedly.[11]

The Agüero Sisters: Highlighting Gender-Based *Mestizaje*

In her second novel, *The Agüero Sisters*, issued five years after the publication of her widely acclaimed *Dreaming in Cuban*, a finalist for the National Book Award, Cristina García ties together the national and diasporic realms, a bridging that paves the way for the participation of the Cuban diaspora in the national as well as transnational meaning-making process. This section sets out to explore García's use of geographical locations on the island laden with historical and cultural meanings as a way of giving prominence to transculturation processes. While three exiled characters in the novel accomplish a brief *regreso* to Cuba, two as mercenaries and a third to recover Agüero's diary, perhaps just as significant is the gesture of revisiting narratives of national and cultural import. Multiple passages in the novel referencing relevant dates, events, and icons entwined with Cuban history and culture all point in this direction.[12]

García offers a narrative framed within the history of Cuba since independence. Constancia and Reina Agüero's father, Ignacio, is born on the day that Estrada Palma, the first president of the Cuban republic, stops in his hometown to preside over a parade. In a magical realist episode charged with symbolism, an owl picks up the mother's placenta and flies away with it, sprinkling the crowd and the president himself with birthing blood. As a result, symbolic blood ties develop between Ignacio Agüero and the republic. Reina and Constancia, his professed offspring, do not fare much better at extricating themselves from a web of historical events. For instance, Reina's insomnia begins coincidentally on the thirty-seventh anniversary of the attack on the Moncada barracks that celebrates the launching of the revolutionary uprising led by Castro in 1953. And the third generation is not saved from political maelstrom either. Silvestre, Constancia's son by her first husband, is sent to the United States through Operation Pedro Pan in the early 1960s. Not until a year later do Constancia, her second husband Heberto, and their baby daughter reunite with Silvestre, whose biological father is Heberto's brother. In the interim, Silvestre runs a high fever that causes him to lose his hearing. Many years later, still bitter from various forms of neglect, he would take the life of his ailing, bedridden father, a onetime mercenary who had taken part in the U.S.-orchestrated Bay of Pigs invasion in 1961. Heberto, too, would lose his life in another attempt, this time in the 1990s, to rid the island of the Castro regime.

Critic Teresa Derrickson accounts for additional passages in which historic events are interwoven specifically with women's bodies: Constancia gives birth the same day that her husband's shipping company is nationalized by the government, and she stops lactating the day she and her family flee Cuba on a boat. Meanwhile, Reina loses her ability to have orgasms at the time of her own defection to the United States in the early 1990s (Derrickson 481). While Derrickson's insightful and persuasive analysis dissects the correlation between woman and nation, it is the Agüero family as a whole that is caught up in a larger net, as the above examples illustrate. Moreover, Ignacio Agüero's profession as an eminent naturalist is linked to nation-building efforts and enhancing Cuba's stature among international museums and scientific institutions. His scientific interests rest not in unmarked fauna and flora but in those that can be cataloged explicitly as Cuban, as the titles of his publications proclaim (Derrickson 483).

In addition to intersecting with the Cuban epic, the Agüero microcosm also resonates with a few of the all-encompassing, foundational narratives of the Cuban nation. Their world is implanted in an unofficial, subterranean, and parallel usable history where the politics of gender and race, often silenced, converge and spring to life. The conflicts within the Agüero family are mired in Cuba's contested gender and racial scripts, as several articles focusing on the novel's characters have revealed.

Another way of unpacking the gender and race connection is by looking at the island locations inscribed in the plot. In the final part of this section I delve into the historical and cultural resonances of those places that serve as settings for the action to see how they contribute to framing the search for a usable past and the forging of a space for progressive diasporic voices. Through the enactment of a vicarious return that emboldens the protagonists to confront conflicting accounts, the novel ultimately defends the idea that a sector of the Cuban diaspora may, through progressive politics, participate in constructing or unveiling alternative narratives. The novel draws from the archive of the nation's foundational myths to zero in on some that are more in line with syncretism and hybridity and thus capable of expanding the space for the recognition of diverse Cuban subjectivities. If Blanca Agüero indeed stands for somewhat marginalized elements such as women's autonomy and *mestizaje*, and the two Agüero sisters are instrumental in exposing the vulnerability and invisibility of those elements, then an argument can be made about the sisters' positive role in bringing an elusive truth—both in the personal and cultural domains—to light.

Pursuit of the truth at both concrete and metaphorical levels moves the narrative forward. At the plot level, this quest is evident from the start, when the reader learns, in a third-person prologue to the novel, that, purposefully or not, Ignacio Agüero shot his wife and decided to conceal the murder, claiming instead that Blanca Agüero died by drowning. The two biologists were by themselves at the Ciénaga Swamp on 8 September 1948, tracking down a rare avian specimen. While Reina, one of the Agüero sisters, upon seeing the body inside a coffin, grows up with the strong suspicion that Ignacio, her purported father, was in fact the murderer, Constancia, the other, is unaware of such a crime, believing until the very end that Blanca had shot herself. This is the version that she learns as a child from Ignacio himself, who demands that she keep the secret of the "true" cause of her mother's demise.

The quest for veracity is at the center of the novel, pulling together the various strands, in each of which a questioning takes place. Emanating from a host of characters, comments to this effect dot the narrative. As Ignacio—ironically indeed—declares just before taking his life two years after Blanca's murder, "The quest for truth . . . is far more glorious than the quest for power" (*Agüero Sisters* 13). For her part Reina, who "can stand anything but lies" (36), revels at the admiration "the image of the image of herself" elicits in men. By the same token, Reina's daughter, Dulcita, wishes only that "we could dismiss all the false histories pressed upon us, accumulate our true history like a river in rainy season" (144).

However, certainties and lies prove to be difficult to separate for all three generations; they appear to be as connected as will and fate, health and disease, survival and extinction, life and death. Such a notion is captured in an oxymoronic assertion: "We are all radiant with disease" (43). The true account, in the novel, is buried both figuratively and physically. The diary in which Ignacio Agüero offers details of the crime has been buried in Cuban soil, specifically at a farm belonging to the family in Camagüey, on the eastern part of the island. Entries from the diary are interspersed throughout the present of the narrative, focused on the 1990s, so that it is not until the end, when Constancia hires someone to take her back to Cuba illegally on a boat, that a thorough account of Blanca's assassination is recovered.

The factual is also hidden behind images that mask true identities and appearances. After marrying twice in Cuba and leaving the island with her second husband, Constancia has managed to become a successful saleswoman of beauty products at a department store in New York. Later on, after her husband sells his tobacco shop and they resettle in Miami, Constancia relies on her entrepreneurial skills to create a complete line of face and body lotions called "Cuerpo de Cuba." With her treatments "Ojos de Cuba," "Senos de Cuba," "Cuello de Cuba," "Codos de Cuba," and "Muslos de Cuba," Constancia meets the needs of clients who seek to hide some imperfection, including those related to aging. As she remarks, her beauty line can have a magical effect: "A dab of concealer and powder, and the need for surgery is temporarily camouflaged" (19). Constancia, nonetheless, undergoes plastic surgery and, as a result, acquires her mother's face. While the transformation signals the impossibility of getting rid of the past, of severing the ties to the family's turbulent history, taking on another's identity jibes with the trope of appearance versus reality.

The novel establishes a counterpoint not only between appearance and reality but also between the eastern and western parts of the island, identified with contrasting agricultural products. The persistent tension recalls Cuban ethnologist Fernando Ortiz's arguments in *Contrapunteo cubano del tabaco y el azúcar*. In Ortiz's analysis, the two agricultural products leading the Cuban economy at the time he wrote his essay generated strikingly different ways of life, each relying on different production means and labor configurations. Tobacco, an indigenous plant grown in *vegas* that require no machinery, only steady, constant supervision, resulted in a strong attachment to the land. Its cultivation was based on free white labor. The tobacco-growing areas were settled by white immigrants from Spain, especially the Canary Islands, and by peasants with roots in these areas. Sugar, on the other hand, a perennial grass imported at the beginning of the sixteenth century that thrived in Cuban soil, called for industrial plants, sometimes large-scale *ingenios* or sugar mills, which perforce necessitated large contingents of workers. Unlike tobacco, these could be administered by *hacendados* from abroad and could easily become prey to foreign control, alien to Cuban values and interests. Espousing an unwavering nationalist ideology, Ortiz was concerned with the rising influence of a U.S.-dominated sugar market—on both the producing and receiving ends. Just as important, the sugar mills employed large numbers of black slaves as disposable labor, crucial for their smooth functioning. Hence, as Ortiz points out, there are racial overtones to the modern production of tobacco and sugar. Manifold significations, therefore, underlie each of these two key products of the Cuban economy.[13]

Racial dimensions of the counterpoint are of primary interest in this particular reading of García's novel. It is worth noting how some of their ramifications play out in geographical terms, for if the western part of the island is typically identified with tobacco, the central and eastern sections gave rise to a proliferation of sugar mills. This is far from saying that each region was exclusively dedicated to tobacco or sugar, but that there was a predominance of one over the other in each. Robert Dyer, for instance, states in an article published in 1956 that "eastern Cuba has three-fourths of the new mills founded in the country" (179). He adds that "since Independence, the great economic activity is along the eastern frontier" (179), that is, where sugar is produced.

In *The Agüero Sisters*, Reinaldo Agüero, Ignacio's father, becomes a *lector* at El Cid Cigar Manufacturers Company in the western province of Pinar del Río after settling in Cuba from Galicia. It is in Pinar del Río where he and his wife resided when, the day of Ignacio's birth at the onset of the Republic, the first president of Cuba visited their town. As *lector*, the elder Agüero used to read Spanish classics such as *El Cid* and Cervantes's *Don Quixote* (as well as Dickens and Hugo, given the *lectores*' intellectual curiosity and well-rounded culture) to the cigar makers while they cut and rolled the leaves to manufacture the world-famous *habanos*. In the novel, there is a reference, tinged with nostalgia, to the changing climate around 1918 when sugar cane growers became millionaires overnight thanks to soaring prices on the world market, while tobacco workers were losing their jobs to falling tobacco prices (113). Ortiz's concerns would seem to echo in passages like this one.

Whereas the Agüero family background recalls a purely Hispanic, white environment such as the one associated with tobacco, as soon as Ignacio falls under the spell of Blanca Mestre, the racial landscape shifts toward the miscegenation that is an essential part of Cuban culture—as if "sugar," with its multiplicity of meanings, were taking over. As Stephen Knadler notes, "Blanca serves as a sign of an alternative Cuban history"—due to her race as well as to her indifference toward gender norms and expectations. The daughter of a *mulata* descended, in part, from French colonists who had settled in Santiago de Cuba after fleeing Haiti in 1791, Blanca is a stunning mixed-blood who unselfconsciously breaks the hearts of men; even calculating, shrewd natural scientists lose their minds over her. She is also a dedicated biologist whom we get to know, by and large, through Ignacio, who offers an eyewitness account of Blanca's actions and enigmatic behavior, an "other's" behavior, in the diary he keeps and later buries. Ignacio, though, merely records what he watches, for he seems incapable of understanding the reasons behind Blanca's actions, including her unapologetic and bewildering disregard for motherhood, at the same time that he tries to "'capture' and possess her like so many of his scientific specimens" (Derrickson 484).

Blanca abandons Constancia five months after giving birth and comes back two and a half years later, carrying another child, Reina, whose father, it turns out, is an unidentified black man. Critic Amparo Marmolejo-McWatt claims that Blanca—in contrast to Ignacio's white, Hispanic heritage—stands for Oshún, one of the Santería orishas, who is recognized in the Catholic religion as Our Lady of Charity of El Cobre, patroness of Cuba. Oshún is "the independent *mulata* no man can resist. She is the symbol of *Cubanidad*" (Marmolejo-McWatt 90).

There are numerous references to Our Lady of Charity in the novel, beginning with the date of her feast, 8 September. Blanca is murdered on 8 September 1948. Moreover, it is forty-three years later, in September 1991, when Constancia decides to return to Cuba to recover Ignacio's diary and Heberto's body after his abortive attempt to invade Cuba. On 8 September she arrives in Camagüey, where a procession is under way, awash with the color associated with Oshún: "All the girls wear yellow dresses. Have flowers braided through their hair. The boys, also in yellow, carry a statue of their beloved patron saint. Others offer pumpkins and strands of amber beads to La Virgen de la Caridad del Cobre" (*Agüero Sisters* 296). At that moment, Constancia remembers that it was on this day that her son Silvestre was born thirty-four years earlier.

Recurrent references to the celebration point to the foundational narrative built upon the reported apparition, in the early seventeenth century, of Our Lady of Charity to three Cuban nationals. Different versions of the legend identify them as two Indians and one black or as an Indian, a black, and a white man. It was in the town of El Cobre, "the only fully recognized Afro-Cuban *pueblo* in the island's history," according to María Elena Díaz

(49), where the shrine to the effigy was built, following her apparition in the sea. The story became an emblem of the Cuban nation. The dark-skinned Lady empowering the races that make up Cuban identity could be all but dismissed as "a unitary (and modern) symbol of Creole syncretism as well as an early and immanent manifestation of the (ontological) essence of the Cuban nation—of *cubanía*" (María Elena Díaz 46). She is the embodiment of Cuban syncretism. Whereas renowned cultural critics such as Ortiz, José Juan Arrom, and Antonio Benítez-Rojo as well as Cuban historian Olga Portuondo have read Our Lady of Charity in these terms, a sanitized version emerges on the U.S. side of the Straits. The filtering is reflected in a large mural painted in the hermitage built to the Virgin in Miami by the Cuban exile community. Underscoring the role played by "major figures" of the Cuban nation, the mural depicts a rather truncated narrative:

> In the visual text of this mural, Indians are relegated to the initial screen of colonization and blacks perhaps to the legendary figure in the mythical canoe. Allegedly, forty-four (racially invisible and mostly nineteenth-century) "major figures" in a conventional "great-men approach" to Cuban historical tradition spin around the central Christian Marian/mother symbol of the nation. (María Elena Díaz 46)

The critic further writes that the Miami chapel "has come to represent a diasporic space of Cubans in exile, one often also charged with strong political meanings regarding the present and the past" (46). However, diasporic spaces cannot presume to be terse, homogeneous, and monologic. Against the "orthodox, conventional, and conservative formulation of the nation" (46) imprinted in the mural, progressive diasporic voices may want to symbolically present a human landscape more in tune with the mixed-race portrayal of the nation through Our Lady of Charity. This is the case with García.

Remarkably, it is in El Cobre where, in December 1990, Reina, the offspring of Blanca, a *mestiza*, and a black Cuban man, finds herself working as an electrician. Shortly after an accident occurs in the mines where the former slaves were brutally exploited centuries earlier, Reina decides to leave the island and join her sister in the United States. It is the accident at El Cobre that prompts Reina's decision to follow her sister in exile and, in so doing, sets in motion Constancia's eventual return to Cuba. Being close to the eastern end of the island, El Cobre, chiefly, but also Santiago de Cuba and Camagüey reverberate with the racial politics alluded to by Fernando Ortiz in connection with sugar.

If sugar is in fact packed with racial meanings, as Ortiz declares, by situating the mixed-blood Agüero women in the sugar-producing region of Cuba and making them play a major role, the narrative projects a *mestiza* paradigm—in the feminine, given the obvious gender concerns. It simultaneously tones down the white Hispanic components, such as those depicted in the Miami shrine's mural. Being of Spanish stock, this is likely the white culture juxtaposed with tobacco as well as, one may add, with masculinity, as it is Ignacio who harkens back to Pinar del Río and Heberto who is the owner of a tobacco shop in New York City where he illegally keeps a steady supply of *habanos*. The gesture underscores the syncretic character of Cuban culture and religion. Simultaneously, Santería, the Afro-Cuban syncretic religion, is practiced widely by many a character in the novel. Constancia, Reina's lover, and even Ignacio honor it when dealing with obscure affairs of the heart.

Thus it would appear that the cultural thrust of the novel is folded into the notion of *transculturation*, a term coined by Fernando Ortiz. As it is widely known, Ortiz proposed the adoption of this neologism, which best describes, in his view, the outcome of the cultural negotiation that takes place in zones of contact such as Cuba. For Ortiz, the label that was used to describe a similar type of transaction at the time—*acculturation*—failed to capture the complexity of the process. Unlike acculturation, which implied leaving behind a native culture to adapt to a host culture, transculturation stood for mixing. As it is widely known, he used the metaphor of the *ajiaco*, or Cuban stew, to describe the mixing, as the many ingredients that go into the stew keep their unique flavor yet produce entirely different fare.

Various foundational stories such as the counterpoint between tobacco and sugar, the Our Lady of Charity icon, and the concept of transculturation resonate in García's novel, providing a usable past that calls into question the silencing of the *mestiza* by violent means, exposes the myth of whiteness of the Cuban community at home and abroad, and showcases the role of diasporic women in bringing these issues to the fore. In the latter respect, it should be noted that it is Constancia, not Heberto, who retrieves the diary containing the story of the Agüero family. It is Constancia, not Heberto, the invader, who brings to light the true account of her *mulata* mother's death at the hands of her father, the Creole ornithologist. And it is Constancia, a Cuban American harboring qualms about exile politics and the sterile nostalgia found in the Miami enclave, who becomes the point person for the final elucidation of the secret. As Dalia Kandiyoti writes, "Constancia's nostalgia and return differ from the scripted versions about invasion, reconquest, and recovery that dominate the collective imagination of Garcia's exiles. For Constancia's return is marked by reconciliation with her history" (88). The critic adds that Constancia's return "leads instead to an understanding of the past as a complex construction, both an edifice of lies and a landscape of competing, not single, truths" (89). The concluding episode would seem to assign an important role to a character that, although coming in from the cold north, seeks to literally excavate the truth.

Giving this interpretation another turn of the screw, the passage suggests a role for transnational subjects in the overhauling of national stories. And certain readings of transculturation would allow for the kind of participation that the novel insinuates. For instance, for Rafael Rojas, Ortiz's metaphor stresses "the blending of cultures," not a "process of synthesis" or "teleological narrative," as it is commonly understood ("Transculturation and Nationalism" 70). Rather than reaching a climax, the process is ongoing. Rojas's assessment of Ortiz's concept seeks to emphasize that national culture is not the outcome of a teleological process. From this vantage point, "[t]he infinite migratory tissue of Cuban society always 'differs,' and will always differ, 'from the consolidation of a definitive and basic national homogeneity'" (70).[14] It follows, then, that in this time of increasing migration worldwide, and specifically in Cuba, the diaspora could be taken as another element—another ingredient—contributing to the (trans)national stew. The *ajiaco* can be enriched by the contribution of the diaspora.

Hence García engages with a borrowed history that can be turned into a usable past and present, a usable past that is more racialized and woman-centered than many would acknowledge. Her vicarious return through Constancia reveals a desire to hold on to that history. The act of going back reaffirms a space for the apt exploration of a past not written in stone, subject to undergoing revisions, even if from abroad. The author stakes her right to a Cuban imaginary rich with syncretic, hybrid symbols and redeploys it in ways that demonstrate a diasporic consciousness. In this case, the diasporic viewpoint brings to light issues of race and gender germane to a Cuban nation that has often sanitized their significance.

Days of Awe: Highlighting Non-Mainstream Religions

While the previous novel served to highlight the intersection of gender and *mestizaje*, my aim in this section on Achy Obejas's *Days of Awe* is to examine how the novel's intense probing of the marginalized Sephardic tradition in Cuba overlaps with a diasporic identity. I argue that the exploration of the Jewish faith long either repressed or practiced underground by the protagonist's ancestors on the island unpredictably throws the main character into a journey of self-discovery. The search culminates with the embrace of a rediscovered national and religious identity, gainfully attained by surveying a usable past that safeguards collective memory. As the novel's narrator points out, referring to herself and her father, they are "afflicted with a feverish kind of racial memory that compels [them] to constantly glance backward" (39). The protagonist uses this "affliction" to her advantage.

As in the previous two novels, there are historical references that serve as a backdrop to the story. The protagonist and narrator, Ale, short for Alejandra San José, was born on the day of the triumphal march into Havana of the revolutionary army led by Fidel Castro in 1959. Unhappy with the turn of events, her parents decide to leave Cuba on a boat provided by her father's boss, a Jew. The timing of the family's escape from Cuba coincides with the initial skirmishes of the invading army financed by the Kennedy administration to destabilize the Castro government in 1961. The failed intervention would go down in history as the Bay of Pigs invasion, although the Cubans would name it Playa Girón, the site where the invading forces suffered their final defeat. Years later, in 1980, Ale's paternal grandfather is found behind the gates of the Peruvian embassy, taking part in the incident that triggered the Mariel boatlift. Finally, the son of Moisés Menach, Ale's father's best friend, loses his life trying to reach U.S. shores during the raft crisis of 1994. The dates (1961, 1980, and 1994) highlight key moments in the history of the Cuban exodus.

The historical intricacy conveyed in the novel is not fortuitous. It is meant to accentuate the links between past and present, the private and the public, and Cuba and the United States. In addition, Castro himself makes a cameo appearance in an episode set in 1939. The episode occurs in the countryside, where Alejandra's ancestors settled near the Castros' farm in a rural area near Mayarí, in Oriente Province. A very young Fidel is astounded when he comes face to face with the young Enrique, who is swimming naked in a nearby river. As a Jew, Enrique is circumcised, and this is what surprises Fidel, whom the novel presents as ignorant of the Jewish religion, like most of the folks in that Eastern region. In the novel, even the future Máximo Líder, who twenty years later would take over the reins of the multicultural nation, is unaware of the Jewish presence on the island.

One of the narrative strands of the novel surveys the unacknowledged history of Sephardic Jews in Cuba through the San José family, some of whose members practice Jewish rites. The crypto-Sephardic, converted family recalls a legacy of the Inquisition that almost wiped out Jewish life in the Americas and, before that, in Spain. Armed with historical memory, it is no wonder that most of the San José clan is in a bind: "to survive as Jews they had to pretend to be otherwise" (*Days of Awe* 121). They had to hide or camouflage whatever remaining rites the family had managed to preserve. Only Enrique's grandfather, Ytzak, wants to keep the flame of their religious faith from dwindling, taking it upon himself to instill his beliefs and values in his grandson. Trying to perpetuate his faith, he separates Enrique from his parents and takes him to Havana, where there is a more widespread recognition of the miscellaneous religions that have contributed to making Cuban culture a unique mix. In the capital, they would be able to be openly Jewish.

Despite Ytzak's efforts, though, there is no doubt that Enrique wears his Jewishness uneasily. At one point, frightened by a mob that hails Hitler, Enrique is asked point-blank whether he is a Jew. Not only does he deny it but he also joins the mob, gesturing along. While the incident constitutes the only time that Enrique actually lies about being a Jew, he is far from proclaiming his identity at any time, always keeping it to himself, maintaining it *sotto voce* until the end of his life, when he finally "comes out."

Interpreting Enrique's silence as a purely individual act misses the point, for secrets interact with larger collective predicaments. They are "negotiated: continual decisions about whom to tell, how much to tell, and whom not to tell describe social worlds, and the shape and weight of interactions therein" (White 11). Secrets pulsate with broader implications, as marginalized populations are well aware. As stated, Enrique's efforts to conceal his identity are due to the record of repression of Jews in Spain as well as the New World. Although not known as an anti-Semitic society, Cuba had its bouts of openly discriminating toward the Jews, who were called *polacos* (Polish) in popular parlance. According to Margalit Bejarano, discrimination stemmed primarily from the Spanish upper-class minority in Cuban society during the prerevolutionary period, the Republic, portrayed as the past in Obejas's novel. However, the fact that Cuba was the only Latin American country voting against the partition of Palestine in 1947 suggests that there were differences of opinion among its citizens. Not all Cubans backed the establishment of the state of Israel. Although the situation improved with the 1948 election of Carlos Prío Socarrás and even further with the return to power of Fulgencio Batista in 1952, there were nonetheless periods of anti-Semitism orchestrated by the Spanish, pro-Arab, and Lebanese sectors of Cuban society, as well as, to some extent, the Catholic Church. Jews did not participate in public life and preferred to keep to themselves, joining mostly Jewish social clubs and synagogues. There was some ambivalence toward Jews in Cuban society.[15]

Given this context, it is not surprising that, in the novel, Enrique wants his daughter Ale to be thoroughly "Cuban" (*Days of Awe* 9) from the start, being evasive at all times about her Jewish Sephardic roots. He most likely perceives Cuban identity to be of one piece, within precise contours and therefore less problematic than his own Jewish identity. Enrique wants Ale not to struggle with an identity that by its very nature is ambiguous, as the literature on this subject indicates, due to its long history of diasporic locations. Using the work of Daniel and Jonathan Boyarin as a source, critic Caroline Bettinger-López writes about the interstitial nature of Jewish identity, which by definition circumvents straightforward categories of analysis such as the national, genealogical, and religious (142). Because she is just "Cuban," Ale's upbringing in the United States is devoid of references to her Sephardic background. She discovers only belatedly and accidentally her father's worship practices, and it is only after her first trip to Cuba in 1987 that she begins to dig deeper into that vital part of her heritage.

Ale's return trips to Cuba in the late 1980s and 1990s allow her to activate her national Cuban identity through an exploration of the Sephardic religion of her ancestors. In a way similar to Ruth Behar's in *An Island Called Home* (see chapter 2), Ale discovers anew on the island what it is to be Cuban by coming into contact with her Jewish heritage and reclaiming both identities. It is Enrique's old friend and confidant, Moisés Menach, whose family becomes Ale's support network in Havana, who leads her down the path of awareness at the request of Enrique. In a letter, he asks Moisés to fill her in. Through Moisés, she learns about her father's faith and also about a Cuba steeped in the Special Period after the dismantling of the Soviet Union. Obejas uses a familiar template, in fact, to offer a fresh perspective on the relationship between Cuba, Jewish identity, and diaspora. According to Kandiyoti, who has published about the role of Sephardism in Latina Literature, "Sephardism works to bring together Jewish and Latina diaspora literature and criticism, which are seemingly disconnected but actually overlapping narrative imaginaries" ("Sephardism in Latina Literature" 235). This is what Achy Obejas and Kathleen Alcalá, whose novels are the focus of Kandiyoti's essay, show in their work.

Ale's first trip to Cuba after twenty-six years takes place at the behest of a group of progressive Chicago politicians and activists. As fearful exiles, her parents are reluctant to let her go, fearing the worst. Ale appeases them by saying that traveling to Cuba is no different for her than going to Spain, Bolivia, or Senegal. As a child in Chicago, she used to study the maps of Havana, learning about its grid, but she quickly outgrew the need. Havana faded and her "Cuban self vanished" (*Days of Awe* 56) to the point where she considers her being Cuban as "an accident of timing and geography" (67). A disengaged returnee in Havana, she assumes the role of a mere interpreter:[16]

> If a local Cuban asked me a direct question, I'd quickly translate the words into English like an automaton, and if they protested that it was meant for me personally, I'd define the rules of my job: That I was invisible, that I had no opinion or judgment, that I was there simply to convert one language into another and that they should never address me as an individual but always focus their pronouncements on the other person. (76)

Using her profession as a buffer, as a subterfuge for not getting personally involved, Ale is left with no words or emotions of her own, and she does nothing but observe from a safe distance. She is conscious of her otherness, due not so much to her accent as to the cadence of her enunciations and to her privilege as a visitor. However, once she comes into contact with Menach and is drawn into his sprawling family, Ale begins to develop an interest in both her family's past and present-day Cuba. It is Menach's charge to slowly but surely shed light on Ale's Sephardic roots, seeking to fill "the void of memory for Sephardic Cuban Jews" (Johnson 37). At the same time, he and his relatives make Ale aware of Cuba's day-to-day struggle in the hair-raising 1990s. After Ale's first trip to Cuba, she reconstructs her ancestors' history from the letters that Menach sends to her. As the scion of the San José family, she becomes the repository of its history in the diaspora.[17]

This interweaving of experiences, coming from subjects of both the Jewish and Cuban diasporas, is what Kandiyoti calls a "connective" thematic component of Latina/Sephardic literature. She describes it as one of the narrative strategies deployed in these works. These texts, Kandiyoti claims, are connective because they capitalize on the intersection between Sephardic Jewish history and the history of the Americas ("Sephardism" 240). Diaspora, Kandiyoti seems to imply, fuels this kind of reflection about making connections. And indeed, at a very concrete level, this is what Ale does when she draws parallels between the Jewish and Cuban diasporas, backed up by the oft-repeated claim that Cubans are the Jews of the Caribbean (*Days of Awe* 103). For Licia Fiol-Matta, the idea of return provides the main bridge between the two diasporas in *Days of Awe*, since the novel creates "a parallel between the biblical prohibition of return to the promised land, and the difficulty that Cuban diasporans have experienced with ... physically returning to Cuba after the Revolution, even for a visit" (711). Ale's mother, for one, is denied a permit that would allow her to enter the island after Ale's father dies.

Still, the narrative downplays whatever difficulties might ensue from the political rift and allows the protagonist to reach Cuban territory more than once, since it is on the island that the secrets about the San José family are disclosed and Ale reclaims her homeland. Fiol-Matta argues that the novel promotes a notion of Cubanness as essential to the self and it is only in Cuba where one can come to an understanding of national and cultural identity (711). That may be true, but in all fairness it needs to be clarified that once Ale gains awareness of her hybrid identity, she engages Cuba from a diasporic position that does not take labels for granted. This is the conclusion Carolyn Wolfenzon implicitly reaches in her insightful essay about *Days of Awe*, in which she claims that indetermination is what best describes the state in which both Ale and her father live (108). Partaking of more than one tradition, as diasporic subjects they defy strict definition. Little by little, Ale embraces a diaspora consciousness, part of which leads her to actively take part in concrete transnational transactions. We see her, for instance, sending vitamins, food, and jeans for Menach's children and grandchildren, corresponding with them, making telephone calls, and exchanging family news and photographs. At no point does she seek to return to Cuba permanently.

Through the Menach family, Ale makes peace with her Cuban self and becomes familiar with the political situation on the island, about which she is increasingly critical. If prior to her first trip Havana had faded, by the end of the novel it has come back to her in full color. It is to Havana where she takes Enrique's ashes after he is cremated. Ale is asked by her father to spread his ashes over the flowing waters of Havana Bay. On his deathbed in Chicago, Enrique finally concedes his faith in front of his daughter and asks her to say kaddish (Hebrew prayers for the dead) for him. On this occasion, Moisés Menach closes the circle and not only takes Ale to a Sephardic synagogue in the capital but also fulfills his vow to Enrique to not withhold any information from Ale. Hence both Enrique and Ale reach the end of their journeys of self-discovery and acceptance. Having "come out" with their own complex identities, they have both healed.

In this, her second novel, Obejas reviews the history of Jews in Cuba through the microcosm of a family to offer her tale of displacement and redemption in a new land. The novel narrates the process of self-discovery through which Ale gradually comes to terms with her own multiculturalism (Goldman 69). Obejas's choice of title befits the outcome. The expression "days of awe" or days of repentance refers to the period in the Jewish calendar from Rosh Hashanah, the Jewish New Year, to Yom Kippur, the Day of Atonement. In Dara E. Goldman's words, the title of the novel "underscores the process of self-examination and awareness that the protagonist realizes" (67). Expanding upon its significance, Wolfenzon writes that the days of repentance are not part of the Hebrew calendar and therefore fall outside linear, normal time. Obejas uses this time out of time, the critic claims, as "a metaphor of diasporic Cubans and explores it as a conflictive but enriching place where the multiple elements that constitute identity can become integrated" (105). In sum, the days of awe designate a time to mend one's ways, a time for the regeneration of personal and collective self-knowledge from a religious point of view, an undertaking that extends to other areas of the self. Appropriately, Obejas uses the cloak of the Jewish religion, with its evocation of diaspora, to offer a secular Cuban-American tale of self-awareness, rebirth, and growth.

Loving Che: Highlighting Revolutionary Icons

Of the three authors, Ana Menéndez is the youngest and the only one from the second generation. Yet most of her fiction revolves, thus far, around the Cuban-American population in the South Florida enclave of Little Havana. Her first short story collection, *In Cuba I Was a German Shepherd,* was praised for its sensitivity toward exile angst, felt through characters that keep their dignity in the face of adversity. The title of the book, as well as of the main story, refers to a mutt that brags about having been a purebred in Cuba. The joke illuminates the Cuban exiles' penchant for magnifying losses as they transitioned into their new milieu. Asked by Álvarez Borland about the prominent place of the older exile generation in her writing, Menéndez said: "Maybe I just needed to exorcize those ancients before I could get on with my own story." And she added: "In fact, this novel I'm working on now [*The Last War*] begins in a very autobiographical vein. It eventually veers off into total invention, but it is interesting . . . that it took two books before I could get down to my 'own' story. Of course, the novel has nothing at all to do with Cuba" ("Crossing the Crest" 178–79).

Menéndez's first novel, though, has a great deal to do with Cuba and the Cuban-American community in the United States; in fact, that is its centerpiece. Her empathy for Cuban exiles makes her choice of subject, Che Guevara, all the more mystifying. At the same time that Che is idolized by multitudes around the world as the archetypal symbol of revolutionary fervor, many who fled Cuba in the early 1960s remember him as a cold-blooded man involved in firing squads and summary executions. He is both revered and reviled, depending on the lens. It is therefore astonishing that a young writer with direct links to the Cuban community would turn Che into a character with erotic appeal. Here, *eros* and *epicus* appear side by side. Like *The Agüero Sisters,* Menéndez's novel seems to open up a space for counternarratives.[18]

Published in 2003, *Loving Che* has a minimalist plot. The novel, more meditative than action-driven, is about Teresa de la Landre, a visual artist who presumably had a love affair with Che Guevara, the narrator's putative father. Neither the reader nor the narrator gets to know Teresa except through her writing. Teresa allowed her baby daughter to leave for Miami with her grandfather while she stayed behind waiting for the return of Che from one of his trips abroad. The daughter, who remains nameless in the novel, returns to Cuba only many years later as a young woman insistently looking for her mother. She is induced once again to go to the island after receiving a package that contains Teresa's diary, some photographs, and cryptic verses. The diary, taking up a good portion of the novel, is rooted in a history that goes back to the 1940s and stretches well into the 1990s, however briefly, when Teresa is in her sixties. Thanks to this account, the story we read serves as an overlay to a historical canvas that affords a usable past.

For obvious reasons, official history rarely acknowledges the personal, but personal diaries, a genre associated with women's writing, can easily incorporate public events even if, as Álvarez Borland argues, they do so in order to stress "the importance of the individual's story over the collective official record we call history" ("Figures of Identity" 38). The story Teresa writes about is tied to Cuba's history of revolutionary struggle. A daughter of privilege, Teresa is alert all the same to political developments on the island and feels attracted to figures that played an important role in those developments. These are figures such as Eddy Chibás and José Antonio Echeverría, who sought to overturn the corrupt political system during the Republican period in the first half of the twentieth century. In fact, Teresa's self-awareness as a woman is connected to her growing awareness of this history: "Eddy Chibás, unlucky Eddy who even now rests under an unlucky sign, is the first man I love" (*Loving Che* 33). Chibás, the object of young Teresa's infatuation, is only the first link in a chain of attractions that betray Teresa's interest in men who played a significant role in public affairs.[19]

Later, student leader José Antonio Echeverría's collapse at the beginning of the insurrection against Batista, during the attack on the presidential palace in 1957, keeps Teresa awake for two nights while barely surviving on milk and sugar (44).[20] Even though she never gets to meet Chibás nor Echeverría personally, Teresa has no trouble twisting together national and personal realms. Both leaders impact her directly. Teresa owns up to the difficulty of constructing a narrative out of disconnected events: "Memories like these remind us that life is also loose ends, small events that have no bearing on the story we come to write of ourselves" (48). But by carefully choosing key events, she passes on a personal history that can be only imperfectly understood outside those events, for in this text mother and motherland are linked.

Admittedly, this piece of fiction writing is not the first to feature a woman who abandons her child for the sake of romantic love or some other reason;

recent examples include García's *Dreaming in Cuban* and *The Agüero Sisters* as well as Isabel Allende's short story "Tosca." In her reading of *Dreaming in Cuban*, O'Reilly Herrera entwines the theme of maternal loss with national losses ("Women and the Revolution" 73). Likewise, in Menéndez's novel such despicable behavior seems tied to the historical narrative constructed by Menéndez. Teresa's extramarital affair with Che, lasting several years, is the logical culmination of her preoccupation with other famous male figures in Cuban history, legendary men who died in heartbreaking circumstances. The relationship between Teresa and Che is prefigured in those other imagined relationships.

At a metaphorical level, by stringing together the private and the public, story and history, woman and politics, the novel suggests that both mother and motherland are capable of abandoning their offspring to a tragic fate. More than a Penelope, forever awaiting the return of her lover, Teresa can be read as a metaphor for a not-too-loving nation that demands sacrifice, violence, and separation as a means of achieving the intangible goal of accomplishing a national, inclusive, and democratic community. Teresa's behavior as a detached mother is nothing but baffling if this broader context is evaded. Why would she abandon her baby by staying in Cuba? Why would she, at the same time, be infatuated with martyrs attempting to bring nationalism to fruition? Or is she simply so smitten with Che that everything else loses meaning? It would seem that *Loving Che* is in the same league as other ethnic novels that enlarge the role of the mother figure in order to make it stand for and represent broader entities such as the motherland (Davis, "Back to the Future" 62). Teresa's aberrant behavior is replicated at the national level. In the book, neither motherhood nor the motherland is for the fainthearted.

Segments of the diary revolving around the adult life of Teresa de la Landre serve as a tool for situating the iconic Che Guevara within a personal story with national overtones. One should be mindful that Che, a complex and controversial hero of global scope, but especially of the Cuban revolution, is one whom conservatives and exiles love to loathe. The hub of Cuban exile, Miami, as the narrator notes, "was not a city for romantic heroes; here, an association with the revolution was something to be hidden, denied, and ultimately forgotten" (*Loving Che* 158). Yet, by placing Che third in line after Chibás and Echeverría, both of whom inspire similarly passionate feelings in Teresa as well as deferential reactions among Cubans of all stripes,

Menéndez reclaims him as part of a genealogy that sought to effect change for the public good. Surely there must be something good in a (hi)story that a mother wants to bequeath to her child as a way of restoring what was taken away from her. As Teresa writes to her child: "I took a history from you" (155). And now she wants to give it back, in a beautifully wrapped package, with Che as a parent and a lover.[21]

While the author clings to a pantheon of heroes that is gender-scripted, she also gives Che back his human condition, much like Walter Salles's *Motorcycle Diaries* did for Che on the screen. The novel highlights Che the lover, capable of awakening Teresa to the daily sounds, sights, and smells around her, as well as arousing and fulfilling Teresa's erotic desires:

> I move to kiss him, part his lips with my tongue. He murmurs, moves his hand down my spine, down. He pulls me into his body. I let myself sink onto him. He looks up at me: My love, he murmurs. The light is beginning to fade from a window that now catches our reflection between its blinds. I am above him, watching him, this man who is not a hero or a photograph; who is only warm, smelling of moss ground, his body before me, freckled and soft, his skin tacky to the touch with dried sweat. (*Loving Che* 100–101)

As in this scene, Che appears enveloped in a mix of revolutionary halo and sensual, primordial demeanor, as if he were the earth itself: "In that small room, his smell overtakes me again: mountains and dirt and unwashed skin and heat" (96). His presence always appeals to the senses: "that smell, like wet leaves, old earth, metal" (65). Although Menéndez's Che also includes the compassionate young man who cares about the disempowered and later the *guerrillero* who has scruples about killing (if we are to believe Che the character in the novel, when he refers to one such incident), the emphasis here is on passionate, adulterous love, hence the lyrical and introspective quality of the writing. Such an intimate portrait of Che is clearly nonconventional in the exile environment and possibly in Cuba as well. Even the memoir of Hilda Gadea, Che's Peruvian first wife, entitled *My Life with Che: The Making of a Revolutionary*, overlooks the personal realm to privilege instead the political ideology to which both dedicated their lives.

The projected image is reinforced by the accompanying photographs of the *guerrillero* in a variety of situations. Often the narrative serves as a caption to the photographs, all of which seem to be authentic. Except that the photographs are reinserted into a new context, thereby "clearly reinventing Ernesto Guevara for the reader," as Álvarez Borland notes ("Figures of Identity" 38). Some project him as the public man that he was: Che speaking into a microphone; peeking into an office and clad in military fatigues; addressing the militia from atop a jeep. But other photographs portray him as a private individual: undressed from the waist up, in bed, propped on one elbow while sipping *mate*; clean shaven, with a shirt and tie and puffing on a cigar; and a final picture of Che—after he was killed. The latter photographs inject a measure of prosaic humanity into the iconic Che.

This is the Che that Teresa impresses upon the narrator, even if it may be just a fantasy. In fact, critics have noted the fictive nature of the love affair between Teresa de la Landre and Che, contending that Teresa's account is an attempt "to create a particular image of herself that she wanted her daughter to accept and remember" (Álvarez Borland, "Figures of Identity" 42). There are enough references throughout the book to history as mirage to warrant disbelief. Dr. Caraballo, a scholar of Cuban history whom the narrator consults about Teresa's diary, says at one point in the novel: "I can understand how, in the absence of a past, one might be tempted to invent history" (173). Similarly, with regard to Teresa's account of her relationship with Che, Menéndez states: "I suppose in a way Teresa's story is all about the sustaining power of fantasy" ("Crossing" 177). Although at the end we are left with no certainty about the relationship, the diary contains the story by which Teresa wanted her daughter to remember her, and this turns it into a meaningful story. Moreover, the Che that Menéndez constructs might well have been all along a persona who has little resemblance to the real Che, but the fact is that the novel has manufactured an alternate *guerrillero* with an all-too-human face. This outcome is what makes it a transgressive story in the Cuban-American context. Menéndez has picked one truth among several and turned it into a novel or into a usable past.

And what is the significance of the past for the narrator? It is to search for her mother that the narrator travels to Cuba several times prior to receiving a parcel with her mother's diary and once afterward. Her trips provide a window into the Cuba of the Special Period, suspended in tediousness and daily struggle amid the collapsing infrastructure. On her last trip, she succeeds in finding her mother's old servant, who confirms only part of the story. With regard to Teresa's affair with Che, though, she is unable to offer any proof. It is plausible, indeed, that the love affair between Teresa and Che never took place and that Teresa stayed on the island out of hope and faith for a brighter future.

Unable to ascertain an absolute truth, the narrator leaves Cuba and moves on with her life. On a trip to Paris, she goes into an antique shop where she comes across a photograph of Che, the *guerrillero* in military fatigues, standing in the forest with a camera flung across his chest. It is an image that restores the revolutionary aura to Che, placing him within a much broader public history: "There he stands for all eternity, the young soldier with a yearning to record the world that lies before him, his hands light on the camera, his eyes searching ahead" (*Loving Che* 226–27). She comes across this souvenir from her assumed past so far from home that it is as if she had found herself walking among ghosts (226). Still, the Che image that has traveled the world over finds a place in her luggage, where it helps to prop up an identity that is usable as well as portable. Grounded in the specific time and place that saw him soar, yet timeless and global, Che is part of the narrator's post-history, one she clearly claims, through her maternal side.

Hence rewriting the past has value for the narrator as well as for the enigmatic Teresa. For Menéndez, who dared tackle a sensitive subject, the vicarious return to present-day Cuba through the narrator as well as to the *Cuba de ayer* through Teresa leads to a history that bridges the personal and the collective, the private and the public, redefining the terms in which historical figures are read. While the novel falls short of creating a space for the active, public participation of women in history, it does sift recent history through a woman's eyes, offering a reappraisal of a legendary figure.

Conclusion

Written against the grain of mainstream narratives, the three examined novels are built upon returns, both literal and metaphorical. The emphasis in them is on times past. Their interest lies not in the transition between exile and ethnicity but in how to rewrite the past from the diaspora. Their gaze toward an earlier period, though, differs from the nostalgic bent among exile writers who sing the praises of a glorified nation lost in mist. Rather, it shares a semantic field with the Welsh word *hiareth*, which refers to a long-lost homeland, to pining for a home that does not quite exist. Lois Parkinson Zamora points out that the concern with the past stems from a culture that chooses not to discard it easily. While this may be accurate with regard to historical narratives in the Americas in general, our three authors' position at this moment in time, as I have argued, brings about an exploration of a past that happened in Cuba for the most part. In addition to their diasporic position, multiculturalism and the current Cuba "boom" in the United States have a bearing on their selection of subject matter.

Given their location, García, Obejas, and Menéndez are aware of the need to restore a sense of genealogy and of the importance of the imagination in achieving this goal. The manifold difficulties that they face in recovering a sense of genealogy are highlighted in the novels by various means, including the disappearance of the older characters. Notice how in the three novels considered here one or both parents pass away, and only one of natural circumstances, leaving behind orphaned, diasporic characters who often rely on diaries, letters, and photographs to fill the gaps or, conversely, to serve as a springboard to their accounts. The authors are invested in the restorative power of the written word, of literature. They seem to agree with Caren Kaplan, who writes: "When the past is displaced, often to another location, the modern subject must travel to it, as it were. History becomes something to be established and managed through... forms of cultural production" (35). The instrumental function of fiction is evident in the three novels analyzed.

The Agüero Sisters focuses on women's apprehensions and *mestizaje*. While critics have noted how García's engagement with feminist concerns comes across in the development of the novel's female characters, the actual mapping of the novel's action supports this observation. As a backdrop to the narrative is Fernando Ortiz's essay on the configuration of the sugar and tobacco industries, located in disparate regions, which serves to bring the figure of the *mestiza* to the readers' notice. *Days of Awe* foregrounds the Jewish religion to explore how such a marginalized faith can lead the novel's young female protagonist to come to terms with her Cuban subjectivity, as diasporic as her Jewish identity. And *Loving Che* highlights the figure of Che Guevara as a mythic creation that can inspire both idealistic and disparaged views of this global icon. The three therefore "go back" to Cuba and Cuban discourses and join in crafting revisionist views of Cuban cultural and political history responding to a mediated but usable past. In so doing, they broaden the limits of what is defined as Cuban.

By including the younger Menéndez in the chapter and reading her novel using a parallel approach that shows points in common, I suggest that the dividing lines between generations are not as clear-cut as the usual classifications would make them seem. Some overlapping can and does occur in this and other cases, hence validating O'Reilly Herrera's term Cub*and* for those born and raised off the island. They, too, see Cuba as distant but somehow inexplicably alluring.

6

Toward a Boomerang Aesthetic

The View from the Island

> Un día tío volvió de la otra orilla,
> cargando con su espíritu gregario,
> y ya no le dijeron más gusano,
> porque empezó a ser un comunitario.
> [One day uncle returned from the other shore,
> bringing along his gregarious spirit,
> and he was no longer called *gusano*,
> because he became a *comunitario*.]
> Frank Delgado, "La otra orilla" (1997)

> No soy de aquí,
> ya no soy de allá,
> no aprendo a vivir
> en el va y viene y va
> [I'm not from here
> I'm no longer from there,
> I'm not learning how to live
> in the comings and goings and comings.]
> David Torrens, "Ni de aquí, ni de allá" (2002)

For those who choose it, returning is nothing but the last step of an undertaking that begins with departure, the culmination of a travel experience viewed with circumspection on the island until recent times. Cubans who left in the wake of the revolution were deemed to be abandoning the motherland for good while those who stayed, bidding a final adieu, faced the monumental challenge of constructing a new society requiring their undivided attention and supreme loyalty. Accommodating émigrés was not part of the plan, so the subject was kept out of most narratives, taken up only as an aside.

The above paradigm provided the backbone for many a story, including Tomás Gutiérrez Alea's classic film, *Memories of Underdevelopment* (1968), based on the novel by Edmundo Desnoes. Readings of the film have highlighted the protagonist's dilemma as an intellectual whose life has been turned upside down by the revolution and who does his best to make sense of the turmoil brought about by the new social order. However, recent interpretations address other factors contributing to the protagonist feeling adrift. The departure of his wife, best friend, and parents throw him into a state of *insilio* or internal exile that had been bypassed in the discussion. Critics now argue that not only does the film foreground the trials of adjusting to emerging social codes; it also wrestles with the grueling impact of migration (Martínez San Miguel 209–15; Ana M. López 7).

In Gutiérrez Alea's film, migration found a way in through the back door, inconspicuously. But although at first migration took a backseat to topics considered more urgent, the subject has been gradually gaining ground both at the level of plot and in the field of hermeneutics, opening up a space for both a discourse on émigrés and its contestation and reconfiguration. As one would expect, Cubans do not speak with one voice regarding migration.

Lyrics by Cuban singers Frank Delgado and David Torrens used as epigraphs of this chapter point to noteworthy changes that have been making their way into the cultural production in Cuba with respect to views of migration as well as return, views that have a bearing on the interaction with returnees and its representation. The initial portrayals of émigrés in literature and popular culture are not cause to celebrate, relying, as they do, on overly politicized, stereotypical, and injurious images. At this stage, the need for the inclusion of émigrés in the symbolic production, due to their sheer volume and dimension in the Cuban/Caribbean context, was as desirable as their banal and disparaging treatment was undesirable. The émigré was discursively constituted in openly "injurious terms," as other liminal subjects have been portrayed. Although the phrase, from Judith Butler (123), refers to attitudes toward subjects exhibiting nonnormative sexual behaviors, its effects, as well as the nonconformist reaction it provokes, are similarly felt in other spheres. In light of the call for unity, on the one hand, and of the émigrés' involvement in attempts to oust the Castro regime, on the other, that treatment, in the case of Cuban exiles, was mediated by politics.[1]

Given that migration waves since the 1980s have been less politically driven, the depiction has evolved, acquiring more subtlety, in part because migration is no longer perceived as a treacherous or definitive act. On the contrary, displacement takes on even a constructive slant, as it allows those who leave to come back with not only material possessions but also nonmaterial assets resulting from exposure to more global ways of life. David Grubin's documentary *Havana, Havana* (aired on PBS in July 2012), on four well-liked musicians (Raúl Paz, Kelvis Ochoa, Descemer Bueno, and David Torrens) who years after having left return and perform for the Cuban public, underlines less the undeniable human cost of migration than the benefits reaped from being exposed to diverse influences around the world, capitalizing on what can be gained from that exposure. The music sphere seems to have been an advantageous recipient of the kind of thinking that, at a time of diminishing state control, values openness in recent times.

Appreciating the back and forth movement undergirds what I propose to call a boomerang aesthetic. The eclectic fusion of musical forms resulting from cultural exchange, positively appraised, contrast with the dictates to keep foreign influences at bay, especially those of the United States, during the early days of the revolution and beyond. While Cuban music has been historically a creole product, disdainful of borders or border-free, what is remarkable in post-Soviet times is the plethora of Cuban musicians who have relocated in cities around the world, each with its own musical tradition. A musical give-and-take ensues, one that is likely to make its way back to the island, especially when some of the musicians themselves come back to perform in Havana venues.[2]

The songs by Delgado, a popular Cuban singer/songwriter born in 1960, and Torrens, born in Guanabacoa in 1966, serve to illustrate some of the vexing issues. Faced with a revamped policy toward émigrés in Cuba that began to take shape in the late 1970s, the speaker in Delgado's "La otra orilla," from the album *La Habana está de bala* (1997), expresses his dumbfounded confusion using the songwriter's customary style, a combination of "aggressively critical lyrics" and "biting humor" (Shaw 44–45). The lyrics display the transmutation of the exile from a devious, shadowy figure worthy of contempt to an embraceable member of the Cuban-American community, a *comunitario*. Because family ties and friendship are of utmost importance in a majority of works dealing with returnees from a Cuban perspective—as Carlos Varela's familiar composition "Foto de familia" reminds us—the subject of "La otra orilla" is the speaker's uncle, no longer viewed as a worm or *gusano*, which was the blanket label bestowed on exiles. The lyrics unmask the motives behind the morphing of the exile, cynically pointing to the bankrupt nation's eagerness to lay its hands on the hard currency that presumably lines the pockets of the return migrant. Since the exodus has continued, the speaker notes, subsequent waves of émigrés—*marielitos* and *balseros*—are expected back, to further contribute to the nation's coffers. The return of those who left in 1980 prompts sharp comments about their mutation from scum or *escoria* to the more mellifluous *marielito*.

As if presenting the spectacle of the turnaround in lexicon alone were not enough to make the listener cringe with discomfort, the speaker alludes in passing to his own participation in mass protests directed to those who left toward the United States via the port of Mariel. The prospective émigrés were then subjected to all kinds of rebuffs on the part of co-workers, neighbors, and friends. One can only imagine what someone who was moved, for whatever reasons, to participate in the *actos de repudio* designed to sow fear and bring shame on their targets must have felt in the face of the shift marked by the deferential treatment toward the formerly despised exiles. Although many would prefer to sweep them under the rug, the despicable actions and reprimands many undertook have left an ill feeling among countless Cubans, one that moves artists and writers alike to revisit these actions time and again.

In the reprimand, as Judith Butler writes, the subject attains not only recognition but also "a certain order of social existence, in being transferred from an outer region of indifferent, questionable, or impossible being to the discursive or social domain of the subject" (122). Reprimands can actually generate disobedience and a certain empowerment (123). Indeed, the events surrounding departures from Mariel, as we shall see, come back to haunt victims and victimizers alike as those who left on a boat feel it is high time for a visit.

While Delgado's "La otra orilla" hints at some of the mutations that the figure of the exile has endured, it still draws the line between *cubano* and *comunitario*, or between those who stayed and those who fled, who find themselves on different shores. On the other hand, David Torrens's "Ni de aquí, ni de allá" introduces a more supple, transnational perspective on migration and return. The song was included in the album by the same title, released in 2001. Torrens, who left Cuba for Mexico in 1995, has moved between the two countries with apparent ease. "Ni de aquí, ni de allá" could have been inspired by his own ambivalence as a singer who wrestles with a transnational reality: "Yo no soy de aquí / Ya no soy de allá / No aprendo a vivir / en el va y viene y va," the refrain states. [I'm not from here / I'm no longer from there / I'm not learning how to live / in the comings and goings and comings.][3] The stanzas waver between the advantages and disadvantages of leading such a life, as well as addressing the roots of his nomadic existence, which can be attributed to either a personal relationship that fell apart or a paternalistic socialist state: "Me acostumbraste a comer de tu mano / Cual perro manso y feliz de su dueño." [You got me used to eating from your hand / like a friendly dog, happy with his master.] Consequently, the speaker now distrusts love and feels dehumanized due to his uprootedness: "Y aunque viajo por el mundo / soy menos humano / ya no encuentro amor tan grande / y si hoy me lo dan ya no lo comprendo." [Bumming around the world / has made me less human / I no longer find love so healthy / and if they gave it to me today, I wouldn't understand it anymore.] Yet he is the captain of his wandering ship.

Torrens sings from Mexico (*aquí*) toward Cuba (*allá*) as he moves between the two countries, fully aware of the challenges of going back and forth. Far from glorifying his newfound freedom, Torrens acknowledges the tribulations of being from neither here nor there. But because of the speaker's mobility, this song becomes an example of self-representation. There is no need for someone else, grounded in Cuba, to imagine what it is like to come or to go. It is interesting how, at this point in post-Soviet Cuba, the increased fluidity inherent to two-way travel bears on issues of representation and self-representation. Thanks to the fluidity, the returning émigré that was the object of representation is now in charge of the utterance. He who was the "other" is now an actor, a potential agent of material and symbolic changes.

The subject of this chapter is of principal interest to observers of return experiences. As Juan Flores notes, "Beyond what the returnee encounters it is necessary to ask what the society encounters in the returnee, and what impact this presence has on the life of the country and place of origin" (36). The chapter sets out to review an array of examples from the literature, feature films, documentaries, and lyrics from popular songs in order to parse that presence. Returning is never easy, with the same critic describing the reception in the "home" country, in general terms for all émigrés of the Hispanic Caribbean, as a complex situation where "[i]ntense emotions mingle: rejection and resentment alternate with acceptance and inclusion... a place is made at the table, but not without lingering discomfort and suspicions" (45). Anders H. Stefansson, too, makes more than one reference to widely diverse contexts where the social distance between returnees and "stayees" can only be described as fraught (9–10). Even descriptions of the creation of returnee enclaves and the "re-diasporization" process that some returnees have experienced in the homeland find their way into the literature (10). Cuban émigrés are not alone in facing a thorny reencounter.

Additionally, this chapter seeks to demonstrate the striking changes detectable in the discursive representation and self-representation of returnees on the island, as illustrated in the above lyrics. An arc is clearly traced between beginning and end of the experiments on representation, with each migratory wave unwittingly taking on a different burden, largely determined by the historical context informing its flight from the island and first official responses to that flight. There is no question that also informing the representation is the moment at which it is taken up. Both temporalities dialectically influence the thrust of the representation.

In the works that I have examined, exiles who left voluntarily in the 1960s and 1970s are stand-ins for an antinationalist, opportunistic, and materialist culture. Some of these characters abandoned their children to their fate for selfish reasons, and others have obscure, twisted motives for returning. The sons and daughters of the first exiles are not to blame for the decision made by their parents to leave and therefore are seen in a different light. These are the Cubans of the one-and-a-half generation, who have received their share of mixed attention in the literature. These being the book's main concern, I have deemed it appropriate in any case to provide a wider context so as to account for a changing perspective. The next migration wave, represented by the *marielitos*, is part of a different dynamic that still wrestles with the mass rejection to which they were originally subjected, although at this stage the dichotomies informing earlier representations begin to taper off. The response to the departure through Mariel and subsequent ones affords more flexibility and openness in the representation, becoming at times humorous and lighthearted.

Presently, emigration is less of a politically charged issue, and characters do not appear as tainted by their wish to flee.[4] Whereas this change began to take shape in the 1990s (D. Díaz 38), the trend has become more pronounced in the new millennium, especially when some of the artists who spend time abroad are involved in formulating counterdiscourses framing the signification and value of migration. These artists' self-proclaimed identity enables a different formula for self-representation, one that encompasses transnational, global processes impacting cultural practices. From neither here nor there is how singer David Torrens describes his status. Another well-known singer, Descemer Bueno, owns a home in Miami, but his performances require frequent travel to Cuba and Spain. Musical traditions found in all of these places contribute to the hybridity that characterizes Bueno's repertoire (Borges-Triana 105). Hopscotching across continents and hemispheres is now routine practice for these and many other Cuban singers, as musicologist Susan Thomas wrote in 2005.

The cover of Habana Abierta's 2005 CD album *Boomerang* evokes a similar mobility. It identifies three cities, Havana, Miami, and Madrid, on a colorful boomerang whose outline recalls the contours of the island. The curved shape is surrounded by water, across which the peripatetic object may be ricocheting, always on the move. Although the song is actually about a love triangle, the album cover transposes the triangle to a bright, imaginary map.

The same curved object occupies center stage in an installation by visual artist Abel Barroso titled *Teoría de tránsito del arte cubano*, part of the collection of the Museo Nacional de Bellas Artes in Havana. In this 1995 piece, a number of small boomerangs raggedly delineate the silhouette of the island, each carrying the name of a visual artist of Barroso's generation (Flavio Garciandía, the late Belkis Ayón, Tonel, and José Bedia, among others). Some of these artists have temporarily or permanently emigrated, thereby justifying the presence of objects conventionally associated with travel, including airmail envelopes and stamps (however rare their use has become in the digital age), plane tickets, suitcases, and blimps. The boomerangs that only imperfectly delimit the outline of Cuba evoke the return of those who left, opening up insular space to ideas and objects brought in through correspondence and personal contact. The arched artifacts can easily be converted into bridges if held upright, but the conversion, with the inherent fixity of the bridge, does little to replicate the flowing movement that the boomerang outlines and that is at the heart of this aesthetic.

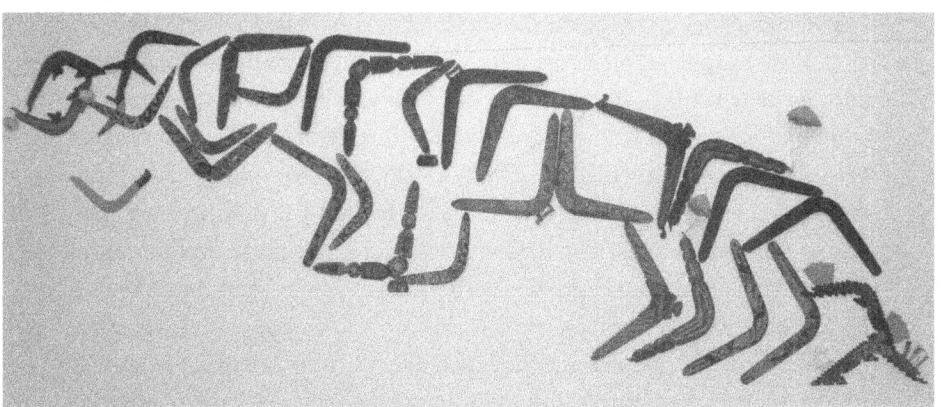

Figure 6.1. Abel Barroso, *Teoría de tránsito del arte cubano* (1995). Woodcut, paper, print, objects. Photograph by Vitalina Alfonso. Part of the collection of the Museo Nacional de Bellas Artes, Havana.

As a work of art, Barroso's *Theory of the Transit of Cuban Art* connotes rather than denotes, seeming to interrogate long-established paradigms of severance between those who left and those who remained on the island. Indeed, its boomerang aesthetic, inconceivable twenty-five years ago, points to a different standard for taking up migration and return. It is an aesthetic more attuned to the varied forces of globalization and transnationalism with the potential of bringing about change, of opening up the island to the world and vice versa. The boomerang, then, serves as a symbol of individual mobility as well as the ability to absorb and mix homegrown and outside traditions regardless of their origin. I will come back to it at the end.[5]

Not every Cuban, of course, enjoys the mobility and concomitant access to foreign currency claimed by the above artists, and some who wish to return are not allowed in even at this time. There are still barriers in place to block the movement of boomerangs. But notwithstanding the negative reactions that differential access to privilege may provoke or the possible coercion and backlash that dissidence may encounter, these incipient comings and goings may be foreshadowing a more natural relationship to travel and migration for many. And when their time comes to return, prospective émigrés will be less likely to face an incongruous reception, as recent local representations suggest. They are in a better position to resignify the terms of the relationship.

Cultural products made outside of Cuba, too, have not failed to take notice of the change in the status quo. Venezuelan director Fina Torres dips into the new landscape in her 2010 film *Habana Eva*, about the return to Cuba of Jorge, an émigré who for the past thirty years has been a resident of Caracas, where he settled as a child of six. Upon arrival in Havana, Jorge meets Eva, a young woman whose apathy toward her dull surroundings brings her into his arms. Unbeknownst to her, Jorge is the heir of a wealthy family that has entrusted him to take stock of the family's former sprawling real estate in Havana with an eye toward recovering it. Soon Eva discovers that Jorge has left the country unexpectedly, leaving an envelope stuffed with money for her. But in addition to money, in the process he has given her something more precious—the confidence and determination to follow her dreams.

Soon after she and a former boyfriend join forces to open a private business, Jorge, who has experienced pangs of conscience for his deplorable actions, arrives in Havana a second time. Eva is then torn between the two men. In a key scene, she confesses her love for both men, conceding to the émigré: "You opened up the world for me, but it was he [her boyfriend] who helped me build it." The film, which draws from magical realism, ends with the three marrying. As in Jorge Amado's *Doña Flor and Her Two Husbands*, the final scene shows Eva, in her wedding gown, sitting in a vintage convertible between the two handsome men as they drive down the Malecón in Havana.

The narrative, then, is an allegory about present-day Cuba, where the adoption of new economic measures has had an exponential effect in other areas. The happy ending seems to imply that forging ahead requires a collective effort, one where both insiders and outsiders are expected to take part. As a result, the émigré in the film, which in all likelihood is among the younger members of the one-and-a-half generation, can also play a role, as a co-protagonist, in the construction of a future for Cuba.

Other sites envisaging crucial changes in the discursive representation of returnees are worth scrutinizing. Being circumstantial, part of the cultural materials I shall examine may not withstand the test of time, but all of it helps to feel the temperature of Cuban reality during a period of manifest transition. The move is toward a gradual coming to terms with migration and return and, with it, interaction on a global scale.

Trapped in Cubanidad: Exiles' Flawed Attempts at Reconciliation

Representations of the first exile wave are ensnared in the nationalist ideology fueling the Cuban revolution, which, as a sweeping change, gave rise to the political polarization of society. As early as June 1961, Castro articulated in his speech "Palabras a los intelectuales" a bedrock principle of the Cuban revolution: everything inside the revolution, nothing outside of it. There would be zero tolerance toward those who tried to undermine the political and cultural processes set in motion in 1959. The line drawn between the inside and the outside of the revolution has shifted ever so slowly over time. But those who opted for exile in the 1960s were allegedly anti-Castro and antirevolutionary and therefore the regime's foes. With the financial backing of the United States, many were involved in attempts to topple the Cuban government, a fact that did not contribute to dispelling the neat binary corralling the political imagination.[6]

Indeed, the binary lasted well into the 1990s, even within the cultural arena. It infused a speech by writer Abel Prieto, then president of UNEAC (National Union of Cuban Writers and Artists), who addressed an audience of over two hundred Cuban émigrés in the government-sponsored conference La nación y la emigración. The spring 1994 event sought to foster a more open relationship with "la comunidad cubana en el exterior." Speaking to nonresident nationals hailing from about seventy countries, Prieto, who was to be promoted to minister of culture in 1997, serving in this capacity until 2012, delved into the differences between *cubanidad* and *cubanía*. He was building on a distinction made by Fernando Ortiz in his seminal essay, "Los factores humanos de la cubanidad," published in 1939. While *cubanidad* designates a generic, taken for granted Cubanness, *cubanía* is the outgrowth of consciousness and a sense of responsibility toward the nation.[7] Only the second, *cubanía*, can be consciously attained. The two labels would reverberate in films and other cultural products depicting the visit of émigrés in Cuba.

In the same vein, Prieto proposes in his essay a distinction between *cultura plattista* and *cubanía*.[8] To the contingency of the *cultura plattista*, which does not hesitate to compromise national sovereignty, *cubanía* responds with a strengthening of nationalist ideals. The difference between the two stances manifests itself in the sense of temporality (*cubanidad* or *cultura plattista* emphasizes the day-to-day, and *cubanía* what lies ahead); in ethics (*cubanidad* resonates with annexation while *cubanía* is tied to a high moral ground); and in geopolitics (*cubanidad* pleads for appeasement while *cubanía* advocates for whatever struggle it would take to convert Cuba into a beacon for freedom) (73–75). The atmosphere radiating from each of these realms lies, too, in opposite fields: *cubanidad* is bounded by haziness, and *cubanía* by luminosity. And each is made up of layers. Thus *cubanidad* subsumes

> todo un complejo de símbolos, mitos, actitudes, estados anímicos y modos de pensar, y una representación peyorativa del ser nacional, conjugada con una exaltación de todo lo extranjero y en especial del imperio del norte y de su papel en los destinos de Cuba [a set of symbols, myths, attitudes, mental states, and ways of thinking, as well as a pejorative representation of the national being, combined with an exaltation of the foreign, especially of the empire to the north and of its role in the destiny of Cuba]. (40–41)

It is evident that outlining the debate in such political, essentialist terms can conceivably give rise to some misconceptions, such as accusing anyone who enjoys U.S. popular culture but defends Cuba's right to self-determination of pandering to *cubanidad*. There is no continuum able to account for reasonable ambiguities.[9] Prieto went on to deconstruct common views on the exile, offering a list of stereotypes found on the island, which range between the golden exile and the *gusanera*.[10] Refurbishing these terms, Prieto recalls the pun making the rounds in Havana at the time about the metamorphosis of *traidores* (traitors) into *traedólares* (carriers of dollars), and points out that the golden exile has turned into a pudgy Santa Claus, loaded with presents (81). Such stereotypes, he said, must be questioned. Yet, even when taking a stab at being even-handed, a skewed image emerges out of the analysis.

If I have devoted some space to summarizing Prieto's lengthy address, it is because its underpinnings carry over and serve to unmask the representation of the Cuban exile in those works where he or she appears as a character. Indeed, those representing the first wave of exiles fit the description of *cubanidad* or *cultura plattista* advanced in Prieto's words. For the most part, the exile is trapped in a cluster of values: he is "pragmático, medroso, siempre llamando a la cordura y a las concesiones, enemigo de ideales y utopías" [pragmatic, fainthearted, always favoring sanity and concessions, an enemy of ideals and utopias] (41). In contrast, *cubanía* belongs to those tilting at windmills.

One of the earliest examples in Cuban cinema of that specimen, aligned with *cubanidad*, who returns temporarily, is the character of the mother in *Lejanía*, a film directed by Cuban writer and filmmaker Jesús Díaz in 1985.[11] *Lejanía* depicts the return of Susana, a middle-aged woman who comes to the island to visit her son, Reinaldo, after ten years of separation. His parents and sister had left without him when he turned sixteen, believing that they would eventually reunite. Although Susana is haunted by feelings of guilt and inadequacy given the family history, she is holding out an olive branch, trying, in her own way, to redeem herself.

However, the way the character pursues her goal brings to light the divergent social values each of the two characters has come to harbor. The young man is married to a darker-skinned young woman who has a daughter from a previous marriage. These two factors—race and civil status—render the young woman suspect in the eyes of the mother, adding to the tension between mother and son. On the other hand, Susana tries to compensate for lost time and opportunity through material means, by bringing with her a cornucopia of presents for her loved ones, in a gesture that captures the transformation grasped in popular slang. Soon after arriving, she shows a home video of a child's birthday party in Miami where we get a peek at a piñata shaped like Uncle Sam's tall hat. The scene projects the stereotypical image of the exiles reviewed in Prieto's speech.

The son is not about to fall for the five suitcases overflowing with consumer goods that the mother has brought, nor is he moved to compassion in the face of her other actions. Hence the path toward reconciliation is strewn with obstacles for the two, who always talk past each other. The *lejanía* (meaning distance or remoteness in Spanish), which at first connotes physical distance, ensues in ethical terms as well. At the end, the unhomely atmosphere inside the house is untenable, and Reinaldo leaves hastily on a trip to the eastern end of the island to further contribute with his work to the bright future in store for Cuba. "Siento como si me hubiera pasado el día entre fantasmas" [I feel as if I had spent the day among ghosts], the son remarks before taking off. The main characters inhabit the conflicting temporality sketched by Abel Prieto between *cubanidad* and *cubanía*, with the mother standing in for a past enveloped in fog and the son marching toward the luminosity of the future.[12]

A similar sensibility permeates *Reina y Rey*, where even the association between exiles and ghosts made in *Lejanía* is upheld. Released in 1994, the film was directed by another esteemed Cuban filmmaker, Julio García Espinosa. The title refers to a humble, middle-aged woman by the name of Reina who, at the height of the Special Period, can hardly feed herself, much less her only companion, a darling little dog, Rey, that runs away in search of food. At this critical moment, Carmen and her husband, who had left Reina, their former domestic servant, in charge of their comfortable residence in Havana, decide to make a return trip to the island after a twenty-year period. Carmen's words upon entering her former home, "No somos fantasmas que regresan" [Those returning are not ghosts], are uttered as a way of ascertaining themselves—as well as her real, albeit devious, motives for returning. Like apparitions, the exiles seem to be looming in the dark, ready to strike when least expected.

Although Reina is caught by surprise, Carmen has come from exile to take her former domestic to Miami with her and charge her with the care of her yet-to-be-born grandchild. Carmen and her husband have brought suitcases filled with presents for Reina: "Vamos a ver lo que te trajo Santa Claus" [Let's see what Santa Claus has brought you], Carmen exclaims. In order to ingratiate themselves, they take Reina out to tourist attractions around Havana, allowing her to experience the bright side of the city, a sample of better things to come should she accept their offer, amid the despair brought about by the depths of the crisis.

Despite all the attention, however, Reina declines to leave, in part due to the realization that even after twenty years of separation from her past employers, the terms of the relationship have remained virtually unchanged. The way out of the pervading misery—made worse by a particular kind of violence ensuing from survival tactics—that Carmen and her husband offer Reina implies a return to the totality of the past and therefore is out of the question. Addressing Carmen with a formal *señora* all along, Reina grasps that the past is close at hand (Fowler, "Identidad, diferencia" 26).

At one point Carmen remarks, "Al final los de Miami no hacen más que pensar en los de La Habana y los de aquí en los de Miami. Hay que abrir la ventana y dejar que entre un poco de aire." [After all, those here are always in the mind of those in Miami and vice versa. We have to open a window so air can come in.] The remark is part of the rhetoric of reconciliation, one that flies in the face of the actual encounter in the film. Paradoxically, what the movie shows flies in the face, too, of the real encounters that travelers witness upon arrival at the José Martí airport in Havana, with relatives standing outside of the crowded terminal for hours on end just to extend a welcome to the returning kin. These are public gestures of reconciliation like none other—or so they seem.

Yet even in works released after the end of the Cold War, like *Reina y Rey*, one finds cartoonish renderings of first-wave exiles partaking of a *cubanidad* that is nothing but regressive at its core. It is clear that a firmly rooted ideology prevailed over affect in the two cases examined here, one that gave way to what appears to be a disarticulation between representation and reality, and proof that representation is nothing but embroiled in multiple negotiations.

The "Redeemable" One-and-a-Half Generation

Members of the one-and-a-half generation do not share the same responsibility as their parents for leaving Cuba, and return narratives in which they appear are not as weighed down by parameters of *cubanidad*, although politics and ideology are still at play. Jesús Díaz, who, apart from his views on the older émigrés, became intrigued by the unanticipated return of the sons and daughters of Cuban exile, explored their fate in both film and printed text starting at the end of the 1970s. He delved into the subject in the documentary *55 hermanos* (1978), the book of testimonials *De la patria y el exilio* (1979), and the feature film *Lejanía* (1985), where a younger character plays a minor but illustrative role.

Díaz was at the airport with his cameraman in December 1977 when the first contingent of the Antonio Maceo Brigade landed on the island, and he set out to understand its members' aspiration to reconnect with their native land. The film crew of *55 hermanos* sympathetically follows the young Cubans who, coming from around the world, abide by the protocols of return, such as visiting their former homes and reacquainting themselves with family members with whom they had lost touch. Given the political dimension of the trip, the *brigadistas* also show their willingness to help build a new future for a Cuba that purportedly would include them by working at a construction site alongside Cuban workers.

The interaction of the members of the Brigade with Cubans on the island drew a distinction between the older and the younger generations, a difference underscored by the inclusive title that Díaz chose for the film. *55 hermanos* opened the audience's eyes to the existence of a more heterogeneous exile community than they ever thought possible given the Cuban media's prejudiced reporting about those departing, as the director and writer expressed in his interview with Oliva Collmann (162). If reconciliation was not feasible with the former amid the trappings of their *cubanidad*, with the latter it was possible to hold a dialogue: What were they really looking for? Were they capable of sustaining a fierce *cubanía*? In their public statements, the *brigadistas* highlight sad episodes of their lives in the United States, implicitly comparing the two countries to the detriment of their adopted land. Throughout the documentary, there is a tension between the young Cubans' eagerness to understand and support social policies implemented by the revolution and their emotional need not only to reminisce about their childhood in neighborhoods around Havana but also to become relevant actors in the present landscape. They aspire to recognition of their Cuban nationality. Coming from a place to which they sense they do not belong, given subjective feelings of attachment to place, they have arrived at another that has some qualms about taking them in as its own. In a meeting with Fidel Castro at the end of the trip, one of the Brigade's members voices his desire to return permanently to Cuba. Whereas the desire is understandable, the Comandante responds, the *brigadistas* need to comprehend that they are most useful to the motherland from abroad, where they can disseminate their kind vision of Cuba. The returnees, then, are asked to honor the nation's pressing needs from afar, and the tension between the personal and the political endures. Still, this film remains one of the best attempts at what Martínez San Miguel identifies as the search for a common language that engenders discursive exchanges between Cubans on the island and the diaspora (226).

Other works confirm the out-of-reach return for the same generation, including the Díaz film critiqued above, *Lejanía*. Accompanying the mother in her trip to visit her son Reinaldo is Ana, Reinaldo's cousin, with whom communication is viable. In a climactic scene, she confides to him her ambivalence for her adopted country and specifically the metropolis where she has lived, New York. New York may be a big and filthy city, but it is a magical place, Ana remarks. She then quotes the last stanza of Lourdes Casal's poem "Para Ana Veltfort" in recognition of her dual cultural allegiance.

Díaz's representation pictures a new hybrid subject who, thanks to the difference he or she entails, has the potential of escaping the *cubanidad* vs. *cubanía* conundrum, since this new subject, by his or her very nature, partakes of both. Partaking of *cubanía*, they are at once inevitably drawn to "innocuous" forms of *cubanidad*. Ana, for instance, sees the "magic" of New York and subscribes to Casal's dual perspective. Indeed, the filmmaker tackles a concern dear to the one-and-a-half generation, that of bicultural awareness. Ana's character introduces a dissonance that will be taken up, rather unsuccessfully, in later works by other filmmakers and writers. She disturbs what had become a familiar storyline. Since the concern that drives the plot in *Lejanía* is primarily the mother's guilt, impossible to discard given the framework within which it is handled, one that excludes redemption, the narrative highlights what Ana lacks—guilt—not what she can integrally offer. Still, free of the original "sin" of voluntarily fleeing, Ana does not share the blame, as she was taken out of Cuba as a child. Although she is a sympathetic character who articulates her hybrid identity over her conversations with Reinaldo, Ana's divided loyalty gives rise to feelings of disorientation rather than contentment or empowerment.

(That hybrid subjectivities can be theorized as a source of contentment and empowerment is the topic of Antonio Vera León's essay "The Garden of Forking Tongues: Bicultural Subjects and an Ethics of Circulating In and Out of Ethnicities." Vera León plays with the double meaning of *di-vertido*—both "to turn in another direction" and "to amuse"—to argue about the festive character of bicultural locations. The *di-vertido* subject is uniquely positioned to draw from the cultures and subject positions he or she intimately knows and benefits from this knowledge. On the contrary, most of the examples appearing in island lore focus attention on the drawbacks of coming into contact with U.S. culture.)[13]

The lack of culpability of the sons and daughters of Cuban exile does not quite ease the reinsertion on the island of another contemporaneous character, Mayra, in Alberto Pedro Torriente's play *Weekend en Bahía* (1987). Mayra unexpectedly stumbles upon Esteban, her former sweetheart, over the course of her first trip to Cuba. Their personal relationship was cut short by Mayra's parents' decision to leave for the United States. It has been nineteen years since they left. It is safe to assume that the action takes place around the time the play appeared, shortly after *Lejanía*'s and prior to the onset of the Special Period. Since Mayra fled Cuba as a teenager in the late 1960s, she is a member of the one-and-a-half generation.

The play's setting is a room occupied by Esteban, which he enters accompanied by Mayra, late at night. At the beginning, Esteban and Mayra are poised to resume their relationship, but as they chat, differences begin to surface. She has changed for the worse, according to Esteban, who has to comment on her "odd" behavior. She slips easily into English, takes out a marijuana joint, and resists Esteban's sexual advances, but at the same time she insists on staying with him. Gradually, Esteban comes to the realization that she is an outsider—or at least someone who has changed beyond recognition. They talk about their jobs and come to the conclusion that neither is happy. Mayra invites him to leave Cuba with her, but Esteban refuses, arguing about the benefits of raising his child in Cuba. At the end, Mayra's visit serves to reconfirm the advantages of staying put, revealing what can be lost with banishment as well as exposure to capitalism's ills. As soon as that lesson is learned, Esteban goes back to his routine.

Mayra, therefore, is used almost as a prop to demonstrate the rewards of living in Cuba. She comes across as alienated, incoherent, even confused. Although Mayra is far from being the epitome of *cubanidad*, her bilingualism makes her suspect, especially when it brings in tow unbecoming habits learned in exile. Neither character is unambiguously positive, but as a product of hybrid culture, Mayra is a loser and remains a cypher at best.[14]

The challenges of coming to terms with the Anas and Mayras that Cuban literature and popular culture might contemplate further materialize in *Miel para Oshún* (2001), a feature film by renowned director Humberto Solás. The film's main character, Roberto, leaves Cuba as a child with his father on a boat through Camarioca. Having been led to believe that Roberto's mother had abandoned them, Roberto returns to Havana only thirty-two years later, in the 1990s, and once there discovers that he has been deceived. He then decides to track down his mother with the help of his cousin. Following a lead from a *Santería* priestess, they finally discover Roberto's mother in Baracoa, site of one of the oldest settlements in Cuba, located at the eastern end of the island, where the emotional reconciliation takes place.

The movie stands for an allegory in which mother and nation merge, using the same trope as in *Loving Che*. As the film director sets him on his journey, Roberto wonders about his identity, agonizing over his off-kilter Cubanness: "No he tenido una vida feliz. No sé quién soy, si cubano, si americano.... Ustedes por lo menos saben quiénes son, aunque esto esté malo, aunque tengan problemas.... [He venido] a encontrarme yo, a encontrar mis raíces." [I have not been happy. I do not know who I am, whether Cuban or American. You know who you are even in the midst of difficulties. I came to my homeland to find myself, to find my roots.] Roberto's confession takes place in a public square where its residents have gathered, being a collective witness to the voyage of (re)discovery of the young man, as well as the beneficiary of the veiled warning radiating from Roberto's monologue: beware of the perils of cultural hybridity.[15]

Entwining the pursuit of mother and motherland, the film takes a compassionate look at this "orphaned" character. Reestablishing the bonds takes time and effort. So, in order to reach his goal, Roberto needs to be tested: he travels from one end of the island to the other using whatever transportation he can manage to obtain; bathes in crystalline rivers and explores the dense mountains dotting the Cuban countryside; is subjected to the depth of the crisis hitting fellow Cubans in the 1990s; and begins to symbolically jettison his hard-won but "confusing" identity. Crowning his apprenticeship is the loss of both his U.S. passport and his personal belongings, without which he is restored to an unmarked, primordial state. Given a blank slate, he is in a position to reclaim both his mother and his motherland.

Deserving of a Special Mention in the 2001 Havana Film Festival and an award for best feature film in Mexico in 2002, the well-intentioned but clueless *Miel para Oshún* has been hailed as emblematic of the desire for reconciliation among Cubans on both sides of the divide, and indeed there is an ideal of inclusion undergirding the film. Alas, enabling this elusive accomplishment is the waning of Roberto's complex subjectivity. The journey in which he embarks strips Roberto of the bicultural identity that seals his membership in the one-and-a-half generation. In order for reconciliation to take place, Roberto needs to make a "viaje a la semilla" or voyage to the source and assume an unadulterated Cuban identity grounded on the island. Only then can he be reabsorbed and assimilated within the geographic borders of the nation.

This being the 1990s, a period thick with more pressing, less ideological demands that call for survival skills, *Miel para Oshún* circumvents the *cubanidad* versus *cubanía* predicament traversing earlier movies. Yet misunderstandings persist about the true nature of the one-and-a-half generation. The representation of the children of exile in the above cinematic and literary examples wavers between a disconcerting look at someone who appears to be the same yet is different, in which case perplexity is sustained and confusion acknowledged, and the inclination to strip him or her of otherness, to eradicate heterogeneity, in an effort to dissolve that ambiguity. There was no question they were a challenge brought to life because, as José Quiroga writes, "Epistemologically, you were something else, other than Cuban, even if Cuba was always the ontology that gave some meaning to existence" (191). Seen as the flip side of the representation of return in the literature of the one-and-a-half generation, the above examples reaffirm, to an extent, the elusiveness of home, of a home that encompasses and consents to the diversity embodied by these subjects. The ambivalence enveloping the search for home comes across vividly in examples such as these. The quest to do away with ambivalence, nevertheless, lives on in both sides.[16]

The Deferral Strategy

Whereas most of the quests for home fail, there is one narrative strategy used in some of the works reviewed that serves to overcome the glitch of representing an "other" marked by departure and return. I call this the deferral strategy, one that avoids the trap of representing an unknown subject. Among these works is a segment of *Mujer transparente* (1990), which comprises a number of vignettes on female characters, each under the direction of a different filmmaker. The one dealing with a returnee, "Laura," directed by Ana Rodríguez, follows the main character as she drives toward a Havana hotel to meet up with her best friend, Ana, who left Cuba as an adolescent in the late 1960s. References to the period pepper the film, from the 1966 French production of *Who Are You, Polly Maggoo?* to the Beatles and the Spanish singer Massiel, whose voice is heard in the background. The segment moves back and forth between the past and the present, with the former—relived through photographs and Laura's voiceover—characterized by the carefree lives of the two young women and their friends, who eventually part ways. It is Ana's return in the 1980s that triggers Laura's memories. The two friends have pursued different paths in life. In a letter to Laura, she complains about the pressures to get ahead in Miami, noting that there is something lost, in human terms, with migration. The last images of Ana, appearing in photographs taken in Miami, which she sent to Laura in Cuba, convey a freewheeling lifestyle that seems to be the opposite of her friend's levelheaded approach to life.

Laura is conscious of the potential problems inherent to political polarization, including the pull to dig one's heels in and only *pretend* that reconciliation is possible. Her reflections reveal that she is not immune to these missteps, and she even fears turning Ana into the enemy. Moreover, once Laura arrives at the hotel, she must navigate the minefield of an economic structure geared toward the expansion of family visits and tourism, both laced with the restricted use of the dollar (limited to nonresidents at the time), *jineterismo*, and the weakening of moral standards, among others. Laura feels the urge to leave the area, but refrains from doing so. She then resolutely calls Ana from the lobby and asks her to meet her there. The segment ends with a photograph, taken just before Ana fled Cuba, of the two friends in an embrace.

Embrace notwithstanding, the viewer can only speculate about the outcome of the reencounter, since it remains outside the field of representation and visualization. That reencounter is necessary because it serves to give closure to the initial rift, with the potential reconciliation having the added impact of broadening the borders of the Cuban national community (Martínez San Miguel 243). In spite of its significance, or perhaps because of it, the reluctance to make the reunion visible should not be cause for concern. On the contrary, given the pitfalls of representing exiles, the choice to leave out the two friends' actual reunion can in fact be construed as a wise decision, especially when their life histories lead the viewer to anticipate manifold differences that might obstruct communication. At the same time, reconciliation between the two friends is not ruled out, as the final photograph suggests. The reencounter may or may not have a happy ending.

Such a strategy of uncertainty has the advantage of evading the difficulties of representing the exile as "one of us" (as in the final scenes of *Miel para Oshún*) or an "other" (as in *Weekend en Bahía*), both of which bolster the inside/outside dichotomy which not only radical politics but also classic notions of nationalist belonging are likely to reinforce. The dichotomy cancels out the claims of a diaspora that seeks a less rooted, more fluid, and perhaps transnational relationship with the nation. For this reason, the reluctance or reticence to speak for the exile or the returnee, which defers definition, can be an enticing narrative strategy, one that has not been lost on other writers, artists, and filmmakers. It is compelling because it resists hegemonic discourses—while concurrently falling short of radically unsettling them.

Mariel and Beyond: Leveling the Playing Field

Two additional works that build upon the deferral strategy are "Diente por diente," a short story by Nancy Alonso, and Humberto Padrón's short film, *Video de familia* (2001), the latter of which, representing a later migration wave, will be addressed further below. Included in the groundbreaking anthology of Cuban women's writings *Estatuas de sal* (1996), edited by Mirtha Yáñez and Marilyn Bobes, and later appearing in Alonso's collection *Tirar la primera piedra* (1997), "Diente por diente" utilizes the egg motif to revisit the mass hysteria ignited through infamous *actos de repudio* during the Mariel exodus. Used to signify the loathing lavished upon the *marielitos*, the motif becomes a powerful symbol of open rejection toward those fleeing, who were the targets of others wielding the eggs. But the situation has evolved, and in the 1990s, when the narrative is set, amid so many calamities, nourishment can no longer go to waste.[17]

Alonso's story revolves around a character, Pepe Cruz, who took part, albeit with reservations, under social pressure, in an *acto de repudio* against a co-worker, Armando, who chose to leave Cuba when the opportunity arose, surprising everyone who knew him. Armando himself had shown his resolve against those choosing to flee, so his about-face left his friends stunned. Given that the two men show hypocrisy and dubious moral standards through actions, neither one is beyond reproach, thus leveling the playing field. There is no longer a situation where the once-revolutionary character is situated in high moral ground.

Armando comes back to visit years later, bringing back memories of cowardly behavior for Pepe, who let himself be thrown into the abominable *acto de repudio* staged for Armando. Armando, however, remains only a trace throughout the story, without ever materializing as a character of flesh and bone. He drops off a dozen eggs at his former co-worker's house, leaving just his name. But the name suffices for Pepe to sense what the visit is about. Only at the end of the story does Pepe open the package left by Armando, which, ironically, saves the day, as he had no food left in the house. The narrative, then, points to the role played by émigrés in post-Soviet Cuban economy, as some of the aforementioned works also do, but this time neither one of the two characters measuring each other up is a shining example of ethical behavior. Blurring the line drawn between victim and victimizer, the moral stalemate yields a more sober representation of both sides.[18]

Alonso's story insinuates a sharing of responsibility for past actions whose denouement could be no other than the disastrous today of the narrative. With Pepe cornered by the ex-*marielito*, whose payback for past deeds remains but a gesture, at least poetic justice has been served. Writers such as Alonso thus "occupy" the official discourse on *marielitos*: "Occupied by such terms and yet occupying them oneself risks a complicity, a repetition, a relapse into injury, but it is also the occasion to work the mobilizing power of injury, of an interpellation one never chose" (Butler 123). Mobilizing so as to preserve historical memory through culture is indeed what some of the Cuban writers and songwriters are undertaking.[19]

Failure to expose a shameful action also looms large in Leonardo Padura's *La novela de mi vida* (2002), a complex novel liable to be read in a number of ways. Because it is an elaborate piece of fiction by one of Cuba's most admired novelists, it calls for a somewhat lengthier analysis. The novel's alignment with Padura's highly praised detective fiction stems from the search for a lost manuscript, conducted by the main character, Fernando Terry, a scholar on Cuba's preeminent nineteenth-century romantic poet, José María Heredia. Given this chapter's overriding concern, I am interested in Fernando as a *marielito* who feels he has no option but to flee, returning to his native land after nearly two decades in diaspora. His ouster from the University of Havana following an accusation regarding his knowledge of a gay friend's plans to take off by boat illegally precipitated Fernando's departure. He suspects that someone in his close circle of friends betrayed him. Unable to clear his name and secure employment in accordance with his qualifications, he gets on a boat leaving from the Mariel harbor. After spending four years in the United States, Fernando settles in Madrid, where he succeeds in securing a university post. Fernando returns to Cuba for a month only after hearing that he might finally get hold of the lost manuscript, an autobiography, authored by Heredia. There he renews his friendships, although since it is unclear who denounced him, the relationships at first stand on shaky grounds. Gradually, though, and after confronting them one by one, he crosses all of his friends' names off his list of possible collaborators. Meanwhile, Fernando has rekindled his relationship with the woman, who is now a widow, he had always loved.

The narrative goes back and forth between Fernando's chasing Heredia's manuscript—as well as attempting to uncover the truth about Fernando's downfall—and Heredia's apocryphal *novela de mi vida*, segments of which are interspersed throughout the book. Heredia (1803–39) was forced to leave Cuba as a result of his membership in the Soles y Rayos de Bolívar masonic lodge, which sought to end Spanish colonial rule on the island. He was denounced for his efforts to achieve independence for Cuba. The parallel narrative brings about an analogy between exile at two different times in Cuban history, presenting a far from glowing picture of a nation whose powers that be force out real and hypothetical dissidents. The novel is unequivocal, especially on the sections regarding the nineteenth century, about the pervasiveness of the convenient "solution" that exile represents. Those mentioned as also suffering exile then include such leading lights in colonial Cuba as Félix Varela, José Antonio Saco, and Félix Tanco. As a critic notes, Heredia was a groundbreaker; he was one of the first Cuban intellectuals to be banished as well as one of the first to practice self-censorship as a means to avoid the wrath of a tyrannical regime that kept him off the island (González Acosta 291). If exile is one of the main themes of Padura's novel, as I posit, it makes sense to link Heredia and Fernando Terry.

The two characters are linked in other ways. Just as troubling as expulsion is the fact that no one truly confronts it or sides openly with the victims. No one did with respect to Heredia, if we are to believe Padura's fictionalized account, and no one does regarding Terry. Neither Fernando's former colleagues at the University of Havana nor anyone else raises his voice to try to right the wrong done to Fernando, and they are therefore to blame for not taking a stand. This argument is put forth by one of Fernando's former professors whose ranking at the university would have allowed her to demand his reinstatement: "Y en ese momento no hice lo que tenía que hacer: poner mi renuncia contra tu regreso. . . . Me di cuenta de que todos nosotros, los que podíamos haber hecho algo, pero sobre todo yo, éramos los culpables de perderte" (Padura 279). [And at that moment I did not do what was required of me: threaten to resign unless you were reinstated. . . . I realized that all of us, who could have done something, I especially, were as much to blame for having lost you.] Punctuating the two parallel narratives on

Fernando and Heredia is the idea that those who stay on the island share the responsibility for the drain that constitutes exile, whether as the outcome of betrayal, rejection, silence, or inaction.

Nowhere is the connection between Heredia and Terry more explicit than at two scenes where a vicarious encounter occurs. As soon as he gets back to Havana, Terry heads to the city's sea wall and, from there, watches a man who, passing by on a sailboat, fixes his eyes on him: "Aquel desconocido, que lo observaba con tan escrutadora insistencia, alarmó a Fernando y le hizo sentir, como una rémora capaz de volar sobre el tiempo, el dolor que debió de embargar a José María Heredia" (Padura 17). [That unknown man who observed him with insisting scrutiny alarmed Fernando and made him feel, like a fish capable of flying over time, the sorrow that must have overcome José María Heredia.] In a contrapuntal fashion, Heredia, in his manuscript, describes his last departure from the island. Leaning his elbow on the ship's railing, the poet sees a man on shore following the vessel's movement with his eyes:

> Por un largo momento nuestras miradas se sostuvieron, y recibí el pesar recóndito que cargaban aquellos ojos, una tristeza extrañamente gemela a la mía, capaz de cruzar por encima de las olas y el tiempo para forjar una misteriosa armonía que desde entonces me desvela, pues sé que fuimos algo más que dos hombres mirándose sobre las olas. [We locked eyes on each other and I was overcome with a sadness eerily similar to mine, capable of defying the waves as well as time in order to forge a mysterious harmony that from then on has kept me awake, because I know that we were more than two men gazing at each other over the waves.](Padura 332)

With that gaze across space and time involving the two characters, Padura succeeds in merging both Heredia's and Terry's sentiments about exclusion from their beloved island. Note that the two scenes, serving as bookends, occur toward the beginning and end of the novel, underscoring the influence of exile (and return) within it.

There is yet another similarity between the nineteenth-century poet and the twentieth-century scholar, and that is their fervor for Cuba. Heredia feels at home nowhere else but on the island despite the fact that he spent far more years in exile in Mexico than in his birthplace; that he, moreover, was born to Dominican parents who had settled in Santiago de Cuba. On the other hand, Fernando Terry goes through a period of estrangement upon his return. Refamiliarizing himself with Havana proves to be difficult. He remembers little about his old stomping grounds, almost unrecognizable after almost two decades. And it is no wonder that he finds Havana *ajena* or strange (Padura 84), as during his absence Cuba had seen the collapse of the Soviet empire and the advent of a new economic order that wreaked havoc on the island. Fernando wanders around the city like an outsider, taking note of new developments (113). However, his initial distancing diminishes at the same rate as his involvement in both his friends' and lover's lives increases, and he becomes nostalgic for the past and more attuned to his surroundings. Toward the end of the novel, Fernando begins to fancy a permanent return. The challenges to readapting to the rigor of life in Cuba are enormous, but going back to the "loneliness and silence" of his life in Madrid, about which we learn remarkably little, is terrifying (Padura 298). And so, rejecting a diasporic form of existence, he envisions a future that does not rule out a permanent return: "Una sensación de paz envolvió a Fernando y pensó que volvería tantas veces que al final se quedaría, porque, en realidad—y ahora tenía la certeza—, él no se había ido nunca" [Feelings of peace enveloped Fernando, who thought that he would come back so many times that at the end he would stay because, in truth—and now he has no doubt—he had never left] (298). Although Fernando's permanent return is postponed, by the end of the novel we are led to believe that he has made up his mind about his eventual reinsertion on the island.

With its two main characters unable or unwilling to imagine a home away from home, *La novela de mi vida*, then, reaffirms a rooted form of cultural belonging at the same time that, ironically, it acknowledges the hybrid quality of Cubanness by focusing in part on Heredia. The unhomely feelings of both Heredia and Terry after their return soon dissipate, and despite the vicissitudes of living under regimes with the potential of "betraying ideals and the best of just causes" (Padura 125), the fictional characters stake a claim within the boundaries of the island. Despite the impediments, homeland eclipses diaspora.

Padura is not alone in holding on to a classic notion of insular nationalism. Odette Casamayor-Cisneros perceptively points out that among contemporary writers, Abilio Estévez, Senel Paz, Marilyn Bobes, and Alexis Díaz-Pimienta, too, craft fictional characters whose contentment is contingent upon their being grounded on the island (163). The satisfaction they derive from being rooted stands in opposition to the discontent and incompleteness felt by those who have left Cuba. This is the case with Padura's characters. But while the superimposition of nationality and territory is no doubt one way of imagining ethnicity, as prescribed by a modern nationalist ideology, other works contemporaneous with Padura's novel go beyond the requirement to imagine alternative outcomes. The sample of videos, lyrics, and works of art that follow amplify this other space in order to entertain diasporic realities.

Humberto Padrón's fifty-minute film *Video de familia* (2001) revisits some of the ideas reviewed before. Like "Laura," of *Mujer transparente*, and Alonso's "Diente por diente," *Video* keeps the return of the émigré lurking on the margins, as deferred action, in addition to seeming to come to terms with a Cuban diaspora. It utilizes the video format to keep kin living elsewhere abreast of family developments and have them tune in for joyful occasions. This time, a family is celebrating the birthday of Rauli, the absent son, who left Cuba on a boat four years earlier, in the mid-1990s, possibly during the *balsero* crisis. They have prepared some food, the ingredients of which they bought in the black market. They are keen to show the young man what they have prepared since it was with his remittances that they have been able to afford it. The father, however, is kept out of the loop, as he is an old-fashioned militant whose loyalty to timeworn values puts him at odds with this type of illegal but widespread activity. Neither can he tolerate Rauli's homosexuality nor the dark color of the skin of his daughter's boyfriend, major revelations that are made over the course of filming the video, causing uproar in the group, with everyone else trying to appease the authority figure. Cultural critic Dean Luis Reyes, in an essay published in 2003, noted that *Video de familia* privileges the point of view of a generation that resents impositions and dogmas because it has outgrown its adherence to a unanimous, collective national project (13).

The family discussion over the course of filming the video evidences concerns about the current situation on the island, ranging from social evils such as prejudice toward homosexuality, racial discrimination, authoritarianism, and machismo to economic issues such as the de-penalization of the dollar and reliance on family remittances. Incensed at the discovery of his son's sexual orientation, the father threatens to keep Rauli out of the house during his upcoming visit to the island. Compounding the problem is his son's partner, the cameraman, who at one point gets in front of the camera and hints at his own plans to join Rauli abroad. At the same time, the mother pleads with her husband to accept the changing values, pointing out that the family cohesiveness ought to be his priority.

Still, despite his homophobia, the father eventually relents, surrendering, albeit reluctantly, to the mother's pleas to come to terms with their son's sexuality and take him in as a legitimate member of the family. This is as far as the shooting of the video inside *Video de familia* goes, but *Video de familia* itself ends with a series of still photographs that depict the family reunion once the gay son gets back. The photographs show he and his siblings, mother, and grandmother embracing, although some hurdles do remain, evinced by the father's visible discomfort in the photograph where he appears flanked by his son and his son's partner. Nonetheless, the mother's insistence on the major role the family plays in matters of the heart brings about the wordless family reunion at the end.

As in *La novela de mi vida,* once the road to reconciliation has been cleared, *Video de familia* extends a more or less welcoming hand to the émigré. Like Fernando Terry, Rauli asserts his right to come back. But he is unlikely to propound a permanent return given not only the uneasiness that his difference still provokes but also his partner's ostensible wishes to join him in the diaspora. As Reyes suggests, for Humberto Padrón the problem is not fleeing per se but the scruples to come together in spite of the disagreements (13). The film eschews the discord for the most part, as the director chooses to offer visual rather than audible glimpses of the reunion. Once again, the deferred action has served to skirt an awkward reunion.

Back to the Future of Return

An even more accepting view of fleeing and returning is encoded in some examples drawn from contemporary Cuban music, a field that has faced multiple challenges in recent times. Cosmopolitan and transnational in character as it is in essence, Cuban music has been impacted by the relocation of a disproportionate number of musicians abroad and shifting perceptions of the role of those living in the Cuban diaspora, in addition to advances in communication and technology. As Susan Thomas argues, the process has been affected "by migration, politics, global economics, and an evolving perception among Cubans abroad and on the island of the meaning—and the location—of Cubanness, emigration, and exile" (109–10).

There are surely new demands placed on the cultural sphere in post-Soviet Cuba, not the least of which is the depletion of liberal state allocations. Changes are afoot, as can be heard in the song "Isla," by the Lien and Rey duo: "Isla / basta ya de viejas soluciones / *del que va y no regresa* / de la sociedad perfecta / sobredosis del hombre sin el hombre" [Island /enough of old solutions / *of he who flees not to return* / of perfect society / of an overdose of man without man] (Ibarra 59).[20] The aspiration to a perfect society is no longer feasible. And the line *del que va y no regresa* sums up the frustration over the way migration has been conceptualized in terms of a one-way trip, outlawing return.

Taking advantage of the shifts inside Cuba, some have overcome this frustration and over the past decade turned their journeys into two-way trips. The four musicians in Grubin's documentary *Havana, Havana*—Paz, Ochoa, Bueno, and Torrens—validate Lien and Rey's hope of finding new solutions to old problems for the benefit of ordinary men and women. Above all, and unlike previous generations, they feel entitled to come and go and to live wherever they choose without compromising their Cuban identity. As Raúl Paz nails it in his interview with Eva Silot Bravo: "In a way, we eliminated the incongruous term of definitive departure." And even when musicians do not go back physically, they maintain their ties to the island and with each other.

Grubin's documentary opens with a "Havanization" concert in Havana in December 2011, which brought together Paz, Ochoa, Bueno, and Torrens. After spending more than a decade abroad in France, Spain, the United States, and Mexico, respectively, all four singers decided to return to Cuba, some to stay, others to visit.[21] It was only appropriate that they would open the concert with Torrens's song "Ni de aquí, ni de allá," a hymn to the uprooted. Although focusing mostly on Raúl Paz's journey from humble beginnings to celebrity, the film stresses throughout the benefits of opening up to the world without apprehension and assuming what I label a "boomerang aesthetic." It calls attention to the fact that Cuban music is quintessentially the outcome of ethnic and cultural mixing, so there is no point in keeping foreign influences at arm's length, a credo Paz and the others sustain with their music innovations. Writing about this cohort, Silot Bravo notes that in general terms its influences range from jazz to reggae, Argentinian and U.S. rock, funk, and pop. On the Cuban side, these performers are influenced by "feeling," the *trova*, and jazz musicians such as Emiliano Salvador,

Chucho Valdés, Bobby Carcassés, and Gonzalo Rubalcaba, among others. Finally, they draw inspiration from Afro-Cuban music, specifically *timba* and hip-hop.

The film also emphasizes generational change, arguing that the "generación perdida" to which the singers belong ("lost" generation or second generation under the revolution, so called because it did not have much of a public voice) has the same right as previous generations to forge its own future. Raúl Paz's "Mama," about a young man who leaves home to follow his own path, aptly became one of the singer's first hits in Cuba after his return. Not knowing what awaits him, the young man proceeds nonetheless to design his own future: "No sé muy bien si mi tiempo será largo, mamá / lo que vendrá, lo que seré / caminaré sin pensar y sin decir a buscar lejos lo que sea nuevo / sonreiré cuando a veces me acuerde de ti / de lo que fue, de lo que vi, de lo que sé." [I'm not sure if I'll go away for long, mama / nor what will come, what I'll be / I will walk far without thinking or saying much until I find something new / I will smile whenever I think of you / of what was, of what I saw, of what I know.] His future will not hew to a script.

But if the young man in "Mama" felt the urge to explore other horizons on his own, at some point he also chose to come back home, as captured in the 2006 song "En casa," featured in *Havana, Havana*: "Nada mejor que volver a casa / nada mejor que volverte a ver." [Nothing tops going back home / nothing tops seeing you again.] Paz himself left for Paris in the 1990s to continue his studies in classical music, but after a while began to feel nostalgic for Cuba, and his homesickness propelled him to write his own songs, which were well received in that European city. Paz returned to Cuba as soon as he was authorized to do so after overextending his permit to stay abroad. The first album he recorded in Cuba, *En vivo*, appeared in 2007. "En casa" encapsulates the exhilaration felt by those who return "home" to reunite with loved ones. Returning fills one with a smile and hits one close to one's heart: "llena la sonrisa y se te pega en la camisa."

The documentary leads the viewer to believe that Paz went home indeed. In another video, based on the song "Mama" of the album *Revolución* (2005), Cubans of all walks of life sing along with Paz, who shares the lyrics with them as he ambles down the streets of Havana. Theirs becomes a collective, public performance, with Paz fully inscribed in the city landscape. Besides nostalgia, another reason for returning may be, as the video suggests, how well the singer can blend with his public and, in contrast with

European countries, how recognizable he is in the island's familiar environment. At home, he is a celebrity, enjoying the dividends that come with it. Cubans of all ages come out to greet him as he walks by exuding warmth and familiarity. The "French Cuban," as he is called by some of his peers, is an example of the boomerang aesthetic.

Despite Paz's successes in the Old World, he chose a two-way solution to his troubles. For him, there was the added advantage of collaborating with singers of his own generation with whom he shared not only the experience of exile but also an entirely different perspective on leaving and returning. Their take on this issue is made explicit in interviews with the singers conducted for the video. Since fleeing was not the outcome of an openly political confrontation, they are not as invested as the first exile wave in staying away. Their disposition to leave aside, for whatever reasons, what today seem rigid ways of thinking politically as well as professionally explains that after the successful Havanization concert in Havana (there was a first delivery of the concert in Toulouse, France), they traveled to Miami for a repeat performance in February 2012, followed by a final one in New York later that year. The tour across continents and hemispheres recalls the trajectory of the boomerang featured in the Habana Abierta album cover and Abel Barroso's installation. This possibility marks a sea change with respect to the comportment of historical exile whose return was contingent on regime change on the island. Homecoming may be just as complicated for recent émigrés (for one, they may be perceived as privileged and out of touch with Cuban reality or they may be committed to a changing of the guard and therefore suffer isolation), but those advocating cyclical migration today are in a better position to occupy preexisting discourses, tinkering with them and effecting change. They can rearticulate the representation of returning émigrés from within. It remains to be seen whether their direct participation in articulating that experience will bring about a far-reaching change in the symbolic representation of hybridity and return and, more important, on the national discourse on *lo cubano*.

Conclusion

The narratives included in this chapter cover a wide spectrum in the representation of émigrés. They range from the flattened and unflattering portrayal of first-generation exiles to the more nuanced of the post-Soviet migrants. In-between the two, there are the mixed appraisals of the one-and-a-half generation, who inspired Cuban writers and filmmakers to grapple with an unforeseen event, that of the return of the children of exile. One of their better-equipped interpreters was Jesús Díaz, who explored its significance within the parameters laid down by Lourdes Casal in "Para Ana Veltfort." However, it was the downside of Casal's ruminations on an identity grounded in two places at once that caught the attention of Díaz and those who followed in his footsteps. This imbalance is not surprising, as many of the representations have as an undercurrent a nationalist sentiment that hinders imagining an identity not bounded by the geographical limits of the nation. Envisioning other options functions, indeed, as a counterweight to the neat confluence of nationalism and territoriality that has seized the Cuban imagination for centuries despite the vast migration waves the country has experienced throughout its history.

A tension emerges if the island-generated representations of émigrés are made to interact with narratives written on the U.S. side of the Straits. At the end of the period examined here, however, one comes to the realization that recent émigrés are inching closer toward other ways of representing cultural locations not superimposed squarely on the island. The expression *Ni de aquí ni de allá* recalls, in fact, some of the reflections made by Gustavo Pérez Firmat in his *Life on the Hyphen: The Cuban-American Way*. Neither Cuban nor "American" or both at the same time is, after all, what Cuban Americans are all about (on top of other subjectivities hard to disregard—those of class, race, gender, and the like). Except that more of the recent émigrés do not seem to be as hesitant to return as exiles are, nor do they have to bide their time for decades before they make it back. This new scenario will no doubt continue to influence the relationship between migrants and homeland. If the trend continues, returning will necessarily take on other shapes, different from the ones pictured by the one-and-a-half generation. In a post-Soviet era celebrated by the collapse of what seemed like impregnable walls, the more recent expatriates are better positioned to bring to fruition the boomerang aesthetic that informs their work.

Epilogue

The Cuban-American narratives examined in *Impossible Returns* illustrate the dynamics of returning even when they fall within the purview of *volver* or metaphorical return. These dynamics are shaped by historical factors. Of special import for the one-and-a-half cohort are its inextricable links to post-1959 exile, without which it cannot be understood. Be it by resisting or embracing the exile ethos championed by the previous generation, the return narratives of the one-and-a-half generation still wrestle with political rift, a relic of the belligerence of times past. On the other hand, the Cuban leadership's ambition to achieve socialism, not at any time or place, but in the throes of the Cold War and in an underdeveloped island under the sphere of influence of the United States, is another factor weighing on the terms of engagement and the subject of return.

Intransigence on both sides of the conflict erected solid barriers to communication and contact. In contrast to the opportunities and prospects that exist today, however limited, returning to the island for family reunification purposes or just to visit was nothing short of unimaginable for decades. A number of factors conspired against this laudable goal: military interventions and the adversarial nature of the relationship between Cubans on the island and abroad, the U.S. economic embargo, travel restrictions, the lack of bilateral relations, the Cold War, and the effacement of exiles from the island's revolutionary imagination. Some of these drawbacks are still standing. From the United States, Cuba seemed as out of reach as another galaxy, at least until 1979. When those who left Cuba as children or adolescents were able to return and engage Cuba in revolution, defying every rule of exile, they were met with hostility in the Cuban-American community as well as denied full citizenship rights by the island nation. If "home is the place where, when you have to go there, they have to take you in," as Robert Frost intuited, then Cuba was not entirely home. Despite the tensions, though, the sympathetic members of Grupo Areíto and the Antonio Maceo Brigade, among others, established a foothold in the 1970s and soon after others would follow.

Further conspiring against a seamless homecoming was the passage of time. When the sons and daughters of exile reached Cuba, the former homeland no longer felt like home. Driven by an all-too-human homing desire nonetheless, their return narratives draw from elliptical tropes that throw the fissures into relief. These include the post-indexical ties revealed in chapter 2 in memoirs by Ruth Behar, Román de la Campa, Emilio Bejel, and Tony Mendoza, who in their repeated trips (save Mendoza) to Cuba come face to face with a transformed island containing little of what was reminiscent to who they were as children or young adults. At times, all there seems left are crumbs of home. The authors rely on what is meaningful to them today to make sense of their trips: the Jewish diaspora experience, the implications of a growing Latino population in the United States, autobiographical narratives on nonnormative sexualities, and abundant photographic representations of the Cuban plight.

The gaps are unveiled as well in the faint traces of artwork by Ana Mendieta in Cuba tracked down in chapter 3, an erasure that is counteracted by the collective memory shared by groups and individuals at the fringes of institutional recognition and by the artist's allure among young Cuban artists. These seek out whatever leftovers of the iconic Mendieta remain in the isolated sites where she carved her earth sculptures. As sites imbued with meaning, they are loci generative of memory.

The fissures are further highlighted in Cuban childhoods that saddle the adult, as seen in chapter 4. Both visual artists Ernesto Pujol and María Brito and writers Carlos Eire and Gustavo Pérez Firmat go back to the past in search of explanations as to their present selves only to discover the ruptures, more than the continuities, at play in the transition. Reinforcing the ruptures is the determination of the last three to refrain from reinserting themselves in the current Cuba. Their absence can only exacerbate the rift.

Finally, chapter 5 shows the reliance on post-memory in fiction writers Cristina García, Achy Obejas, and Ana Menéndez, the first two at the younger end of the one-and-a-half generation and the last of the second generation. Yet all three betray a diasporic consciousness redressing downplayed cultural components of several discourses on Cubanness. The authors' hybridity uniquely positions them to both feed from and problematize received versions of narratives of historical significance. The female perspective permeating these novels makes the intervention in historical accounts all the more intriguing. As argued, Menéndez shares so much ground with García and Obejas that she exemplifies the resilience of the Cuba allure hold that critics have noted even among members of the second generation in exile.

Both an unbridgeable gap and a desire to close that gap animate all of the above narratives. They express the deterritorialization of Cuban subjectivities while looking to Cuba as partly enabling that subjectivity. Because diaspora can hardly extricate itself from the homeland, chapter 6 tracks down the representation of exiles in Cuban cultural production after 1959. To the reductive representation of the older exiles, incapable of embodying *cubanía*, followed a more nuanced portrait of both the subsequent generation and other migration waves. Acknowledging the evolving subjectivity of émigrés, such as the hybridity of the one-and-a-half cohort, as well as the definite perks that exile can deliver, has been difficult for Cuba-based writers and filmmakers. Instead, they have focused on the alienation and losses it can entail, sometimes with a built-in didactic intention. Implicit in the representation is the unwanted provocation to an idea of national belonging that values rootedness.

At the same time, the distance between those representing and those represented has contracted in recent times. Post-Soviet realities have changed the rules of the game. Migration is no longer deemed a shameful action, and with the adoption of new changes in migration laws Cubans can now engage in two-way travel. The inside/outside dichotomy is considerably impaired as a result. The space that the two-way travel opens up allows this critic to detect a "boomerang" aesthetic coming into being, an aesthetic consenting to fusion, eclecticism, and a mix of influences in the arts.

The new label is just one more proposal among several others that aim to expand the parameters within which to make sense of the (trans)national body. Rather than depending on metaphors conceived around "roots, uprootedness, transplants, the mother earth, and the trunk of national culture" (Duany, "Reconstructing Cubanness" 17), which suggest the idea of a Cuban identity tethered to the island, critics have clamored for alternative paradigms more accommodating to the fluidity of Cuban subjectivities abroad as well as, one might add, on the island. Being implicated in the scheme, critics from the one-and-a-half generation have sought to loosen the link. Among those reviewed in the book are proposals by Duany (with his call for aerial and aquatic metaphors), Cámara and Fernández (*lo cubano*), Behar (the bridge and portable identities), and O'Reilly Herrera (the tent). Others include *Cuba (tras)pasada* (Rivero) and a culture of translation (Pérez Firmat). As diverse as these propositions are, what unites them is the plea to rethink the metaphors employed in narrating Cuban national identity given a growing, vibrant diaspora whose ties, however figurative, to the island nation cannot be dismissed.

Thus far the demands to revise the metaphors have come from writers in the diaspora, and they have been written in English, although there are exceptions. Ambrosio Fornet calls for a resolution to what he identifies as a "bicephalous" or two-headed criticism unable to consolidate diverse territorial and extraterritorial narratives. With the two-way migration that many have begun to envision on the island and the rise of transnational practices, the time may come when the appeals for new paradigms dictated from within and drafted in the native tongue will cease to be rare. These new narratives of the nation, sensitive to dislocation and dispersal, will then reach a much broader readership. A daunting test for all is to extend full recognition to diaspora while accepting the markers that render it different, quite a challenge for a nation that has routinely exhibited a siege mentality and therefore puts a premium on a show of unity and uniformity.

Diaspora is the term used throughout the book to name the Cuban communities abroad. Although not every Cuban American subscribes to the label, opting instead to retain the exile tag, diaspora appears to be the most inclusive. Many Cuban Americans have forged transnational ties with Cuba, a development that some of the works analyzed here openly illuminate. Others, however, hold on to an exilic vantage point that still draws the line between Cuba and the other shore, wherever that may be. This is the case even within the one-and-a-half generation, politically as diverse as any other. Rather than adhering to *transnationalism* as a term to define the community because not all Cubans practice it, or to *exile* because numerous others have outgrown it, many Cuba scholars now employ *diaspora*.

The rubric can be extended to the more recent migratory waves. Although still infrequent thus far, the return narratives of Cubans who grew up under the revolution and fled in post-Soviet times show the nurturance of ties with the island. Hence it is also transnational. This is the case with Carlos Acosta, whose memoir, *No Way Home: A Dancer's Journey from the Streets of Havana to the Stages of the World* (2007), a rags-to-riches story, is also a return narrative. Now a world-famous classical dancer, Acosta describes his humble background as the son of a black truck driver and a white homemaker who made their home in a poor neighborhood in the outskirts of La Habana. Given his remarkable talent, as a teenager Acosta was offered the opportunity to study and perform abroad. He has since reached the pinnacle of classical ballet, working as a principal dancer for world-renowned companies. Today Acosta lives in London but travels to Cuba often. Despite the low-key nationalism that saturates his memoir, Acosta wants his daughter to be proud of her heritage, and he plans to eventually return to live on the island to create an arts complex with the wherewithal amassed abroad. The strong, uninterrupted relationship with the homeland in both emotional and material terms that Acosta has managed to maintain is what makes *No Way Home* dissimilar to the return narratives analyzed in my study, whose social and political backdrop is emphatically different. Acosta's narrative is comparable to some of the lyrics discussed in the previous chapter. In both of these cases, the stakes are high on account of their potential "boomerang" effect.

Although the evidence is still sparse, foreseeing a changed landscape of frequent visits or cyclical migration is not far-fetched. The return of the one-and-a-half generation, the children of post-1959 exile, may well be a chapter that has run its course in the history of returns. Cuban émigrés are increasingly mirroring other émigrés. If some time ago migration from the island was starkly different from that of other Caribbean nations, characterized by irregular waves over a period of time, and with exiles as outliers, whatever return narratives there may be in the pipeline are likely to herald more of a convergence these days. Cuban nationals continue to leave the island, but they, as diasporic subjects, do not relinquish their right to return—physically and metaphorically. Frequent visits and cyclical migration are already commonplace in sectors of Cuban society. The narratives surveyed both influence and are influenced by the resulting diasporic imaginary, one that need not bide its time to face the travails intrinsic to the reencounter. With variations, those demands upon the returnee have been portrayed in literature since the beginning of civilization. In this instance, they are worth scrutinizing if for no other reason than to gauge what exactly an island in the Caribbean, small in size but big in dreams, and its diaspora are capable of contributing to the literature on returns.

Notes

Introduction: The Poetics of Return

1. There are variables to be considered regarding the statement. The timing of the return trip, whether in times of relative bonanza, like the 1980s, or during the economic crisis in the 1990s, is one of the variables. Arriving in Cuba in the 1990s made undue demands on the traveler, generally taking her way outside of her comfort zone. Also, notwithstanding the undeniable peculiarities of the one-and-a-half generation, there are commonalities among all returnees, such as the search for a shared identification that they feel they are missing in their current lives. Many honor the same rituals, such as seeking out their relatives and former homes and other spaces associated with their past.

2. According to the 2009–11 U.S. Census American Community Survey, the breakdown is as follows: 49.4 percent entered the United States before 1990, 19.4 percent between 1990 and 1999, and 31.1 percent after 2000. From a total Cuban-American population of 1,829,495, there were 1,066,300 born outside of the United States.

3. Notwithstanding the common ground, bear in mind that, as Mette Louise Berg notes drawing from Karl Mannheim's theoretical work on generations, the one-and-a-half generation is not "an actually existing social group" but rather a group with a "shared migration trajectory" (45)—a trajectory upon which the notion of an imagined community is built. The shared migration history is what makes it an identifiable generation, as the group is diverse with regard to social extraction, political sympathies, and even their assumptions about acculturation.

4. Operation Pedro Pan or Peter Pan ran between 1960 and 1962. It supported the airlift of 14,048 unaccompanied children to the United States in order to save them from presumably being brainwashed by the Communist regime. More about the program is found in chapter 1. It was the largest exodus of unaccompanied minors tout court (M. A. Torres, *The Lost Apple* 88, 250), without the qualifier "organized," until recently. However, the Cuban exodus cannot compare with the several thousand Central American children crossing the border seeking to escape not only

extreme poverty but also gang violence emboldened by drug trafficking. If they make it across the Mexico-U.S. border after the long, treacherous trek, these other children are likely to face deportation. The result is a humanitarian crisis of unprecedented proportions.

5. I borrow the phrase "homing desire" from Avtar Brah, who uses it in her *Cartographies of Diaspora: Contesting Identities* (1996). Her experience living in a number of countries across four continents inspired, I suspect, her usage of the phrase, which captures the ineffability of an elusive aspiration.

6. In his article "Ages, Life Stages, and Generational Cohorts: Decomposing the First and Second Generation in the United States," Rumbaut proposes a breakdown consistent with age at time of arrival, fractioning the second generation into 1.25, 1.5, and 1.75, with the latter being close to the U.S. born.

7. See Elías Miguel Muñoz's essay "Flags and Rags (On Golden Lake)," in which the author confesses his fear of "not being able to continue inventing—idealizing—the Island on the basis of memories" (199).

8. The elements Safran lists are the following: "(1) They, or their ancestors, have been dispersed from a specific original 'center' to two or more 'peripheral,' or foreign, regions; (2) they retain a collective memory, vision, or myth about their original homeland—its physical location, history, and achievements; (3) they believe that they are not—and perhaps cannot be—fully accepted by their host society and therefore feel partly alienated and insulated from it; (4) they regard their ancestral homeland as their true, ideal home and as the place to which they or their descendants would (or should) eventually return—when conditions are appropriate; (5) they believe that they should, collectively, be committed to the maintenance or restoration of their original homeland and to its safety and prosperity; and (6) they continue to relate, personally or vicariously, to that homeland in one way or another, and their ethnocommunal consciousness and solidarity are importantly defined by the existence of such a relationship" (88–89).

9. According to a report in the *Café Fuerte* blog, 1,000 émigrés are repatriated yearly. See "Cuba: Mil emigrados retornan cada año para quedarse en el país." The article lists the application procedures for a permanent return.

10. This is not to say that all Cubans in the United States are either diasporic or transnational. As Tölölyan observes, the population includes assimilated members, ethnics, and a large number of exiles, some of whom display "the full range of diasporic behavior, engage actively in political and cultural self-representation, and care about maintaining contact with Cuba and Cuban communities in other countries, like Puerto Rico, Mexico, and Spain" ("The Contemporary Discourse of Diaspora Studies" 653). Here, too, transnationalism, in the form of contact with Cuba, conflates with diaspora; it counts as one of the manifestations of diasporic behavior.

11. On the island Ambrosio Fornet, who has promoted the literature of the

one-and-a-half generation in Spanish translation when necessary, has also moved toward assuming the label for reasons he has made clear in his essay "The Cuban Literary Diaspora and Its Contexts: A Glossary": "I myself for years resisted using diaspora because it seems to me that to do so would mean, first, taking it out of context, and second, that this would serve only to occlude the connotations of the traditional terms, especially those of a political nature. The question of political connotations, however, was what finally made me adopt it, because I became aware that its 'semantic neutrality,' so to speak, facilitated its insertion into a terrain—that of literary criticism—where it was necessary to work without preconceived ideas, without prejudice. Besides, today the Cuban diaspora is a hybrid of exile and emigration, to which we would have to add unclassified displacements, from the sociological point of view, such as the so-called Peter Pan children, forced by their parents to emigrate while still young" (92). Fornet privileges diaspora as a more neutral as well as inclusive term, a notion with which Víctor Fowler also agrees (see Fowler's "Miradas a la identidad en la literatura de la diaspora").

12. The exile label as an umbrella term is under siege, too, because it leaves many Cubans out. Nancy Raquel Mirabal argues for a more flexible model than the one provided by post-1959 exile, which in her view disregards the history of the pre-1959 Cuban diaspora (368). Mirabal points out that pre-revolutionary migration to the United States must be taken into account if we want to arrive at a comprehensive understanding of the long-standing Cuban presence in the United States, one that discloses other push and pull factors besides political expatriation. For a study of the Cuban presence in the U.S. prior to 1959, see also Gerald E. Poyo.

13. For Rojas see *Isla sin fin* (1999) and for O'Reilly Herrera, her introduction to *Cuban Artists across the Diaspora: Setting the Tent against the House* (2011). I will comment further on the latter in chapter 5.

14. See Fornet's *Memorias recobradas: introducción al discurso literario de la diaspora* (2000), a commendable collection of writings by Cuban Americans edited by the critic. Prior to the publication of this volume, Fornet was the editor of a series of dossiers on the same subject that appeared in *La Gaceta de Cuba* in the 1990s.

15. "Cuban-American literature of exile" implies that there is something distinct, even exceptional, marked by the addition of the word *exile*, about Cuban-American literature that sets it apart from other ethnic literatures, including Latino/a literature. This claim is hardly unique to Álvarez Borland, as there has been some reluctance among critics to include the works of Cuban exiles under the rubric of Latino/a literature due to its politically conservative slant. Given its early conceptualizations as a literature of resistance in the 1960s, it is hard for these critics to imagine how Latino/a literature could possibly house, paraphrasing Pérez Firmat, "appositional," not "oppositional," literature under its label (*Life on the Hyphen* 6). Inherent to these arguments are broad generalizations with the potential of having the unintended

effect of pigeonholing a whole area of studies. Other critics, however, argue in favor of the inclusion of Cuban-American literature into the burgeoning field of Latino/a studies. Two such critics are Marta Caminero-Santangelo and Eliana Rivero ("[Re]Writing Sugarcane Memories: Cuban Americans and Literature").

16. My intention is not to offer a comprehensive overview of dystopian returns. Left out of my summary, for instance, is Guillermo Cabrera Infante's *Mapa dibujado por un espía* (2013) about the author's trip to Havana from Belgium, where he was representing Cuba as cultural attaché, upon hearing about his mother's passing. There, he confronts the transformation of his city along the lines of others depicting a fraught return: "Estaba en su país pero de alguna manera su país no era su país: una mutación imperceptible había cambiado las gentes y las cosas por sus semejantes al revés: ahí estaban todos pero ellos no eran ellos, Cuba no era Cuba" [He was in his homeland, but somehow his homeland was not his homeland: an imperceptible mutation had changed the people as well as things for their reverse, they were all there but they were not themselves, Cuba was not Cuba] (157).

17. Ponte's story is very much in keeping with the *ingravidez* or weightlessness that Odette Casamayor-Cisneros identifies as a hallmark of post-Soviet Cuban literature. The works that the critic examines go beyond dystopia to account for a moment of much uncertainty, without a blueprint for the future. See Casamayor-Cisneros's book on the subject.

18. An exception to the paucity of studies is the interest of scholars in the 1840 return narrative of Mercedes Santa Cruz y Montalvo, the Condesa de Merlín, *Viaje a La Habana*. There are various studies and critical editions of this account, including one by Adriana Méndez Rodenas for the publisher Stockcero.

19. Race relations is also the topic of the more recent *Unbecoming Blackness: The Diaspora Cultures of Afro-Cuban America* (2012), by Antonio López, a book that explores the dynamics of race in Cuban-American literature as well as the lives of prominent Afro-Cubans in the United States, such as Eusebia Cosme, Arturo O'Farrill, and Rómulo Lachatañeré, who forged alliances with African Americans and Afro-Latinos. Taking his cue from critical race theory and the fertile insights of Afro-American writers, López argues about the capacious ability of black characters in many works of literature to both record and elide racial contradictions (190).

20. See Jorge Duany, "Becoming Cuba-Rican," and Pedro Pérez Sarduy, "Writing from Babylon," as examples of narratives from Puerto Rico and London, respectively.

Chapter 1. An Uphill Battle: The Contentious Politics of Return

1. Of course, Castro's revolution has not been the only reason people left Cuba. Toward the end of the nineteenth century, many Cubans sought to escape the political turmoil unfurled by the fight for independence, taking advantage of the opportunities afforded by the burgeoning cigar industry in Key West and Tampa. While there

were 620 residents of Cuban origin in Tampa in 1880, the number had increased to 5,532 by 1890. In New York, a premier magnet for Cuban migration, the census of 1870 reported 15,650 persons of Cuban origin. By the middle of the twentieth century, the population of Cuban origin in the United States was 32,200 (Aja 99–105). The mass exodus triggered by the Castro takeover, however, more than dwarfed that influx.

2. It is a little known fact that on account of the high expectations unleashed by the revolution, more Cubans returned than left the island in 1959. The difference was 12,345 persons in favor of those who returned (Aja 117). There were 81,665 Cubans living in the United States in 1950.

3. The 1970 figure approximates the "less than 3 percent" provided by María Cristina García in *Havana USA* (44) and the 2.8 percent offered by Lourdes Casal and Yolanda Prieto in their essay on black Cubans in the United States (343).

4. Based on the 2004 American Community Survey, the Pew Hispanic Center reported that 86 percent of Cubans in the United States identified themselves as white, and 8 percent chose "some other race." These figures may not correlate faithfully with racial phenotypes, as whiteness is viewed as a measure of success in the adopted country. They are, however, an indication of the racial imbalance within the community. See the Pew Hispanic Center's Fact Sheet *Cubans in the United States*, 3–4.

5. For literature on the differentiated profiles of Cuban migration waves in the United States, see Portes and Bach, *Latin Journey: Cuban and Mexican Immigrants in the United States* (1985); Portes and Rumbaut, *Immigrant America: A Portrait* (1990); García, *Havana/USA: Cuban Exiles and Cuban Americans in South Florida, 1959–1994* (1996) and "The Cuban Population of the United States: An Introduction"; Pedraza, *Political Disaffection in Cuba's Revolution and Exodus* (2007) and "Cuba's Refugees: Manifold Migrations"; Grenier and Pérez, *The Legacy of Exile: Cubans in the United States* (2003); Eckstein, *The Immigrant Divide: How Cuban Americans Changed the U.S. and Their Homeland* (2009), and Y. Prieto, *The Cubans of New Jersey: Immigrants and Exiles in a New Jersey Community* (2009).

6. Papers on Cubans in Canada, Western Europe, and Copenhagen, among other countries, were presented by Jean Stubbs, Nadine Fernández, Mette Louis Berg, and others as part of a panel, "The New Cuban Diaspora," at the Thirtieth International Congress of the Latin American Studies Association in 2012.

7. The numbers for Venezuela are provided by Holly Ackerman (102n1), who points out that there were about twice as many Cubans in the country in the early 1980s. The figures for other cities were cited by Stubbs et al. in their 2012 presentations.

8. For a useful overview of the history of travel restrictions, see Mark P. Sullivan's 2014 Congressional Research Service Report for Congress, "Cuba: U.S. Restrictions on Travel and Remittances," especially 1–15.

9. A total of thirty-eight issues of the journal appeared over a decade. After ceasing publication in New York in 1984, *Areíto* reappeared in Miami under the leadership of

Andrés Gómez, who gained prominence as a vocal member of the Antonio Maceo Brigade. The magazine has closed ranks and is now clearly identified with the Cuban revolution. In the 1970s there was also *Nueva Generación*, which preceded *Areíto*, as well as *Joven Cuba*, another magazine published by young Cuban Americans who advocated for social justice and the rights of U.S. minorities.

10. For an outline of Casal's political trajectory and a selection of her writings, see María Cristina Herrera and Leonel Antonio de la Cuesta's edited volume *Itinerario ideológico*.

11. See Jenna Rose Leving Jacobson's dissertation, "Confessing Exile: Revolution and Redemption in the Narratives of the Cuban *(Re)encuentro*," for a perceptive reading of Grupo Areíto's *Contra viento y marea* as confessional writing, in part meant to gain a foothold as worthy Cubans on the island's revolutionary process. I am grateful to Jacobson for providing me with a copy of her dissertation.

12. See *Baraguá* 2, no. 1 (1979), which includes several articles on the 1979 trip.

13. With an eye to the future, the Brigade was given permission by the Cuban authorities to also organize trips to the island for second-generation Cuban-American children called the Maceítos. The Maceítos Brigade trips took place in 1979 and the early 1980s.

14. It is no coincidence that many documented returns assert the relevance of the house. Among the videos that document the ritual of visiting the former home are Stephen Olsson's *Our House in Havana* (2000) on the return of Silvia Morini, Ruth Behar's *Adio Kerida: Goodbye Dear Love* (2002), Allie Humenuk's *Shadow of the House: Photographer Abelardo Morell* (2007), and Eduardo Lamora's *Cuba, el arte de la espera* (2007).

15. The surname Veltfort was subsequently misspelled in the poetry volume and in other publications. For a possible explanation of the misspelling and the search for the individual behind the name, see Negrón-Muntaner and Martínez San Miguel.

16. See the Bernardo Benes Papers at the Cuban Heritage Collection, box 14, folder 116. See also Mirta Ojito, who chronicles in her memoir the events leading up to the Mariel exodus in 1980, including Benes's role in the historic dialogue. About terrorist activities, see María de los Ángeles Torres's *In the Land of Mirrors*, 100–102.

17. Many of the essays in the volume are written by women, who seem to favor the personal essay over the book-length memoir. It is worth noting that the *Bridges* project began as a 1994 double issue of the *Michigan Quarterly Review*, edited by Ruth Behar in collaboration with her colleague Juan León. The book, however, is edited by Behar alone. For a study of the essays included in this and other volumes, see my article "Reading Lives in Installments: Autobiographical Essays by Women of the Cuban Diaspora." Additional writers covered in the article are Madeline Cámara,

Lourdes Casal, Carlota Caulfield, Kenya Dworkin, María Cristina García, Andrea O'Reilly Herrera, and Eliana Rivero.

18. As I was making last-minute corrections to the manuscript, President Obama and Raúl Castro held simultaneous press conferences in Washington, D.C., and Havana to announce the beginning of a new era. The statements were made after months of secret negotiations between the two parties. Although the embargo will still be enforced, the reopening of ties is likely to facilitate travel.

19. Estela Bravo, a well-known American documentary filmmaker, has directed other videos such as *Miami-Havana* (1992) about divided Cuban families and *Fidel* (2001). She has lived in Cuba for several decades.

20. See California Pedro Pan's video *Pedro Pan of California Responds to Bravo's Documentary*.

21. The intersection of politics and children and the polarizing interpretations of Operation Pedro Pan are precisely the focus of Anita Casavantes Bradford's book, *The Revolution Is for the Children: The Politics of Childhood in Havana and Miami, 1959–1962* (2014).

22. See Kimberly Ramírez's doctoral dissertation, "The Lost Apple Plays: Performing Operation Pedro Pan."

23. As of late, the media has been busy reporting the changing attitude of key individuals regarding Cuba travel. Florida gubernatorial candidate Charlie Christ surprised his supporters in February 2014 when he stated his opposition to continuing the embargo and his plans to consider a trip to Cuba. Likewise, U.S. Chamber of Commerce President and CEO Thomas Donohue led a delegation to Havana in May 2014 to assess the island's business climate. And among Cuban Americans, sugar tycoon Alfonso Fanjul from Palm Beach, Florida, revived his relationship with his homeland during trips to the island in 2012 and 2013. Fanjul is said to have explored business opportunities as well.

24. On the other hand, 63 percent of Cuban Americans believe that Cuba should remain on the U.S. State Department list of countries that sponsor terrorism. See the Cuban Research Institute, School of International and Public Affairs at Florida International University, webpage for poll results over the years.

25. A record high 48 percent of Cuban Americans in Florida voted for Barack Obama, the Democratic candidate, in 2012. The overwhelming support is likely to help reshape U.S. policy toward Cuba. The election to Congress of the first Cuban-American Democrat, Joe Garcia, who defeated Republican David Rivera in 2013, was also held as proof of the more moderate views emerging from within the community (Campo-Flores). However, García lost his seat to the Republican contender in the 2014 midterm elections.

26. The Multilateral Investment Fund of the Inter-American Development Bank estimates that over $8 billion in remittances were sent to the Caribbean region as a whole in 2012 (see the graph on p. 20 of *Remittances to Latin America and the Caribbean*). There has been a remarkable upward trend in the figures for Cuba. In 1998 Cuba received nearly $800 million in transfers (Aja 73). In 2001, the figure was $813 million, based on a World Bank estimate (Pedraza, *Political Disaffection* 207). By 2012, remittance flows to Cuba had soared to $2.6 billion USD (see Morales, "Cuba: 2.6 Billion"). The Havana Consulting Group LLC found that remittances in goods only, or in-kind, rose to $3.5 billion USD in 2013 (see Morales, "Emigrados cubanos enviaron más de 3,500 millones de USD en remesas"). Data on remittances, still sketchy, has not been gathered consistently over time.

27. Additionally, Cuba residents are allowed to stay abroad for a period of twenty-four months (with the option to renew) without losing their rights to property and essentially turning into émigrés. Only those considered a threat to "national security," as well as the doctors, scientists, and other professionals whose absence would trim a qualified workforce, might be held back. Additionally, the law extended the period of time that émigrés can stay on the island from 30 to 90 days (also with the option to renew), and those with a PRE (Permiso de Residencia en el Exterior) may do so for up to 180 days. Cubans who left the country illegally since 1994 may now return for a visit after eight years.

28. The statistics on travel and the breakdown on type of travelers published in even reliable studies as well as reports on projected travel disclose noticeable gaps. It appears that statistics have not been systematically collected over time, in part because the Cuban government refrains from providing detailed information. Travelers are lumped together on the basis of countries where travel originates. I am grateful to Jorge Duany, director of the Cuban Research Institute at Florida International University, and Bob Guild, of Marazul Charters, for the clarification. Exact figures and cumulative statistics are hard to come by. According to Guild, there are various totals for those arriving on charter flights from the United States, but these omit the number of Cuban Americans traveling via third countries (e.g., the Cayman Islands, Cancun, and Nassau), which have been very high during certain years. Still, the Havana Consulting Group LLC, whose mission is to study Cuba's markets, provides cumulative data on their web page, drawing vaguely from the Oficina Nacional de Estadísticas de Cuba and "their own sources." Data covering the period 2007–12 can be accessed on their web page. See particularly Emilio Morales's "Miami Leads in Sending Flights to Cuba." Apparently, the Group, led by Morales, ex-president of the Cuba-based CIMEX, has begun to keep tabs steadily on travel-related matters, including the number of visitors. For 2012, this consulting body reports the arrival of 475,936 Cuban nonresident nationals in Cuba, with 521,314 projected for 2013. On the

other hand, researcher María Dolores Espino reports the arrival of 384,200 Cuban nonresident nationals in Cuba in 2012, based on statistics provided by the United Nations World Tourism Organization for a category of visitors called "Other Caribbean" (after accounting for tourist arrivals in Cuba from individual Caribbean countries). There is an unexplainable discrepancy of over 90,000 visitors in 2012 between both reports.

Chapter 2. Daring to Go Back: In Search of Traces

1. Saltzman draws from the work of Rosalind Krauss, who had previously applied the notion of the index to contemporary art, defining it as follows: "By index I mean that type of sign which arises as the physical manifestation of a cause, of which traces, imprints, and clues are examples" (211).

2. Bejarano offers slightly different statistics: the numbers went from "more than 10,000" before the revolution to about 3,000 by the end of 1963 (40). All of these figures, Robert M. Levine argues, are perforce merely approximations due to the practice of counting only those identified and affiliated as Jews (115, 120–21).

3. See Antonio López, *Unbecoming Blackness*, for comments about the "Afro-Cuban-occupied house," a trope the critic has identified in several memoirs and films evoking a return, among them those of de la Campa, Behar, and Pérez Firmat.

4. *Paladares* are small restaurants that have opened in private houses, *jineteras* are the women who sell their bodies to tourists in exchange for dollars or consumer goods, and *boteros* are collective taxis. They are all fixtures in post-Soviet Cuban society.

5. Another memoir attempting to restore indexical ties, this time through mouth-watering Cuban cuisine, is Eduardo Machado's *Tastes Like Cuba: An Exile's Hunger for Home* (2007). It was not among those selected for this chapter because it is a memoir written in collaboration with another writer, Michael Domitrovich, whose play *Artfuckers* was put onstage under the direction of Machado in 2007. In 2014 they switched roles, with Domitrovich directing Machado's play *Worship*. It is not clear where Domitrovich's contributions end and Machado's begin in *Tastes Like Cuba*.

6. For the evolving relationship between the state and the church in Cuba during the period surveyed in Bejel's narrative and up until the visit of Pope John Paul II, see Yolanda Prieto, "The Catholic Church and the Cuban Diaspora."

7. To the best of my knowledge, the video *Going Back* has not been commercially released but has made the rounds in exhibitions and seminars. It was first shown at the 1998 New York Video Festival.

8. Mendoza admits as much in an essay, "Going Back," published in O'Reilly Herrera's volume *ReMembering Cuba*. He writes that his focus "shifted," and he became interested in the daily lives of Cubans during the post-Soviet period (82).

Chapter 3. Ana Mendieta: Chiseling (in) Cuba

1. See Ambrosio Fornet's "El quinquenio gris: revisitando el término," for an overview of this period marked by coercion and censorship. Fornet is credited with coining the term *quinquenio gris*. The essay was written in 2007 as a response to a heated discussion on Cuban cultural politics triggered by the reappearance on a television program of a cultural commissar from the 1970s. The digital journal *Criterios* published a dossier on the subject. In addition to Fornet's, the dossier includes essays by Desiderio Navarro, Mario Coyula, Eduardo Heras León, Arturo Arango, and Norge Espinosa, among others.

2. See the interview with Ana's sister Raquelín Mendieta in *Fuego de tierra*, a documentary by Kate Horsfield et al. I also draw from a telephone interview with Raquelín on 28 February 2013 for my comments on Ana's first trip.

3. These documents can be found in Veigas's archives at his home in Marianao, Havana.

4. See the articles by Ángel Tomás and Roger Ricardo Luis that appeared in the Cuban press.

5. The interview with Tony Mendieta was conducted in Varadero on 28 May 2011.

6. Interview with José Veigas Zamora on 28 June 2010.

7. Correspondence with Flavio Garciandía dated 27 July 2010.

8. The two projects that were left pending are the G and Farallones del Castillo del Príncipe Project and the Topes de Collantes Project. The former consists of ten to twelve sculptures etched in the *farallón* with the goal of creating a mural while the latter has to do with sculptures made in limestone similar to the one found in Jaruco. Mendieta had the second project in mind for the "Salón de Paisajes" celebrated in 1982, but she never got around to tackling it. A copy of both proposals can be found in Veigas's archives in Havana.

9. The interview with Bedia took place in his Miami studio on 9 July 2010.

10. The correspondence with Garciandía is dated 2 August 2010.

11. Among the art books are Olga Viso's two lavishly illustrated volumes focusing exclusively on Mendieta. Additional examples are José Veigas Zamora's and Camnitzer's books that incorporate her figure in their comprehensive studies of Cuban art—the former including the diaspora and the latter circumscribed to insular production.

12. Having received the 2010 National Prize for the Visual Arts, Rodríguez has distinguished himself for his innovative artistic and pedagogical work. See his interview with Antonio Eligio Fernández in *La Gaceta de Cuba*.

13. García Socarrás follows Mendieta in the use of the body, a form of art that emerged in the 1960s and the 1970s around the time that Ana was taking her first steps in the art world. Both subscribe to the premises of ephemeral, *in situ*, performance,

often outside of galleries and museums, with its implicit denunciation of formal purity as well as the veneration of art objects linked to a market economy and the making of canonical art. Although both men and women have espoused the critique, as art critic Martin Jay points out, for the latter the naked body serves other purposes. It is used as an instrument to reclaim the control of the aesthetic process with the aim of displacing the center of attention from the sublimated, passive body as an object of desire and consumption throughout the centuries to an anti-normative representation of the feminine body, capable of provoking a different kind of gaze (59). Its aim is to free the body from centuries' worth of encrustations laid on it by art and inertia.

14. According to a telephone conversation with the artist, 21 June 2010. Rodríguez later shared with me a video of that visit to Escaleras de Jaruco and another of his students' performances, some inspired by Mendieta.

15. Bruguera was on the faculty at the Department of Visual Arts of the University of Chicago between 2003 and 2010. She makes frequent trips to Cuba. In 2009 she caused a stir in Havana during a performance, "Tatlin's Whisper," by inviting the public to speak up in front of a microphone. Members of the audience took advantage of the opportunity to demand freedom of expression. In December 2015 she startled everyone by calling on fellow Cubans to assemble at a public space, the emblematic Plaza de la Revolución, for a reenactment of "Tatlin's Whisper." Bruguera's intention was to test the limits of the Cuban government's tolerance toward free speech only days after Barack Obama's and Raúl Castro's press conferences on the resumption of diplomatic relations between the United States and Cuba. The artist was detained briefly by Cuban authorities before she had a chance to show up at the plaza. She was arrested again, and her passport was taken away from her after she refused to give up on her efforts to stage the performance. Prior to leaving for Cuba, Bruguera had been using art to call attention to the plight of immigrants through a program funded by the Queens Museum of Art in New York. Her work is at the intersection of art and politics.

16. See Alexandra Gonzenbach for an application of Julia Kristeva's theory of the abject to an analysis of Mendieta's work.

17. Two anthologies of critical essays on Cuban art published recently suggest that Tonel's idea of the "major map" is gradually gaining ground. Both volumes reveal the positive impact of displacements, postmodern, and postcolonial discourse on the appreciation of difference and the blurred boundaries between center and periphery. The influence of such discourse helps to project the deterritorialization of Cuban culture and the simultaneous recognition of artists from the diaspora in a more favorable light. See Andrés Isaac Santana as well as Magaly Espinosa and Kevin Power for their treatment of this topic.

Chapter 4. Cuban Childhood Redux

1. Similarly, Raul Rodriguez, the Miami architect about whom David Rieff writes in *The Exile: Cuba in the Heart of Miami* (1993), recognizes the healing power of return: "The more I go to Havana . . . the less I am the eleven-year-old I was and the more I am able to behave as the person of forty-four that I am today" (57–58). It was looking for a way out of the sense of disconnectedness between his childhood in Havana and his adulthood in Miami that Rodriguez made a number of trips to Havana (71).

2. I draw from my interview with Pujol on 17 April 2012 for my account of his returns to Cuba. In this section on Pujol, the words in quotation marks are his unless otherwise indicated. See also Pujol's brief introductory essay in the *Taxonomías/Taxonomies* catalog.

3. For a sociological study of the Cuban community in Puerto Rico, see Cobas and Duany. For a personal take on the community, see Duany's "Becoming Cuba-Rican," which describes some of the ideological differences between the older exiles and their children. Among the latter, many question Puerto Rico's neocolonial status as well as the animosities between the United States and Cuba.

4. See Espacio Aglutinador's website at http://www.espacioaglutinador.com/. The gallery opened in 1994 in the home of Sandra Ceballos and Ezequiel Suárez with the purpose of disseminating unofficial, alternative points of view in the visual arts in Cuba.

5. To get a sense of the impact of local exile politics on the artistic community in Miami, see Jenni Lukac's interview with María Brito, César Trasobares, María Lino, and other artists, in which they offer their candid opinions about the complex intersection of art and politics.

6. I am alluding to *Improper Conduct*, a 1984 documentary by Néstor Almendros and Orlando Jiménez Leal about the persecution of homosexuals and dissidents, some of whom were sent to special labor camps in the 1960s. This being the 1990s, proper conduct had more to do with politics *tout court* rather than homosexual behavior, no longer as much of a taboo.

7. Accused of being traitors to the motherland, émigrés had been torn away from collective memory and thrown into the dustbin of national history. The infamous *Diccionario de la literatura cubana* (1980) left out the entry for Guillermo Cabrera Infante, an avowed dissident writer, among others. There have been improvements in the way writers such as Cabrera Infante are treated in Cuba nowadays, with some being gradually restored to their hard-won place in the Cuban literary canon. However, it appears that what is being published is still rather selective.

8. The two exhibitions were *Latin American Art, a Woman's View: María Brito-Avellana, Ana Mendieta, Elena Presser*, in 1981, and *Transcending the Borders of Memory:*

María Brito, María Magdalena Campos-Pons, María Martínez-Cañas, Ana Mendieta, in 1994 (Martínez 86).

9. Personal conversation with the artist, 19 November 2013, at the closing of *Body of Work*, a group exhibition at the Kresge Gallery, Ramapo College of New Jersey.

10. These are Brito's words in an e-mail addressed to O'Reilly Herrera.

11. See Brito's explanation of her installation *The Garden and the Fruit*, in her essay "Merely a Player," inspired by the harrowing experiences of a political prisoner in Cuba.

12. For background information on Cuba's involvement in the Angolan war, see Piero Gleijeses, *Visions of Freedom: Havana, Washington, Pretoria, and the Struggle for Southern Africa, 1976–1991* (2013).

13. The skewed way in which blame is assigned in the book has raised a few eyebrows. A case in point, writing about autobiography as an important resource for historians, Paula S. Fass notes both the richness of details found in Eire's first book of memoirs and his "deeply biased" (111) opinions about the Cuban revolution. Historians should beware, Fass warns. It appears that the tendency to pit memory against reason, objectivity, or even restraint is not exclusive of Eire. David Rieff contends that it is also present in other Cuban-American memoirs such as Pablo Medina's (*The Exile* 70). While the conundrum would appear to be part and parcel of the "Exile's Childhood," Gene Bell-Villada takes issue with the assumption, offering Vladimir Nabokov's memoir as an example of self-control (27).

14. It is ironic when after experiencing a scary incident with a pervert in his neighborhood in Havana, Eire blames the revolution for not having succeeded in changing the Cuban people for the better as it had promised to do (*Waiting for Snow* 322). Similarly, the revolution, or rather Fidel Castro, is also at fault when an incident of the same nature occurs in the Chicago subway years later, when Eire is fifteen. This, on top of his already dire situation, elicits a sarcastic expression of gratitude: "Thank you, Fidel. Thank you very much. Muchas gracias, compañero" (*Waiting for Snow* 205).

15. Pérez Firmat's memoir features a similar episode of sexualization of the only (black?) maid making an appearance in his family's dwelling in Havana. See Antonio López's critical reading of the gendered and racial connotations of this passage (195–97).

16. For further considerations on the concept of cultural citizenship, see William Flores and Rina Benmayor. It refers to the battle for the recognition of cultural rights among minorities.

17. The resulting detachment between nation and national identity falls in line with calls from a range of critics for an expanded notion of *lo cubano*, as argued in the introduction. For a theoretical framework of the nation as a discursive construction

that is always in the process of being composed, see the postcolonial critic Homi K. Bhabha as well as the French philosopher Étienne Balibar.

18. A prolific writer, Pérez Firmat has drawn largely from personal experience for his poetry, fiction, and essays, and that experience is deeply connected with the Cuban-American culture of the one-and-a-half generation. See especially *Carolina Cuban* (1987), *Anything but Love* (2000), and *Scar Tissue* (2005), in addition to his memoir, which was nominated for the 1995 Pulitzer Prize for nonfiction.

19. For the development of Miami under Cuban exiles, see Guillermo J. Grenier and Alex Stepick III, *Miami Now!* (1992); Alejandro Portes and Alex Stepick's *City on the Edge: The Transformation of Miami* (1993); and Robert M. Levine and Moisés Asís, *Cuban Miami* (2000). David Rieff's *The Exile* provides a more introspective view of the enclave.

20. It is hard to say how widespread the identification with a displaced homeland is among Cuban Americans, but it would appear not to be an exceptional case among diasporic communities. A scholar of the Pakistani diaspora, Mark-Anthony Falzon, asserts that cities other than the country of origin can become the "cultural heart" of a diaspora even while the diasporic people maintain a nostalgic and emotional attachment to their homeland. This is the case with Bombay, which has become another homeland for displaced Pakistanis. Moreover, when members of the community move to other places, they return to the adopted city for family, business connections, socializing, and even matchmaking efforts (Falzon 672). The fluid sense of place accomplished by the Pakistani diaspora urges the critic to argue for decentering the notion of homeland, both geographically and analytically (Berg 182), that is, for imagining the homeland anew. However, for many reasons Bombay is not Little Havana. It would be appealing to extrapolate from Falzon's comments, if only for the glimpse they afford of what a decentered homeland might look like, but there are differences between the two diasporas. Among these are the historical origins of the Cuban diaspora, the ongoing Cuban exodus, the continuance of the regime that sparked the various waves of migration, and the seeming lack of interconnectedness among Cubans throughout the world. Still, Cuban Miami is an important node for the Cuban diaspora, and some of Falzon's observations may apply.

21. Evidently, the South Florida location has been transformed over the years. As critics claim, Miami has become less Cuban and more Latino. See Rieff, *The Exile*. It is doubtful that more recent émigrés from the island feel the same pull, probably preferring instead to head to Havana and other Cuban cities to quench their thirst for shared memories.

22. My gratitude to Gustavo Pérez Firmat for sending me a copy of "A Cuban in Mayberry," his keynote address at the South Atlantic Modern Language Association Congress in Durham, North Carolina, on 9 November 2012. At the congress, which was devoted to memoirs, there was a panel dedicated to him, where I presented this

section of the chapter on his autobiography. The critic expanded his views on *The Andy Griffith Show* and the fit between person and place in *A Cuban in Mayberry: Looking Back at America's Hometown* (2014).

Chapter 5. Vicarious Returns and a Usable Past in *The Agüero Sisters, Days of Awe,* and *Loving Che*

1. See O'Reilly Herrera's introduction to *Cuban Artists across the Diaspora: Setting the Tent against the House* (2011), in which she elaborates on Bourriaud's notion of the *radicant*, a term applied to a species of plants that grow roots as they press forward. Like the ivy, the Cub*ands'* identity is both rooted and portable, 12–13.

2. See critical essays and interviews by Alfonso, Araújo, Campuzano, Leyva, and Alfredo Prieto.

3. Obejas's work has appeared in translation on the island as well. Editorial Letras Cubanas published in 2009 a collection of her stories, written between 1994 and 2007, titled *Aguas y otros cuentos*. A review by Vitalina Alfonso appeared in UNEAC's *La Gaceta de Cuba* in 2010.

4. In his essay "El retorno de las yolas," Silvio Torres Saillant elaborates on the idea that the Dominican diaspora has the potential to help modify the conceptual parameters of the discourse on Dominican identity through their exposure to other ways of living and thinking (38). See also Torres Saillant's "Antelación: sobre la perspectiva diaspórica," in which the critic claims the existence of a diasporic perspective in connection with the Dominican diaspora (398–401). In the same vein, I argue that Cuban-American writers are invested in the interrogation of aspects of the discourse pertaining to Cuban identity. Eliana Rivero alludes to this reconceptualization process among Cubans of the diaspora when she writes: "In our case, as the Cuban diasporic interpretive community, it would behoove us to remember that we [Cuban-American writers and critics] are reformulating and reweighing (in the original Latin/Romance meaning of *repensare*, to rethink and to weigh again, *sopesar* in Spanish) the very meaning of Cubanness, questioning its inherent essentialism and proposing a more inclusive and extensive signification for the term and its derivatives" ["In Two or More (Dis)places" 197].

5. Additional parallels appear across novels by these writers, such as the role of journals and letters in transmitting fragments of a family history in *Dreaming in Cuban, The Agüero Sisters, Days of Awe,* and *Loving Che*; the use of the trope of the "bad" or absent mother; the infatuation with historical male figures in both *Dreaming in Cuban* and *Loving Che*; and the distrust of grand narratives. There seems to be a zeitgeist at work here, strengthened by the female perspective in all of these works.

6. Other Cuban-American works featuring a vicarious return are, in no particular order, Oscar Hijuelos's *The Mambo Kings Play Songs of Love* (1989) and *Beautiful María of My Soul* (2010); Pablo Medina's *The Return of Felix Nogara* (2000); Uva

de Aragón's *Memoria del silencio* (2002); short stories by Sonia Rivera-Valdés in her collection *Las historias prohibidas de Marta Veneranda* (2001); Elías Miguel Muñoz's *Brand New Memory* (1998); Margarita Engle's *Singing to Cuba* (1993) and *Skywriting* (1995); and Roberto G. Fernández's *El príncipe y la bella cubana: los amores de don Alfonso de Borbón y Battenberg y doña Edelmira Sampedro y Robato* (2014). Among plays and performances are Carmelita Tropicana's performance piece *Milk of Amnesia/Leche de Amnesia* (1994); Nilo Cruz's drama *Hortensia and the Museum of Dreams* (2005); Pedro Monge Rafuls's play *Nadie se va del todo* (written in 1991, after Monge's first trip to Cuba, and published in 1995); Héctor Santiago's piece *Balada de un verano en La Habana* (1992); Carmen Peláez's one-woman show *Rum and Coke* (2008); and last but not least, one of the earliest works to tackle the subject, René Alomá's play *A Little Something to Ease the Pain* (1981). Alomá's play was first produced by Toronto Arts Productions at the St. Lawrence Center in November-December 1980 and later translated into Spanish as *Alguna cosita que alivie el sufrir*. Peláez's *Rum and Coke* played at the Abingdon Theatre Company in New York City in February-March 2008. I am grateful to Peláez for sending me a copy of the manuscript. Together, all of these works comprise close to three decades of contemplating return, and even reconciliation, through fiction.

On the island, the act of returning appears as well in short stories such as "El regreso" (1962), by Calvert Casey; "Viaje a La Habana" (1995), by Reinaldo Arenas; novels such as Leonardo Padura's *La novela de mi vida* (2002), built around two parallel narratives, the return to Cuba of José María Heredia in the nineteenth century and of a recent Cuban émigré; in the documentaries, films, and testimonies of Jesús Díaz, specifically *55 hermanos* (1978), *Lejanía* (1985), and *De la patria y el exilio* (1979); in addition to *Desde los blancos manicomios* (2008), by Margarita Mateo Palmer, who, like de Aragón's novel *Memoria del silencio*, focuses on two sisters separated by exile who reunite at the end (see chapter 6 for additional titles). Moreover, there are a number of plays by Alberto Pedro Torriente and lesser known playwrights that address the subject, as Vivian Martínez Tabares makes clear in her essay "El reencuentro: un tema polémico," published in 1999. In other works, such as *Posesas de La Habana* (2004), by Teresa Dovalpage, or *La isla de los amores infinitos* (2006), by Daína Chaviano (both now living in the United States), there is a return to situations, recollections, affective ties, and cultural codes that link Cubans on the island with those in the diaspora. This partial listing suggests a thematic interest that spans both shores.

7. From García's answers to questions posed by an anonymous interviewer. They appear in "A Conversation with Cristina García," part of A Reader's Guide, an addendum to the 1998 Ballantine edition of *The Agüero Sisters*.

8. I thank Karen S. Christian for reminding me of Benítez-Rojo's comments. His

reflections also resonate nicely with the bilingual publications of some of the writers explored in the book. Their double consciousness manifests itself linguistically, too.

9. Outside of Cuba, though, the worshipping of Martí has been the object of revisionist accounts of his ideas as well as the uses of Martí by various political factions. See Lillian Guerra, *The Myth of José Martí: Conflicting Nationalisms in Early Twentieth-Century Cuba* (2005), and Francisco Morán, *Martí, la justicia infinita: Notas sobre ética y otredad en la escritura martiana* (2014).

10. See Raúl Rosales Herrera for a fruitful application of post-memory to the work of Cecilia Rodríguez Milanés, a second-generation Cuban-American writer whose credits include *Marielitos, Balseros, and Other Exiles* (2009). Like Menéndez, Rodríguez Milanés explores topics dear to the Cuban-American pathos.

11. See Menéndez's interview with Alfredo Prieto, in which she expands on this idea.

12. In her first novel, too, García draws a parallel between the private and public spheres, between the family story and History. See O'Reilly Herrera, "Women and the Revolution," for a detailed reading of the novel along these lines.

13. Foreign control of Cuba's natural resources by the United States, which had been rapidly expanding in the first few decades of the twentieth century, is of utmost concern to Ortiz. The ethnographer decries its deleterious effect on Cuban society, given how absolved it is of direct accountability and responsibility toward Cubans. For an analysis of how the status quo played out within the framework of Cuban nationalism, see Rojas, "Transculturation and Nationalism."

14. The quotations in Rojas's text are from Fernando Ortiz's *Etnia y sociedad*.

15. Another incident was the 1939 denial of entry to Jews on board the SS *St. Louis*, an ocean liner with over nine hundred Jews that was forced to return to Europe after Cuba, the United States, and Canada, refused to let them land. Robert M. Levine claims that Jews were excluded from some professions as well as from the social clubs founded by the Cuban elite (120).

16. See both Maya Socolovsky's and Kelli Lyon Johnson's essays on the relevant role of translation in the novel.

17. Ale's role resembles the one played by Pilar Puente, the main character in Cristina García's *Dreaming in Cuban*. Pilar, too, serves as the storehouse of her family's annals, even if from abroad. She, by the way, is intertextually mentioned in the novel as a U.S.-based Cuban-born artist with whom Menach's granddaughter Deborah collaborates (*Days of Awe* 322).

18. Menéndez has been called very unsavory names by bloggers in the Miami Cuban community because of her choice of subject. For them, the novel has an unquestionably oxymoronic title.

19. Eddy Chibás was a politician, radio commentator, and leader of the Ortodoxo

party, who denounced government corruption indefatigably and, frustrated by his inability to substantiate his claims, shot himself during a radio broadcast in 1951.

20. José Antonio Echeverría was co-founder of the Directorio Estudiantil, a clandestine student organization that offered resistance to the Batista dictatorship. He died in 1957 during an organized assault on the presidential palace.

21. One could speculate as to why the author chose Che Guevara, instead of other revolutionary heroes of the time, to be at the forefront of that history. A possible answer may be that many identify Che with revolutionary idealism and courage, that is, with Revolution as a utopic, liberating space more than with revolutionary praxis sustained over time and exposed to arbitrariness, corruption, and failure. It is also true that by choosing Che as a putative father, Teresa hands down a kinship that transcends Cuba given Che's international stature.

Chapter 6. Toward a Boomerang Aesthetic: The View from the Island

1. The trite treatment of émigrés is hardly unique to Cuban culture. Silvio Torres Saillant, for instance, notes that émigrés in the Dominican Republic are blamed for fomenting idleness through remittances as well as for deforming the Spanish language. Dominicans visiting or returning to the island may also be perceived as aggravating criminality and corruption (*El retorno* 42–54). Torres Saillant is in favor of recognizing the contributions of émigrés to countering retrograde ideas such as a racist ideology and the maintenance of social inequality. He argues that migration can play a positive role in redefining Dominicanness (*El retorno* 22–98). Likewise, Juan Flores exposes the predicament of a Puerto Rican diaspora that feels like a stranger in its own land, pointing out that its presence "all too often spurs resentment, ridicule and fear, and even disdain and social discrimination with clear racial and class undertones" (5). Flores, too, feels that returning migrants can intervene positively and critically in their native culture. While the three diasporas from the Hispanic Caribbean share some common ground, nowhere is the salience of politics as noticeable as in the Cuban case.

2. See Susan Thomas's essay "Cosmopolitan, International, Transnational: Locating Cuban Music" for a description of some of the ways in which Cuban music has absorbed and redefined new sounds since the eighteenth century. Thomas recognizes, however, that the scenario has changed since the 1990s due to increased migration. See also Borges-Triana, 103–6, and Silot Bravo. Other musicians who have returned in recent times are Diana Fuentes, who went back to Cuba from Puerto Rico to introduce her new album, *Planeta Planetario*, to a Cuban audience in June 2014. Others have returned permanently. Such is the case with Manuel González Hernández, better known as Manolín, el Médico de la Salsa, who went back in October 2013 after leaving for Miami in 2001. Isaac Delgado and Tanya Rodríguez have likewise returned on a permanent basis.

3. The lyrics appear in English translation in Osmel Almaguer's article on Torrens in havanatimes.org.

4. The noted attenuation of politics should not be extended to all areas and subject matters. The music sphere especially has seen the rise of groups highly critical of the regime in recent times, though not all share the same goals. These groups use public spaces available to them to voice popular grievances against the Castro government, sometimes in an attempt to mobilize people in casting doubt on the legitimacy of the system. See Nora Gámez Torres on the Cuban hip-hop group Los Aldeanos.

5. An additional example of musical projects across borders is Gema and Pavel's album *Art Bembé* (2003), for which tracks were recorded in three locations, Madrid, New York, and Havana. See Thomas, 116.

6. Lillian Guerra writes about the recruitment of Cubans from the early ranks of exile for the "world's largest CIA station at the University of Miami with an annual budget of $50 million, a staff of four hundred agents, and a payroll of perhaps ten to fifteen thousand informants, saboteurs, and self-appointed political saviors"(*Visions of Power* 4) between 1960 and 1965. These efforts were directed at engineering invasions and fomenting counterrevolution in Cuba.

7. Both labels have been subjected to critique in recent times. The ideological use of *cubanidad* and *cubanía* in the political discourse in both the island and exile has motivated some to opt for the more neutral *lo cubano*. See the introduction to *Cuba, the Elusive Nation*, by Damián J. Fernández and Madeline Cámara Betancourt, especially pages 5–6.

8. An appendix to the first republican constitution of 1901 and later repealed in 1934, the Platt Amendment, from which the adjective *plattista* derives, recognized the right of the United States of America to intervene in Cuba, giving it also access to national territory for the establishment of coal mines and naval bases.

9. Essence, binary, and teleology are built into Prieto's discourse, but other sections of his address are a bit more nuanced. He takes into account his audience, clarifying that not all exiles share the culture attached to *cubanidad*, the same way that not all island residents are examples of *cubanía*. Additionally, in the discussion that followed his speech, which is included in the volume on the conference proceedings, Prieto recognized that his essay, which sought to present the Cuban revolution as the end result of a historical process fraught with irreconcilable, dueling views of the nation, had to rely on a particular rhetoric helping to throw into relief the triumph of *cubanía* made possible by the 1959 takeover. From Prieto's vantage point, revolutionary Cuba had finally achieved nationalist closure, turning into a bastion of *cubanía*.

10. Prieto makes a reference to the terms used by Jorge Duany in his article "Neither Golden Exile nor Dirty Worm: Ethnic Identity in Recent Cuban-American Novels."

11. Perusing earlier works, I came across a couple of short stories that make no effort whatsoever at bringing subtlety into play in their depiction of the returning émigré. The title of one short story by Raúl González de Cascorro, "El chulo regresa" [The Pimp Returns], says it all. The character's flaws pile up. Not only is the returnee someone whose former livelihood as a pimp makes him suspect; he is also a criminal mercenary coming to invade the island. In another story, "La huida," by Arístides Gil Acejo, the character who returns on a motorboat had just abandoned a group of fellow citizens in the open seas at the first sight of the Cuban coast guard. Both stories are included in an anthology, *Cuentos del mar* (1981), edited by Gustavo Eguren. It should be noted that stereotyping also pervaded works about the insurrection against Batista, with writers who sympathized with the nascent revolutionary movement, such as Guillermo Cabrera Infante, Lisandro Otero, and Edmundo Desnoes, depicting the revolutionaries as virtuous and the *batistianos* as abominable (see Rojas, *Essays in Cuban Intellectual History* 128–29).

12. In his positive review of *Lejanía*, which appeared in *Revolución y cultura* following the release of the film, Eliseo Alberto attributes a waxlike quality to the character of Susana, who resembles a museum object. She is a representative, Alberto claims, of a world driven by greed that disappeared a quarter of a century ago. Stuck in the past and unable to understand the "New Man" being built by the revolution, Susana is a prime example of mere *cubanidad* in this Jesús Díaz movie. It is interesting to note that intellectuals like Díaz and Alberto, both of whom would leave Cuba years later to become highly critical of the revolution from abroad, were caught up in a discourse that projected the exiles as a monolithic bloc, the target of serious accusations. Their indictment of exiles overlaps rather neatly with the one advanced by official discourses, making them complicit with the construction of a prototype for national and international consumption. The exiles are, in essence, a symbol of the prerevolutionary Republican period and thus, in the internal logic of the episteme, deserving of scorn. Intellectuals who backed Cuba's nationalist and social justice program, among them the revolutionary but also critical and astute Díaz and Alberto, assisted in its logic, rarely remaining above the fray. After being very active as a writer and filmmaker in Cuba until the 1990s, Jesús Díaz went on to live in Berlin and Madrid, where he continued to publish and was named co-editor of the journal *Encuentro de la Cultura Cubana*, whose first issue came out in 1996. Eliseo Alberto fled Cuba in 1990, settling in Mexico, where he published several important books, including *Informe contra mí mismo* (1997) and *Caracol Beach* (Premio Alfaguara de Novela 1998). Both writers died prematurely.

In an interview with Lilliam Oliva Collmann conducted in 1996 and published in the journal *Cuban Studies/Estudios cubanos* in 1998, Díaz talks candidly about the many prejudices he held toward the Miami Cuban population, which he claims to have conquered right after his first visit to the enclave in 1994, when he came in contact with former acquaintances who had relocated in the city.

13. Like Vera León, the artists grouped around CAFÉ, an acronym for Cuban-American Foremost Exhibitions, value positively the new elements they have been able to incorporate in their work. Led by Leandro Soto and others, the artists have organized more than a dozen exhibitions since 2001. They are the subjects of O'Reilly Herrera's *Cuban Artists across the Diaspora*. As the critic states referring to the benefits derived from contact zones, "Rather than emphasizing loss and rupture, this alternative response to displacement stresses the fertile nature of dispersion, scattering, and change. It celebrates the creative potential of the blending of new and old cultural elements, and the positive aspects of movement, dislocation, and cultural exchange" (199). See also Pérez Firmat's classic study *Life on the Hyphen* (1994) about the rewards of biculturalism (4–5).

14. Rolando Pérez Betancourt's *Mujer que regresa* (1986) is among the first narratives to address the return of the one-and-a-half generation. The novel features the return of a woman twenty years after leaving with her family in the 1960s. She renews an old relationship and conceives a child. However, she dies while giving birth months later in the United States. Returning and renewing old relationships, we are led to believe, lead to mortal danger.

15. Like Solás, some Cuban writers abroad view coming into contact with other cultures in a negative light, as an experience that provokes anxiety and confusion. See Fowler, "Miradas a la identidad en la literatura de la diaspora," which reviews various takes on the process. Although, on the other hand, there are more balanced assessments, this is the predominant view in Cuban literature and film.

16. One such attempt is Fornet's *Memorias recobradas*, meaning recovered by Cuba, to which these pieces of collective memory fabricated in the diaspora are entrusted. As noted, this was a praiseworthy project that sought to make Cuban-American writers such as Gustavo Pérez Firmat, Eliana Rivero, Roberto G. Fernández, Lourdes Gil, and Emilio Bejel, among others who began to publish after fleeing Cuba, known to island-based readers. There are obvious discrepancies between the reflections on Cuban-American culture and literature made by these writers and their image in some of the works discussed in this chapter. Should these writings be considered also a return, one wishes there would have been more of them, and earlier, and that they would have been widely circulated. The challenge is to "recover" all of these bits without divesting them of their difference.

17. The egg motif is also utilized in a play by Ulises Rodríguez Febles, *Huevos* (2007), and in a song by Erick Sánchez with the mundane title of "Los huevos que te tiramos cuando te fuiste con la escoria." Sánchez's lyrics, from the 1990s, echo both Alonso's short story and Frank Delgado's "La otra orilla" with its references to

the appreciation of eggs wasted on a character, a *marielita* who suffered rejection at the hands of her classmates. As far as I know, the song has not been commercially recorded. I obtained the lyrics through the Centro de la Torriente Brau, in Havana, which promotes the work of *trovadores*.

18. A more subtle representation of the returnee that left via Mariel also appears in Enrique Pineda Barnet's film *La anunciación* (2009), about a Cuban family separated by exile. The film, which endorses reconciliation, deals with a situation somewhat similar to *Reina y Rey*, but here it is not the exile or émigré who is driven by dark motives but the child's grandmother in Cuba, who wants her daughter, visiting from the United States, to become a surrogate mother at the cost of separating father and son.

Another balanced portrayal of a *marielito* appears in *Mi tío el exiliado* (2012), by Yerandy Fleites Pérez, a playwright born in 1982. In the play, a gay man who left through Mariel returns thirty years later to his sister and her family. Ailing with AIDS, he has come home to die, determined to assert his right to rest in his native country. Conflicts within the family and with neighbors arise, with some wanting to take economic advantage of the sick man's visit. Although in his final days, the *marielito* is not stripped of dignity. But he has waited until he no longer has anything to lose to assert that right, turning it into a pyrrhic victory. The play was staged at Sala Rita Montaner, in Havana, where I saw it in December 2012.

19. Two additional short stories by women writers who erupted in the Cuban literary scene in the 1990s (see Luisa Campuzano, "Narradoras cubanas") adopt a similar strategy of deferment or suspension. Anna Lidia Vega Sarova's "Erre con erre" describes in shorthand, in a brief post-scriptum titled "Escena prescindible," the reencounter of a young woman who returns to her ten-year-old son and mother-in-law. Despite the severe past tension affecting the family unit due to the woman's *jineterismo*, which led her to a female tourist who brought her to the United States, this "unnecessary" and unexpected ending describes their emotional reunion. The breach between past tension and present excitement is left out of the narrative, and what happens after the initial embrace can go either way.

Marilyn Bobes's "Pregúntaselo a Dios," too, revolves around a newly married *jinetera* who, at the beginning of the 1990s, follows her husband to "Tulús," the French town where he lives with his mother. From there she writes to her girlfriend on the island, keeping her up to date regarding the downside of the arrangement. As an "other," she has had to face scores of racial and class prejudices. As her disillusionment grows, so does her deep yearning for her former life. She finally goes back to visit, but all the reader gets to "see" are the tears of the woman, resigned to a fate to which the precarious circumstances engendered by the crisis has condemned her, as she is sitting on Havana's sea wall next to her girlfriend. Here, too, the returnee is almost unrepresentable, but her tears speak volumes about the value she places on the homeland, the space containing all that she emotionally craves.

20. The lyrics by Lien Rodríguez (Matanzas, 1975) and Reinaldo Pantoja (Bayamo, 1977) can be found in *Quiero una canción: Jóvenes trovadores cubanos* (2012), an anthology edited by Manuel Leandro Ibarra.

21. The Havanization concert did not mark the first time that Cuban musicians based on the island and abroad came together. Prior collaborations occurred in Madrid in 2003, when Carlos Varela and his band were joined onstage by Kelvis Ochoa and Athanai (Thomas 116), and in Havana that same year when the Habana Abierta band, based in Madrid, played at the Tropical, which filled to capacity (Thomas 117). The digital magazine *What's On Havana* reported in its February 2014 issue that Habana Abierta had played recently at the Habana Café Cantante. The composition of the group has changed over the years. Kelvis Ochoa and Boris Larramendi left to pursue solo careers, and on stage this time around were Vanito Brown, Alejandro Gutiérrez, Luis Alberto Barbería, and José Luis Medina.

Works Cited

Author's Note: Although the *MLA Handbook for Writers of Research Papers* (2009) does not require URLs in citations, I have provided them for the few sources for which a Google search did not yield the targeted website.

Ackerman, Holly. "Different Diasporas: Cubans in Venezuela, 1959–1998." O'Reilly Herrera, *Cuba* 90–106.
Acosta, Carlos. *No Way Home: A Dancer's Journey from the Streets of Havana to the Stages of the World*. New York: Scribner, 2007. Print.
Ahmed, Sara, Claudia Castañeda, Anne-Marie Fortier, and Mimi Sheller, eds. *Uprooting/Regroundings: Questions of Home and Migration*. Oxford: Berg, 2003. Print.
Aja Díaz, Antonio. *Al cruzar las fronteras*. Havana: CEDEM and UNFPA, 2009. Print.
Alabau, Magali. 1992. *Hemos llegado a Ilión*. 2nd ed. Madrid: Editorial Betania, 2013. Print.
Alberto, Eliseo. *Caracol Beach*. Madrid: Alfaguara, 1998. Print.
———. "Elogio de *Lejanía*." *Revolución y cultura* (Aug. 1985): 8. Print.
———. *Informe contra mí mismo*. México, D.F.: Alfaguara, 1997. Print.
Alfonso, Vitalina. *Ellas hablan de la Isla*. Havana: Ediciones Unión, 2002. Print.
———. "Redescubrimiento de la infancia desde una mirada testimonial." *La Gaceta de Cuba* 6 (Nov./Dec. 2011): 42–46. Print.
Almaguer, Osmel. "David Torrens on the HT Musical Bridge from Cuba." *Havana Times* 6 Feb. 2011. Web. 29 June 2013.
Almendros, Néstor, and Orlando Jiménez Leal, dirs. *Improper Conduct*. Les Films du Losange and Antenne 2, 1984. Film.
Alomá, René. *A Little Something to Ease the Pain*. Toronto: Playwrights Canada, 1981. Print.
Alonso, Nancy. "Diente por diente." *Estatuas de sal: cuentistas cubanas contemporáneas*. Ed. Mirta Yáñez and Marilyn Bobes. Havana: Ediciones Unión, 1996. 223–32. Print.
———. *Tirar la primera piedra*. Havana: Editorial Letras Cubanas, 1997. Print.

Álvarez Borland, Isabel. *Cuban American Literature of Exile: From Person to Persona.* Charlottesville: University of Virginia Press, 1998. Print.

———. "Displacements and Autobiography in Cuban-American Fiction." *World Literature Today* 68.1 (1994): 43–48. *JSTOR.* Web. 25 Jan. 2014.

———. "Figures of Identity: Ana Menéndez's and Guillermo Cabrera Infante's Photographs." Álvarez-Borland and Bosch 31–45.

Álvarez Borland, Isabel, and Lynette Bosch, eds. *Negotiating Identities in Art, Literature, and Philosophy: Cuban Americans and American Culture.* New York: SUNY Press, 2009. Print.

Aparicio, Eduardo. "Fragments from Cuban Narratives: A Portfolio by Eduardo Aparicio." Behar, *Bridges to Cuba* 142–58.

Aparicio García, Bernardo. "A Better Homeland." Rev. of *Learning to Die in Miami*, by Carlos Eire. *Touchstone: A Journal of Mere Christianity* 24.5 (2011): 64–65. Print.

Aragón, Uva de. "Distancia no quiere decir olvido: Viajes a la semilla." *Cultura y letras cubanas en el siglo XXI.* Ed. Araceli Tinajero. Madrid: Iberoamericana, 2009. 203–13. Print.

———. *Memoria del silencio.* Miami: Ediciones Universal, 2002. Print.

Aranda, Elizabeth M. *Emotional Bridges to Puerto Rico: Migration, Return Migration, and the Struggles of Incorporation.* Langham: Rowman and Littlefield, 2006. Print.

Araújo, Nara. "I Came All the Way from Cuba So I Could Speak Like This? Cuban and Cuban-American Literatures in the U.S." *Comparing Postcolonial Literatures: Dislocations.* Ed. Ashok Bery and Patricia Murray. New York: St. Martin's Press, 2000. 93–103. Print.

Arenas, Reinaldo. *Antes que anochezca.* Barcelona: Tusquets, 1992. Print.

———. "Viaje a La Habana." *Viaje a La Habana (novela en tres viajes).* Miami: Ediciones Universal, 1995. 95–153. Print.

Arrom, Juan José. *Mitología y artes prehispánicas de las Antillas.* México, D.F.: Siglo XXI Editores, 1975. Print.

Bachelard, Gaston. 1958. *The Poetics of Space.* Trans. Maria Jolas. Boston: Beacon Press, 1994. Print.

Balibar, Étienne. "The Nation Form: History and Ideology." *Race, Nation, Class: Ambiguous Identities.* Ed. Étienne Balibar and Immanuel Wallerstein. London: Verso, 1991. 86–106. Print.

Barr, Lois. "Review of *An Island Called Home: Returning to Jewish Cuba.*" Rev. of *An Island Called Home*, by Ruth Behar. *Shofar: An Interdisciplinary Journal of Jewish Studies* 27.3 (2009): 209–10. *Project Muse.* Web. 15 June 2012.

Barthes, Roland. *Camera Lucida: Reflections on Photography.* Trans. Richard Howard. New York: Hill and Wang, 1981. Print.

Basch, Linda, Nina Glick Schiller, and Cristina Szanton Blanc. *Nations Unbound:*

Transnational Projects, Postcolonial Predicaments, and Deterritorialized Nation-States. Langhorne: Gordon and Breach, 1994. Print.

Behar, Ruth, dir. *Adio Kerida/Goodbye Dear Love: A Cuban Sephardic Journey*. Women Make Movies, 2002. Film.

———, ed. *Bridges to Cuba/Puentes a Cuba*. Ann Arbor: University of Michigan Press, 1995. Print.

———. "The Girl in the Cast." *Imagined Childhoods: Self and Society in Autobiographical Accounts*. Ed. Marianne Gullestad. Oslo: Scandinavian University Press, 1996. 217–39. Print.

———. "Going to Cuba: Writing Ethnography of Diaspora, Return, and Despair." *The Vulnerable Observer: Anthropology That Breaks Your Heart*. Boston: Beacon Press, 1996. 136–60. Print.

———. *An Island Called Home: Returning to Jewish Cuba*. New Brunswick: Rutgers University Press, 2007. Print.

———. "Juban América." *Poetics Today* 16.1 (1995): 151–70. *JSTOR*. Web. 2 Feb. 2012.

———. "Queer Times in Cuba." Behar, *Bridges to Cuba* 394–415.

———. *Traveling Heavy: A Memoir in between Journeys*. Durham: Duke University Press, 2013. Print.

———. "While Waiting for the Ferry to Cuba." *The Jewish Diaspora in Latin America and the Caribbean: Fragments of Memory*. Ed. Kristin Ruggiero. Portland: Sussex Academic Press, 2005. 124–38. Print.

Behar, Ruth, and Lucía M. Suárez, eds. *The Portable Island: Cubans at Home in the World*. New York: Palgrave Macmillan, 2008. Print.

Bejarano, Margalit. "Antisemitism in Cuba under Democratic, Military, and Revolutionary Regimes, 1944–1963." *Patterns of Prejudice* 24.1 (1990): 32–46. Print.

Bejel, Emilio. *Gay Cuban Nation*. Chicago: University of Chicago Press, 2001. Print.

———. *El horizonte de mi piel*. Cádiz: Editorial Aduana Vieja, 2005. Print.

———. *The Write Way Home: A Cuban-American Story*. Trans. Stephen J. Clark. Andover: Versal Books, 2003. Print.

Bell-Villada, Gene H. "Paradise Lost." Rev. of *Waiting for Snow in Havana: Confessions of a Cuban Boy*, by Carlos Eire. *Commonweal* 130.11 (6 June 2003): 26–27. *ProQuest Religion*. Web. 6 Dec. 2013.

Benítez-Rojo, Antonio. *The Repeating Island: The Caribbean and the Postmodern Perspective*. Trans. James E. Maraniss. Durham: Duke University Press, 1996. Print.

Berg, Mette Louise. *Diasporic Generations: Memory, Politics, and Nation among Cubans in Spain*. New York: Berghahn Books, 2011. Print.

Bettinger-López, Caroline. *Cuban-Jewish Journeys: Searching for Identity, Home, and History in Miami*. Knoxville: University of Tennessee Press, 2000. Print.

Bhabha, Homi K., ed. *Nation and Narration*. New York: Routledge, 1990. Print.

Bleys, Rudi C. *Images of Ambiente: Homotextuality and Latin American Art, 1910–Today*. London: Continuum, 2000. Print.
Blocker, Jane. *Where Is Ana Mendieta? Identity, Performativity, and Exile*. Durham: Duke University Press, 1999. Print.
Bobes, Marilyn. "Pregúntaselo a Dios." *Alguien tiene que llorar*. La Habana-Bogotá: Casa de las Américas/Colcultura, 1995. 61–69. Print.
Boero, Patricia. "Cubans Inside and Outside: Dialogue among the Deaf." Behar, *Bridges to Cuba* 189–96.
Bok, Sissela. *Secrets: On the Ethics of Concealment and Revelation*. New York: Pantheon Books, 1983. Print.
Booher, Bridget. "Living on the Hyphen: Gustavo Pérez Firmat." *Duke Magazine* (May/June 1996). Web. 5 June 2012.
Borges-Triana, Joaquín. *Músicos de Cuba y del mundo: nadie se va del todo*. Lexington: Ediciones ConCierto Cubano, 2012. Print.
Bosch, Lynette M. F. *Cuban American Art in Miami: Exile, Identity, and the Neo-Baroque*. Burlington: Lund Humphries, 2004. Print.
Bourriaud, Nicolas. *The Radicant*. Trans. James Gussen and Lili Porten. New York: Sternberg Press, 2009. Print.
Boym, Svetlana. *The Future of Nostalgia*. New York: Basic Books, 2001. Print.
Bradford, Anita Casavantes. *The Revolution Is for the Children: The Politics of Childhood in Havana and Miami, 1959–1962*. Chapel Hill: University of North Carolina Press, 2014. Print.
Brah, Avtar. *Cartographies of Diaspora: Contesting Identities*. London: Routledge, 1996. Print.
Bravo, Estela, dir. *Los que se fueron*. Instituto Cubano de Radio y Teledifusión, 1980. Film.
———, dir. *Operación Pedro Pan: Volando de vuelta a Cuba*. Bravo Films, 2010. Film.
Braziel, Jana Evans, and Anita Mannur. "Nation, Migration, Globalization: Points of Contention in Diaspora Studies." *Theorizing Diaspora: A Reader*. Ed. Jana Evans Braziel and Anita Mannur. Malden: Blackwell, 2003. 1–22. Print.
Brett, Guy. "One Energy." Viso, *Ana Mendieta* 181–202.
Brink-Dahan, Marcy. "Review of *An Island Called Home: Returning to Jewish Cuba*." Rev. of *An Island Called Home*, by Ruth Behar. *Journal of Jewish Identities* 2.2 (2009): 81–82. Print.
Brito, María. "The Juggler." Interview by Lynette M. F. Bosch and Jorge J. E. Gracia. Gracia, Bosch, and Álvarez Borland 42–53.
———. "Merely a Player." O'Reilly Herrera, *ReMembering Cuba* 54–57.
Bruguera, Tania. "Postwar Memories." *By Heart/De memoria: Cuban Women's Journeys in and out of Exile*. Ed. María de los Ángeles Torres. Philadelphia: Temple University Press, 2003. 169–89. Print.

Bueno, Salvador. *Leyendas cubanas*. Havana: Editorial Arte y Literatura, 1978. Print.
Burns, Dan. "MN Congressmembers Sign On to Better Cuba Policy." 3 May 2013. Web. 28 Aug. 2013. http://mnprogressiveproject.com/mn-congressmembers-sign-on-to-better-cuba-policy/.
Butler, Judith. *Bodies That Matter: On the Discursive Limits of "Sex."* New York: Routledge, 1993. Print.
Cabrera Infante, Guillermo. *Mapa dibujado por un espía*. Barcelona: Galaxia Gutenberg, S.A., 2013. Print.
California Pedro Pan. "Pedro Pan of California Responds to Bravo's Documentary." 29 June 2011. Web. 5 June 2014. https://www.youtube.com/watch?v=s1-tbZyKnHg.
Caminero-Santangelo, Marta. "Contesting the Boundaries of Exile Latino/a Literature." *World Literature Today* 74.3 (2000): 507–17. *JSTOR*. Web. 3 Dec. 2012.
Camnitzer, Luis. *New Art of Cuba*. 2nd ed. Austin: University of Texas Press, 2003. Print.
Campa, Román de la. *Cuba on My Mind: Journeys to a Severed Nation*. London: Verso, 2000. Print.
Campo-Flores, Arian. "Cuban-Americans Move Left." *Wall Street Journal*. 9 Nov. 2012. A6. Print.
Campuzano, Luisa. "Cristina García: bordes y desbordes de lo nacional." *La Gaceta de Cuba* 6 (2007): 34–39. Print.
———. "Narradoras cubanas de fines de los 90: un mapa temático/bibliográfico." *Mujeres de Cuba: Actas del Coloquio de Burdeos*. Ed. Jean Lamore y Omar Guzmán. Burdeos-Santiago de Cuba: Universidad Michel de Montaigne/Universidad de Oriente/Editorial Oriente, 2002. 162–74. Print.
Cantú, Norma. *Canícula: Snapshots of a Girlhood in la Frontera*. Albuquerque: University of New Mexico Press, 1995. Print.
Casal, Lourdes. *Palabras juntan revolución*. Havana: Casa de las Américas, 1981. Print.
———. "Para Ana Veltfort." *Areíto* 3.1 (Summer 1976): 52.
———. "Para Ana Veldford [sic]." Casal 60–61.
Casal, Lourdes, with the assistance of Yolanda Prieto. "Black Cubans in the United States: Basic Demographic Information." *Female Immigrants to the United States: Caribbean, Latin American, and African Experiences*. Ed. Delores M. Mortimer and Roy S. Bryce-Laporte. Washington, D.C.: RIIES Occasional Papers No. 2, Smithsonian Institution, 1981. 314–48. Print.
Casamayor-Cisneros, Odette. *Utopía, distopía e ingravidez: reconfiguraciones cosmológicas en la narrativa postsoviética cubana*. Madrid: Iberoamericana-Vervuert, 2013. Print.
Casey, Calvert. "El regreso." *El regreso (cuentos)*. Havana: Ediciones R, 1962. 107–24. Print.

Cavafy, C. P. "Ithaka." *Collected Poems*. Trans. Edmund Keeley and Philip Sherrad. Princeton: Princeton University Press, 2009. 67–69. Print.

Chamberlain, Mary. *Narratives of Exile and Return*. New York: St. Martin's Press, 1997. Print.

Chambers, Iain. *Migrancy, Culture, Identity*. London: Routledge, 1994. Print.

Chaviano, Daína. *La isla de los amores infinitos*. New York: Vintage Español, 2006. Print.

Chirino, Willy. "Nuestro día (ya viene llegando)." *Cubanísimo*. Sony U.S. Latin, 2005. CD.

Christian, Karen S. "La lengua que se repite: Pushing the Boundaries of Cuban/American Literature." *Caribe: Revista de Cultura y Literatura* 13.2 (2010–11): 17–38. Print.

———. *Show and Tell: Identity as Performance in U.S. Latina/o Fiction*. Albuquerque: University of New Mexico Press, 1997. Print.

Clark, Stephen J. *Autobiografía y revolución en Cuba*. Barquisimeto: Fondo Editorial Río Cenizo, 1999. Print.

Clearwater, Bonnie. "Introduction: *The Rupestrian Sculptures* Photo Etchings." *Ana Mendieta: A Book of Works*. Miami Beach: Grassfield Press, 1993. Print.

Clifford, James. *Routes: Travel and Translation in the Late Twentieth Century*. Cambridge: Harvard University Press, 1997. Print.

Cobas, José, and Jorge Duany. *Cubans in Puerto Rico: Ethnic Economy and Cultural Identity*. Gainesville: University Press of Florida, 1997. Print.

Coe, Richard N. "Childhood in the Shadows: The Myth of the Unhappy Child in Jewish, Irish, and French-Canadian Autobiography." *Comparison* 13 (1982): 3–67. Print.

———. *When the Grass Was Taller: Autobiography and the Experience of Childhood*. New Haven: Yale University Press, 1984. Print.

Cohen, Robin. *Global Diasporas*. London: Routledge, 1997. Print.

Conde, Yvonne. *Operation Pedro Pan: The Untold Exodus of 10,048 Cuban Children*. New York: Routledge, 1999. Print.

Cruz, Nilo. *Hortensia and the Museum of Dreams*. New York: Dramatists Play Service, 2005. Print.

"Cuba: Mil emigrados retornan cada año para quedarse en el país." *Café Fuerte* 24 Oct. 2012. Web. 29 Aug. 2014.

Cuban Research Institute, School of International and Public Affairs at Florida International University. FIU Cuba Polls, 1993–2014. Web. 28 Aug. 2014.

Davis, Rocío G. "Back to the Future: Mothers, Languages, and Homes in Cristina García's *Dreaming in Cuban*." *World Literature Today* 74.1 (2000): 60–68. JSTOR. Web. 11 July 2012.

———. "Between Home and Loss: Inscribing Return in Ruth Behar's *An Island Called Home*." Oliver-Rotger 44–57.

———. "Vulnerable Observation in *An Island Called Home*: Ruth Behar's Story of the Jews of Cuba." *Prooftexts* 31 (2011): 263–86. *JSTOR*. Web. 2 Feb. 2012.

Delgado, Frank. "La otra orilla." *La Habana está de bala*. Nuestra América (distributor), 1997. CD.

Derrickson, Teresa. "Women's Bodies as Sites of (Trans)National Politics in Cristina Garcia's *The Agüero Sisters*." *Modern Fiction Studies* 52.3 (2007): 478–500. Print.

Díaz, Desirée. "El síndrome de Ulises: El viaje en el cine cubano de los noventa." *La Gaceta de Cuba* 6 (2000): 37–40. Print.

Díaz, Jesús. *De la patria y el exilio*. Havana: Ediciones Unión, 1979. Print.

———. "Entrevista con Jesús Díaz." By Lilliam Oliva Collmann. *Cuban Studies/Estudios cubanos* 29 (1998): 155–75. Print.

Díaz, Jesús, dir. *55 hermanos*. ICAIC, 1978. Film.

———, dir. *De la patria y el exilio*. ICAIC, 1979. Film.

———, dir. *Lejanía*. ICAIC, 1985. Film.

Díaz, María Elena. "Rethinking Tradition and Identity: The Virgin of Charity of El Cobre." Fernández and Cámara Betancourt 43–59.

Diccionario de la literatura cubana. Vol. 1. Havana: Editorial Letras Cubanas, 1980. Print.

Dopico, Ana María. "Picturing Havana: History, Vision, and the Scramble for Cuba." *Nepantla: Views from South* 3.3 (2002): 451–93. Print.

Dorson, Melanie. "Comedy Is Your Weapon: Performance Artist Carmelita Tropicana's Oppositional Strategies." N.d. Web. 10 Jan. 2014.

Dovalpage, Teresa. *Posesas de La Habana*. Los Angeles: Pureplay Press, 2004. Print.

Duany, Jorge. "Becoming Cuba-Rican." Behar and Suárez 197–208.

———. *Blurred Borders: Transnational Migration between the Hispanic Caribbean and the United States*. Chapel Hill: University of North Carolina Press, 2011. Print.

———. "Neither Golden Exile nor Dirty Worm: Ethnic Identity in Recent Cuban American Novels." *Cuban Studies/Estudios Cubanos* 23 (1993): 167–83. Print.

———. "Networks, Remittances, and Family Restaurants: The Cuban Diaspora from a Transnational Perspective." O'Reilly Herrera, *Cuba* 161–75.

———. "Reconstructing Cubanness: Changing Discourses of National Identity on the Island and in the Diaspora during the Twentieth Century." Fernández and Cámara Betancourt 17–42.

Dyer, Donald R. "Sugar Regions of Cuba." *Economic Geography* 23.2 (1956): 177–84. Print.

Eckstein, Susan Eva. *The Immigrant Divide: How Cuban Americans Changed the U.S. and Their Homeland*. New York: Routledge, 2009. Print.

Eckstein, Susan, and Lorena Barbería. "Grounding Immigrant Generations in History: Cuban Americans and Their Transnational Ties." *International Migration Review* 36.3 (2002): 799–837. Print.

Egan, Susanna. *Mirror Talk: Genres of Crisis in Contemporary Autobiography*. Chapel Hill: University of North Carolina Press, 1999. Print.

Eguren, Gustavo, ed. *Cuentos del mar*. Havana: Editorial Letras Cubanas, 1981. Print.

Eire, Carlos M. N. *Learning to Die in Miami: Confessions of a Refugee Boy*. New York: Free Press, 2010. Print.

———. *Miami y mis mil muertes: Confesiones de un cubanito desterrado*. New York: Free Press, 2010. Print.

———. "Thinking in Images." Interview by Isabel Álvarez Borland. Gracia, Bosch, and Álvarez Borland 121–33.

———. *Waiting for Snow in Havana: Confessions of a Cuban Boy*. New York: Simon and Schuster, 2003. Print.

Engle, Margarita. *Singing to Cuba*. Houston: Arte Público Press, 1993. Print.

———. *Skywriting*. New York: Bantam, 1995. Print.

Espín, Oliva. *Latina Realities: Essays on Healing, Migration, and Sexuality*. Boulder: Westview Press, 1997. Print.

Espino, María Dolores. "Diaspora Tourism: Performance and Impact of Nonresident Nationals on Cuba's Tourism Section." *Cuba in Transition: Papers and Proceedings of the Twenty-Third Annual Meeting Association for the Study of the Cuban Economy*. Miami, 1–3 Aug. 2013. Web. 6 Jan. 2014.

Espinosa, Magaly, and Kevin Power, eds. *Antología de textos críticos: el nuevo arte cubano*. Santa Monica: Perceval Press, 2006. Print.

Fadraga Tudela, Lillebit. "Fragmentación y otros vicios secretos en la obra de Tania Bruguera." *La Gaceta de Cuba* 6 (2000): 41–43. Print.

Falzon, Mark-Anthony. "'Bombay, Our Cultural Heart': Rethinking the Relation between Homeland and Diaspora." *Ethnic and Racial Studies* 26.4 (2003): 662–83. Print.

Fass, Paula S. "The Memoir Problem." *Reviews in American History* 34.1 (2006): 107–23. *Project Muse*. Web. 6 Dec. 2013.

[Fernández], Antonio Eligio ("Tonel"). "La isla, el mapa, los viajeros: Notas sobre procesos recientes en el arte cubano." Espinosa and Power 239–45.

———. "René Francisco: Del arte a la pedagogía." *La Gaceta de Cuba* 5 (Sept./Oct. 2010): 18–23. Print.

Fernández, Damián J. Introduction. *Cuba Transnational*. Ed. Damián Fernández. Gainesville: University Press of Florida, 2005. xiii–xviii. Print.

Fernández, Damián J., and Madeline Cámara Betancourt. "Interpretations of National Identity." Fernández and Cámara Betancourt 1–13.

Fernández, Damián J., and Madeline Cámara Betancourt, eds. *Cuba, the Elusive Nation*. Gainesville: University Press of Florida, 2000. Print.

Fernández, Roberto G. *Entre la ocho y la doce.* New York: Cengage Learning, 2000. Print.

———. *El príncipe y la bella cubana: los amores de don Alfonso de Borbón y Battenberg y doña Edelmira Sampedro y Robato.* Madrid: Editorial Verbum, 2014. Print.

Fiol-Matta, Licia. "Achy Obejas." *Latino and Latina Writers.* Ed. Alan West-Durán. New York: Charles Scribner's Sons, 2004. 699–715. Print.

Flores, Juan. *The Diaspora Strikes Back: Caribeño Tales of Learning and Turning.* New York: Routledge, 2009. Print.

Flores, William, and Rina Benmayor, eds. *Latino Cultural Citizenship: Claiming Identity, Space, and Rights.* Boston: Beacon Press, 1997. Print.

Fornet, Ambrosio. "La crítica bicéfala: un nuevo desafío." *La Gaceta de Cuba* 1 (Jan./Feb. 2002): 20–25. Print.

———. "The Cuban Literary Diaspora and Its Contexts: A Glossary." *Boundary 2* 29.3 (2002): 91–103. Print.

———. "El quinquenio gris: revisitando el término." *Criterios.* 30 Jan. 2007. Web. 3 July 2014.

Fornet, Ambrosio, ed. *Memorias recobradas: introducción al discurso literario de la diáspora.* Santa Clara: Ediciones Capiro, 2000. Print.

Fowler, Víctor. "Identidad, diferencia, resistencia: a propósito de *Madagascar* y *Reina y Rey.*" *La Gaceta de Cuba* 34.3 (1996): 22–26. Print.

———. "Miradas a la identidad en la literatura de la diáspora." *Temas* 6 (1996): 122–32. Print.

Franqui, Carlos. *Retrato de familia con Fidel.* Barcelona: Seix Barral, 1981. Print.

Fusco, Coco. "El Diario de Miranda/Miranda's Diary." Behar, *Bridges to Cuba* 198–216.

Gadea, Hilda. 1972. *My Life with Che: The Making of a Revolutionary.* 2nd ed. New York: Palgrave Macmillan, 2008. Print.

Galarza, Ernesto. *Barrio Boy.* Notre Dame: University of Notre Dame Press, 1971. Print.

Galeano, Eduardo. "La memoria viva." *Memorias y desmemorias.* 22 Nov. 2010. Web. 28 Aug. 2014.

Gámez Torres, Nora. "'Rap is War': Los Aldeanos and the Politics of Music Subversion in Contemporary Cuba." *Trans: Revista Transcultural de Música* 17 (2013): 2–23. Print.

García, Cristina. *The Agüero Sisters.* New York: Ballantine Books, 1997. Print.

———. "And There Is Only My Imagination Where Our History Should Be." Interview by Iraida H. López. Behar, *Bridges to Cuba* 102–14.

———. "At Home on the Page: An Interview with Cristina García." Kevane and Heredia 69–82.

———. "Con frecuencia se simplifica el tema cubano-americano." Alfonso 151–58.

———. *Dreaming in Cuban.* New York: Ballantine Books, 1992. Print.

———. *A Handbook to Luck*. New York: Alfred A. Knopf, 2007. Print.
———. *King of Cuba*. New York: Scribner, 2013. Print.
———. *The Lady Matador's Hotel*. New York: Scribner, 2010. Print.
———. *Monkey Hunting*. New York: Alfred A. Knopf, 2003. Print.
García, María Cristina. "The Cuban Population of the United States: An Introduction." O'Reilly Herrera, *Cuba* 75–89.
———. *Havana USA: Cuban Exiles and Cuban Americans in South Florida, 1959–1994*. Berkeley: University of California Press, 1997. Print.
García Bedolla, Lisa. "Do Cubans Swing? The Politics of Cuba and Cubans in the United States." *Una ventana a Cuba y los estudios cubanos*. Ed. Amalia Cabezas, Ivette N. Hernández-Torres, Sara Johnson, and Rodrigo Lazo. San Juan: Ediciones Callejón, 2010. 47–64. Print.
García Calderón, Myrna. *Espacios de la memoria en el Caribe hispánico y sus diásporas*. San Juan: Ediciones Callejón, 2012. Print.
García Espinosa, Julio, dir. *Reina y Rey*. ICAIC, 1994. Film.
Gastón, Mariana. "La casa vieja." *Areíto* 4.3–4 (1978): 32–33. Print.
Getsy, David J. "Mourning, Yearning, and Cruising: Ernesto Pujol's *Memorial Gestures*." *PAJ: A Journal of Performance and Art* 30.3 (2008): 11–24. Print.
Giberga, Maritza. "En Ariguanabo, esta vez como constructora." *Areíto* 9.36 (1984): 21. Print.
Gil, Lourdes. "Against the Grain: Writing Spanish in the USA." O'Reilly Herrera, *Cuba* 177–79.
Gil Alejo, Arístides. "La huida." Eguren 342–46.
Gilroy, Paul. *The Black Atlantic: Modernity and Double Consciousness*. Cambridge: Harvard University Press, 1993. Print.
Gleijeses, Piero. *Visions of Freedom: Havana, Washington, Pretoria, and the Struggle for Southern Africa, 1976–1991*. Chapel Hill: University of North Carolina Press, 2013. Print.
Goldman, Dara E. "Next Year in the Diaspora: The Uneasy Articulation of Transcultural Positionality in Achy Obejas's *Days of Awe*." *Arizona Journal of Hispanic Cultural Studies* 8 (2004): 59–74. *JSTOR*. Web. 3 Dec. 2013.
Goldman, Shifra M. "Ana Mendieta: A Return to Natal Earth." *Dimensions of the Americas: Art and Social Change in Latin America and the United States*. Chicago: University of Chicago Press, 1994. 236–38. Print.
Gómez Cortés, Olga Rosa. *Operación Peter Pan: cerrando el círculo en Cuba*. Havana: Casa de las Américas, 2013. Print.
González Acosta, Alejandro. "Heredia: iniciador de caminos." *Encuentro de la cultura cubana* 26–27 (2002–2003): 283–94.
González de Cascorro, Raúl. "El chulo regresa." Eguren 210–19.
González Mandri, Flora. "A House on Shifting Sands." Behar, *Bridges to Cuba* 76–79.

Gonzenbach, Alexandra. "Bleeding Borders: Abjection in the Works of Ana Mendieta and Gina Pane." *Letras femeninas* 37.1 (2011): 31–46. Print.
Gracia, Jorge J. E., Lynette M. F. Bosch, and Isabel Álvarez Borland, eds. *Identity, Memory, and Diaspora: Voices of Cuban-American Artists, Writers, and Philosophers.* Albany: SUNY Press, 2008. Print.
Greenbaum, Susan D. *More than Black: Afro-Cubans in Tampa.* Gainesville: University Press of Florida, 2002. Print.
Grenier, Guillermo J., and Lisandro Pérez. *The Legacy of Exile: Cubans in the United States.* Boston: Allyn and Bacon, 2003. Print.
Grenier, Guillermo J., and Alex Stepick III, eds. *Miami Now! Immigration, Ethnicity, and Social Change.* Gainesville: University Press of Florida, 1992. Print.
Grillo, Evelio. *Black Cuban, Black American: A Memoir.* Houston: Arte Público Press, 2000. Print.
Grubin, David, dir. *Havana, Havana.* David Grubin Productions, 2012. Film.
Grupo Areíto. "Dos semanas en Cuba: Entrevista con Lourdes Casal." *Areíto* 1.1 (1974): 21–28. Print.
———. *Contra viento y marea.* Havana: Casa de las Américas, 1978. Print.
———. "Una vez más en Cuba: Entrevista con Mariana Gastón y Regina Casal." *Areíto* 1.3 (1974): 2–10. Print.
Guerra, Lillian. *The Myth of José Martí: Conflicting Nationalisms in Early Twentieth-Century Cuba.* Chapel Hill: University of North Carolina Press, 2005. Print.
———. *Visions of Power in Cuba: Revolution, Redemption, and Resistance, 1959–1971.* Chapel Hill: University of North Carolina Press, 2012. Print.
Gutiérrez Alea, Tomás, dir. *Memorias del subdesarrollo.* New Yorker Video, 1968. Film.
Guzmán, Manolo. "'Pa La Escuelita Con Mucho Cuida'o y por la Orillita': A Journey through the Contested Terrains of the Nation and Sexual Orientation." *Puerto Rican Jam: Essays on Culture and Politics.* Ed. Frances Negrón-Muntaner and Ramón Grosfogel. Minneapolis: University of Minnesota Press, 1997. 209–28. Print.
Habana Abierta. *Boomerang.* EMI Latin, 2006. CD.
Halbwachs, Maurice. *On Collective Memory.* Ed. and trans. Lewis A. Coser. Chicago: University of Chicago Press, 1992. Print.
Halevi-Wise, Yael, ed. *Sephardism: Spanish Jewish History and the Modern Literary Imagination.* Redwood City: Stanford University Press, 2012. Print.
Hall, Stuart. "Cultural Identity and Diaspora." *Identity: Community, Culture, Difference.* Ed. Jonathan Rutherford. London: Lawrence and Wishart, 1990. 222–37. Print.
———. "Introduction: Who Needs Identity?" *Questions of Cultural Identity.* Ed. Stuart Hall and Paul Du Gay. London: SAGE Publications, 1996. 1–17. Print.
Hernández-Reguant, Ariana. "Return to Havana: *Adió Kerida* and the Films of the

One-and-a-Half Generation." *Journal of Latin American Anthropology* 9.2 (2004): 495–98. Print.

Herrera, María Cristina, and Leonel Antonio de la Cuesta, eds. *Itinerario ideológico: Antología de Lourdes Casal*. Miami: Instituto de Estudios Cubanos, 1982. Print.

Hijuelos, Oscar. *Beautiful María of My Soul*. New York: Hyperion, 2010. Print.

———. *The Mambo Kings Play Songs of Love*. New York: Farrar, Straus and Giroux, 1989. Print.

Hirsch, Marianne, and Leo Spitzer. "'We Would Not Have Come Without You': Generations of Nostalgia." *Contested Pasts: The Politics of Memory*. Ed. Katherine Hodgkin and Susannah Radstone. London: Routledge, 2003. 79–95. Print.

Hirsch, Marianne, and Nancy K. Miller, eds. *Rites of Return: Diaspora Poetics and the Politics of Memory*. New York: Columbia University Press, 2011. Print.

Hoffman, Eva. "The New Nomads." *Letters of Transit: Five Authors Reflect on Exile, Identity, Language, and Loss*. Ed. André Aciman. New York: New Press, 1999. 35–63. Print.

Horsfield, Kate, Nereyda García Ferraz, and Branda Miller, dirs. *Ana Mendieta: Fuego de Tierra*. Women Make Movies, 1987. Film.

Humenuk, Allie, dir. *Shadow of the House: Photographer Abelardo Morell*. Center for Independent Documentary, 2007. Film.

Ibarra, Manuel Leandro, ed. *Quiero una canción: Jóvenes trovadores cubanos*. Holguín: Ediciones La Luz, 2012. Print.

Ibieta, Gabriela. "Fragmented Memories: An Exile's Return." O'Reilly Herrera, *Re-Membering Cuba* 69–78.

Jacobson, Jenna Rose Leving. "Confessing Exile: Revolution and Redemption in the Narratives of the Cuban *(Re)encuentro*." Diss., University of Chicago, 2014. Print.

Jay, Martin. "Somaesthetics and Democracy: Dewey and Contemporary Body Art." *Journal of Aesthetic Education* 36.4 (2002): 55–69. JSTOR. Web. 3 Dec. 2013.

Johnson, Kelli Lyon. "Lost in *El Olvido*: Translation and Collective Memory in Achy Obejas's *Days of Awe*." *Bilingual Review* 27.1 (2003): 34–44. Academic Search Premier. Web. 28 Mar. 2013.

Kandiyoti, Dalia. "Consuming Nostalgia: Nostalgia and the Marketplace in Cristina García and Ana Menéndez." *MELUS: The Journal of the Society for the Study of the Multi-Ethnic Literature of the United States* 31.1 (Spring 2006): 81–97. JSTOR. Web. 16 April 2013.

———. "Sephardism in Latina Literature." Halevi-Wise 235–55.

Kaplan, Caren. *Questions of Travel: Postmodern Discourses of Displacement*. Durham: Duke University Press, 1996. Print.

Kevane, Bridget, and Juanita Heredia, eds. *Latina Self-Portraits: Interviews with Contemporary Women Writers*. Albuquerque: University of New Mexico Press, 2000. Print.

King, Russell. "Generalizations from the History of Return Migration." *Return Migration: Journey of Hope or Despair?* Ed. Bimal Ghosh. Geneva: UN and IOM, 2000. 57–99. Print.

Klas, Mary Ellen. "Families Protest Crackdown on Cuba Travel." *Miami Herald* 11 June 2008. Web. 20 June 2008.

Knadler, Stephen. "'Blanca from the Block': Whiteness and the Transnational Latina Body." *Genders* 41 (2005). Web. 28 Oct. 2012.

Knauer, Lisa Maya. "Audiovisual Remittances and Transnational Subjectivities." *Cuba in the Special Period: Culture and Ideology in the 1990s.* Ed. Ariana Hernández-Reguant. New York: Palgrave Macmillan, 2009. 159–77. Print.

Kozer, José. "Retrato sideral de mi casa." *Carece de causa*. Buenos Aires: Ediciones Último Reino, 1988. 35–39. Print.

Kristeva, Julia. *Powers of Horror: An Essay on Abjection*. New York: Columbia University Press, 1982. Print.

Kundera, Milan. *The Book of Laughter and Forgetting*. Trans. Aaron Asher. New York: Perennial Classics, 1999. Print.

———. *Ignorance*. Trans. Linda Asher. New York: HarperCollins, 2000. Print.

La Fountain-Stokes, Lawrence. "Queer Diasporas, Boricua Lives: A Meditation on Sexile." *Review: Literature and Arts of the Americas* 41.2 (2008): 294–301. Print.

Lamora, Eduardo, dir. *Cuba, el arte de la espera*. Eduardo Lamora and Injam Films, 2007. Film.

Lejeune, Philippe. *Le Pacte Autobiographique*. Paris: Seuil, 1975. Print.

Lerner, Gerda. *Women and History*. New York: Oxford University Press, 1993. Print.

Levine, Robert M. "Identity and Memories of Cuban Jews." Halevi-Wise 115–23.

Levine, Robert M., and Moisés Asís. *Cuban Miami*. New Brunswick: Rutgers University Press, 2000. Print.

Leyva, Waldo. "Trópico de semejanzas: Conversando con Cristina García y Achy Obejas." *La Gaceta de Cuba* 5 (1995): 54–57. Print.

López, Ana M. "Memories of a Home: Mapping the Revolution (and the Making of Exiles?)" *Revista canadiense de estudios hispánicos* 20.1 (1995): 5–17. *JSTOR*. Web. 23 Dec. 2013.

López, Antonio. *Unbecoming Blackness: The Diaspora Cultures of Afro-Cuban America*. New York: New York University Press, 2012. Print.

López, Iraida H. "Reading Lives in Installments: Autobiographical Essays by Women of the Cuban Diaspora." Álvarez-Borland and Bosch 61–75.

López Labourdette, Adriana. "Volver a la ciudad: Espacios urbanos e identidad(es) en la literatura del retorno." *La Siempreviva* 16 (2013): 30–37. Print.

Lowinger, Rosa. "Repairing Things." Behar, *Bridges to Cuba* 98–101.

Loyola, Marilén. "In Search of Cuba: Remembering and Returning in the Writings of Three Cuban Novelists in Exile." *Cuba: contrapuntos de cultura, historia y sociedad*.

Francisco A. Scarano and Margarita Zamora, eds. San Juan: Ediciones Callejón, 2007. 319–47. Print.

Luis, Carlos M. "Mendieta quiere asombrar a Miami con fogatas en Lowe." *El Miami Herald* 27 Nov. 1982. 4. Print.

Luis, Roger Ricardo. "Muy orgullosa de mi Cuba, de la Cuba de hoy." *Granma* 28 Jan. 1981. 3. Print.

Luis, William. "Exile, Memories, and Identities in Gustavo Pérez Firmat's *Next Year in Cuba*." Álvarez Borland and Bosch 93–107.

Lukac, Jenni. "Interview: Lydia Rubio, César Trasobares, Ricardo Zulueta, Ricardo Viera, María Brito, and María Lino." *Art Papers* 17.1 (1993): 17–20. Print.

Machado, Eduardo, with Michael Domitrovich. *Tastes Like Cuba: An Exile's Hunger for Home*. New York: Gotham Books, 2007. Print.

Mannheim, Karl. 1952. "The Problem of Generations." *Essays on the Sociology of Knowledge: Collected Works of Karl Mannheim*. Vol. 5. Ed. P. Kecskemeti. London: Routledge, 1997. 276–322. Print.

Markowitz, Fran, and Anders H. Stefansson, eds. *Homecomings: Unsettling Paths of Return*. Lanham: Lexington Books, 2004. Print.

Marmolejo-McWatt, Amparo. "Blanca Mestre as Ochún in *The Agüero Sisters*." *Afro-Hispanic Review* 24.2 (2005): 89–101. *JSTOR*. Web. 23 May 2013.

Martínez, Juan A. *María Brito*. Los Angeles: UCLA Chicano Studies Research Center Press, 2009. Print.

Martínez San Miguel, Yolanda. *Caribe Two Ways: Cultura de la migración en el Caribe insular hispánico*. San Juan: Ediciones Callejón, 2003. Print.

Martínez Tabares, Vivian. "El reencuentro: un tema polémico." *De las dos orillas: teatro cubano*. Ed. Heidrun Adler and Adrián Herr. Madrid: Vervuert Iberoamericana, 1999. 177–85. Print.

Masud-Piloto, Félix R. *From Welcomed Exiles to Illegal Immigrants: Cuban Migration to the U.S., 1959–1995*. Langham: Rowman and Littlefield, 1995. Print.

Mateo Palmer, Margarita. *Desde los blancos manicomios*. Havana: Editorial Letras Cubanas, 2008. Print.

Matos, Húber. *Cómo llegó la noche*. Barcelona: Tusquets, 2004. Print.

Medina, Pablo. 1990. *Exiled Memories: A Cuban Childhood*. 2nd ed. New York: Persea Books, 2002. Print.

———. *The Return of Felix Nogara*. New York: Persea Books, 2000. Print.

Meluzá, Lourdes. "Un regreso a la naturaleza." *El Miami Herald* 20 Nov. 1982. 10. Print.

Méndez Rodenas, Adriana. "En búsqueda del paraíso perdido: La historia natural como imaginación diaspórica en Cristina García." *Modern Language Notes* 116.2 (2001): 392–418. *JSTOR*. Web. 3 Dec. 2013.

———. "Identity and Diaspora: Cuban Culture at the Crossroads." O'Reilly Herrera, *Cuba* 143–60.
Mendieta, Ana. "Art and Politics." Moure 167–68.
———. "The Struggle for Culture Today Is the Struggle for Life." Moure 171–76.
Mendieta, Raquel ("Raquelín"). "Childhood Memories: Religion, Politics, Art." Moure 223–28.
Mendieta Costa, Raquel ("Kaki"). "Silhouette." Behar, *Bridges to Cuba* 72–75.
Mendoza, Tony. *Cuba: Going Back.* Austin: University of Texas Press, 1997. Print.
———. *A Cuban Summer.* San Francisco: Capra Press, 2013. Print.
———. "Going Back." O'Reilly Herrera, *ReMembering Cuba* 78–82.
Menéndez, Ana. *Adiós, Happy Homeland!* New York: Black Cat, 2011. Print.
———. "Crossing the Crest of Forgetting." Interview by Isabel Álvarez Borland. Gracia, Bosch, and Álvarez Borland 173–79.
———. *In Cuba I Was a German Shepherd.* New York: Grove Press, 2001. Print.
———. *The Last War.* New York: HarperCollins, 2009. Print.
———. *Loving Che.* New York: Grove Press, 2003. Print.
Mirabal, Nancy Raquel. "'Ser de aquí': Beyond the Cuban Exile Model." *Latino Studies* 1.3 (2003): 366–82. Print.
Mishra, Sudesh. *Diaspora Criticism.* Edinburgh: Edinburgh University Press, 2006. Print.
Monge Rafuls, Pedro R. "Nadie se va del todo." *Teatro: 5 dramaturgos cubanos.* Ed. Rine Leal. New York: Ollantay Press, 1995. 109–58. Print.
Moraga, Cherríe. "Giving Up the Ghost." *Heroes and Saints and Other Plays.* Albuquerque: West End Press, 1994. 1–35. Print.
Morales, Emilio. "Cuba: 2.6 Billion in Remittances in 2012." *Havana Times.* 11 June 2013. Web. 28 Aug. 2014. http://www.havanatimes.org/?p=94444.
———. "Emigrados cubanos enviaron más de 3,500 millones de USD en remesas en especie en el año 2013." The Havana Consulting Group. 24 June 2014. Web. 28 Aug. 2014 http://www.thehavanaconsultinggroup.com.
———. "Miami-Cuba Flights Are Booming." *Havana Times* 7 Aug. 2013. Web. 26 Aug. 2013. http://www.havanatimes.org/?p=97556&utm_source=August+23+blast&utm_campaign=August+23%2C+2013+Blast&utm_med ium=email.
———. "Miami Leads in Sending Flights to Cuba." The Havana Consulting Group. N.d. Web. 15 Mar. 2013. http://www.thehavanaconsultinggroup.com/index.php?opt ion=com_content&view=category&id=36&lang=en&utm_source=March+15%2C+2013+Blast+&utm_campaign=March+15+2013+Bl ast&utm_medium=email.
Morán, Francisco. *Martí, la justicia infinita: Notas sobre ética y otredad en la escritura martiana (1875–1894).* Madrid: Editorial Verbum, 2014. Print.

Morejón, Nancy. "Ana Mendieta." *Looking Within/Mirar adentro: Selected Poems/Poemas escogidos.* Ed. Juanamaría Cordones-Cook. Detroit: Wayne State University Press, 2003. 113–17. Print.

Mosquera, Gerardo. "Ernesto Pujol: Cuba Visited Once More." *Cuba Update* 16.4–5 (July–Oct. 1995): 43. Print.

———. "Esculturas rupestres de Ana Mendieta." *Areíto* 7.28 (1981): 54–56. Print.

———. "Mi tierra/My Homeland." Introduction. *Taxonomías/Taxonomies.* México, D.F.: Galería Ramis Barquet, 1994. N.p. Print.

———. "Resucitando a Ana Mendieta." *Poliéster, pintura y no pintura* 4.11 (1995): 52–55. Print.

Moure, Gloria, ed. *Ana Mendieta.* Barcelona: Ediciones Polígrafa, S.A. and Centro Gallego de Arte Contemporáneo, 1996. Print.

Moya, Rogerio. "Areíto." *La Nueva Gaceta,* 2ª. época, nos. 11–12 (1984): 22. Print.

Multilateral Investment Fund. *Remittances to Latin America and the Caribbean: Differing Behavior across Subregions.* N.d. Web. 28 Aug. 2014.

Muñoz, Elías Miguel. *Brand New Memory.* Houston: Arte Público Press, 1998. Print.

———. "Flags and Rags (On Golden Lake): Excerpts from a Book of Memoirs in Progress." O'Reilly Herrera, *ReMembering Cuba* 196–202.

———. *Vida mía.* Cádiz: Editorial Aduana Vieja, 2006. Print.

Negrón-Muntaner, Frances, and Yolanda Martínez San Miguel. "In Search of Lourdes Casal's 'Ana Veldford.'" *Social Text* 92 (2007): 57-84. JSTOR. Web. 22 Nov. 2014.

Neubauer, John, and Borbála Zsuzsanna Török. *The Exile and Return of Writers from East Central Europe: A Compendium.* New York: Walter de Gruyter, 2009. Print.

Nora, Pierre. "Between Memory and History: *Les Lieux de Mémoire.*" *Representations* 26 (1989): 7–24. JSTOR. Web. 2 Dec. 2012.

Obejas, Achy. "Achy Obejas: Nacer en La Habana, una definición." Alfonso 131–48.

———. "A Conversation with Achy Obejas." By Ilan Stavans. Reprinted in Achy Obejas, *Days of Awe.* New York: Ballantine Books, 2001. Print.

———. *Days of Awe.* New York: Ballantine Books, 2001. Print.

———. *Havana Noir.* New York: Akashic Books, 2007. Print.

———. "In 'Awe': Achy Obejas on Her New Work." Interview by Gregg Shapiro. *Windy City Times* 8 Aug. 2001. 20, 33. Web. 28 Dec. 2013.

———. *Memory Mambo.* San Francisco: Cleis Press, 1996. Print.

———. *Ruins.* New York: Akashic Books, 2009. Print.

———. *We Came All the Way from Cuba So You Could Dress Like This?* San Francisco: Cleis Press, 1994. Print.

Ojito, Mirta. *Finding Mañana: A Memoir of a Cuban Exodus.* New York: Penguin, 2005. Print.

Oliver-Rotger, Maria Antònia, ed. *Identity, Diaspora and Return in American Literature.* New York: Routledge, 2015. Print.

Olney, James. "On Telling One's Own Story; or, Memory and Narrative in Early Life-Writing." *Imagined Childhoods: Self and Society in Autobiographical Accounts.* Ed. Marianne Gullestad. Oslo: Scandinavian University Press, 1996. 41–61. Print.
Olsson, Stephen, dir. *Our House in Havana.* CEM Productions, 2000. Film.
O'Reilly Herrera, Andrea. *Cuban Artists across the Diaspora: Setting the Tent against the House.* Austin: University of Texas Press, 2011. Print.
———. "The Politics of Mis-ReMembering: History, Imagination, and the Recovery of the *Lost Generation.*" O'Reilly Herrera, *ReMembering Cuba* 176–93.
———. "Women and the Revolution in Cristina García's *Dreaming in Cuban.*" *Modern Language Studies* 27.3–4 (1997): 69–91. *JSTOR.* Web. 19 May 2014.
O'Reilly Herrera, Andrea, ed. *Cuba: Idea of a Nation.* Albany: SUNY Press, 2007. Print.
———, ed. *ReMembering Cuba: Legacy of a Diaspora.* Austin: University of Texas Press, 2001. Print.
Ortiz, Fernando. 1940. *Contrapunteo cubano del tabaco y el azúcar.* Havana: Editorial de Ciencias Sociales, 1983. Print.
———. *Etnia y sociedad.* Havana: Editorial de Ciencias Sociales, 1993. Print.
———. "Los factores humanos de la cubanidad." 1939. *La Habana Elegante* 51 (2012). Web. 4 Nov. 2012.
Otero, Solimar. *Afro-Cuban Diasporas in the Atlantic World.* Rochester: University of Rochester Press, 2010. Print.
Ortuzar-Young, Ada. "The Roots/Routes of Ana Menéndez Narratives." Oliver-Rotger 149–69.
Oxfeld, Ellen, and Lynellyn D. Long, "Introduction: An Ethnography of Return." *Coming Home? Refugees, Migrants, and Those Who Stayed Behind.* Ed. Lynellyn D. Long and Ellen Oxfeld. Philadelphia: University of Pennsylvania Press, 2004. 1–15. Print.
Padilla, Heberto. *La mala memoria.* Barcelona: Plaza y Janés Editores, 1989. Print.
Padura, Leonardo. *La novela de mi vida.* Barcelona: Tusquets Editores, 2002. Print.
Paternostro, Silvana. "Carlos Eire." BOMB 90 (2005): n.p. 24 April 2012. Web. 11 Sept. 2012.
Paz, Raúl. *En casa.* Naïve, 2006. CD.
———. *Revolución.* Naïve, 2005. CD.
Pedraza, Silvia. "Cuba's Refugees: Manifold Migrations." *Origins and Destinies: Immigration, Race, and Ethnicity in America.* Ed. Silvia Pedraza and Rubén G. Rumbaut. Belmont: Wadsworth, 1996. 479–91. Print.
———. *Political Disaffection in Cuba's Revolution and Exodus.* New York: Cambridge University Press, 2007. Print.
Padrón, Humberto. *Video de familia.* ICAIC, 2001. Film.

Peirce, Charles Sanders. "Prolegomena to an Apology for Pragmaticism." *Peirce on Signs: Writings on Semiotic by Charles Sanders Peirce*. Ed. James Hoopes. Chapel Hill: University of North Carolina Press, 1991. 249–52. Print.
Peláez, Carmen. "Rum and Coke." Manuscript.
Pérez, Lisandro. "Cuban Miami." Grenier and Stepick III 83–108.
Pérez Betancourt, Rolando. *Mujer que regresa*. Havana: Editorial Letras Cubanas, 1986. Print.
Pérez Firmat, Gustavo. *Anything but Love*. Houston: Arte Público Press, 2000. Print.
———. *Carolina Cuban*. Tempe: Bilingual Press, 1987. Print.
———. *Cincuenta lecciones de exilio y desexilio*. Miami: Ediciones Universal, 2000. Print.
———. "A Cuban in Mayberry." South Atlantic Modern Language Association Congress. Research Triangle, N.C., 9 Nov. 2012. Keynote address.
———. *A Cuban in Mayberry: Looking Back at America's Hometown*. Austin: University of Texas Press, 2014. Print.
———. *Life on the Hyphen: The Cuban-American Way*. Austin: University of Texas Press, 1994, 2012. Print.
———. *Next Year in Cuba: A Cubano's Coming of Age in America*. New York: Anchor Books, Doubleday, 1995. Print.
———. *Scar Tissue*. Tempe: Bilingual Press, 2005. Print.
———. "What Sounds Good Also Rings True." Interview by Isabel Álvarez Borland. Gracia, Bosch, and Álvarez Borland 134–44.
Pérez Jr., Louis A. *On Becoming Cuban: Identity, Nationality, and Culture*. New York: Harper Perennial, 2001. Print.
Pérez Sarduy, Pedro. "Writing from Babylon." *The Portable Island: Cubans at Home in the World*. Behar and Suárez 153–60.
Perl, Jeffrey M. *The Tradition of Return: The Implicit History of Modern Literature*. Princeton: Princeton University Press, 1984. Print.
Petro, Pamela. "Dreaming in Welsh." *Paris Review* 18 Sept. 2012. Web. 26 Nov. 2013.
Pew Hispanic Center. *Cubans in the United States*. 25 Aug. 2006. Web. 28 Aug. 2014.
Pineda Barnet, Enrique, dir. *La Anunciación*. ICAIC and Taller de Creación Arca, Nariz, Alhambre, 2009. Film.
Ponte, Antonio José. "Viniendo." *Un arte de hacer ruinas y otros cuentos*. Prologue, bibliography, and notes by Esther Whitfield. México, D.F.: Fondo de Cultura Económica, 2005. 109–24. Print.
Portes, Alejandro, and Robert L. Bach. *Latin Journey: Cuban and Mexican Immigrants in the United States*. Berkeley: University of California Press, 1985. Print.
Portes, Alejandro, and Rubén G. Rumbaut. *Immigrant America: A Portrait*. Berkeley: University of California Press, 1990. Print.

Portes, Alejandro, and Alex Stepick. *City on the Edge: The Transformation of Miami.* Berkeley: University of California Press, 1993. Print.
Poter, Robert B., Dennis Conway, and Joan Philips, eds. *The Experience of Return Migration: Caribbean Perspectives.* Burlington: Ashgate, 2005. Print.
Poyo, Gerald E. *With All, and for the Good of All: The Emergence of Popular Nationalism in the Cuban Communities of the United States, 1848–1898.* Durham: Duke University Press, 1989. Print.
Prieto, Abel. "Cultura, cubanidad, cubanía." *Conferencia "La nación y la emigración."* Ed. Iraida Aguirrechu, Blanca Zavala, and Ana R. Gort. Havana: Editora Política, 1994. 38–97. Print.
Prieto, Alfredo. "La condición cubano-americana (a tres voces: Cristina García, Ana López y Ana Menéndez)." *La Gaceta de Cuba* 6 (Nov./Dec. 2010): 34–40. Print.
Prieto, Yolanda. "The Catholic Church and the Cuban Diaspora." Georgetown University Cuba Occasional Paper Series, No. 1, Dec. 2001, Caribbean Project, Center for Latin American Studies.
———. *The Cubans of New Jersey: Immigrants and Exiles in a New Jersey Community.* Philadelphia: Temple University Press, 2009. Print.
Prieto Taboada, Antonio. "Cómo vivir en ningún sitio: entrando y saliendo del exilio con Reinaldo Arenas." *Revista Hispánica Moderna* 55.1 (2002): 168–87. *JSTOR.* Web. 29 Aug. 2013.
Pujol, Ernesto. "Taxonomías/Taxonomies." *Taxonomías/Taxonomies.* México, D.F.: Galería Ramis Barquet, 1994. N.p. Print.
Quiroga, José. *Cuban Palimpsests.* Minneapolis: University of Minnesota Press, 2005. Print.
Raine, Anne. "Embodied Geographies: Subjectivity and Materiality in the Work of Ana Mendieta." *Generations and Geographies in the Visual Arts: Feminist Readings.* Ed. Griselda Pollock. New York: Routledge, 1996. 228–49. Print.
Ramírez, Kimberly. "The Lost Apple Plays: Performing Operation Pedro Pan." Diss., City University of New York, 2009. Print.
Reyes, Belinda I. *Dynamics of Immigration: Return Migration to Western Mexico.* San Francisco: Public Policy Institute of California, 1997. Print.
Reyes, Dean Luis. "La nación viajera: Manifiesto contra la teleología insular." *La Gaceta de Cuba* 4 (2003): 12–15. Print.
Rieff, David. *The Exile: Cuba in the Heart of Miami.* New York: Simon and Schuster, 1993. Print.
———. "Will Little Havana Go Blue?" *New York Times Magazine* 13 July 2008. 46–51. Print.
Risco, Enrique del. *Siempre nos quedará Madrid.* New York: Sudaquia Editores, 2012. Print.

Risech, Flavio. "Political and Cultural Cross-Dressing: Negotiating a Second Generation Cuban-American Identity." Behar, *Bridges to Cuba* 57–71.

Rivera, David. Testimony of the Honorable David Rivera before the House Judiciary Committee, Subcommittee on Immigration Policy and Enforcement. 31 May 2012. Web. 1 June 2012. http://judiciary.house.gov/index.cfm/2012/5/hearing-on-h-r-2831-to-amend-public-law-89-732-to-modify-the-requirement-for-a-cuban-national-to-qualify-for-and-maintain-status-as-a-permanent-resident-o.

Rivera Valdés, Sonia. *Las historias prohibidas de Marta Veneranda*. New York: Siete Cuentos, 2001. Print.

Rivero, Eliana. "Cuba (tras)pasada: Los imaginarios diaspóricos de una generación." Rivero, *Discursos desde la diáspora* 31–44.

———. *Discursos desde la diáspora*. Cádiz: Editorial Aduana Vieja, 2005. Print.

———. "In Two or More (Dis)places: Articulating a Marginal Experience of the Cuban Diaspora." O'Reilly Herrera, *Cuba* 194–214. Print.

———. "(Re)Writing Sugarcane Memories: Cuban Americans and Literature." *Paradise Lost or Gained? The Literature of Hispanic Exile*. Ed. Fernando Alegría and Jorge Ruffinelli. Houston: Arte Público Press, 1990. 164–82. Print.

Rodríguez, Ana, dir. "Laura." *Mujer transparente*. ICAIC, 1990. Film.

Rodríguez Febles, Ulises. *Huevos: El concierto y otras obras*. Havana: Editorial Letras Cubanas, 2007. 141–99. Print.

Rodríguez Gutiérrez, Milena. "Prólogo: Magali Alabau es Perséfone Pérez o cómo volver a Ilión." Alabau 7–20.

Rodríguez Milanés, Cecilia. *Marielitos, Balseros, and Other Exiles*. New York: Ig, 2009. Print.

Rojas, Rafael. "Diaspora and Memory in Cuban Literature." O'Reilly Herrera, *Cuba* 237–52.

———. *Essays in Cuban Intellectual History*. New York: Palgrave Macmillan, 2008. Print.

———. "From Havana to Mexico City: Generation, Diaspora, and Borderland." Behar and Suárez 94–104.

———. *Isla sin fin: Contribución a la crítica del nacionalismo cubano*. Miami: Ediciones Universal, 1999.

———. "Transculturation and Nationalism." *Cuban Counterpoints: The Legacy of Fernando Ortiz*. Ed. Mauricio A. Font and Alfonso W. Quiroz. Lanham: Lexington Books, 2005. 65–71. Print.

Rosales Herrera, Raúl. "Remembering and Imagining in Contemporary Mariel Writing: Postmemory and the Case of Cecilia Rodríguez Milanés." *Caribe: Revista de Cultura y Literatura* 13.2 (2010–11): 53–70. Print.

Ruggles, Steven, J. Trent Alexander, Katie Genadek, Ronald Goeken, Matthew B. Schroeder, and Matthew Sobek. *Integrated Public Use Microdata Series: Version 5.0*

[Machine-readable database]. Minneapolis: University of Minnesota, 2010. Web. 22 Nov. 2014. <https://usa.ipums.org/usa/>.

Rumbaut, Rubén D., and Rubén G. Rumbaut. "Self and Circumstance: Journeys and Visions of Exile." *The Dispossessed: An Anatomy of Exile*. Ed. Peter Isaac Rose. Amherst: University of Massachusetts Press, 2005. 331–55. Print.

Rumbaut, Rubén G. "Ages, Life Stages, and Generational Cohorts: Decomposing the First and Second Generation in the United States." *International Migration Review* 38.3 (2004): 1160–1205. *JSTOR*. Web. 10 May 2014.

Safran, William. "Diasporas in Modern Societies: Myths of Homeland and Return." *Diaspora* 1.1 (1991): 83–99. Print.

Said, Edward W. "Reflections on Exile." *Reflections on Exile and Other Essays*. Cambridge: Harvard University Press, 2000. 173–86. Print.

Saltzman, Lisa. *Making Memory Matter: Strategies of Remembrance in Contemporary Art*. Chicago: University of Chicago Press, 2006. Print.

Sánchez, Luis Rafael. "La guagua aérea." *La guagua aérea*. San Juan: Editorial Cultural, 1994. 11–22. Print.

Santa Cruz y Montalvo, Mercedes (Condesa de Merlín). *Viaje a La Habana*. Ed. Adriana Méndez Rodenas. Doral: Stockcero, 2008. Print.

Santana, Andrés Isaac. *Nosotros, los más infieles: Narraciones críticas sobre el arte cubano (1993–2005)*. Murcia: Centro de Documentación y Estudios Avanzados de Arte Contemporáneo, [2007]. Print.

Santiago, Héctor. "Balada de un verano en La Habana." *Teatro: 5 dramaturgos cubanos*. Ed. Rine Leal. New York: Ollantay Press, 1995. 160–215. Print.

Schnapper, Dominique. "From the Nation-State to the Transnational World: On the Meaning and Usefulness of Diaspora as a Concept." *Diaspora* 8.3 (1999): 225–54. Print.

Serra, Ana. "Strangers in the Family Home: Spanish Former Immigrants Imagine a Return to Cuba." *Canadian Journal of Latin American and Caribbean Studies* 36.72 (2011): 9–33. Print.

Shapiro-Rok, Ester Rebeca. "Finding What Had Been Lost in Plain View." Behar, *Bridges to Cuba* 85–95.

Shaw, Lauren E. "The *Nueva Trova*: Frank Delgado and Survival of a Critical Voice." *Proceedings of the Conference Cuba Today: Continuity and Change since the Período Especial*. Ed. Mauricio A. Font. New York: Bildner Center for Hemispheric Studies, CUNY, 2004. 41–50. Web. 16 July 2013.

Silos Ribas, Lorena. *La voz en la memoria: La construcción del sujeto literario a partir de los recuerdos infantiles en la literatura escrita por mujeres en Suiza desde 1970*. Munich: LINCOM Europa, 2008. Print.

Silot Bravo, Eva. "¿Se 'habaniza' Miami? Entrevista a Raúl Paz, integrante y coordinador del proyecto Habanization." *Cubaencuentro* 13 Feb. 2012. Web. 24 July 2013.

Socolovsky, Maya. "Deconstructing a Secret History: Trace, Translation, and Crypto-Judaism in Achy Obejas's *Days of Awe*." *Contemporary Literature* 44.2 (2003): 225–49. *JSTOR*. Web. 24 May 2014.

Solás, Humberto, dir. *Miel para Oshún*. ICAIC, 2001. Film.

Stefansson, Anders H. "Homecomings to the Future: From Diasporic Mythographies to Social Projects of Return." *Homecomings: Unsettling Paths of Return*. Ed. Fran Markowitz and Anders H. Stefansson. Lanham: Lexington Books, 2004. 2–20. Print.

Stubbs, Jean. "New Diasporic Routes: Cuban Migration to Canada and Western Europe." XXX International Congress of the Latin American Studies Association. San Francisco. 23 May 2012. Paper.

Suárez, Virgil. *Spared Angola: Memories from a Cuban American Childhood*. Houston: Arte Público Press, 1997. Print.

Suchlicki, Jaime. "La libertad cuesta muy cara." *El Nuevo Herald* 2 Feb. 2012. Op-Ed page. Print.

Sullivan, Edward J. "The Sacred and the Profane." *ARTnews* (Mar. 2000): 122–25. *Academic Search Premier*. Web. 3 Dec. 2013.

Sullivan, Mark P. "Cuba: U.S. Restrictions on Travel and Remittances." Research Service Report for Congress. 19 Aug. 2014. Web. 28 Aug. 2014.

Tamayo, Juan O. "Bid to Tighten Cuba Travel Dropped from Budget Bill." *Miami Herald* 15 Dec. 2011. Web. 5 Mar. 2012.

Thomas, Susan. "Cosmopolitan, International, Transnational: Locating Cuban Music." *Cuba Transnational*. Ed. Damián J. Fernández. Gainesville: University Press of Florida, 2005. 104–20.

Tölölyan, Khachig. "The Contemporary Discourse of Diaspora Studies." *Comparative Studies of South Asia, Africa, and the Middle East* 27.3 (2007): 647–55. *Project Muse*. Web. 6 Jan. 2014.

———. "The Nation-State and Its Others: In Lieu of a Preface." *Diaspora* 1.1 (1991): 3–7. Print.

———. "Rethinking Diaspora(s): Stateless Power in the Transnational Moment." *Diaspora* 5.1 (1996): 3–36. Print.

Tomás, Ángel. "El arte como refugio." *El caimán barbudo* (Apr. 1981): 26. Print.

Torrens, David. *Ni de aquí, ni de allá*. EMI Music, 2002. CD.

Torres, Fina, dir. *Havana Eva*. Alterproducciones, 2012. Film.

Torres, María de los Ángeles. "Beyond the Rupture: Reconciling with Our Enemies, Reconciling with Ourselves." Behar, *Bridges to Cuba* 24–42.

———. "The Convergence of Time: Being Cuban in the Present Tense." Behar and Suárez 161–67.

———. "*Encuentros y encontronazos*: Homeland in the Politics and Identity of the Cuban Diaspora." *Diaspora* 4.2 (1995): 211–38. Print.

———. *In the Land of Mirrors: Cuban Exile Politics in the United States*. Ann Arbor: University of Michigan Press, 1999. Print.

———. *The Lost Apple: Operation Pedro Pan, Cuban Children in the U.S., and the Promise of a Better Future*. Boston: Beacon Press, 2003. Print.

Saillant, Silvio Torres. "Antelación: sobre la perspectiva diaspórica." Saillant, *El retorno de las yolas*. 393–404.

———. "The Latino Autobiography." *Latino and Latina Writers*. Ed. Alan West-Durán. New York: Charles Scribner's Sons, 2004. 61–79. Print.

———. "El retorno de las yolas." Saillant, *El retorno de las yolas*. 22–98.

———. *El retorno de las yolas: ensayos sobre diáspora, democracia y dominicanidad*. Santo Domingo: Librería La Trinitaria, Editora Manatí, 1999. Print.

Torriente, Alberto Pedro. "Weekend en Bahía." *Tablas* 2 (Apr.–June 1987): Libreto No. 14, 1–15. Print.

Tropicana, Carmelita. "Milk of Amnesia/Leche de Amnesia." *I, Carmelita Tropicana: Performing between Cultures*. Boston: Beacon Press, 2000. 52–71. Print.

Tsuda, Takeyuki. *Diasporic Homecomings: Ethnic Return Migration in Comparative Perspective*. Stanford: Stanford University Press, 2009. Print.

Valdés Figueroa, Eugenio. *Cuba: The Maps of Desire*. Vienna: Kunsthalle Wien, 1999. 147–63. Print.

Vaquera-Vázquez, Santiago. "'The Inextinguishable Longings for Elsewheres': The Impossibility of Return in Junot Díaz." Oliver-Rotger 170–88.

Varela, Carlos. "Foto de familia." *Como los peces*. Ariola International, 1995. CD.

Vega Serova, Anna Lidia. "Erre con erre." *Catálogo de mascotas*. Havana: Editorial Letras Cubanas, 1998. 99–115. Print.

Veigas Zamora, José, Cristina Vives, Adolfo V. Nodal, Valia Garzón, and Dannys Montes de Oca. *Memoria: Cuban Art of the 20th Century*. Los Angeles: California/ International Arts Foundation, 2002. Print.

Vera León, Antonio. "The Garden of Forking Tongues: Bicultural Subjects and an Ethics of Circulating in and out of Ethnicities." *Postmodern Notes/Apuntes posmodernos* 3.2 (1993): 10–19. Print.

Viso, Olga, ed. *Ana Mendieta: Earth Body, Sculpture, and Performance, 1972–1985*. Washington, D.C.: Hirshhorn Museum and Sculpture Garden, Smithsonian Institution, 2004. Print.

———. *Unseen Mendieta: The Unpublished Works of Ana Mendieta*. Munich: Prestel Verlag, 2008. Print.

Wakamiya, Lisa Ryoko. *Locating Exiled Writers in Contemporary Russian Literature*. New York: Palgrave Macmillan, 2009. Print.

Watson, Scott. "Ernesto Pujol in Conversation with Scott Watson." *Cuba: The Maps of Desire*. Vienna: Kunsthalle Wien, 1999. 259–67. Print.

Weimer, Tanya N. *La diáspora cubana en México: Terceros espacios y miradas excéntricas*. New York: Peter Lang, 2008. Print.

White, Luise. "Telling More: Lies, Secrets, and History." *History and Theory* 39.4 (2000): 11–22. *Academic Search Premier*. Web. 28 Dec. 2013.

Whitehead, Anne. *Memory*. London: Routledge, 2009. Print.

Wolfenzon, Carolyn. "*Days of Awe* and the Jewish Experience of a Cuban Exile: The Case of Achy Obejas." *Hispanic Caribbean Literature of Migration: Narratives of Displacement*. Ed. Vanessa Pérez Rosario. New York: Palgrave Macmillan, 2010. 105–18. Print.

Wood, Yolanda. "La aventura del silencio en Tania Bruguera." *Arte Cubano* 3 (2000): 34–37. Print.

Zamora, Lois Parkinson. *The Usable Past: The Imagination of History in Recent Fiction of the Americas*. Cambridge: Cambridge University Press, 1997. Print.

Zaya, Octavio. "Tania Bruguera in Conversation with Octavio Zaya." *Cuba: The Maps of Desire*. Vienna: Kunsthalle Wien, 1999. 240–55. Print.

Index

Page numbers in *italics* indicate illustrations.

ABC. *See* American-Born Cuban
Acosta, Carlos, 229
Adio Kerida/Goodbye Dear Love: A Cuban Sephardic Journey (Behar), 28, 67, 69, 73
"Ages, Life Stages, and Generational Cohorts: Decomposing the First and Second Generation in the United States" (Rumbaut), 232n6
The Agüero Sisters (García, Cristina), 188; agricultural products in, 174–75, 178; Cuba's continuing centrality in, 169–70; Cuba's past in, 163–68; family secrets in, 162–63; females in, 161, 169, 245n5; gender-based *mestizaje* in, 171–79; overview, 31, 159–62, 171–79, 191–93, 245n5; post-independence Cuban history and, 171–72; transculturation and, 171, 178, 179. *See also* Novels of return
Alabau, Magali, 25–26
Alberto, Eliseo, 250n12
Alonso, Nancy, 214–15
Álvarez Borland, Isabel, 19, 31–32, 137, 142, 151, 186, 187, 233n15
American-Born Cuban (ABC), 153, 159–60
American writers, and usable past, 163–64
Ana Mendieta (Viso), 114, *114*
The Andy Griffith Show, 156, 244n22
Angolan Civil War, 138

Añoranza (nostalgia and ignorance of birthplace), 123
Antes que anochezca (Arenas), 24, 82
Antonio Maceo Brigade, 41, 43–44, 60, 75, 207–8, 236n13
Aparicio García, Bernardo, 144
Aranda, Elizabeth M., 13
Areíto, 41–45, 47, 60, 100, 235n9
Arenas, Reinaldo, 23–24, 25, 82
Armarios (Pujol installation), 128
Art: body, 91, 96, 112, 240n13; politics and, 97. *See also* Cuban art; Nature in art; Performance art
Artists: post-indexical and diasporic, 65. *See also* Cuban artists
Autobiografía y revolución en Cuba (Clark), 32
Autobiographical narratives: by Cuban and Cuban-American exiles, 19; deracination of, 64; diasporic intimacy of, 64; intertextual nature of, 66–67; by one-and-a-half generation, 7, 31–32, 61–89; overview, 30, 32, 33, 226; post-indexical ties and, 63–67; transnational relationship in, 63. *See also* Childhood narratives; *specific autobiographical narratives*

Bacayú sculpture, *112*, 112–13
Barroso, Abel, 200
Batista, Fulgencio, 182, 187, 248n20
Bay of Pigs, 36

Behar, Ruth, 14, 15, 27, 57, 236n17; *Adio Kerida* of, 28, 67, 69, 73; autobiographical narrative of, 19, 20, 62, 63, 67–74, 88; *Bridges to Cuba* of, 49–51, 67, 73, 236n17; on childhood narratives, 123; on Cuban diaspora, 68–73; Cuban identity of, 89; "Going to Cuba: Writing Ethnography of Diaspora, Return, and Despair" of, 73; *An Island Called Home: Returning to Jewish Cuba* of, 19, 20, 67–74, 88; on Jewish diaspora, 68–73; Jews in Cuba and, 67–73; "Juban América" of, 70; Jubans and, 69, 70, 72, 74; memory and, 71–72; *The Portable Island: Cubans at Home in the World* of, 73; *Traveling Heavy: A Memoir in Between Journeys* of, 28

Bejel, Emilio: autobiographical narrative of, 19, 20, 62, 63, 66, 67, 79–82, 89; on diaspora, 78–82; on family, 80–81; *Gay Cuban Nation* of, 80; on home and homeland, 79–82; homosexuality and, 79–82, 89; *El horizonte de mi piel* of, 79; *The Write Way Home: A Cuban-American Story* of, 19, 20, 79–82, 89

Benes, Bernardo, 48
Berg, Mette Louise, 157, 231n3
Bhabha, Homi, 16, 244n17
Black Cubans, 32, 37, 85, 234n19, 235n3
Bobes, Marilyn, 252n19
Body art, 91, 96, 112, 240n13
Boero, Patricia, 50
The Book of Laughter and Forgetting (Kundera), 159
Boomerang, 200
Boomerang aesthetic, 224; Cuban émigré artists and, 31, 200–201; Cuban émigré writers and, 31; Cuban music and, 196, 223, 249n5
Bosch, Lynette, 134
Boteros (collective taxis), 77, 239n4
Boym, Svetlana, 64, 159
Brah, Avtar, 232n5
Bravo, Estela, 51, 90, 237n19

Bridges to Cuba/Puentes a Cuba (Behar), 49–51, 67, 73, 95, 236n17
Brigadistas, 44, 46, 207, 208. *See also* Antonio Maceo Brigade
Brito, María: assemblages of, 132–33; childhood visual narratives of, 30, 121, 124, 131–36, 157–58; Eire and, 136; exhibitions including art of, 131, 242n8; exile concept in art of, 136; *Feed* painting and sculpture of, 135, 135–36; feminism of, 131; fragmentation in art of, 131, 132; houses and household objects in art of, 131–34; immigration theme in art of, 134; installations of, 131, 133, 133–36, 137; overview, 131, 157–58; paintings of, 131, 135, 135–36; *Party at Goya's/First Arrivals* sculpture of, 131–32; *El Patio de mi Casa* installation of, 133, 133–36, 137; Pérez Firmat and, 136; as Peter Pan child, 131, 133; *The Room Upstairs: Self-Portrait with Two Friends* assemblage of, 132–33; sculptures of, 131–32, 135, 135–36; *Self-Portrait in Grey and White* assemblage of, 132

Bruguera, Tania, 115–18, 117, 241n15
Bueno, Descemer, 200

Cabrera Infante, Guillermo, 234n16, 242n7
CAFÉ. *See* Cuban-American Foremost Exhibitions
Cámara, Madeline, 17
Camnitzer, Luis, 93, 108
Caribbean, 27, 28, 29
Caribe Two Ways: Cultura de la migración en el Caribe insular hispánico (Martínez San Miguel), 23, 28
Cartographies of Diaspora: Contesting Identities (Brah), 232n5
Casal, Lourdes, 5–6, 20–21, 41–42, 47, 224, 236n15
Casal, Regina, 43
Casey, Calvert, 22–23
Castro, Fidel, 3; Cuban-American exiles

and, 18, 40, 203, 208; in *Days of Awe*, 180; in *Waiting for Snow in Havana*, 139, 243n14
Castro, Raúl, 3, 237n18
Cavafy, Constantine P., v ("Ithaka"), 33, 122
Central American children, 231n4
Chambers, Iain, 17
Che. *See* Guevara, Ernesto "Che"
Chibás, Eddy, 187, 247n19
Childhood, textual representation of interrupted, 139–43
"The Childhood" (childhood memoir genre), 137, 138
Childhood memoirs: "Exile's Childhood" as sub-sub-genre of, 124, 136–39, 243n13; as genre called "the Childhood," 137, 138; overview, 30–31, 121–24, 226; "the Writer's Childhood" as sub-sub-genre of, 137–38. *See also* Childhood visual narratives; Eire, Carlos M. N.; Pérez Firmat, Gustavo
Childhood narratives: Behar on, 123; symbolic truth in, 138. *See also* Childhood memoirs
Childhood visual narratives, 30, 121–24, 226. *See also* Brito, María; Pujol, Ernesto
Children, and politics, 138
Children of exiles, 4; politics of return and, 41–47; travel to Cuba and, 41–47, 49–50, 55, 59–60. *See also* One-and-a-half generation
Chirino, Willy, 3
Christian, Karen S., 66
Círculo de Cultura Cubana, 92, 93, 100
Citizenship, cultural, 143, 243n16
Clark, Stephen J., 32
Clifford, James, 11–12
Cocineras mulatas (Pujol), 127
Coe, Richard N., 137, 138
Cohen, Robin, 11
Cold War, 40, 225
Collective memory, 91, 102, 104, 242n7
Conservative Cubans, 40
Contra viento y marea, 42
Costa, "Kaki" Mendieta, 95

Cuarta Pragmática student trip, *112*, 112–14, *114*
Cuba: continuing centrality in novels of return, 169–70; Cuba's past in novels of return, 163–68; socialist, 85, 239n8; Special Period, 56, 83, 85; struggle for sovereignty, 46–47; terrorism and, 237n24; travel by Cuban exiles and government of, 56–57, 238n27. *See also* Havana
Cuba: Going Back (Mendoza), 19, 20; overview, 82–88; photographs of, 82–88, *86*, *87*; video of, 85, 239n7
Cuban Adjustment Act, 38, 54–55
Cuban-American art: community, 129. *See also* Cuban art
Cuban-American artists, 21. *See also* Cuban-American visual artists; Cuban returnee artists
Cuban-American autobiography, 32, 33. *See also* Autobiographical narratives
Cuban-American childhood narratives. *See* Childhood memoirs
Cuban-American diaspora, 4, 13–14, 228, 232n10, 233n12; as distinctive population, 39–41; provisions in roots/routes debates, 15–17
Cuban-American exiles: attitudes toward returning, 2–3; autobiographical narratives by, 19; Castro, Fidel, and, 18, 40, 203, 208; Cuban identity of, 18–19, 34, 45–46, 54, 76, 228, 244n20; after Cuban revolution of 1959, 18, 34–39, 62, 235n1; diversity of, 2; memory trap of, 18; percent wishing to return, 4, 231n2. *See also* Cuban exiles
Cuban-American Foremost Exhibitions (CAFÉ), 251n13
Cuban-American literature, 16, 33; of exile, 19, 233n15; Latino/a literature and, 233n15; race relations in, 32, 234n19. *See also* Literature of return
Cuban-American Literature of Exile: From Person to Persona (Álvarez Borland), 32

Cuban-American narratives, 164, 225; Cuban representations of émigrés and, 224. *See also* Cuban-American autobiography; Cuban-American literature; Cuban-American writers

Cuban-American return narratives, 225. *See also* Cuban return narratives

Cuban Americans: Cuban returnees and, 225; Cuban visits by, 4, 13, 44–45, 236n14; population of, 39; race of, 235n4; transnationalism of, 13–14, 62

Cuban-American visual artists, 21. *See also* Childhood visual narratives; Cuban returnee visual artists

Cuban-American works: vicarious returns in, 245n6. *See also* Cuban-American artists; Cuban-American narratives

Cuban-American writers, 7, 14, 19, 121; Cuban identity and, 160–61, 245n4; Cuban natives and, 251n16. *See also* Cuban-American narratives

Cuban art: Mendieta, Ana, and, 91, 95–97, 104, 120; minor map and major map of, 120, 241n17

Cuban artists, 30; boomerang aesthetic and Cuban émigré artists, 31, 200–201; Mendieta, Ana, and, 30, 91, 93, 96, 101–5, 112–19; Miami, 131. *See also* Cuban-American artists; Cuban returnee artists; Volumen I artists

Cuban children. *See* Children of exiles; Operation Pedro Pan

Cuban cultural productions, about émigrés, 248n1; films, 195; music, 195, 196, 220–23; overview, 195–96, 227. *See also* Cuban narratives, about émigrés

Cuban cultural productions, about returnees: films, 198–99, 205–10, 212–14, 219–20, 252n18; music, 196–98, 220–23; of one-and-a-half generation, 207–12; overview, 195, 198–99. *See also* Cuban representations, of returnees

Cuban culture, 240n1; cultural exchange, 92, 93; in Miami, 155, 244n21; in *Next Year in Cuba*, 150, 153, 154, 155; in *Waiting for Snow in Havana*, 141–43

Cuband, 160, 193, 245n1

Cuban diaspora, 13–14, 161, 232nn10–11, 233n12, 245n4; Behar on, 68–73; de la Campa on, 75, 76, 78; Jewish diaspora and, 68–73, 180, 183–85; Latino diaspora and, 76; Little Havana and, 155, 244n20; of one-and-a-half generation, 9, 39; overview, 228; provisions in roots/routes debates, 15–17; worldwide, 39–41, 235n7. *See also* Cuban-American diaspora

Cuban émigrés, 4, 229; artists and boomerang aesthetic, 31, 200–201; Cuban natives and, 194–95; after Cuban revolution of 1959, 1, 2, 34–39, 235n1; erased from collective memory, 242n7. *See also* Cuban exiles; Cuban migration; Cuban returnees

Cuban émigré writers: boomerang aesthetic and, 31. *See also* Cuban narratives, about émigrés

Cuban exiles, 4, 14–15, 233n12; autobiographical narratives by, 19; Cubans and, 100; de la Campa on Miami, 75–76; flawed attempts at reconciliation, 203–7; in *Loving Che*, 186; mindset and ideological divide, 2; one-and-a-half generation and, 9, 225; trapped in *cubanidad*, 203–7; U.S.-Cuba relations and, 40, 203, 249n6. *See also* Children of exiles; Cuban-American exiles; Cuban émigrés; Cuban migration; Cuban returnees; One-and-a-half generation; Travel to Cuba, by Cuban exiles

Cuban films: about émigrés, 195; about returnees, 198–99, 205–10, 212–14, 219–20, 252n18

Cubangst, 6

Cuban history: *The Agüero Sisters* and post-independence, 171–72; background to Cuban return, 28–30, 34–89

Cubanía (conscious Cubanness), 15, 17, 46, 47, 249n7; in cultural productions about Cuban returnees, 203, 205; one-and-a-half generation returnees and, 208, 209, 211; overview, 203–5, 249n9

Cubanidad (generic Cubanness), 15, 17, 31, 249n7; Cuban exiles trapped in, 203–7; in cultural productions about Cuban returnees, 203, 205, 250n12; one-and-a-half generation returnees and, 207, 208, 209, 211; overview, 203–4, 249n9

Cuban identity: *Areíto* and, 47; of Behar, 89; of Cuban-American exiles, 18–19, 34, 45–46, 54, 76, 228, 244n20; Cuban-American writers and, 245n4; *Days of Awe*, Jewish identity and, 180–85; Miami and, 153; Pérez Firmat and, 153, 155, 157

A Cuban in Mayberry: Looking Back at America's Hometown (Pérez Firmat), 156–57, 244n22

Cuban language, 85

"The Cuban Literary Diaspora and Its Contexts: A Glossary" (Fornet), 232n11

Cuban literature: post-Soviet, 24, 234n17. *See also* Cuban-American literature; Literature of return

Cuban migrants: views of returns based on U.S. arrival dates, 62. *See also* Cuban émigrés

Cuban migration, 227, 228, 229; after Cuban revolution of 1959, 34–39, 235n1; historical background to, 29–30, 34–89; one-and-a-half generation and, 38. *See also* Cuban émigrés; Cuban exiles; Cuban return

Cuban music: boomerang aesthetic and, 196, 223, 249n5; cultural exchange and, 196, 221–22, 248n2; about émigrés, 195, 196, 220–23; politics and, 249n4; about returnees, 196–98, 220–23

Cuban musicians, 195, 197–98, 220, 222–23; émigrés, 220–23, 253n21; returnees, 196, 221, 248n2, 253n21

Cuban narratives. *See* Cuban-American narratives; Cuban native narratives; Cuban return narratives

Cuban narratives, about émigrés: overview, 31, 194–95. *See also* Cuban cultural productions, about émigrés

Cuban narratives, about returnees: deferral strategy in, 212–20, 252n19; from Mariel exodus, 214–20; of one-and-a-half generation, 207–12, 251n14; one-and-a-half generation return narratives compared to, 212, 251n16. *See also* Cuban cultural productions, about returnees; Cuban representations, of returnees

Cuban native narratives: Cuban revolution of 1959 and, 195. *See also* Cuban narratives, about émigrés; Cuban narratives, about returnees

Cuban natives: Cuban-American writers and, 251n16; Cuban émigrés and, 194–95; Cuban returnees and, 225–26; Cuban revolution of 1959 and, 194; one-and-a-half generation returnees and, 207–12

Lo cubano (Cubanness), 8, 17, 30, 160, 223, 243n17, 249n7

Cuban opposition, 40

Cuban Palimpsests (Quiroga), 6

Cuban representations, of émigrés: Cuban-American narratives and, 224; Cuban revolution of 1959 and, 203; overview, 31, 195–96, 223–24, 227. *See also* Cuban cultural productions, about émigrés

Cuban representations, of returnees: of one-and-a-half generation, 211–12, 224; overview, 195, 198–200. *See also* Cuban cultural productions, about returnees

Cuban return: counterpoints between politics and, 41–48; historical background, 29–30, 34–89; U.S.-Cuba relations and, 225

Cuban returnee artists, 21; overview, 30–31. *See also* Cuban returnee visual artists

Cuban returnees: Cuban-American community and, 225; Cuban natives and, 225–26; cultural productions about, 202; in 1959, 235n2; overview, 1–2, 194; permanent returns, 232n9; questions concerning, 1; reacquaintance with homeland, 61–62. *See also specific returnee topics*
Cuban returnee visual artists, 21. *See also* Mendieta, Ana
Cuban return narratives, 19–21; array of, 17–22; dystopian, 22–27; in English or Spanish, 66; family scenes, 2; homosexuality in, 22, 23, 25, 79–82, 219–20; one-and-a-half generation return narratives compared to other, 2, 231n1; overview, 1–2, 26–27, 225–30; vicarious returns in, 245n6. *See also* Autobiographical narratives; Cuban narratives, about returnees; Literature of return; One-and-a-half generation return narratives
Cuban revolution of 1959, 249n9, 250n12; Cuban-American exiles after, 18, 34–39, 62, 235n1; Cuban émigrés after, 1, 2, 34–39, 235n1; Cuban migration and, 34–39, 235n1; Cuban native narratives and, 195; Cuban natives and, 194; Cuban representations of émigrés and, 203; Cuban returnees in 1959, 235n2; social achievements of, 42, 44; Soviet-Cuban relations after, 35–39; U.S.-Cuba relations and, 34–36, 203; *Waiting for Snow in Havana* and, 139, 140, 243nn13–14. *See also* Castro, Fidel; Guevara, Ernesto "Che"
Cubans: Cuban exiles and, 100; Latinos and, 74, 76; in Puerto Rico, 125, 242n3; transnationalism of, 12–14
Cuban studies, on returns, 28–29, 234n18
A Cuban Summer (Mendoza), 88
Cuban visits: by Cuban Americans, 4, 13, 44–45, 236n14; to former homes, 44–45, 236n14; of 1970s and 1980s, 45
Cuban visual artists, 21, 93. *See also* Cuban-American visual artists

Cuban writers: on other cultural contact, 251n15. *See also* Cuban-American writers; Cuban émigré writers
Cuba on My Mind: Journeys to a Severed Nation (de la Campa), 19, 20; as hybrid memoir, 74–75; overview, 74–78, 88–89
Cultural citizenship, 143, 243n16
Cultural exchange: Cuban, 92, 93; Cuban music and, 196, 221–22, 248n2. *See also* Boomerang aesthetic
Cultural productions, about Cuban returnees: *cubanía* in, 203, 205; *cubanidad* in, 203, 205, 250n12; made outside of Cuba, 202. *See also* Cuban cultural productions, about returnees
Cultura plattista, 203, 204, 249n8
Culture: Cuban writers on contact with other, 251n15; hybridity of Mendieta, Ana, 98, 100; in *Next Year in Cuba*, 149, 150, 153, 154, 155; one-and-a-half generation and counterculture, 42; transculturation, 171, 178, 179; U.S. culture in *Learning to Die in Miami*, 141–45, 148; in *Waiting for Snow in Havana*, 141–43. *See also* Cuban culture

Days of Awe (Obejas), 247n17; Castro, Fidel, in, 180; Cuban and Jewish diaspora in, 180, 183–85; Cuban and Jewish identity in, 180–85; Cuba's continuing centrality in, 169–70; Cuba's past in, 163–68; family secrets in, 162–63; females in, 161, 169, 245n5; Jews in Cuba in, 180–85; non-mainstream religions in, 180–85; overview, 31, 159–62, 191–93, 245n5; U.S.-Cuba relations in, 180. *See also* Novels of return
De Aragón, Uva, 19, 29
Death of a Chicken performance art, 117, 118
Deferral strategy, 212–20, 252n19
De la Campa, Román: autobiographical narrative of, 19, 20, 62, 63, 66, 67, 74–78, 88–89; on Cuban diaspora, 75, 76, 78; on Cuban Miami exiles, 75–76; *Cuba on My Mind: Journeys to a Severed Nation* of, 19,

20, 74–78, 88–89; *De la patria y el exilio* and, 75; on greater Cuba in hemispheric context, 74; on Latinos, 74, 76–78; Miami and, 74–76, 78
De la patria y el exilio, 45, 46, 75
Delgado, Frank, 194–97
Deracination, of autobiographical narratives, 64
Deuteragonists, 5
Diálogo negotiations, 48–49
Diaspora, 8; Bejel on, 78–82; Cohen on, 11; Dominican, 245n4; exile compared to, 14–15, 232n11, 233n12; Fornet on, 232n11; homeland aspect of, 10–11, 232n8; homosexuality and, 79–81; Latino, 77, 78; overview, 10–14, 228; Pakistani, 244n20; Puerto Rican, 78, 248n1; toward rhetoric of, 14–15; Safran on, 10–11, 232n8; transnationalism compared to, 9–14, 228. *See also* Cuban diaspora
Diaspora, 11
Diaspora theories: on returns, 17, 27; roots/routes debates, 11, 15–17
Diasporic artists, writers, and postindexical, 65
Diasporic communities, and homeland identity, 161, 244n20
Diasporic intimacy, of autobiographical narratives, 64
Diasporic returns, 27
Diasporic sensibility, in one-and-a-half generation return narratives, 19–21
Díaz, Jesús, 45, 75, 205, 207–9, 224, 250n12
Diaz-Balart, Mario, 55, 59
Diccionario de la literatura cubana, 242n7
"Diente por diente" (Alonso), 214–15
"Distancia no quiere decir olvido: Viajes a la semilla" (de Aragón), 29
Dominican diaspora, 245n4
Dominican Republic émigrés, 248n1
Domitrovich, Michael, 239n5
Dopico, Ana María, 85–86

Dreaming in Cuban (García, Cristina), 171, 188, 245n5, 247n17
Duany, Jorge, 16–17, 58, 228
Dystopian return narratives, 22–27

Earth art, 115; of Mendieta, Ana, 91, 92, 96, 105, 111. *See also Rupestrian Sculptures*
Echeverría, José Antonio, 187, 248n20
Eckstein, Susan E., 3, 4
Egg motif, 214, 251n17
Eire, Carlos M. N., 75; Brito and, 136; childhood memoirs of, 121, 123–24, 136–48, 157–58; "Exile's Childhood" genre and, 124, 136–39; family of, 139–40; *Learning to Die in Miami: Confessions of a Refugee Boy* of, 139, 143–48, 157–58; Operation Pedro Pan and, 139, 143; overview, 136–39, 157–58; Pérez Firmat and, 136–37, 151; textual representation of interrupted childhood of, 139–43; *Waiting for Snow in Havana: Confessions of a Cuban Boy* of, 139–45, 151, 157–58, 243nn13–14
Embargo against Cuba, 36, 41, 53, 57
Émigrés: nostalgia and ignorance of birthplace of, 122–23. *See also* Cuban émigrés; Exiles
"En casa," 3, 222
English: Cuban return narratives in, 66; Mendieta, Ana, use of, 98
En vivo, 222
"Erre con erre" (Sarova), 252n19
Escaleras de Jaruco (national park), 105, 109, 110, 112
Espacio Aglutinador (Cuban art gallery), 128, 242n4
Espin, Oliva, 64
Exhibits and exhibitions: of Brito, 131, 242n8; CAFÉ, 251n13; of Mendieta, Ana, 96, 97, 100, 101, 108; of Pujol, 127–30, 129; of Volumen I artists, 93, 97, 104
The Exile: Cuba in the Heart of Miami (Rieff), 34, 155, 242n1, 243n13

Exiled Memories: A Cuban Childhood (Medina), 121, 138
Exiles: attitudes toward returning, 2; concept in art of Brito, 136; Cuban-American literature of, 19, 233n15; diaspora compared to, 14–15, 232n11, 233n12; exile theories on returns, 17, 19; one-and-a-half generation and memories of, 65–66; one-and-a-half generation narratives espousing, 63. *See also* Cuban exiles; Émigrés
"Exile's Childhood" (sub-sub-genre of childhood memoirs), 243n13; Eire and, 124, 136–39; overview, 124, 136–39; Pérez Firmat and, 124, 136–39

Falzon, Mark-Anthony, 244n20
Family: Bejel on, 80–81; of Eire, 139–40; of Pérez Firmat, 148–50, 152, 154–56; scenes, 2; secrets in novels of return, 162–63
Fass, Paula S., 141, 243n13
Feed (Brito painting and sculpture), *135*, 135–36
Females: feminine figure and nature in art of Mendieta, Ana, 113; in novels of return, 161, 169, 245n5. *See also* Gender
Feminism: of Brito, 131; of Mendieta, Ana, 30, 102, 117
Fernández, Antonio Eligio ("Tonel"), 120, 241n17
Fernández, Damián J., 17, 86
55 hermanos, 207, 208
Films, about returnees, 202. *See also* Cuban films: about returnees
Finding Mañana (Ojito), 138
Fiol-Matta, Licia, 184
"Flags and Rags (On Golden Lake)" (Muñoz), 232n7
Fleites Pérez, Yerandy, 252n18
Flores, Juan, 12, 198, 248n1
Fornet, Ambrosio, 16, 228, 232n11, 251n16
Fragmentation, in art of Brito, 131, 132
The Future of Nostalgia (Boym), 159

Galeano, Eduardo, 90
Gans Grin, Jaime, 72
García, Cristina, 21, 54; *The Agüero Sisters* of, 31, 159–79, 188, 191–93, 245n5; *Dreaming in Cuban* of, 171, 188, 245n5, 247n17; novels of, 170, 247n12; overview, 31, 159–62, 191–93. *See also* Novels of return
García, Joe, 237n25
García Espinosa, Julio, 206
García Socarrás, Yamisleisy "Yami," 112–13, 119, 240n13
Gastón, Mariana, 43, 44–45
Gay Cuban Nation (Bejel), 80
Gender: *mestizaje* in *The Agüero Sisters*, 171–79. *See also* Females
Geo-Imago solo exhibit, 96, 100, 101, 108
Getsy, David J., 124
Gil, Lourdes, 14
Gil Alejo, Arístides, 250n11
Gilroy, Paul, 11
"Going Back" (Mendoza), 239n8
"Going to Cuba: Writing Ethnography of Diaspora, Return, and Despair" (Behar), 73
Goldman, Shifra M., 107, 108
Gómez Cortés, Olga Rosa, 51
González, María Elena, 65
González de Cascorro, Raúl, 250n11
González Mandri, Flora, 122
Goya, Francisco, 131
Greater Cuba, 74
Grubin, David, 196, 221
Guerrillero (guerrilla fighter), 189, 190, 191
Guevara, Ernesto "Che," 186, 188–92, 247n18, 248n21
Gutiérrez Alea, Tomás, 195

Habana Abierta, 200
Habana Eva, 202
Halbwachs, Maurice, 91
Hall, Stuart, 11
Havana, 5, 24, 94; in *Next Year in Cuba*,

148–52, 154–56; photographs of, 85–86, 86, 87. *See also* Cuba
Havana, Havana, 196, 221–22
Havanization concert, 221, 223, 253n21
Hemos llegado a Ilión (Alabau), 25–26
Heredia, José María, 215–18
Hernández-Reguant, Ariana, 73
Higher Institute of Art (ISA), 115; Cuarta Pragmática student trip, *112*, 112–14, *114*
Los hijos de Pedro Pan (Pujol exhibit), 127–28, *129*, *130*
Hiraeth (homesickness), 6
Hirsch, Marianne, 28, 166
Hoffman, Eva, 61, 62, 121
Homecoming: Schutz on, 83–84. *See also* Return
"Homecomings to the Future" (King), 27
Homeland: aspect of diaspora, 10–11, 232n8; Bejel on home and, 79–82; Cuban returnees' reacquaintance with, 61–62; identity among diasporic communities, 244n20; returnees' impact on, 18; transnationalism and, 12
Homeland return. *See* Return
Homes: Bejel on homeland and, 79–82; Mendoza's Cuban family, 84
Homing desire, 6, 7, 232n5
Homosexuality: Bejel and, 79–82, 89; in Cuban return narratives, 22, 23, 25, 79–82, 219–20; diaspora and, 79–81; in fiction of Obejas, 170; Pujol and, 124, 125, 129
El horizonte de mi piel (Bejel), 79. *See also The Write Way Home: A Cuban-American Story*
Houses and household objects, in art of Brito, 131–34
Hybridity: *Cuba on My Mind* as hybrid memoir, 74–75; identity and subjectivities, 209; Mendieta, Ana, and cultural, 98, 100

Ibieta, Gabriela, 121
Identity: diasporic communities and homeland, 161, 244n20; hybrid, 209; *Learning to Die in Miami* and conflicts in, 145–46. *See also* Cuban identity
The Immigrant Divide: How Cuban Americans Changed the U.S. and Their Homeland (Eckstein), 3
Immigration: theme in art of Brito, 134; U.S. and, 32–33
Improper Conduct, 242n6
In Cuba I Was a German Shepherd (Menéndez), 186
Index, 65, 239n1
Indexical markers, 30; post-indexical markers, 30, 64, 65
Installations: by Barroso, 200, *201*; of Brito, 131, *133*, 133–36, *137*; of Pujol, 125, 127–28, *129*, *130*, *133*, 133–36
ISA. *See* Higher Institute of Art
"Isla," 221, 253n20
An Island Called Home: Returning to Jewish Cuba (Behar), 19, 20; overview, 67–74, 88; photographs in, 71–73, *72*
"Ithaka" (Cavafy), v, 33, 122

Jaruco limestone caves, 91, 93, 105, 107, 108, *112*, 112–15, 118–19
Jewish Cuban (Juban), 69, 70, 72, 74
Jewish diaspora, 10; Behar on, 68–73; Cuban diaspora and, 68–73, 180, 183–85
Jewish identity, and Cuban identity, 180–85
Jews in Cuba: Behar and, 67–73; in *Days of Awe*, 180–85; discrimination against, 182, 247n15; Sephardic, 180–85; statistics, 67, 239n2
Jineteras (prostitutes), 77, 239n4
Juban, 69, 70, 72, 74
"Juban América" (Behar), 70

Kandiyoti, Dalia, 179, 183, 184
Kaplan, Caren, 192
King, Russell, 27
Knauer, Lisa Maya, 13
Kozer, José, 1

Krauss, Rosalind, 239n1
Kundera, Milan, 123, 153, 159

Latin America, 27
Latino/a literature, 160, 233n15
Latino diaspora, 76, 77, 78
Latinos: Cubans and, 74, 76; de la Campa on, 74, 76–78; memoirs of, 143; in Miami, 244n21
"Laura" (segment of *Mujer transparente*), 212–13
Learning to Die in Miami: Confessions of a Refugee Boy (Eire): conflicting identities in, 145–46; death and resurrection theme in, 143–48; overview, 139, 143–48, 157–58; trauma in, 147–48; U.S. culture in, 144–45, 148
Lejanía, 205, 206–9, 250n12
Lerner, Gerda, 169
Lien and Rey duo, 221
Lieux de mémoire (sites of memory), 91, 109–11, 119
Life on the Hyphen: The Cuban-American Way (Pérez Firmat), 4, 8, 150
Literature: Latino/a, 160, 233n15; representation in, 139–43, 159. *See also* Cuban literature
Literature of return, 22, 198, 230; stereotyping in, 250n11. *See also* Novels of return
Lite sexile, 80, 81
Little Havana, 148, 149, 151, 152, 154, 155, 244n20
López, Antonio, 234n19, 239n3
López Labourdette, Adriana, 22, 27, 29
Loving Che (Menéndez): Cuban exiles in, 186; Cuba's continuing centrality in, 169–70; Cuba's past in, 163–68; family secrets in, 162–63; females in, 161, 169, 245n5; *guerrillero* in, 189, 190, 191; Guevara in, 186, 188–92, 247n18, 248n21; highlighting revolutionary icons in, 186–91; overview, 31, 159–62, 191–93, 245n5. *See also* Novels of return

Machado, Eduardo, 239n5
Making Memory Matter: Strategies of Remembrance in Contemporary Art (Saltzman), 64
"Mama," 222
Mankekar, Purnima, 12
Mannheim, Karl, 231n3
Mapa dibujado por un espía (Cabrera Infante), 234n16
Mariel boatlift, 37
Mariel exodus, 49, 197, 214–20, 252n18
Marielitos (Mariel refugees), 37, 197, 199, 214, 215, 252n18
Maroya sculpture, *106*, 107, 113
Martí, José, 166, 247n9
Martínez, Juan A., 131, 134
Martínez San Miguel, Yolanda, 23, 28
Mayol, Humberto, 71
"Mazapán de Matanzas" sketch, 98, *99*, 100
Medina, Pablo, 121, 138, 243n13
Memoirs, 30–31; Latino, 143; in return migration studies, 31–32. *See also* Autobiographical narratives; Childhood memoirs
Memorias recobradas (Fornet), 251n16
"La memoria viva" (Galeano), 90
Memories of Development, 195
Memory, 65; Behar and, 71–72; collective, 91, 102, 104, 242n7; of exile of one-and-a-half generation, 65–66; national, 102–3; post-memory, 21, 166–67, 247n10; sites of, 91, 109–11, 119; trap of Cuban-American exiles, 18
Memory Mambo (Obejas), 167
Mendieta, Ana, 21, 136; art and politics of, 97; art books including works of, 111, 240n11; art using nature and feminine figure of, 113; backdrop to return story of, 92–93; body art of, 91, 96, 112, 240n13; Bruguera's art and, 115–18, *117*; Cuban art and, 91, 95–97, 104, 120; Cuban artists and, 30, 91, 93, 96, 101–5, 112–19; cultural hybridity of, 98, 100; earth art of, 91, 92, 96, 105, 111; exhibits of, 96, 97, 100, 101,

108; family of, 93–95, *94*; feminism of, 30, 102, 117; *Geo-Imago* solo exhibit of, 96, 100, 101, 108; glitches to soft landing return, 97–101; Jaruco limestone caves and, 91, 93, 105, 107, 108, *112*, 112–15, 118–19; legacy at century's turn, 112–19; *Maroya* sculpture of, *106*, 107, 113; "Mazapán de Matanzas" sketch of, 98, *99*, 100; overview, 30, 90–92, 120; performance art of, 91–92, 96, 116–18, *117*; personal aspects of return of, 93–95; as Peter Pan child, 91, 92; politics of, 97, 100, 103; Pujol and, 127; Rosa de la Cruz collection, 119; *Rupestrian Sculptures* of, 30, 91, 93, 97, 105, *106*, 107–15, *112*, 118–19; sculptures of, 30, 91, 93, 96, 97, 105, *106*, 107–15, *112*, 118–19, 240n8; use of English, Spanish and Spanglish, 98, 100; Volumen I artists and, 93, 96, 101–5

Mendieta, Carlos, 95

Mendieta, Pablo, 95

Mendieta, Raquelin, 90, *94*, 95

Mendieta, Tony, 97

Mendoza, Tony: autobiographical narrative of, 62, 63, 67, 82–88; *Cuba: Going Back* of, 19, 20, 82–88; Cuban family homes of, 84; *A Cuban Summer* of, 88; "Going Back" of, 239n8; photographs of, 82–88, *86*, *87*; socialist Cuba and, 85, 87, 239n8; Special Period and, 83, 85

Menéndez, Ana, 21; *In Cuba I Was a German Shepherd* of, 186; fiction of, 186; *Loving Che* of, 31, 159–70, 186–93, 245n5; novels of, 170; overview, 31, 159–62, 191–93. *See also* Novels of return

La mesa de Saturno (Pujol exhibit), 128–29

Mestizaje, 171–79

Mexico, 40–41

Miami, 4, 18; Cuban artists, 131; Cuban culture in, 155, 244n21; Cuban exiles, 75–76; Cuban identity and, 153; de la Campa and, 74–76, 78; Latinos in, 244n21; Little Havana, 148, 149, 151, 152, 154; in *Next Year in Cuba*, 148, 151–56

Miel para Oshún, 210–11

Migration: studies on returns, 27–29. *See also* Cuban migration; Émigrés; Return migration

Milanés, Cecilia Rodríguez, 247n10

Miller, Nancy K., 28

Mirabal, Nancy Raquel, 233n12

Mishra, Sudesh, 10–11

Mi tío el exiliado (Pérez), 252n18

Mosquera, Gerardo, 107–10, 115, 118, 125, 128

Mujer que regresa (Betancourt), 251n14

Mujer transparente, 212–13

Muñoz, Elías Miguel, 232n7

Nanas y cunas (Pujol), 127

Narratives of return. *See* Return narratives

National memory, 102–3

Nature in art: Mendieta, Ana, use of feminine figure and, 113. *See also* Earth art

"The New Nomads" (Hoffman), 121

Next Year in Cuba: A Cubano's Coming of Age in America (Pérez Firmat), 18, 243n15; Cuban culture in, 150, 153, 154, 155; culture in, 149, 150, 153, 154, 155; Havana in, 148–52, 154–56; *Life on the Hyphen* and, 150; Little Havana in, 148, 149, 151, 152, 154; Miami in, 148, 151–56; overview, 148–58

"Ni de aquí, ni de allá" (Torrens), 194, 197–98, 221

Nora, Pierre, 91, 109–10

Nosotros, los de entonces, ya no somos los mismos (What We Were Then, We Are No Longer), 104–5, *105*

La novela de mi vida (Padura), 215–19

Novels of return: Cuba's continuing centrality in, 169–70; Cuba's past in, 163–68; family secrets in, 162–63; females in, 161, 169, 245n5; overview, 31, 159–62, 191–93, 226–27, 245n5; usable past and, 31, 159, 163, 164, 166–69, 179; vicarious returns in, 31, 159, 161, 162. *See also* García, Cristina; Menéndez, Ana; Obejas, Achy

No Way Home: A Dancer's Journey from the Streets of Havana to the Stages of the World (Acosta), 229
"Nuestro dia (ya viene llegando)" (Chirino), 3

Obama, Barack, 51, 55, 59, 237n18, 237n25
Obejas, Achy, 21, 245n3; *Days of Awe* of, 31, 159–70, 180–85, 191–93, 245n5; homosexuality in fiction of, 170; *Memory Mambo* of, 167; overview, 31, 159–62, 191–93. *See also* Novels of return
Odysseus, 61
Ojito, Mirta, 138
Olney, James, 137–38
One-and-a-half generation: counterculture and, 42; Cuban diaspora of, 9, 39; Cuban exiles and, 9, 225; *Cubangst* of, 6; Cuban migration and, 38; as deuteragonists, 5; fears of return of, 7, 232n7; *hiraeth* of, 6; homing desire of, 6, 7, 232n5; memories of exile of, 65–66; as neither hardliners nor newcomers, 4–9, 231n3; Operation Pedro Pan and, 3, 5, 231n4; overview, 1–2, 4–9, 231n3, 232n6; transnationalism of, 9. *See also* Children of exiles
One-and-a-half generation literature, 232n11. *See also* Literature of return
One-and-a-half generation narratives: espousing exiles, 63. *See also* Childhood memoirs; One-and-a-half generation return narratives
One-and-a-half generation returnees, 61–62, 229; Cuban cultural productions about, 207–12; *cubanía* and, 208, 209, 211; *cubanidad* and, 207, 208, 209, 211; Cuban natives and, 207–12; Cuban representations of, 211–12, 224; as redeemable, 207–12; self-awareness gained from return, 121–22; time passage between departure and return, 121–22
One-and-a-half generation return narratives, 122; autobiographical, 7, 31–32, 61–89;

Cuban narratives about returnees compared to, 212, 251n16; by Cuban natives, 207–12, 251n14; diasporic sensibility in, 19–21; by Díaz, 207–9; family scenes, 2; mixed viewpoints of, 17–18; other Cuban return narratives compared to, 2, 231n1; overview, 1–2, 6–7, 225, 226; transnational sensibility in, 19–21; *volver, regresar* and *retornar* of, 8–9. *See also* Novels of return
Ong, Aihwa, 11
Operación Peter Pan: cerrando el círculo en Cuba (Gómez Cortés), 51
Operation Pedro Pan, 3, 5, 51–53, 127, 231n4; Eire and, 139, 143; overview, 35–36. *See also* Pedro Pans
O'Reilly Herrera, Andrea, 16, 39, 122, 131, 160, 188, 193, 245n1, 251n13
Ortiz, Fernando, 174, 178
"La otra orilla" (Delgado), 194, 196–97

Padrón, Humberto, 214, 219–20
Padura, Leonardo, 215–19
Paintings: of Brito, 131, 135, 135–36; of Pujol, 125, 126, 127, 128
Pakistani diaspora, 244n20
Paladares (privately owned restaurants), 77, 239n4
"Para Ana Veltfort" (Casal, Lourdes), 47, 224, 236n15
Party at Goya's/First Arrivals (Brito sculpture), 131–32
Paternostro, Susan, 139, 143
El Patio de mi Casa (Brito installation), 133, 133–36, 137
Paz, Raúl, 3–4, 221–23
Pedro Pans, 51–53; Pujol and, 127–28, 130. *See also* Operation Pedro Pan; Peter Pan children
Peirce, Charles Sanders, 64–65
Pérez, Gina M., 27
Pérez Betancourt, Rolando, 251n14
Pérez Firmat, Gustavo, 14, 16; Brito and, 136; childhood memoir of, 30–31, 123–24,

136–39, 148–58; Cuban identity and, 153, 155, 157; *A Cuban in Mayberry: Looking Back at America's Hometown* of, 156–57, 244n22; Eire and, 136–37, 151; "Exile's Childhood" genre and, 124, 136–39; family of, 148–50, 152, 154–56; *Life on the Hyphen: The Cuban-American Way* of, 4, 8, 150; *Next Year in Cuba: A Cubano's Coming of Age in America* of, 18, 148–58, 243n15; overview, 136–39, 157–58, 244n18
Performance art: of Bruguera, 116–18, 117, 241n15; *Death of a Chicken*, 117, 118; of Mendieta, Ana, 91–92, 96, 116–18, 117; *El peso de la culpa*, 117, 118
Perl, Jeffrey M., 61, 62
El peso de la culpa performance art, 117, 118
Peter Pan children: Brito as, 131, 133; Mendieta, Ana, as, 91, 92. *See also* Pedro Pans
Peter Pan's Table (Pujol installation), 128
Petro, Pamela, 6
Photographs: of Havana, 85–86, 86, 87; in *An Island Called Home: Returning to Jewish Cuba*, 71–73, 72; by Mendoza in *Cuba: Going Back*, 82–88, 86, 87
Politics: art and, 97; children and, 138; Cuban music and, 249n4; of Mendieta, Ana, 97, 100, 103
Politics of return: children of exiles and, 41–47; counterpoints in, 41–48; overview of contentious, 34–89; Pujol and, 129
Ponte, Antonio José, 24, 234n17
The Portable Island: Cubans at Home in the World (Behar), 73
Portes, Alejandro, 12
Post-indexical markers, 30; diasporic artists and writers and, 65; ties and autobiographical narratives, 63–67; visual arts and, 64, 65
Post-memory, 21, 166–67, 247n10
"Pregúntaselo a Dios" (Bobes), 252n19
Prieto, Abel, 203–5, 249n9
Progressive Cubans, 41–42
Puerto Rican diaspora, 78, 248n1

Puerto Rico, 13, 27, 125, 242n3
Pujol, Ernesto: childhood visual narratives of, 30, 121, 123–31, 126, 129, 157–58; exhibits of, 127–30, 129; *Los hijos de Pedro Pan* exhibit of, 127–28, 129, 130; homosexuality and, 124, 125, 129; installations of, 125, 127–28, 129, 130, 133, 133–36; Mendieta, Ana, and, 127; *La mesa de Saturno* exhibit of, 128–29; overview, 124–25, 157–58; paintings of, 125, 126, 127, 128; Pedro Pans and, 127–28, 130; politics of return and, 129; *Taxonomías/Taxonomies* collection of, 125, 126, 127; *Trofeos de la guerra fría* exhibit of, 128; *El Vacío* exhibit of, 129, 130; visual art of, 21

Los que se fueron, 52, 90
Quinquenio gris (dull cultural works), 92, 240n1
Quiroga, José, 6, 45, 94, 118, 212

Race: of Cuban Americans, 235n4; relations in Cuban-American literature, 32, 234n19. *See also Mestizaje*
"Reconstructing Cubanness" (Duany), 16–17
Regresar (to return), 8, 9
"El regreso" (Casey), 22
Reina y Rey, 206–7, 252n18
Religions, *Days of Awe* and non-mainstream, 180–85
René Francisco Rodríguez, 103, 112, 115, 118–19, 240n12
Representation in literature, 159; textual representation of interrupted childhood, 139–43. *See also* Novels of return
Representation of exiles, 31; figurative, 23. *See also* Cuban representations, of émigrés
Representation of returns, 2; discursive, 32. *See also* Cuban representations, of returnees
"Rethinking Diaspora(s)" (Tölölyan), 8

Retornar (to return), 8, 9
"El retorno de las yolas" (Saillant), 27–28, 245n4
"Retrato sideral de mi casa" (Kozer), 1
Return: diaspora theories on, 17, 27; exile theories on, 17, 19; healing power of, 122, 242n1; historical background to, 29–30, 34–89; self-awareness gained from, 121–22; staying away compared to, 121; transnationalism and, 17
Returnees: impact on homeland, 18. *See also* Cuban returnees
Return migration, 1, 31–32; studies, 27–29
Return narratives: array of, 17–22; dystopian, 22–27. *See also* Cuban return narratives
Return studies: Cuban, 28–29, 234n18; migration studies and other, 27–29; return migration, 31–32
Revolution: icons in *Loving Che*, 186–91. *See also* Cuban revolution of 1959
Rieff, David, 34, 53–54, 155, 242n1, 243n13
Risech, Flavio, 50
Rivera, David, 54–55, 123, 237n25
Rivero, Eliana, 6, 15, 16, 60, 123, 228, 234n15, 245n4
Rodenas, Adriana Méndez, 15, 165
Rodríguez, Ana, 212–13
Rodriguez, Raul, 242n1
Rodríguez Brey, Ricardo, 93, 101, 103, 105
Rojas, Rafael, 16, 29, 179, 233n13, 250n11
Rok, Ester Rebeca Shapiro, 50
The Room Upstairs: Self-Portrait with Two Friends (Brito assemblage), 132–33
Roots/routes debates, 11, 15–17
Rosa de la Cruz collection, 119
Rubio, Marco, 34, 53–55, 59
Rumbaut, Rubén G., 4, 25, 232n6
Rupestrian Sculptures (Mendieta, Ana), 30, 91, 93, 97, 118–19; *Bacayú* sculpture, *112*, 112–13; Cuarta Pragmática student trip to, *112*, 112–14, *114*; *Maroya* sculpture, *106*, 107, 113; overview, 105, 107–9; as return to *la tierra* and *su tierra*, 105, 107–9; as site of memory, 109–11; *taíno* goddesses and, 107, 108; Tercera Pragmática student trip to, 115

Safran, William, 10–11, 17, 232n8
Said, Edward, 2
Saltzman, Lisa, 64, 65, 239n1
Sánchez, Luis Rafael, 78
Saussure, Ferdinand de, 64, 65
Schnapper, Dominique, 10
Schutz, Alfred, 83–84
Sculptures: of Brito, 131–32, *135*, 135–36; of Mendieta, Ana, 30, 91, 93, 96, 97, 105, *106*, 107–15, *112*, 118–19, 240n8
Self-Portrait in Grey and White (Brito assemblage), 132
Sephardic Jews, 180–85
Serra, Ana, 28
Sexile, 79–80, 81, 82
Sign, taxonomy of, 64–65
Silos Ribas, Lorena, 147
Sites of memory (*lieux de mémoire*), 91, 109–11, 119
Socialist Cuba, 85, 87, 239n8
Solás, Humberto, 210–11, 251n15
Soviet-Cuban relations, 35–39
Soviet Union: post-Soviet Cuban literature, 24, 234n17; Soviet-Cuban relations, 35–39
Spain, 40
Spanglish, 98, 100
Spanish: Cuban return narratives in, 66; Mendieta, Ana, use of, 98, 100
Spared Angola: Memories from a Cuban-American Childhood (Suárez), 138
Special Period, 56, 83, 85
Stefanson, Anders H., 4, 18, 27, 28
Suárez, Virgil, 138

Taíno goddesses, 107, 108
Tastes Like Cuba: An Exile's Hunter for Home (Machado and Domitrovich), 239n5
Taxonomías/Taxonomies (collection of

paintings and installations by Pujol), 125, *126*, 127
Tendedera (Pujol installation), 128, *129*, 130
Teoría de tránsito del arte cubano (Barroso installation), 200, *201*
Tercera Pragmática student trip, 115
Terrorism, 40, 237n24
Tölölyan, Khachig, 8, 10, 11, 161, 232n10
Tonel. *See* Fernández, Antonio Eligio
Torrens, David, 194–98, 200, 221
Torres, Fina, 202
Torres, María de los Ángeles, 22, 50, 53
Torres Llorca, Rubén, 93, 101, 104–5
Torres Saillant, Silvio, 27–28, 143–44, 245n4, 248n1
Torriente, Alberto Pedro, 209–10
Transculturation, 171, 178, 179
Transnationalism: of Cuban Americans, 13–14, 62; of Cubans, 12–14; diaspora compared to, 9–14, 228; homeland and, 12; of one-and-a-half generation, 9; overview, 11–14; of Puerto Ricans, 13; relationship in autobiographical narratives, 63; returns and, 17; sensibility in one-and-a-half generation return narratives, 19–21
Travel ban, 41, 43–44, 51, 53–55. *See also* Travel to Cuba, U.S. policy
Traveling Heavy: A Memoir in between Journeys (Behar), 28
Travel to Cuba, by Cuban exiles, 34, 62; broadening returns, 48–53; children of exiles and, 41–47, 49–50, 55, 59–60; Cuban government and, 56–57, 238n27; growing demand for, 58–59, 238n28; growing support for, 53, 55, 237n24; lingering opposition to, 53–55; in 1970s and 1980s, 43–46, 48–49; overview of political context of, 59–60; Pedro Pans, 51–53; remittances to Cuba by, 56, 238n26; statistics on, 58–59, 238n28; terrorism against, 49
Travel to Cuba, U.S. policy: Cuban opposition and, 40; ebb and flow of, 41; embargo against Cuba and, 41, 53, 57; liberalization of, 51–53; 1990s to present, 49–53; Obama and, 51, 55, 59, 237n18, 237n25; overview, 60; restrictions, 40–41; travel ban, 41, 43–44, 51, 53–55; violations of travel ban, 41, 43–44, 51
Trofeos de la guerra fría (Pujol exhibit), 128
Tropicana, Carmelita, 166
Troyano, Alina, 166

Unbecoming Blackness: The Diaspora Cultures of Afro-Cuban America (López), 234n19
United States (U.S.): Cuban migrants' views of returns based on arrival dates in, 62; culture in *Learning to Die in Miami*, 141–45, 148; immigration and, 32–33
Usable past: American writers and, 163–64; novels of return and, 31, 159, 163, 164, 166–69, 179; overview, 168
U.S.-Cuba relations, 249n8; Cold War and, 40, 225; Cuban exiles and, 40, 203, 249n6; Cuban return and, 225; after Cuban revolution of 1959, 34–36, 203; Cuba's natural resources in, 174, 247n13; in *Days of Awe*, 180; Diálogo negotiations, 48–49; embargo against Cuba, 36, 41, 53, 57; Obama and, 51, 55, 59, 237n18, 237n25; U.S. attempts to topple Cuban government, 203, 249n6. *See also* Travel to Cuba, U.S. policy
Utopian return narratives, 22–24

El Vacio (Pujol exhibit), 129, 130
Varones (Pujol installation), 128
Vega Sarova, Anna Lidia, 252n19
Veigas Zamora, José, 96
Venceremos Brigade, 41, 43
Vera León, Antonio, 209, 251n13
"Viaje a La Habana" (Arenas), 23
Vicarious returns: in Cuban-American works, 245n6; in Cuban return narratives, 245n6; in novels of return, 31, 159, 161, 162
Video de familia, 214, 219–20

"Viniendo" (Ponte), 24, 234n17
Viso, Olga, 93, 97, 114, 240n11
Visual arts: post-indexical and, 64, 65. See also Cuban visual artists
Volumen I artists, 115; dispersal of, 101–2; exhibition by, 93, 97, 104; Mendieta, Ana, and, 93, 96, 101–5; overview, 93
Volver (metaphorical returning), 8–9, 29–33, 225

Waiting for Snow in Havana: Confessions of a Cuban Boy (Eire), 144, 145, 151; Castro, Fidel, in, 139, 243n14; Cuban culture in, 141–43; Cuban revolution of 1959 and, 139, 140, 243nn13–14; overview, 139–43, 157–58; U.S. culture in, 141–43

Weekend en Bahía (Torriente), 209–10
Whitehead, Anne, 102, 109
"Will Little Havana Go Blue?" (Rieff), 53–54
Women. *See* Females
Writers: post-indexical and diasporic, 65; usable past and American, 163–64. *See also* Cuban writers
"The Writer's Childhood" (sub-sub-genre of childhood memoirs), 137–38
The Write Way Home: A Cuban-American Story (Bejel), 19, 20, 79–82, 89

Zamora, Lois Parkinson, 163–65, 167–69
Los zapatos de Amparito (Pujol), 125, 126, 127

IRAIDA H. LÓPEZ is a professor of Spanish and Latino/a and Latin American Studies at Ramapo College of New Jersey. She is the author of *La autobiografía hispana contemporánea en los Estados Unidos*, which received, in manuscript form, the first Research and Dissertation Award of the Latin American Studies Association's Latino Studies Section. López collaborated with Ena Lucía Portela in the critical editions of *El viejo, el asesino y yo*, a compilation of short stories by the Cuban writer, and of *Cien botellas en una pared*, Portela's best-known novel. López's work has also appeared in edited volumes, as well as in peer-reviewed journals in the United States and abroad.